M000298603

The Living Tree
Studies in Modern Orthodoxy

Shlomo Riskin

THE LIVING TREE
STUDIES IN MODERN ORTHODOXY

Ohr Torah Stone
Maggid Books

The Living Tree
Studies in Modern Orthodoxy

First Edition, 2014

Maggid Books
An imprint of Koren Publishers Jerusalem Ltd.

POB 8531, New Milford, CT 06776–8531, USA
& POB 4044, Jerusalem 91040, Israel
www.korenpub.com

© Shlomo Riskin 2014

Cover design: Yehudit Cohen

All rights reserved. No part of this publication may be reproduced,
stored in a retrieval system or transmitted in any form or by
any means, electronic, mechanical, photocopying or otherwise,
without the prior permission of the publisher, except in the case
of brief quotations embedded in critical articles or reviews.

ISBN 978 159 264 408 7, *hardcover*

A CIP catalogue record for this title is
available from the British Library

Printed and bound in the United States

Contents

vi

Dedication and Acknowledgments

The publication of this book is dedicated in honor of Seyma Lederman and in memory of her beloved husband, Arnold Lederman.

Arnold Lederman, of blessed memory, immigrated to Melbourne, Australia from Czestochowa, Poland, shortly before the Second World War. He was a pioneer and innovator in the textile industry, and based on the skills he had brought with him from Poland, together with his business acumen and ingenuity, Arnold established Classweave Industries – an Australian icon in the textile industry.

Arnold Lederman was a wonderful family man and was very active in the Melbourne Jewish community, helping other Jewish emigrants from Europe re-establish their lives after the war. He tragically died of a heart attack in 1969, at the tender age of 48, leaving behind his youthful widow and six young children.

Seyma Lederman, may she live to be 120, was born in Tel Aviv in 1928. Due to the difficult living conditions at that time, her family immigrated to Australia in 1929. She was raised under trying conditions in the small country town of Narrabri, where her family was the only Jewish one. Nevertheless, she was raised to be a proud Jewess, instilled with a love of Jewish life and the newfound State of Israel.

As a young widow in Melbourne, with the support of her wider family, Seyma courageously raised her six children, ensuring that they received the best available Jewish education. She also encouraged them to be actively involved in Jewish youth movements and shul life. Despite the hardship and lonely responsibility, Seyma found the time to be active in many communal organizations, including wizo, Emunah Women, Refuah Meals for Hospitals, and visiting the sick in Melbourne.

In 2013, as a youthful 85-year-old, Seyma fulfilled her lifelong dream of returning to Israel, the land of her birth, as an *olah ḥadasha*. Joining three of her children already in Israel, Seyma lives a happy and meaningful life where she continues to serve as an inspiration to many, respected by all for her grace, generosity and kindness.

"Many women have done valiantly, but you surpass them all" (*Eshet Ḥayil*).

ACKNOWLEDGMENTS

First and foremost I must thank my *rabbeim*, chief among them Rav Joseph B. Soloveitchik, at whose feet I sat for seven years at Yeshiva University and who formed my most fundamental direction in talmudic learning, Jewish philosophy, and the primacy of halakha in Jewish life; Rav Soloveitchik was truly *Lamdan HaDor*. I owe a great deal to Rav Moshe Feinstein, *Posek HaDor*, who unstintingly gave me several hours of his precious time every Friday morning for questions of *psak* during my second year in the rabbinate in the then-fledgling Lincoln Square Synagogue. And certainly I owe much of my professional and existential calling to attempt to reach every Jew with love and without judgment to the Lubavitcher Rebbe, Rav Menahem Mendel Schneerson, *Manhig HaDor*, whose counsel I sought at every important juncture of my life. Whatever is good in this book belongs to them; that which the reader might reject is due to my own deficiencies and misunderstandings.

I am indebted to Rav Shuki Reich, beloved friend and partner at Ohr Torah Stone, for the many hours we spent studying many of the *sugyot* discussed in this work. I am also grateful to Rav Avi Scharf, my faithful assistant, for bringing many important sources to my attention. I thank my editor Channah Koppel for her literary skills as well as for her smiling persistence; without her these essays would not have seen the light of day. As is true of everything that emanates from the office of Ohr Torah Stone and Rabbanut Efrat, nothing would ever happen without the unflappable involvement and round-the-clock dedication of my administrative aid, Micky Mirvis. I am deeply grateful to my faithful friend Matthew Miller and to his staff at Maggid Books, especially Sima Bozin for proofreading the text and Tomi Mager for managing the project. Mostly, I thank my students at Ohr Torah Stone, who heard many of the *shiurim* which developed these writings and challenged many of the ideas therein.

And of course, above all, I thank the Almighty who gave me the privilege of planting in His vineyard.

Introduction

What is Modern Orthodoxy?

What is Modern Orthodoxy? I cannot count the number of times I have been called upon to answer this question by Jewish communities throughout the world. Interest in the topic has only escalated since the highly publicized Pew Research Center's 2013 survey of American Jewry, which clearly demonstrated the extent to which Orthodox Jews are more than reproducing themselves in terms of their commitment to the Jewish future, while every other sector of Jewry suffers mass defections to out-marriage, to the extent that there is reason to fear that Diaspora Jewry may be an endangered species. The Modern Orthodox accomplishment is particularly impressive considering that they are distinguished from the *ḥaredi* sector in that they maintain their fealty to a Torah-observant lifestyle while participating fully in the modernity of Western culture – just as the name Modern Orthodox implies.

Perhaps the best way to begin this essay is by explaining what Modern Orthodoxy is *not*. Firstly, I would not re-name the Modern Orthodox movement with the alternate sobriquet of "Centrist Orthodoxy," as some have proposed. I would rather subscribe to the conundrum recorded in the name of the Rebbe Menaham Mendel of Kotzk: "If I am I and you are you, then I am I and you are you; but if I am I *because* you are you, then I am not I and you are not you." The Kotzker's message is that one's halakhic position within the spectrum of Judaism must be authentic in and of itself, and not dependent upon another, contrasting position; after all, if the *ḥaredi* position on the spectrum moves more to the right, then the centrist position will perforce shift over to the right of what it was initially, causing it to compromise the integrity of its original position. Modern Orthodoxy stands on its own.

Modern Orthodoxy is committed to the ability of halakha to deal creatively, responsibly, and sensitively with the challenges and opportunities which are part of living within the modern world – be they scientifically generated, gender related, or nationally demanded by our return to the center stage of history and the Jewish State after two thousand years of Diaspora living.

Secondly, I do not believe that Modern Orthodoxy is by definition Torah-light or Torah-less. It does not imply less commitment to Torah study, less commitment to communal prayer, or less commitment to modest dress. On the contrary, if one is living in Meah She'arim or Boro Park, one will probably remain an observant Jew even without praying several times a day or dedicating specific times to Torah study. It is the individual who works in finance on Wall Street or in high tech in Tel Aviv, it is the person who spends most of the day in a physics lab or in a hospital operating theatre, who desperately requires the daily regimen of prayer and Torah study to keep him or her anchored and mindful of the Jewish values and ideals which are the ultimate purpose of our nation.

Even more to the point, my mentor Rav J.B. Soloveitchik taught that sanctity, the biblical commandment "to be holy," can only be achieved by profound and passionate commitment to a higher idea, even commitment unto death. Hence, Modern Orthodoxy, which is closely linked to (but not necessarily identical with) religious Zionism, promotes the mitzva of *aliya* for every Diaspora Jew, at least as a mitzva to aspire to, unless one is largely dedicating him or her self to the furtherance of the Jewish community as an educator, rabbi, communal worker, philanthropist, or leader of Jewish affairs – in which case he or she is considered an extra-territorial resident of Israel, according to Rabbi Ovadia Yosef.

Within Israel, the ideals of Modern Orthodoxy require IDF service for all our youth. From this perspective, Modern Orthodoxy demands more commitment than does haredism, and – judging from today's Hesder Yeshiva youth – produces greater sanctification of God's name in the present, and demonstrates profound dedication to the Jewish future in the Jewish land.

From a theological vantage point, the following famous biblical exchange between God and Moses is deeply instructive. When Moses asked God to tell him His name, so that Moses might communicate to the Israelites the nature of the God who was sending him to lead them, God responded, "I will be whomever I will be," or in Hebrew, *Ehyeh asher Ehyeh* (Ex. 3:14). The future tense of the verb *Ehyeh*, to be, suggests that God is presenting Himself (as it were) as the God of becoming, as the God of history, and, in the context of Moses' mission, as the God of freedom and redemption.

Further, the Name is open-ended, saying essentially, "I will be whomever and whenever," because God has empowered His human creations to develop and take responsibility for the world (Gen. 2:15) and has covenanted His nation Israel to be a blessing for all the families of the earth by teaching them God's desire for compassionate righteousness and moral justice, for universal peace and redemption (Gen. 12:2,3; 18:18,19; Isaiah 2; Micah 4; *Aleynu* and *Al Ken Nekaveh* prayers).

It is not we who must wait for God to act; rather, it is God who is waiting for us to not only act but to initiate redemption – as indeed our generation is doing in our return to Israel. God and the Messiah are waiting for us…

Modern Orthodoxy suggests that the same kind of partnership between God and humans which applies to world history and redemption applies to the realm of Torah as well. God has communicated to us His laws and directives via His sacred Torah so that we may become a kingdom of priest-teachers to humanity and a holy, exemplary nation to the world (Ex. 19:5–6, Seforno ad loc).

In addition to the Written Torah, God left room in the Second Tablets for an Oral Tradition of human interpretation and exegesis, of decrees and enactments, so that the input of righteous and pious scholars will retain the relevance of the divine teachings in every generation, in every circumstance, and even for specific human needs and exigencies. (Ex. 34, with Midrash *Mekhilta*).

Rabbi Soloveitchik once described the philosophic school of thought to which he adhered as halakhic existentialism, meaning that halakha must respond to the most basic and universal existential questions of humanity. Hence, there are two separate verses directing Modern Orthodox decision-making. One is, "Ask your father and he will tell you, your grandfather and he will guide you" (Deut. 32:7). This directive recognizes the critical role of past precedent and tradition in retaining the continuity of our rituals from generation to generation. The second verse which guides us is, "If there arises a matter too extraordinary for judgment (that is, a new situation)…you must go up to the judge that there is in those days (who understands the temper of the times and the needs of the hour)…and in accordance with the Torah that he will instruct you…shall you act" (Deut. 17:8–11).

The Modern Orthodox decisor must orchestrate the interplay between both of these directives, taking into account the guiding principles used by the sages of the Talmud in their religio-legal discussions, the meta-halakhic principles such as, "for the sake of the perfection of the world," "in order to respect the integrity of the human being created in the divine image," "for the sake of freeing a wife chained to an impossible marriage the sages found every leniency," "in order to provide spiritual satisfaction for women," and "you must love the stranger and the proselyte."

This path is an expression of the great partnership between God and Israel in moving the world towards redemption, as well as in interpreting the Torah for every generation. Torah must surely be our tree of life, as symbolized by the menora. The menora is made of pure gold, the most precious metal on earth and one that never decays – this represents eternity. The menora has a solid base representing the life-giving support and structure of bygone eras, and extended branches which reach out to the future by giving forth almond blossoms and flowers, offering the world light and warmth and love.

In the words of Rabbi Avraham Yitzḥak HaKohen Kook, words which can well be considered the hallmark of Modern Orthodoxy, "May the old be renewed, and may the new be sanctified."

Section I
Torah for Today

Science and Philosophy in the Beit Midrash

Behold, I have taught you statutes and ordinances, even as the Lord my God commanded me … Safeguard and keep them, since this is your wisdom and understanding in the eyes of the nations, who, when they hear all these statutes, shall say: Surely this great nation is a wise and understanding people" (Deut. 4:5–6).

One of the real tensions in the Jewish religious world has always been how to approach – if at all – secular learning. A visit to a major Jewish library is all one needs in order to understand that it's possible to spend one's entire life absorbed in the study of Jewish religious texts, yet barely skim the surface. Since the study of Torah requires intensive effort, to the extent that only a few rare individuals in each generation can scale the entire mountain of Jewish religious learning, it's not surprising that one school of thought discourages scaling any mountain other than Mount Sinai. Many outstanding religious leaders, especially within the Ashkenazi world, have considered all secular study to be absolutely forbidden (see, for example, *Responsa Rashba* 1, 17).

Thus, in the 1,300 years since the final redaction of the Talmud, the type of knowledge we would now identify with university studies has been deemed outside the scope of most centers of higher talmudic learning. If one wants to practice medicine, a course of study must be pursued outside the framework of the traditional yeshiva. In America, in those *yeshivot* which allow their students to attend night classes at local colleges, the common directive is to take only those courses needed to help one earn a living. In Israel's *ḥaredi* yeshiva world, even high school matriculation is virtually non-existent, making college education an impossibility (although this may be very slowly changing).

At first glance, the verse quoted above would seem to throw its weight on the side of all those who look askance at the pursuit of secular studies. Torah, in the eyes of the nations, is our wisdom. Other nations may have their wisdom, but we Jews have our Torah, and this is what we are supposed to safeguard.

However, in the Talmud we find that the issue is not so clear-cut. In Tractate Berakhot 35b, Rabbi Yishmael counsels the combination of Torah study with professional pursuits (*derekh eretz*), citing the verse "you shall gather your grain" (Deut. 11:14) as an imperative. Presumably, this would include receiving the preparatory instruction or training required to do one's work. Rabbi Shimon bar Yoḥai disagrees, saying, "If you plough in the time of ploughing, plant in the time of planting, reap in the time of reaping, thresh in the time of threshing… when will there be time for Torah?" Ploughing, reaping and threshing, which represent the world of professional training and work, must give way to the study of Torah, which is the ultimate professional pursuit and most meaningful possible occupation for every Jewish male.

The text then records the observations of Abaye and Rava. According to Abaye, many followed Rabbi Yishmael (combining Torah with a worldly occupation) and their efforts met with success, while others followed the path recommended by Rabbi Shimon bar Yoḥai (Torah and only Torah) and their efforts did not meet with success. Rava adds that during the important planting and harvesting months of Nisan and Tishrei he would beseech his students to return to the fields so that they would not be dependent on charity in order to study Torah.

Although this passage clearly acknowledges that Torah study may be combined with a productive occupation, it is conceivable that if it were a question of forsaking Torah study for pure intellectual endeavor, then even Rabbi Yishmael would bow to Rabbi Shimon bar Yoḥai and forbid taking time away from Torah study.

Indeed, in Tractate Menaḥot 99b, Rabbi Yishmael's nephew, Ben Dama, approaches his illustrious uncle and asks what the law would say about someone who had studied the entire Torah – could that person then go out and study Greek wisdom? In response, Rabbi Yishmael quotes the following verse: "This book shall not depart from your mouth, and you shall meditate upon it day and night" (Josh.1:8), adding that if Ben Dama can find a moment that is neither day nor night, then he can study Greek. In a word, Torah and Greek wisdom (or, it would seem, any other academic wisdom) are mutually exclusive.

But there is an alternative view. In Tractate Shabbat 75a, Rabbi Yehoshua ben Levi, quoting Bar Kappara, declares that anyone who is capable of understanding the art of astronomy (the science of Babylon) and does not engage in it, is included among those boors who "regard not the work of the Lord, nor consider the operation of His hands" (Is. 5:12). The underlying philosophic principle here is that science – the study of the natural universe – brings one closer to the Creator of the universe, enabling one to appreciate and love Him.[1] The Gemara then asks how we know that according to the Torah we are commanded to study astronomy, and cites a verse in Deuteronomy – the very same verse quoted above, which seems to suggest that we are supposed to study only Torah! In contrast to the previous interpretation, Rabbi Shmuel bar Naḥmani in the name of Rabbi Yoḥanan turns the verse on its head:

> "Safeguard and keep them since this is your wisdom and understanding in the eyes of the nations." What is wisdom and understanding in the eyes of the nations? This is astronomy (science). (Shabbat 75a)

According to this interpretation, it's not enough to study only Torah. We are also commanded to become experts in those areas of knowledge valued by the nations and able to be observed by the nations. If we don't contribute to physics and the arts and medicine, then why should any nation think of us as a significant people? How can we be a light unto the nations if we don't probe the mysteries of light in both its physical and metaphysical senses?

---

1. See Maimonides, *Sefer HaMitzvot*, Positive Commandment 3.

When the Talmud quotes Isaiah about the importance of studying the work of God's hands (science), the implication is that all knowledge which helps us to recognize the multifaceted work of the Creator is central to our existence, and to our ability to properly acknowledge our Creator. Blindness to the Creation is blindness to the Creator. When reciting the *Shema*, our twice-daily acceptance of Heavenly Kingship, two blessings always precede it: the first deals with the revelation of nature and the second with the revelation of the Torah, teaching that two different paths exist toward the recognition of the Creator, and that each complements the other.[2]

One of the first religious experiences I ever had took place inside a biology lab, and not in a Talmud class. Slides of snowflakes under the microscope revealed that each flake was perfectly hexagonal, blazing with the colors of the rainbow, and that the design and configuration of each snowflake was exquisitely unique. I asked permission to stay behind and lock up the lab, and then spent the next two hours observing hundreds of slides of snowflakes. Tears filled my eyes as I euphorically repeated again and again: "How glorious are Your works, O God!" I sensed that if a snowflake, seemingly so ordinary, could express such sheer wonders of beauty and perfection, then this world could not have developed accidentally and there must be a God who created the infinite complexities of our universe.

Maimonides (Rabbi Moshe ben Maimon, 1135–1204), at the end of chapter 4 of his *Laws of the Fundamentals of the Torah*, speaks of the "great pursuits" and the "small pursuits." What are these small pursuits? The arguments between Rava and Abaye, meaning all the arguments in the Talmud. What are the great pursuits? *Ma'ase Bereshit* (the physical creation) and *Ma'ase Merkava* (a representation of the heavenly spheres), which for him are Aristotelian physics and metaphysics, or our science and philosophy. To be sure, Maimonides does caution that before embarking on the great pursuits, one must first "fill one's belly" with the arguments of Abaye and Rava. Nevertheless, he subsumes these areas of study under the rubric of Gemara, which is the highest level of

---

2. After the *Shema*, we recite the blessing of redemption, which recognizes God's role in history.

the Oral Law (*Laws of Talmud Torah* 1, 12), and sees them as part of the commandment to know and love God (*Laws of the Fundamentals of the Torah* 4, 13).

For Maimonides, yeshiva and university are not two distinct bodies ruled by separate administrations. Rather, the university should be embodied within the yeshiva. If Maimonides were setting up a yeshiva curriculum, alongside and part of the study of Talmud would be classes in science and philosophy whose purpose, no less than the study of our holy texts, would be to awaken the student to a more profound awareness of the Creator and His Creation.

overrule a decision of its fellow court…unless it [the second court] is greater than the former in wisdom and in number.

In effect, this mishna is attempting to explain the editing policy of Rabbi Yehuda HaNasi (c. 200 CE) in redacting the Mishna, in which both the minority and majority opinions on almost every issue are duly recorded. Would it not have been far more logical to have excluded the minority opinion altogether? After all, Exodus 23:2 enjoins us to "decide the law in accordance with the majority" and normative halakha follows majority rule. The answer is that the minority opinion is not to be excluded, for it retains validity within the broad spectrum of the halakhic field; after all, "these and those are the words of the Living God." The mishna expresses this view by making reference to the halakhic principle that one court cannot overrule the opinion of another court unless the latter is greater than the former in wisdom and number (that is, the plurality which votes in favor of the decision must be greater in the second court).

The minority opinion is so important, Maimonides explains in his interpretation of this mishna, that if a court *post facto* rendered a decision in accordance with the minority opinion, a subsequent court cannot choose to switch back to the majority opinion unless it is greater than the first court in both wisdom and number.

The Rabad of Posquieres, in his interpretation of this mishna (ad loc.), even goes one step further: the only time that the second court must be greater than the first in wisdom and in number in order to overrule the decision of the first court is when the first court did not have a dissenting minority opinion. If, however, the second court wished to overturn the first court's ruling on the basis of a minority opinion, it need not be greater than the former in wisdom and number!

If the exigencies of the time and/or the situation demand it, it is certainly permissible for a religio-legal authority (*posek*) to resolve a halakhic problem in accordance with a minority decision. So teaches the Tosefta in the beginning of Tractate Eduyot, and this is the accepted procedure in normative halakha.[4]

---

4. For example, whenever a great financial loss is involved, we may invoke a minority opinion: Rema, Ḥoshen Mishpat, siman 25; Shakh, Yoreh De'ah, siman 242, and

As Rabbi Shimshon of Sens clearly explains in his *Additions to Mishna Eduyot*, a sage of the amoraic period can decide the law in accordance with a minority opinion of the *Tanna'im*, the sages of the earlier mishnaic period, since "these and those are the words of the Living God." The minority opinion is also an aspect of the divine will, and as such it can neither be nullified nor disregarded.

An interesting expansion of this concept is to be found in the Jerusalem Talmud (Y. Sanhedrin 22a), where Rabbi Yannai maintains that if the Torah had been given as a concise list of rules and statutes, without differences of opinion, no one would be able to live by its demands, since the diversity of the human spirit, the exigencies of different generations, and the necessities of specific situations would never be taken into account. The Torah had to be given in a manner which would allow for differences of opinion in order to maintain the necessary flexibility to deal with changing individual needs and historical situations. Indeed, Rabbi Yannai explains that the Torah must be able to be interpreted with "forty-nine prohibitions for impurity and forty-nine possibilities for purity."

According to the Babylonian Talmud (Sanhedrin 17a), in order to qualify as a member of the Sanhedrin, the highest court in the land, one had to have the legal ability to render a normally impure creeping creature ritually pure according to the Torah in a hundred different ways.[5] Additionally, the law required that there always be one member of the Sanhedrin who could begin the debate with a statement in defense of acquitting the defendant.

In other words, should it ever become necessary, due to changing circumstances, to find a halakhic way out, the judge had to be capable

---

Taz, Yoreh De'ah, end of siman 293 concerning the prohibition of *ḥadash* outside of Israel. See also Rema *Responsa* 125 in which he permits a Friday night marriage under extenuating circumstances.

5. Rabbenu Tam (*Tosafot*, ad loc.) dismisses this skill as useless sophistry but Rabbi Moshe Isserles, in Rema *Responsa* 107, maintains that this is not simply a matter of mental gymnastics but rather a reference to the normative halakha of lessening the degree of ritual impurity of small insects. From the talmudic context it seems clear that the intent is for the judge to be able to find a source for acquittal or purity if the nature of the situation warrants it.

of discovering any and every possible way to do so. Only a pluralistic halakha, with a majority and minority opinion, has the potential for such flexibility.

THE OVEN OF AKHNAI: LEGITIMATE VS. ILLEGITIMATE DISPUTES, AND THE PERILS OF DELEGITIMIZATION

The classic story in the Talmud, which sheds much light on the theological underpinning of halakhic pluralism, is the incident of the oven of Akhnai, the subject of a dispute between Rabbi Eliezer and the sages (Bava Metzia 59b). Rabbi Eliezer ruled that the oven in question was ritually pure and all the other sages of his time ruled it was impure.

The Talmud, in a famous and oft-cited passage, records Rabbi Eliezer's invocation of miracles to prove the correctness of his position. A carob tree became uprooted from its place and moved one hundred (or, some say, four hundred) cubits, a water channel reversed the direction of its flow, and the walls of the study hall bent over and threatened to bury those within. But the sages remained steadfast. They rejected the miraculous proofs as irrelevant to halakhic decision-making. Ultimately, Rabbi Eliezer invoked a voice from heaven which declared, "Why are you paining Rabbi Eliezer, since the law is in accordance with his opinion in every instance?" To which Rabbi Yehoshua responded, "It [the Torah] is no longer in the hands of heaven … As Rabbi Yirmiyahu taught, the Torah has already been given on Mt. Sinai; we do not heed voices from heaven, for the Torah itself has already ruled that we follow the majority."

The incident concludes with a remarkable postscript, in which Rabbi Natan meets Elijah the Prophet who, according to rabbinic tradition, never died and shuttles between heaven and earth. Rabbi Natan asked Elijah, "What did the Holy One, Blessed Be He, do at that moment?" Elijah responded, "He laughed and said, 'My children have prevailed over Me, My children have prevailed over Me.'"

The amazing and troubling aspect of this story is that the Almighty Himself is overruled as a result of the halakhic process. The only way to understand such a phenomenon theologically is to posit that both the opinion of the sages and the opinion of Rabbi Eliezer were the words of the Living God; that in the divine Torah there is room for multiple truths. Had the sages been absolutely wrong in their decision, the Almighty could not have rejoiced over their victory. Indeed, the Bible itself mandates the settlement of halakhic disputes "in accordance with the Torah which [the sages of each generation] shall teach" (Deut. 17:8–11).

Hence, it seems as if the Almighty left certain issues open, to be decided by the religio-legal leadership of each generation. And even though He Himself might prefer one view over the other, He nonetheless, in most instances, left the final decision to be decided by the rabbinic majority.

God explains that His response is joyous because, *nitzḥuni banai* – a phrase usually translated as, "My children have prevailed over Me." But the phrase may also be taken to mean, "My children have eternalized Me" (derived from the word *netzaḥ*, eternity). The Almighty rejoices because herein lies the secret of the Torah's survival: Only a halakha which leaves issues open to be decided by the rabbinic authorities of each generation will not become obsolete and atrophied. Only a halakha which is sensitive to the realities of multiple generations will live eternally.

However, this is not the end of the story. There is a critical sequel, which is less well-known but no less significant:

> They said that on that day they brought all of the objects that Rabbi Eliezer had purified and burnt them in fire. They took a vote and excommunicated him… Rabbi Eliezer rent his clothes, removed his shoes, and sat on the ground [as one in mourning]. Tears ran from his eyes and a blight descended upon the world which devastated a third of the olives, a third of the wheat, and a third of the barley.
>
> Imma Shalom, the wife of Rabbi Eliezer, was also the sister of Rabban Gamliel. From that time forward, she would not allow her husband to fall prostrate after the *Amida* in supplication [the *Taḥanun* prayer]. One day she did not stop him – either because she mistakenly thought it was the day of the New Moon, when such prayers are not recited, or because she went to the door to attend to a beggar – and she found her husband prostrate in the midst of his beseechings [i.e., reciting *Taḥanun*]. She said to him, "Rise, you have killed my brother!" When Rabban Gamliel's

death was announced, Rabbi Eliezer asked his wife, "How did you know?" She replied, "I have received this [teaching] from the house of my grandfather: All of the [heavenly] gates are closed [since the Holy Temple's destruction] except for the gate of unjust affliction." (Bava Metzia 59b)

Apparently, the author of the story believed that Rabban Gamliel had caused Rabbi Eliezer undue heartache. Although it may have been necessary to decide the law in accordance with the sages and against Rabbi Eliezer, it was superfluous and unjust to have placed Rabbi Eliezer under sanction. After all, "these and those are the words of the Living God."

All of nature shared in Rabbi Eliezer's pain, by way of the blight which destroyed a third of the basic food crops of the time. Rabban Gamliel later explained that his actions were justified "in order that disputes not increase in Israel." Indeed, Jewish unity was an especially important goal in the period following the Roman destruction of the Holy Temple and the loss of national Jewish sovereignty, and it was imperative that the Torah serve as a central unifying force – but even so, the Almighty decreed that the head of the Sanhedrin was deserving of death for having caused the great Rabbi Eliezer to suffer an unjust excommunication. It was legitimate, in the interest of unity, to decide the law against Rabbi Eliezer but he ought not to have been delegitimized or marginalized.

THE REBELLIOUS ELDER

In the interests of national unity, the Torah does prescribe the death penalty for the *zaken mamrei*, the rebellious elder who disregards the majority opinion (Deut. 17:8–13). However, this law applies only if the elder is qualified to be a member of the Sanhedrin and teaches others to go against the majority decision in practice (Sanhedrin 87, Maimonides, *Hilkhot Mamrim*, chapter 3). However, if the elder merely disagrees on a theoretical plane and urges the majority to change its opinion, he is not culpable but rather praiseworthy for expressing his truth (Maimonides, Laws 6–7).

For example, Mishna Eduyot 5:6 relates four disagreements between Akavya ben Mehalalel and the sages. Only when Akavya disrespectfully accused Shemaya and Avtalyon of showing favoritism to a convert because they themselves were converts, was the possibility of excommunicating Akavya raised. Akavya is not criticized in the mishna for maintaining his minority opinion, but rather praised for remaining steadfast in his beliefs despite the personal cost incurred – he lost his position as chief justice of his court. The mishna concludes that there was no one in Israel as wise and sin-fearing as Akavya ben Mehalalel.

Rabbi Menaḥem Meiri goes one step further than Maimonides and maintains that one can never be condemned as a rebellious elder unless he disagrees with every other member of the Sanhedrin; if even one member of the Sanhedrin agrees with the elder, he is not considered a rebellious elder.

Moreover, the question as to whether the scholar himself may act in accordance with his own view is open to dispute. According to the Babylonian Talmud (Sanhedrin 88b), Maimonides (ibid.), and Nahmanides (Rabbi Moshe ben Naḥman, 1194–1270) (ad loc.), the scholar must, in his personal practice, obey the Sanhedrin even if he is convinced that the halakha is contrary to their ruling.

By contrast, the first mishna in Horayot teaches that if a recognized scholar knows that a decision of the Sanhedrin is incorrect but nevertheless acts in accordance with the majority, he has committed a transgression and must bring a sacrifice. By not following his own minority opinion, the scholar has transgressed!

These two sources seem to be in direct conflict. Can they be reconciled?

The basis for the conflict may be found in two contradictory midrashic teachings. The Bible mandates that it is necessary to follow the rabbinic leaders of one's generation, and to "not deviate from what they tell you, neither right nor left" (Deut. 17:11). Rashi (Rabbi Shlomo Yitzḥaki, 1040–1105) on this verse cites the *Sifrei*: "Even if he tells you that right is left and left is right, you must obey." This view would seem to support the Talmud in Sanhedrin, as well as the views of Maimonides and Nahmanides.

The Jerusalem Talmud, on the other hand, provides an opposite interpretation to the same words: "One might think that even if they [the sages] tell you that right is left and that left is right, you must listen to them. No, that is not the case. It is for this reason that the Torah specifies 'neither right nor left,' in order that you may understand that only when they tell you that right is right and left is left, must you listen to them" (Y. Horayot 1:1).

Rabbi Yaakov Zvi Mecklenburg in his biblical commentary *Ha-Ktav VeHaKabbala*[6] suggests emending the text in Rashi to accord with the Jerusalem Talmud, as does Rabbi Chaim Hirshensohn.[7] The *Torah Temima*[8] makes a fascinating distinction between the two contradictory sources: he says that Rashi and the *Sifrei* are commenting on a situation in which a specific case is open to various interpretations, and although it may appear to the individual that the correct view is different from that of the Sanhedrin, he must nevertheless obey the Sanhedrin, because he agrees that it is also possible that the Sanhedrin's opinion is correct. The Jerusalem Talmud, on the other hand, is commenting on a situation in which an issue is cut-and-dried, and the individual is certain that the Sanhedrin has made an incorrect decision. In such a case, he must follow the dictates of his knowledge and conscience. I suggest, as an added proof, that this might explain the Bible's use of the words "right" and "left," rather than "black" and "white"; the latter are objective categories, whereas the former are more subjective. After all, whether you are standing to my right or to my left depends upon which way I am facing.

Hence, on the theoretical level, halakhic differences of opinion should not only be tolerated but even encouraged, as the necessary outcome of a divine law which contains many truths and allows for each scholar to discover his truth. Whether or not this ideal was to be expressed by giving a scholar the leeway to follow a minority view – at a time when there was a single ruling body, the Sanhedrin, that made unanimity a real possibility – is a moot issue, and perhaps depended on the nature of the dispute.

It is clear that the one area which brooked no disagreement was the calendar, as detailed in the Mishna in Tractate Rosh HaShana (2:8, 9) which tells of the time that Rabban Gamliel forced Rabbi Yehoshua to accede to the will of the majority concerning the date of Yom Kippur.

---

6. Deut. 17:11.
7. *Malki BeKodesh*, vol. 2 p. 74 (New Jersey, 1921).
8. Deut. 17:11, s.v. *u'mevoar mizeh*.

Rabbi Yehoshua's coerced acquiescence was not based on the verse, "you shall not deviate from what they tell you, neither right nor left" (Deut. 17:11) but rather on the verse, "These are the appointed times of God, holy proclamations which you [the courts] shall proclaim at their appointed times" (Lev. 23:4). This suggests that although there is generally latitude for individual expression in halakha within the confines of the injunction "you shall not deviate," on issues relating to the calendar – which preserves the unity of the Jewish people more than anything else – majority decisions must be accepted by all. Without a unified calendar, the people of Israel would never have survived two thousand years of exile.

JUDICIAL ERROR

The legitimacy of difference of opinion in a Jewish world without a unifying Sanhedrin may be illumined by the talmudic distinction between two categories of judicial error (Sanhedrin 33a). If a judge erred in his decision because he overlooked or misread a mishnaic text which has a universally accepted meaning, his decision is invalidated. This is called *ta'ut bedvar mishna*. If, however, a judge erred as the result of improper textual evaluation, i.e., there was a dispute in the mishna and although most authorities using the accepted rules of procedure would decide in accordance with one view, this judge decided in accordance with the other view (*ta'ut beshikul hadaat*, a mistake in judicial discretion) – then the judge's decision remains binding, even though in certain instances he may be liable to pay monetary restitution. This scenario is made possible by the principle, "These and those are the words of the Living God."

The Gemara in Sanhedrin asks whether accepted rulings of the *Amora'im* are to be considered undisputed texts, like the mishna in the first example above. Similarly, the *Rishonim* differ as to whether accepted rulings of *Geonim* are undisputed; *Aharonim* ask the same question about the *Rishonim,* and contemporary authorities debate whether the *Kitzur Shulhan Arukh* or *Mishna Berura* are to be considered undisputed texts about which there can be no argument in later generations.

Rabbi Zerahia HaLevi, the twelfth-century sage known as the Baal HaMaor, quotes a view that represents one extreme: "I heard from one of the sages of the previous generation that today there can be no mistakes in judgment (*ta'ut beshikul hadaat*), for all the laws we have are either from the Talmud or the geonic sages who came after the Talmud...therefore, anyone who errs [nowadays], errs in a matter of the mishna (*ta'ut bedvar mishna*)" (*HaMaor HaGadol*, Sanhedrin 12a). In other words, one could argue that every judicial error nowadays is the result of a misreading of the cut-and-dried decisions of earlier generations and, hence, can be invalidated by later courts. However, Rabbi HaLevi goes on to reject this view.

The most extreme statement of this position was expressed by Rabbi Yair Bachrach in seventeenth-century Ashkenaz: "And so, in these generations [after the *Shulḥan Arukh*] it would be strange to say that they [judges] were mistaken in their judgment [*beshikul hadaat*] since everything said by previous adjudicators is like mishna to us [and hence, their mistake is *bedvar mishna*, it is as if they have misread the mishna and is immediately invalidated]" (*Ḥavot Yair*, responsum 165).

The Rosh (Rabbi Asher ben Yeḥiel, 1250–1327), the great scholar of the thirteenth century who spanned both Ashkenazic and Sephardic schools of thought, disagreed vigorously. The Rosh firmly maintained that wherever the Talmud does not record a final halakhic decision, difference of opinion is legitimate, including disagreement with earlier generations and with the judge's contemporaries.[9] According to the Rosh, as long as there is a post-talmudic source which supports one's minority opinion, that opinion is legitimate.

There are also those who maintain that a halakhic decision is valid despite the incorrect application of the judicial procedure or oversight or incomplete familiarity with relevant rulings. The Rosh even maintains that if an error in judgment becomes known before the ruling has been effected, the decision is still valid, but the Rema, in *Tur Ḥoshen Mishpat* 25, disagrees.

Rabbi Yitzḥak ben Moshe of Vienna, commonly referred to as the *Or Zarua*, on Sanhedrin 5a maintains that an error in judgment that results from a lack of knowledge of some preceding rulings, but in which the correct procedure of legal reasoning was applied, never entails even

---

9. Rosh, *Commentaries* to Sanhedrin 33a. See also *Responsa of Rabbi Abraham ben HaRamban*, no. 97 and Rabbi Yaakov Emden, *Sheilat Ya'avetz*, Sec. 11:20. This is likewise the position of the Gaon of Vilna and of Rabbi Joseph B. Soloveitchik.

liability. We can conclude from the Rosh and the *Or Zarua* that a judgment would be all the more valid if a judge was fully cognizant of the accepted rules of judicial procedure, had reviewed and understood all the relevant sources, and nevertheless became convinced that the truth was to be found in an opinion different from that of the *Kitzur Shulḥan Arukh*!

The very nature of this halakhic conversation and the legitimacy granted to minority, rejected opinions within that conversation is a far cry from some contemporary ḥaredi voices that call for blind faith in the pronouncements of designated leaders, and automatically curtail consideration of other viewpoints. But the tension between pluralistic and monistic views of halakha is perennial. In the twelfth-century work *Sefer HaKabbala*, an attempted history of the transmission of the Oral Law, the author Rabbi Abraham Ibn Daoud wrote in his introduction:

> The purpose of this book is to provide students with evidence that all the teachings of our rabbis of blessed memory, namely, the sages of the Mishna and the Talmud, have been transmitted: each great sage and righteous man, each head of an academy and his school, as far back as the Men of the Great Assembly, who received them [the teachings] from the prophets, of blessed memory. Never did the sages of the Talmud, and certainly not the sages of the Mishna, teach anything, however trivial, of their own invention, except for the enactments (*takkanot*) which were made by universal agreement in order to erect a hedge around the Torah. Now, should anyone infected with heresy attempt to mislead you, saying, "It is because the rabbis differed on a number of issues that I doubt their words," you should retort bluntly and inform him that he is a "rebel against the decision of the court" (*zaken mamrei*); and that our rabbis of blessed memory never differed with respect to a commandment in principle, but only with respect to its details, for they had heard the principle from their teachers but had not inquired as to its details, since they had not served [studied from] their masters sufficiently.

In this last sentence, Ibn Daoud apparently relies on the source in Tractate Sanhedrin and even provides an interesting interpretation to the

Gemara there: disputes arose in Israel because the students of Hillel and Shammai did not sufficiently study the details of their masters' teachings, and it is only concerning the details of the law that there are disputes.

Maimonides, in his *Interpretation of the Mishna*, an introduction to the Order of Zera'im, takes a very different approach. He maintains that there are two major categories of halakhot in the Oral Law. The first category is made up of laws which were communicated by the Almighty to Moses (*halakha LeMoshe MiSinai*), and about which there are no disputes, such as the laws concerning phylacteries and the thirty-nine activities forbidden on the Sabbath. The second category is made up of laws which were developed by the sages of each generation by applying the accepted hermeneutic principles, each sage according to his own individual logic. In this latter category there are naturally differences of opinion. Maimonides condemns those who would maintain that the disputes originated as a result of faulty transmission or insufficient study, calling them men "of no wisdom, devoid of principles, denigrating those from whom they received the commandments."

Apparently, Maimonides maintains that the Almighty purposely, as it were, left room for interpretation, since in so many instances He chose not to communicate an absolute law but rather to allow individual sages to extract the law by means of legal rules and logical analysis. Thus, the sages of each generation would have flexibility in applying the law for their generation and in accordance with their understanding, as Maimonides explicitly states in *Mishneh Torah* (*Hilkhot Mamrim*, 2:1). It is also interesting to note that elsewhere in *Hilkhot Mamrim* (1:4), Maimonides cites Sanhedrin 88, but with a significant difference. He maintains that as long as there was a functioning Sanhedrin in Israel, all disputes were resolved either by unanimous decision or majority rule; once the Sanhedrin was nullified, disputes increased in Israel. The great sage and decisor completely deletes any reference to the idea that insufficient study on the part of the disciples of Hillel and Shammai caused an increase in disputes. Rather, he points to the absence of a unifying halakhic authority for all of Israel as the reason for the increase in disputes.

Moreover, Maimonides emphasizes the fact that with regard to those halakhic issues about which there was no divine transmission (*halakha LeMoshe MiSinai*), each court has the right to decide in accordance with its understanding and the needs of its generation, even if this involves overruling a previous court:

> The Great Court expounded in accordance with one of the hermeneutic principles, according to how the law appeared in its eyes, and arrived at a judgment, and then another court arose after it and another ruling appeared to it more correct and it desired to overturn [the previous judgment]. It may overturn and rule in accordance with its judgment, as is written: "the judge who will be at that time" (Deut.17:12) – you are only obligated to go to the court of your generation. (2:1)

Maimonides believes that the principle that one court cannot overrule the decision of another unless it is greater in wisdom and in number only applies to a decree, an enactment initiated by a specific court (see *Kesef Mishneh* on halakha 2, ibid.); it does not apply to a halakhic interpretation based upon logic, reason, and the exigencies of the time when it was issued. As far as the latter is concerned, we may certainly invoke the axiom, "these and those are the words of the Living God."[10]

Maimonides' opinion is in contradistinction to the passage from *Sefer HaKabbala,* quoted previously, which posits that all of the talmudic material except for the rabbinic enactments emanates from tradition and, "never did the sages of the Talmud, and certainly not the sages of the Mishna, teach anything, however trivial, of their own invention."

---

10. It seems to me that Rabbi Sherira Gaon, in his famous responsum to Rabbi Yaakov ben Rabbi Nissim and the community of Kairouan regarding the genesis of the Oral Law, could very well serve as the basis for Maimonides' position of a component part of halakha, which emerges in accordance with the decisions of the leadership of each generation. The *Gaon* wrote, "With these principles the Talmud continually becomes augmented, generation after generation, since every generation establishes its principles which emanate from the questions which arise" (*Iggeret Rabbi Sherira Gaon*, Levin Edition, p. 66).

HALAKHIC PLURALISM IN THE EYES
OF *RISHONIM* AND *AḤARONIM*

In many of the off-hand remarks of the early commentators, their advocacy of the principle of halakhic pluralism is plain to see, regardless of whether these great authorities stemmed from Ashkenaz, Sepharad, or Provence. They repeatedly express the pluralistic principle of "these and those are the words of the Living God."

Rashi, in his commentary to Ketubbot 57a, writes:

> When two [sages] argue over the statement of one [who was their master], and one sage says that this is what the master said and the other says that this is what the master said, one of them is lying. But when two *Amora'im* argue regarding a civil or ritual halakhic issue, and each one maintains the logic of his position, there is no falsehood. Each one is expressing his logic, the one master giving a reason for permitting and the other master giving a reason for prohibiting, one master compares issue to issue in such a fashion, and the other master compares it in another fashion. It is necessary to say, "these and those are the words of the Living God"; sometimes this logic pertains and sometimes that logic pertains, because the logic changes even on the basis of a small change in the issues at hand.

The Ritba (Rabbi Yom Tov ben Avraham Asevilli, 1250–1330) on Eruvin 13b comments as follows:

> "These and those are the words of the Living God." The rabbis of France asked, How is it possible for both views to be those of the Living God when one prohibits and the other permits? And they answered: When Moses went on high to receive the Torah he was shown forty-nine ways to permit and forty-nine ways to prohibit every object. He asked the Almighty concerning this, and He said, "Let these [matters about which there are so many possibilities] be handed over to the sages of Israel in every generation, and let the resolution be in accordance with their will."

Rabbi Menaḥem Meiri (1248–1316), in his work *Beit HaBeḥira*, commented on Yevamot 14a:

> That which the Torah commanded *lo titgodedu* ("Do not slice yourselves up" – Deut.14:1), even though its principal meaning is not to wound oneself as an expression of mourning for one who has died, there is a nuance [within the word *titgodedu* which may be interpreted to mean] not to turn the commandments into separate divisions [*agudot*], and this is to prohibit several individuals from performing ritual in one way while others perform the ritual in a different way, until it appears as though we are being led by two Torahs. But this prohibition applies only when a city has only one court, and when even this court is itself divided, with one component group deciding in accordance with one view and another component group in accordance with another view. But whenever there are two judicial courts, albeit in one city, and one court is accustomed to deciding in accordance with this view and the other court is accustomed to deciding in accordance with that view, this does not represent separate divisions because it is impossible for everyone to always agree on one opinion. This is certainly true regarding actions based upon custom, where there is no objection if these act in such a way and those in another way.[11]

---

11. It is interesting to note that according to Rabbi Ben-Zion Uziel, the first Sephardic chief rabbi of the State of Israel, in his *Piskey Uziel* (page 26, siman 10), Rashi would permit two different courts – for example, Sephardic and Ashkenazic – in one city, since he explains the prohibition of making divisions "lest it appear that we are acting in accordance with two Torahs" (Rashi on Yevamot 13b) and different communal customs do not suggest two Torahs. Maimonides, on the other hand, would prohibit this since he maintains that the prohibition of making divisions, "that there not be two courts in one city, this one in accord with this custom and that one in accord with that custom, for this matter causes great dissension" (*Mishneh Torah, Hilkhot Avoda Zara*, chapter 12, law 14). Rabbi Avraham Yitzḥak HaKohen Kook, in *Ezrat Kohen*, siman 103, par. 17, rules that the Sephardic and Ashkenazic communities in one city are separate, and the prohibition of making halakhic divisions does not apply to them. Rabbi Kook cites the *Shakh* to *Yoreh De'ah* 242, who limits the prohibition, "Do not slice yourselves up" to dissension within the same court in one city.

Even during the period of the later commentators, the idea of halakhic pluralism finds expression. Admittedly, works such as the *Kitzur Shulḥan Arukh* of Rabbi Shlomo Ganzfried, which records only one authoritative opinion – unlike the original *Shulḥan Arukh*, which includes the opposing views of Rabbi Karo and the Rema – seem to imply a more monistic halakhic approach. A ringing defense of pluralism is to be found in the words of Rabbi Chaim ben Rabbi Bezalel, brother of the Maharal, who studied together with Rabbi Moshe Isserles (the Rema) in the mid-sixteenth century in the yeshiva of Rabbi Shalom Shachna. He wrote *Viku'aḥ Mayim Ḥayim* (usually included at the end of the Rema's *Torat Ḥatat*), in which he vigorously argues against any written halakhic codification reflecting only one halakhic opinion:

> Only after [the decisor] has studied all of the legal disputes which have arisen regarding a specific law can his word run quickly into the sea of wisdom...Moreover, the mind of an individual is not always consistent and perhaps his mind is not disposed to give the same halakhic ruling which he gave yesterday; there is not in this any change or deficiency [which would lead us] to say that through him the Torah is becoming like two Torahs, God forbid. The opposite is the case; this [manner of halakhic investigation, exploring multiple opinions] is the path of Torah, and "these and those are the words of the Living God." (*Alon Mishpat HaIvri*, 37)

A fascinating contrast is to be found in the writings of two cotemporary religious leaders, Rabbi Moshe Feinstein and Rabbi Yitzḥak Hutner. The former, world-renowned halakhic decisor of our generation, utilizes the expression "these and those are the words of the Living God," but nevertheless posits that one argument may ultimately be more correct than the others:

> And this is the matter concerning all of the disputes of our earlier and later sages, when one forbade and the other permitted: whenever the [law] was not resolved in accordance with one [of them], any [rabbi] could rule in his locality in accordance with his

logic, even though the true law is only in accordance with one of them ... Both are the words of the Living God, but the real truth, revealed before heaven, is only like one of them.

Nevertheless, Rabbi Moshe Feinstein insists that with regard to reciting the blessings on learning Torah and fulfilling the commandment to study Torah, no differentiation should be made between texts containing majority opinions and texts containing minority opinions. All Torah texts are worthy since "these and those are the words of the Living God" (*Iggrot Moshe, Oraḥ Ḥaim* 4:9, 24).

Rabbi Yitzḥak Hutner, on the other hand, accepts the talmudic view that disputes arose as a result of insufficient study or forgetfulness, a view which we initially equated with the monistic approach to halakha. Nevertheless, he resoundingly affirms the positive role of disputes in enlarging the scope of Torah and initiating novel ideas therein. He even reads into this view of the origin of halakha a bold concept of halakhic pluralism:

Sometimes, the nullification of Torah is its very confirmation, as it is written, "the tablets which you have broken." [God said to Moses], "May your strength increase because you have broken them; the act of breaking the tablets is an act of confirming the Torah through its nullification." Our sages have said, "Were the tablets not broken, Torah would not have been forgotten in Israel" (Eruvin 54a); we find therefore that the breaking of the tablets contains an aspect of forgetting of the Torah. We learn from this an awesome and novel idea: it is possible for Torah to be increased through its having been forgotten, and it is possible to be blessed with increased strength because of the Torah having been forgotten!

Go out and see what our sages have taught: three hundred laws were forgotten during the mourning period for Moses, and Otniel ben Kenaz restored them with his logic and casuistry (Temura 16a). And even more than that: every dispute in halakha stems from the fact that Torah was forgotten, and nevertheless our sages declared, "Even though these purify and those defile, these invalidate and those permit, these exempt and those obligate, these and those are the words of the Living God." Hence, all different opinions and differing views contribute to the growth of Torah and its majesty, which ... is emphasized to a greater extent by the Oral Law which is revealed in disputes rather than by agreement, because "these and those are the words of the Living God" includes the principle that even the rejected view in halakha remains Torah knowledge as long as it was expressed as part of the give-and-take of the Oral Law... and if there will be a vote afterwards and the decision is in accordance with the rejected view, from then on halakha will be different in truth.

The "battles" within Torah are not simply one of many possible ways of (acquiring) Torah, but rather the positive creation of new Torah values which cannot be found in the words of Torah... And the two sides which clash in halakha become partners in the creation of a new Torah value whose name is "the battle of Torah." (*Paḥad Yitzḥak*, Ḥanukka pp. 36–37)

Despite all this, pluralism is obviously not open-ended. Starting with the biblical story of the Tree of the Knowledge of Good and Evil which opens the Book of Genesis and serves as an introduction to the entire Torah, it is clear that God demands that the definition of what is good and what is evil must emanate from an objective source beyond the subjective individual. Indeed, even though the fruit was "good to eat, a temptation to the eyes, and a desirable way to gain wisdom," the Almighty nevertheless decided that it was evil to partake of it. And from the talmudic period until the Emancipation, the partners to the "these and those are the words of the Living God" disputes each accepted upon themselves an external and objective halakha. Submission to a higher autonomous system was the axiom of halakhic dispute. Hence, a non-Orthodox system cannot claim halakhic legitimacy under the rubric of "these and those are the words of the Living God." While we may certainly learn from serious Jews of any or no religious persuasion, both tradition and logic dictate that halakhic legitimacy can only be accorded to those who accept upon themselves the axioms upon which the halakhic system is based.

Although a non-halakhic theological system cannot claim for itself a voting voice in a forum of halakhic discourse, I believe it is crucial that the tent of Orthodoxy be as broad, open, and inviting as possible. Even a halakhic position which the Orthodox majority rejects, but which, nevertheless, has a legitimate halakhic basis to rely upon, should be given due consideration.

Within the world of halakhic Judaism, the most striking affirmation of the benefits of a pluralistic approach is to be found in the words of Rabbi Avraham Yitzhak HaKohen Kook, in *Olat Re'iya*, volume 1, p. 336:

> The multiplicity of views which arise as a result of the differences of personalities and educational backgrounds is specifically the fact which most enriches and broadens wisdom. Ultimately, all issues will be properly understood, and it will be recognized that it would have been impossible for the Building of Peace [the Third Temple] to have been erected had it not been for all those influences which appeared to have been in conflict.

According to Rabbi Kook, it is the sum total of many different ideas and ideologies which will ultimately lead to a shared vision that expresses true peace; the authentic symphony is the product of many different musical instruments melding together in majestic harmony.

Authority versus Autonomy: On Parents and Children, Masters and Disciples

PREFACE: THE FUNDAMENTAL IDEOLOGICAL SOURCE FOR HONORING ONE'S PARENTS[1]

The Torah emphasizes a child's obligation to honor his parents in two central verses: "Honor your father and your mother, that your days may be lengthened upon the land which the Lord your God gives to you" (Ex. 20:12) and, "A person shall fear his mother and his father, and you shall observe My *Shabbatot*; I am the Lord your God" (Lev. 19:3). According to the sages, the ideological basis for honoring and fearing parents – aside from the gratitude that is due to them for providing care and physical sustenance – rests upon the fact that it is the parents who gave birth to the children; they have "creators' rights."[2] From this perspective, honoring parents is a logical continuation of honoring God. There is a *beraita* (mishnaic source) that teaches this explicitly:

---

1. Gerald Blidstein, *Honor Thy Father and Thy Mother*, Ktav 1975.
2. Therefore, in terms of halakha, honor must be shown to parents after their death – including the customs of mourning and reciting Kaddish – even in the case of parents who abandoned their children or harmed them. Since the parents gave the children life, they are worthy of elementary halakhic respect.

The rabbis taught: there are three partners in [creating] a person: God, his father, and his mother. When a person honors his father and mother, God says: "I consider them as though I dwelled among them and they honored Me." (Kiddushin 30b)

The Gemara also records an illustration of the direct line from Divinity to parenthood: "When he would hear his mother's footsteps approaching, Rabbi Yosef would say: 'I shall stand up before the approaching Divine Presence'" (Kiddushin 31b).[3]

Perhaps the most obvious proof of this close connection between honoring God and honoring parents is the location of the commandment to honor parents within the Ten Commandments: it is grouped in the first half, together with the commandments pertaining to the relationship between man and God: "I am the Lord your God"; "You shall have no other gods"; "You shall not take God's name in vain"; Shabbat; and then honoring parents.

Obviously, since the commandment to honor one's parents is the last of the first five commandments, it also serves as a logical and appropriate bridge to the second group of five commandments, which pertain to inter-personal relations: "You shall not murder"; "You shall not commit adultery"; "You shall not steal"; "You shall not bear false witness"; "You shall not covet." These latter five were grouped together on the second tablet.[4]

According to Maimonides, the very foundation of an authoritarian society – as opposed to an anarchical one – rests upon the principle of honoring parents. If there is no respect for parents, there will be no respect for the law and for the legal system as a whole. Maimonides was an outstanding codifier whose genius is displayed in his magnum opus, *Mishneh Torah*. In this definitive work, one can learn from Maimonides' knowledge of the commandments, his

---

3. From the story of Rabbi Yosef, it would seem that the custom, prevalent among Oriental Jewish communities, to kiss the mother's hand while reciting *Eshet Ḥayil* on Shabbat is derived from the fact that *Eshet Ḥayil* is in fact referring to the Divine Presence, and the mother represents the Divine Presence.
4. According to the *Commentary of Nahmanides* on Ex. 20:12–13.

meticulous formulations and precise definitions, but also from his choice of location for each subject. He discusses honoring parents under the category of Laws of Heretics, after the first four chapters which deal with a heretical elder, and those who rebel against the Sanhedrin. In his *Commentary on the Mishna*, on the words, "These are actions whose dividends a person enjoys in this world, while the capital awaits him in the World to Come; these are they: honoring one's father and mother" (Pe'ah 1:1), Maimonides writes explicitly: "'Whose dividends a person enjoys in this world' – because he thereby creates stable social relations."[5]

Similarly, in the *Shulḥan Arukh*, Rabbi Yosef Karo lists the laws of honoring parents in the section known as *Yoreh De'ah*, before (and as a sort of introduction to) the laws of honoring one's Torah teacher or a Torah sage: sections 240–241 deal with honoring parents, while section 242 discusses the prohibition of teaching others in the presence of one's rabbi, and the obligation to stand up for and give honor to a learned sage. In other words, there is a direct connection between honoring parents and honor for the legislative religious establishment.

SCOPE OF THE OBLIGATION TO HONOR
AND FEAR PARENTS

On one hand, several of the anecdotes recorded in the Gemara would seem to suggest that honoring parents is one of the "commandments that are not quantified." Rabbi Abahu taught:

> Like Avimi, my son ... He had five sons who were ordained as rabbis during his father's lifetime. Rabbi Abahu would come calling at the door, and Rabbi Avimi himself would run to open it for his father, calling "Yes, yes!" until he came in. One day his father said to him: "I would like to drink some water." When Rabbi Avimi brought the water to his father, Rabbi Abahu had fallen asleep. Rabbi Avimi bent down and waited by him, with the water, until he woke up. (Kiddushin 31b)

---

5. Maimonides, *Moreh Nevukhim*, Friedlander edition, Part III p. 41.

The Gemara recounts other, similar stories: "Rabbi Tarfon had a mother for whom, whenever she wished to retire to bed, he would bend down so that she could climb over him" (ibid.). Perhaps the most famous story concerns Duma, the son of Netina, who refrained from disturbing his father's sleep, even though he thereby suffered great financial loss.

On the other hand, if we study carefully the stories in the Book of Genesis – stories about the family that formed the basis for the creation of the nation in the Book of Exodus – we see that the parents were not always right, and the independence of the children was, in many cases, necessary and important. At the very least, we may say that in several instances there is a tension between the principle of obeying a parent and following the right path in the eyes of God.

Let us offer several examples.

According to almost all the midrashim of the sages, Abraham was required to rebel against his father, Terah, and his idolatry, in order to introduce into the world the revolutionary concept of monotheism, belief in the One God of justice and mercy.

The tragedies of Jacob's life – his difficult stay with Laban the Aramean; the exchange of Laban's daughters under the wedding canopy, causing Jacob to marry a woman he did not love; his sons' deception of him concerning the fate of Joseph; Joseph's deception, hiding his identity as Jacob's son – all this arose from Jacob's deception in presenting himself as Esau to his blind father. This is expressed in the very fact that it is only after some twenty-two years away from his father's house that Jacob is ready to establish a monument "to the Lord God of Israel." Until then he had a "Lord of his father," but he did not yet have a Lord for himself. The lengthy severance from his father was necessary, it seems, for him to discover his true identity and his personal God.

The forefathers sometimes made mistakes, as even the sages themselves point out:

> Rabbi Hama bar Guria said, in the name of Rav: A person must never differentiate between one of his children and all the others: because of the weight of two *sela'im* of fine wool that Jacob gave Joseph [i.e., the coat] over and above [what he gave] to his

other children – his brothers were jealous of him, and ultimately our forefathers ended up going down to Egypt. (Shabbat 10b)

Halakhically, too, it is clear that a child is not completely subjugated to his parents: he is free and independent, at the very least when he reaches maturity and can take responsibility for himself (according to the sages, apparently, at the age of twenty), at which point he is considered responsible for his actions in the Heavenly Court, too.[6] In the Mishna we learn (Pesaḥim 10:1), "Even a Jew who is destitute must not eat before first leaning." Rashi explains, "He must not eat on Passover eve until he leans, in the manner of free men." The Gemara (Pesaḥim 108a) explains further:

> A woman at her husband's table does not lean (Rashbam: "for she is subjugated to her husband"). But if she is an important woman, she must lean. A son at his father's table must lean (Rashbam: "For he is not subjugated to such a degree").

According to the Gemara's conclusion, a rabbi's assistant and his student need not lean, because they are likewise considered subjugated – but this is not the case concerning a son at his father's table! A man's son is granted greater independence than the man's disciples.

Let us review the scope of the halakhic obligation of honoring parents as the sages view it, and try to define it in practical terms. The Gemara (Kiddushin 31b) records the following Tosefta:

> The sages taught: What is the definition of "fear," and what is the definition of "honor"?
>
> "Fear" means – [the son] should not stand in [his father's] place, nor sit in his place, nor contradict his words, nor express [agreement or] disagreement with him.
>
> "Honor" means – providing him with food and drink, clothing and shelter; bringing him in and escorting him out.

---

6. See Rashi on Gen. 23:1: "At a hundred [Sara] was like a twenty-year-old in terms of sin: just as a twenty-year-old has no sin, for she is not punishable," based on Yoma 38a.

It is easy to understand that the commandment to honor parents requires compassion and positive assistance, ensuring that parents have all their physical needs taken care of. But is a son actually forbidden to disagree with his father, to think differently from him – even in everyday, practical matters? If this were so, the son would certainly be completely subjugated to his father in the most personal and private sphere possible – that of thought and opinion!

Rashi interprets the entire discussion of "fearing" parents as referring to a public forum:

> "Not to stand in his place" – in the place reserved for his father among the elders, among his colleagues. "Nor to express agreement or disagreement" – if his father and another sage are divided in their interpretation of a matter of halakha, the son should not say, "I would tend to agree with so-and-so." (Rashi ad loc.)

It would seem, according to Rashi, that the prohibition is not to disagree with one's father, but rather to express this disagreement in public, thereby embarrassing him in front of his peers. But it is not prohibited for a son to disagree with his father's views in the context of a private discussion between them.

Rabbi Yosef Karo draws a different distinction to explain the requirements, saying, "He should not contradict his words, nor express agreement or disagreement." According to this great halakhic authority, the prohibition refers not specifically to a public arena, but rather to a situation where the disagreement is expressed "before him" – i.e., in his father's presence, because this causes his father embarrassment. In other words, a son may disagree with his father, but he must not express it to his father's face, in his presence – either in the home or outside of it (*Shulḥan Arukh, Yoreh De'ah*, siman 240:2). The *Shakh* disagrees, commenting there, "It would seem that it is prohibited to contradict him even while not in his presence, as it would seem from the argument in section 4, and as taught explicitly further on, in siman 242:20."

The Vilna Gaon brings irrefutable proof that the halakha is indeed in accordance with Rabbi Yosef Karo's ruling, i.e., that the prohibition of contradicting the parent refers specifically to a situation in which the contradiction is expressed in his presence. He writes:

> For we find [many learned Torah sages] who disagree with their fathers and their Torah teachers – Rabbi disagrees with Rabban Shimon ben Gamliel, and many other such examples. And we rule accordingly. (See Vilna Gaon's commentary on the *Shulḥan Arukh*, ad loc.)

In fact, the possibility of a son disagreeing with his father – even if his father is also his Torah teacher – is discussed explicitly:

> Our sages taught: "And you shall teach them [the words of Torah] diligently" – meaning that the words of Torah should be fluent and clear [literally: "sharp"] in your mouth. As it is written: "The warrior's arrows are sharpened."
>
> It is also written, "Happy is the man who has filled his quiver with them; they shall not be shamed, for he shall speak with the enemies at the gate. What is the meaning of the expression "with the enemies at the gate?"
>
> Rabbi Ḥiya bar Abba said: Even a father and his son, or a rabbi and his disciple, who are studying Torah together at the same gate – they become enemies [opponents] of one another. [Rashi: "Because each raises objections against the other's view, and one need not necessarily accept the view of the other."]
>
> And they do not move from there until they come to love one another, as it is written: "And beloved in a storm [*besufa*]" – read this not as *besufa*, but rather as *besofa* – i.e., in the end. (Kiddushin 30a–b)

Rashi seems to understand from this that a son may disagree with his father even concerning matters of Torah, and even in his presence. He therefore concludes that the only thing that is prohibited is for him to express disagreement with his father in public, in the presence of his father's peers, since this causes him shame.

It appears to me that if a son is encouraged to consolidate and attain his own independent opinion in matters of Torah and halakha, which are the source of authority in society as a whole, he is certainly entitled to his own opinions in material, worldly matters.[7]

Having addressed the definition of "fear," let us now turn our attention to the matter of "honor." According to the Gemara cited above, honor involves providing food and drink, clothing and shelter, and escorting one's parents. In other words, a child should serve his parents so as to ensure that all their vital physical needs are taken care of.

The Gemara in Kiddushin (31b; 32a) poses the obvious question, "On whose account?" In other words, who is responsible for paying for these vital amenities? The son is required to perform the actions involved in providing them – but who is responsible for the funding of all these conveniences, including housing, medications, etc.? The Gemara concludes that it is the parent himself who pays.

In the *Shulḥan Arukh* this conclusion is codified as halakha, with the additional comment: "If the father lacks (the necessary funds) and the son possesses – the son is forced [if necessary] to provide nourishment for the father. And if the son, too, lacks, he is not required to go collecting alms in order to provide nourishment for his father." The Rema adds that if neither the father nor the son is able to pay, but a grandchild has the necessary funds, the grandchild is obligated to pay (*Shulḥan Arukh Yoreh De'ah*, siman 240:5).

LIMITATIONS OF THE OBLIGATION

Is an adult child free to make choices that contradict the views of his parents in such existential questions as where and what to study, where to live, and whom to marry? The halakha answers this question very clearly:

> If a disciple wishes to go to a different place, where he is certain that his studies with the Torah teacher there will be successful, and his father objects out of concern that the proposed place is dangerous – he is not required to obey his father in this matter. (*Shulḥan Arukh*, siman 240:25 to end)

---

7. This, despite the teaching of Rabbi Yisrael ben Yosef al Nakava in *Menorat HaMaor*, p. 19, maintaining that in matters of halakha a son may argue with his father, but not in other matters.

The Rema, outstanding halakhic authority of the Ashkenazi world, adds a similar and even more sensitive scenario, in which a child is not required to obey his parents: "Likewise, if the father objects to his son marrying a certain woman whom he [the son] desires, the son is not required to obey his father" (ibid.).[8] In this matter, the Rema bases his ruling on the great Italian authority known as the Maharik, Rabbi Yosef Kolon (1420–1480), who provides three reasons for his stance (*Responsa*, shoresh 166):

> The verse from the beginning of the Book of Genesis, concerning the first marriage – between Adam and Eve – teaches, "Therefore a man shall leave his father and mother and cleave to his wife, that they may become a single flesh" (Gen. 2:24). This tells us that a person must choose a spouse without parental interference.
>
> The sages deduce from the verse, "A person shall fear his father and his mother, and you shall observe My Shabbatot," that if the parent instructs the child to perform some act that contradicts one of the commandments of the Torah, the parent is not to be obeyed: "A person shall fear his father and his mother" – BUT – "You shall observe My Shabbatot" (i.e., even if the parent instructs that the Sabbath be violated) (Lev. 19:3). The rule is that if we must choose between the words of the Teacher (God) and those of the student (the parent), we follow the words of the Teacher (Bava Metzia 32a).

The Maharik cites the ruling of Rabbi Yehuda in the name of Rav (Kiddushin 41a) that, "A man may not betroth a woman until he sees [has met] her, lest she be loathsome in his eyes, while the Torah teaches, 'You shall love your neighbor as yourself,'" from which the Maharik deduces, in a most romantic fashion, that the Torah itself requires that the bride and groom be in love with one another! This idea is eternalized in one of the seven blessings recited under the nuptial canopy: "Grant joy to these loving companions, as You granted joy to Your creations in the Garden of Eden." Therefore, the Maharik concludes,

---

8. This ruling of the Rema does not apply to marriages that are halakhically forbidden.

if a parent commands his son not to marry his beloved, the parent is giving an instruction that is contrary to the Torah, and the son is not required to obey!

The third reason is a purely halakhic one, defining the essence of the commandment of honoring and fearing parents:

> Thus far the discussion of "on whose account" has concerned only such matters as pertain to the father himself, such as sustaining the father physically and providing his physical requirements. But in matters that do not involve the father himself, such as here [the matter of the son's marriage partner], the father has no right to object to his son's decision – neither on the basis of "honor" nor on the basis of "fear." For "honor" pertains only to such matters as providing food and drink, clothing and shelter… and the like, which involve the father himself. But in matters that do not involve the father himself, it is clear that the father has no right to object to his son's choices.[9]

In summary, the parent has no right to interfere, and the child is certainly not obligated to obey the parent, in such existential matters. The concepts of "honor" and "fear" are relevant only in the sphere of the parent's own physical requirements.

TENSION BETWEEN THE DEMANDS OF THE OLDER GENERATION AND THE NEEDS OF THE YOUNGER GENERATION

What happens when a father claims that his physical health will be affected by his son marrying a certain woman, or engaging in a certain profession? What if the child's "disobedience" will lead to a parent suffering a psychological ailment?

It would seem that the child must still be free and independent to lead his or her own life. The Gemara recounts a fascinating story,

---

9. See also *Ḥiddushei HaRashba* on Yevamot 6a, and the opinion of Rabbi Ḥananel, as quoted by Nahmanidies, both of which say the same thing.

describing a situation in which it is exceptionally difficult for a son to live in the vicinity of his mother:

> Rav Assi had an elderly mother. She said to him, "I want some jewelry." He duly did as she asked. "I want a husband." He promised to seek a husband for her. "I want a husband who is as pleasant as you are." He left his mother and went to Eretz Yisrael. He heard that his mother was following him to Eretz Yisrael. He came before Rabbi Yoḥanan to ask a question. He said to him, "Shall I leave Eretz Yisrael?" He told him, "That is forbidden." He said to him, "In order to escape my mother?" He answered, "I do not know." He waited a little, and then came again to ask. Rabbi Yoḥanan said to him, "Assi, you wish to leave Eretz Yisrael. May God bring you back [after you have sorted out the problem with your mother] in peace." Rav Assi came before Rabbi Elazar, to ask him. He said, "Perhaps, God forbid, Rabbi Yoḥanan was angry with me?" Rabbi Elazar said: "What did he say?" He answered, "May God bring you back in peace." [Rabbi Elazar] told him, "If he was angry with you, he would not have given you a blessing." Having asked all these questions and received answers to them, he left Eretz Yisrael. He then heard that the coffin of his deceased mother was on its way to Eretz Yisrael. He said, "Had I known that my mother was coming to Eretz Yisrael only in a coffin, I would not have left the land." (Kiddushin 31b)

Apparently, Rav Assi understood the moment his mother mentioned her desire for a husband "like him," that his mother's relationship towards him was not a healthy one; it was likely to disrupt his marriage and his normal functioning. He had no choice but to leave Babylon – where his mother lived – and move to Eretz Yisrael. When he heard that his mother was following him to Eretz Yisrael, he received an indirect blessing to leave the land because of her. This story appears to be the source of an important halakha for Maimonides, who adds another significant consideration:

> A person whose father or mother has become demented should try to deal with them in the best possible way in accordance with their perceptions, until He has mercy on them [meaning

either that God heals them, or that He takes them in death]. But
if it is impossible for him to deal with them, on account of their
dementia, he may leave them and go, instructing others to care
for them appropriately. (*Mishneh Torah, Hilkhot Mamrim* 6:10)

What Maimonides adds here is that while a child is permitted to leave
a psychotic parent, he must ensure that there are other people, or an
institution, to take care of the parent.

The Ra'avad, in his comments on Maimonides (ibid.), does not
accept this law and responds in his characteristic style: "Avraham [refer-
ring to himself] says this teaching is not correct. If he [the son] goes and
leaves [the parent], who shall he instruct to care for him?" According
to the Ra'avad, the son must stay – at the very least for long enough to
train a suitable caregiver.

The *Kesef Mishneh* (Rabbi Yosef Karo) disagrees with the Ra'avad
(ibid., in the *Mishneh Torah*), and emphasizes that the source for Maimonides' ruling is the story of Rav Assi quoted above: "If our Teacher
[Maimonides] had invented this law of his own initiative, [Ra'avad's]
comment would be in place. But since he bases it on the actual story of
Rav Assi, the comment has no place."

The Ran similarly has trouble understanding Ra'avad's comment,
since Maimonides bases his ruling on the Gemara itself, on the story of
Rav Assi. But the Ran raises the possibility that perhaps Rav Assi was permitted to leave his mother specifically in order to fulfill the commandment
of going to Eretz Yisrael, even though leaving a mother who is mentally
ill would not otherwise be permissible. However, the Ran himself rejects
this interpretation. Rabbi Yitzhak Or Zarua likewise rules in accordance
with Maimonides, on the basis of the story of Rav Assi (Introduction,
Shiltei HaGibborim in the comments of the Rif on Kiddushin 13b).

Sefer Ḥasidim and *Arukh HaShulḥan* broaden the law to allow a
son to leave a parent even if the parent is not mentally disturbed. The former states (siman 343), "If a father and his son live in strife and anger… it
is better that they not live together." The latter writes (siman 240:33), "If
he [the parent] is not wicked, but simply behaves badly and is regarded
by others as being strange, or if he is drunk, then it is advisable for [the
son] to distance himself from him." All of the above suggests that if, for

objective reasons, the parent is limiting the son's ability to develop in the marital, social, or economic sphere, the son is permitted to leave the parent. If Rav Assi had remained in Babylon, his mother would certainly have been happier – but he nevertheless left and went to Eretz Yisrael.

In summary, it would appear that in the great conflict that may erupt between responsibility for the older generation and the development of the younger generation, the latter must prevail. There is no obligation to accept the instructions – or even to live in the vicinity – of a parent who does not allow a son or daughter to live his or her own life and to choose his or her own destiny.

A SON'S INDEPENDENCE IN MATTERS OF HALAKHA: AKAVYA BEN MEHALALEL AND HIS SON

Akavya ben Mehalalel was an important figure during the tannaitic period who was not afraid of standing up to authority, as the following story illustrates:

> Akavya ben Mehalalel made four halakhic rulings. [The sages] said to him: Akavya, recant those four rulings that you made and we will make you the head of a *beit din* (court of law). He said to them: Better that I be called a fool all my life and not for a moment perform evil in the eyes of God, lest people say, "he recanted for the sake of power."
> …They excommunicated him, and he died in excommunication, and the *beit din* stoned his coffin.
> Rabbi Yehuda said: Heaven forfend that Akavya should be excommunicated! The gate of the courtyard may not be locked before any Jew as wise and fearful of sin as Akavya ben Mehalalel. (Mishna Eduyot 5:6)

The mishna in Tractate Eduyot that immediately follows this one also focuses on Akavya ben Mehalalel. The mishna teaches a lesson of great importance with regard to relations between parents and children. At the same time, we learn something of the manner of study in the period around the time of the destruction of the Second Temple: the stormy debate that rages among the sages indicates the essence of the Oral Law.

> At the time of his death, [Akavya ben Mehalalel] told his son: My son, recant concerning the four matters that I taught. His son answered: Why, then, did you not recant yourself? He answered: I learned from the many, and they [the other sages] likewise learned from the many. I maintained my understanding, and they maintained their understanding. But you have been exposed to the view of an individual [myself, your father] and the view of the many [the other sages, who disagree with me]. It is better that you set the lone opinion aside and adopt the words of the many.
>
> He said to him: Father – recommend me to your colleagues. He answered: I will not recommend. He said: Perhaps you have found some deficiency in me? He answered: No. It is your actions that can cause you to be drawn closer, and your actions that have the power to cause you to be held at a distance. (Mishna Eduyot 5:7)

What is amazing about the above dialogue between the father – an enormously knowledgeable Torah sage – and his learned son, is the complete freedom that the father allows his son in his halakhic rulings, with no connection whatsoever to "family loyalty"; the father makes no effort to force his son to rule as he does. The son leans in his father's presence at the Seder table but he is free before God, and his Torah learning is no less legitimate or valuable than that of his father. Conversely, the son must understand the legitimate price of independence: he must seek acceptance on his own merits, and not by dint of family connections.

AKAVYA BEN MEHALALEL VS. THE SAGES, AND
RABBI ELIEZER VS. RABBAN GAMLIEL

In order to understand this story in depth, it is important to investigate when Akavya ben Mehalalel lived, and how the basis of his disagreement with the sages turned on the very essence of the Oral Law, its content, and the method of its transmission. According to what appears to me to be the most probable opinion, the controversy between Akavya ben Mehalalel and the sages concerning the four laws in question took place during the time of Rabban Gamliel of Yavneh – the period during which the rabbinical establishment succeeded in excommunicating Rabbi Eliezer ben Hyrcanus, known as the "great Rabbi Eliezer."[10]

The accounts are quite similar, if not altogether identical. Rabbi Eliezer never changed his halakhic position concerning the "*akhnai* oven" (Bava Metzia 59b), and as a result he suffered excommunication – exactly the same as Akavya ben Mehalalel, according to one version of the mishna quoted above.[11] It is quite possible that the tension between Rabbi Eliezer, on one hand, and Rabbi Yehoshua and Rabban Gamliel, on the other hand, was of the same variety that the Gemara records as having developed between Akavya ben Mehalalel and the sages. Akavya was opposed to changing his view of the halakha because he was not entitled to change what he had learned from the majority of his teachers – which, for him, was the crux of the Oral Law. By the same measure, Rabbi Eliezer ben Hyrcanus, who was known as a "plastered pit that does not lose a drop" (Mishna Avot 2:8), and who testifies concerning himself that he "never said [taught] anything that he had not learned from his teachers" (Sukka 28a), belongs to the same school of thought. Clearly, his halakhic line of thinking – his definition of the tradition of Oral Law that Moshe received at Sinai – was the one that he had "preserved" from his teachers of the previous generation.

Rabban Gamliel and Rabbi Yehoshua (as well as Rabbi Akiva), on the other hand, established in Yavneh the supremacy of the hermeneutical laws by which the Torah is interpreted, and the superiority of logical argument over ancient tradition. These intellectual giants were not afraid to innovate in various spheres of halakha, and Rabbi Eliezer ben Erekh, who belonged to the school of Rabbi Yehoshua, Rabban Gamliel, and Rabbi Akiva, is described as an "ever-swelling stream" (Mishna Avot 2:8) – the complete opposite of a "lined pit that does not lose a drop."[12]

---

10. Ḥaim Dov Mantel, *Studies in the History of the Sanhedrin*, chapter 3, pp. 128–130, Dvir 1969.

11. For a detailed account of the *akhnai* story, please see the previous chapter, "Dissent in Jewish Tradition."

12. Yitzḥak Gilat, *The Teachings of Rabbi Eliezer ben Hyrcanus and Their Place in the History of the Halakha*, Dvir 1968, especially chapter 5, "Deduction and Logical Argument as Principles and Elements in Halakhic Decision-Making," concerning the scope of the prohibition of leaving leaven in one's house according to Rabbi Eliezer (p. 150), and in general, pp. 316–324.

TRADITION VS. INNOVATION

Around the story of the *"akhnai* oven" (Bava Metzia 59b) we perceive the tension between old tradition and innovative exegesis, between God, who rules in accordance with Rabbi Eliezer, and His children, belonging to the new generation, who emerge victorious: Rabbi Yehoshua and Rabban Gamliel. What Akavya ben Mehalalel is really explaining to his son is that in his generation, the halakhic direction has already been decided in favor of hermeneutical laws and logic. He himself is obligated to follow the majority of his teachers, but his son is free to rule according to the majority in his own generation.

The tension between tradition and innovation, between halakhot transmitted from generation to generation and the logical rules by which the Torah is interpreted, reaches its climax in the story of the *"akhnai* oven"* – an oven which Rabbi Eliezer declared ritually pure, while the rest of the sages declared it impure. In support of Rabbi Eliezer, various miracles occurred. For example, a stream of water, which traditionally represents Torah, ran backwards[13] – perhaps symbolically alluding to the correctness of the previous generation – and the walls of the study hall threatened to collapse on those within, bringing all the writings of previous generations down upon their heads. The walls did not fall, out of respect for Rabbi Yehoshua, nor did they straighten themselves, out of respect for Rabbi Eliezer. They continued to stand, bent over, expressing the inherent tension in the Oral Law between tradition (represented by Rabbi Eliezer) and logical innovation (represented by Rabbi Yehoshua).

A voice from heaven declared that Rabbi Eliezer was correct, but even this did not sway the sages.

> Rabbi Yirmiyah said: Since the Torah was given at Mount Sinai, we do not pay attention to heavenly voices, since You already wrote in the Torah, "You shall follow the majority."

---

13. In Hebrew – *amat hamayim*, which may also be read as *emet hamayim* – the truth of the water. Water refers to Torah; thus, we learn that the truth of Torah is in its flow from generation to generation.

This means that there is no absolute Oral Law that was given at Sinai stipulating the absolute halakha. Since the giving of the Torah at Sinai, there are exegetical rules and rules for halakhic decisions that are based on logic, too – not only on the accepted tradition.[14] The halakha is decided in accordance with the latest generation, which is the beneficiary of the wisdom of former generations as well as the wisdom of the present.

It is further related in the same Gemara that Rabbi Natan met Elijah the Prophet and asked him, "What did the Holy One do at that time?" i.e., at the time of this argument, when the view of the majority of the sages prevailed, as it were, over God's own ruling! Elijah reported that God had laughed and said, "My children have prevailed over Me; My children have prevailed over Me."

It should be noted that the expression "prevailed" (*nitzḥuni*) indicates both victory (*nitzaḥon*) and also eternity (*netzaḥ*). It is specifically the Oral Law, which embodies the possibility of innovation, inducing one matter from another in order to find solutions to the problems of each generation and the challenges and needs of each era – it is specifically this Torah that is eternal. Needless to say, during the period of Yavneh, following the tremendous shock of the destruction of the Temple, innovation in Torah was of critical importance.

Despite his greatness, Rabbi Eliezer was excommunicated by the Great Court, the Sanhedrin, resulting in a blight on the year's crops. The Gemara relates that one day he prostrated himself in prayer and Rabban Gamliel, head of the Sanhedrin, died as a result of the cry of the great Rabbi Eliezer – apparently protesting that he was not deserving of excommunication. The lesson is that while we can understand the victory of Rabbi Yehoshua in halakhic terms – we can understand the need for halakha to be based on logical argument and innovation, in order for

---

14. The source of controversy in halakha is itself argued in the Gemara. In Sanhedrin 88b, we learn that controversy arises principally from the deficiency in the tradition that came about because the disciples of Hillel and Shammai were not sufficiently familiar with their teachings, while Eruvin 13b maintains, in the name of the heavenly voice, "Both these and those are the words of the living God" – i.e., controversy is an integral part of the Oral Law and the divine will.

the Torah to remain an eternally swelling stream – we cannot justify the excommunication of Rabbi Eliezer and the complete delegitimization of his halakhic view in all matters. The authority of tradition cannot serve as the sole factor in the process of the Oral Law, but at the same time, it cannot be completely nullified.

The story concludes in glorious dialectic. The past dare not be denied or obliterated, even as the present and future must be given their due. The death of Rabbi Eliezer ben Hyrcanus, the great Rabbi Eliezer, is recounted in Sanhedrin 68a:

> When Rabbi Eliezer fell ill, Rabbi Akiva and his colleagues came to visit him. He sat under his canopy [since he was excommunicated], while they sat in the room. That day was a Friday, and his son Hyrcanus came in [just before dusk] to remove his father's *tefillin* [so that he would not be wearing them on Shabbat]. Rabbi Eliezer scolded him, and he went out reproached.
>
> He [Hyrcanus, son of Rabbi Eliezer] said to his friends: "It seems to me that my father has lost his mind."
>
> They said to him, "You and your mother may have lost your minds [but Rabbi Eliezer, your father, is quite clear of mind]. How could you have put aside a prohibition punishable by stoning [lighting Shabbat candles to announce the start of Shabbat, and the preparation of hot food] for the sake of engaging in a prohibition of *shevut*?" [The prohibition against wearing *tefillin* on Shabbat is *muktza*, of rabbinic origin, and hence of lesser importance than the biblical injunctions against kindling lights or cooking food on Shabbat.]
>
> When the sages saw that Rabbi Eliezer was in his right mind, they entered and sat before him at a distance of four cubits [as required in the presence of a person who is excommunicated].
>
> Rabbi Eliezer said to them: "Why have you come?"
>
> They answered, "We have come to learn Torah."
>
> He said to them, "Why did you not come until now?"
>
> They said: "We had no time."
>
> He said to them: "I should wonder if you did not all die [in the Destruction, in Bar Kokhba's rebellion, or in the subsequent

Hadrianic persecutions]. You do not honor one another properly, and for this you will be punished."

Rabbi Akiva said, "And what of my death?"

He said to him: "Yours will be even harsher than theirs!"

The Gemara tells us that Rabbi Eliezer was teaching his visitors the laws pertaining to planting cucumbers – apparently a type of magic. Ultimately, they asked Rabbi Eliezer, "What of a shoe that is upon the shoemaker's model?" He answered them, "[It is ritually] pure!" – and his soul departed in purity. It must be remembered that Rabbi Eliezer maintained that the "*akhnai* oven" was pure! Rabbi Eliezer gets the last word and a small measure of poetic redress of the wrongs done him.

The story concludes with Rabbi Yehoshua standing up and declaring, "The vow [excommunication] is annulled; the vow is annulled!" This displays a partial restoration of Rabbi Eliezer's original status. The excommunication against him was removed after his death, or while he was dying, but in the greater picture he lost the battle. The halakha follows Rabbi Akiva, Rabbi Yehoshua, and Rabban Gamliel. Ultimately, in most of the rulings in the halakhic process, as God declared, "My children have prevailed over Me!" Despite the constant tension between fathers and children, between the Written Law and the Oral Law, between the Holy One and the Torah sages, between loyalty to the past and innovation towards the future, it is the sons who prevail – but without excommunicating or nullifying the tradition! The tradition must remain a vital – but not exclusive – element in halakhic decision making.

> The sages teach: [The prophet Elijah, bearer of the tidings of redemption, will come] not to distance nor to bring close, but rather to make peace in the world, as it is written (Mal. 3:23, 24), "Behold, I send to you the prophet Elijah, and he will restore the hearts of the fathers to children, and the heart of children to their fathers." (Mishna Eduyot 8:7)

First – "the heart of the fathers to the children": the previous generation must appreciate and accept the innovation of the younger generation.

Still, thereafter, "the heart of the children to their fathers" – genuine appreciation and fundamental loyalty to the tradition must be passed down from generation to generation.

As Rabbi Kook teaches: "The old must be made new, and the new must be made holy." But the new must take into account – and, to a considerable extent, be based upon – the original tradition. It is only when there is no longer fear of innovation and, at the same time, there is loyalty to tradition, will the ancient aspiration be fulfilled, "to increase Torah and enhance its glory."

Sanctity: Bringing God into this World

One of the most intriguing, absorbing, and significant theological questions is the concept of *kedusha*, sanctity. All who deal with this fascinating subject agree that sanctity is to be found in the encounter between the human and the Divine, for "Holy, holy, holy is the Lord of Hosts" (Is. 6:3) – God is the source of all holiness. And because God is generally perceived as the transcendent, ineffable Master of the Universe, beyond human understanding and beyond the limits of nature, conventional wisdom equates the search for sanctity and spirituality with an attempt to escape the material world in order to enter a distant, ethereal world.[1]

To a great extent, the major commentaries on the biblical command "You shall be holy" (Lev. 19:2) follow this line of interpretation. Rashi, for example, interprets the words "be holy" to mean "be separate," separate yourselves from sin and especially from forbidden sexual relationships. Nahmanides goes even further, advocating general abstention from the excess materialism of this world, suggesting that one ought to separate oneself even from materialistic pleasures which are biblically permissible. According to these views, "holiness" requires separation from the material world in which we live.

---

1. See Rabbi Joseph B. Soloveitchik's depiction of the typological "Religious Man" in his important work, *Halakhic Man* (Jewish Publication Society, 1983).

My teacher and mentor, Rabbi Joseph B. Soloveitchik of blessed memory, provides a very different perspective in his article "Sacred and Profane: *Kodesh* and *Hol* in World Perspective."[2] He rejects escaping, abstaining, and withdrawing from the physical world to find sanctity and spirituality, and prescribes instead expanding and including, bringing God into every aspect of our physical universe. After all, the entire universe belongs to the Holy One, Blessed Be He and "there is no place devoid of the potential for actualizing the presence [of God]." In the words of the famed Rebbe Menahem Mendel of Kotzk, "Where is the place of His glory? Wherever you let Him in!"

In this essay, I hope to follow in the footsteps of Rabbi Soloveitchik and demonstrate how sanctity must be brought into the world through the human encounter with the Divine in the dimensions of time and space.

THE FESTIVALS AND TIME

Let us begin with the dimension of time, as it described in the Torah. Leviticus 23, the chapter which describes the festivals in depth, repeatedly uses the word *mo'ed* for festival which literally means "meeting" or "appointed time."[3] The annual festivals are meetings or encounters in two senses. First, they are time-specific encounters between the Jewish people and God, as it says in Exodus 23:17, "Three times a year, all your males shall be seen before the presence of the Master, Lord." Second, the festivals are encounters between the Jewish people and specific momentous events in its history, specific times when the Divine Presence was especially manifest.

Each of the three festivals of pilgrimage testifies to a different historical event. Passover testifies to our freedom from Egyptian enslavement, Shavuot – to our receiving of the Torah of ethics, morality, and human responsibility at Sinai, and Sukkot – to our survival despite our wanderings through an alien and hostile desert environment. Hence, in

---

2. *Gesher*, Student Organization, Rabbi Isaac Elchanan Theological Seminary (Sivan 5728/June 1966).

3. See, for example, Amos 3:3, "Do two walk together, unless they have agreed to meet (*no'adu*)?"

these moments of time, we encounter the God of Freedom, the God of Torah and Morality, and the God of Protection.

THE SABBATH DAY

The first biblical reference to sanctity is in conjunction with time, specifically the Sabbath: "And God blessed the seventh day and made it holy" (Gen. 2:3). Interestingly, the chapter of the festivals in Leviticus 23 begins with the Sabbath, which the Bible apparently sees as a primary festival, a *mo'ed*; an appointed time of human meeting with the Divine.

> And the Lord spoke to Moses, saying, "Speak to the Children of Israel and say to them: These are the appointed times of the Lord, which you are to proclaim as proclamations of holiness... For six days work may be done, but the seventh day is a Sabbath of Sabbaths (*Shabbat Shabbaton*), a proclamation of holiness. You are not to do any work; it is Sabbath to the Lord in all your dwellings. (Lev. 23:1–3)

It is clear from this passage that the Sabbath, or Shabbat, is a sacred, appointed time of momentous significance, a time which touches eternity.

Time without God is an undifferentiated succession of seconds, minutes, hours, days, weeks, months, and years, which move on inexorably, automatically, impervious to human beings and their experiences; people who live out their lives without divine times are caught between the tick-tocks of a blind and unfeeling master clock. The prophet of futility, Ecclesiastes, says it frighteningly well:

> A generation goes and a generation comes, but the earth abides forever. The sun rises and the sun sets, it aims for its [resting] place, [but then] rises from there. [The wind] goes toward the South, veers round toward the North, round and round goes the wind, and then circles around again. (Eccl. 1:4–6)

Time without God is cyclical and endlessly repetitive, without ultimate meaning. In the words of William Shakespeare, "Tomorrow, and tomorrow, and tomorrow / Creeps in this petty pace from day to day / To the last syllable of recorded time."[4] Time without God creeps at a petty pace instead of progressing as a meaningful march (*halakha*) because it reduces individual life to nothing more substantive than the vapor we exhale on a cold day, the *hevel* bemoaned by Ecclesiastes. It is "a tale told by an idiot, full of sound and fury, signifying nothing."[5]

But this is not the case if life is a tale told by God, if world and life were created by a God of love and purpose. This is the message of that primordial seventh day:

> And God saw all that He had made and behold it was very good; and it was the evening and the morning of the sixth day. Then the heavens and the earth were completed, and all their array. God completed on the seventh day His work which He had made; and He rested on the seventh day from all His work which He had made. And God blessed the seventh day and made it holy, because on it He rested from all His work which God had created to make. (Gen. 1:31–2:3)

What occurred on that momentous and significant seventh day? God recognized the goodness of the material world that He had created, and that there was no need to repeat what had already been accomplished without ever arriving at a finish line. The seventh day described in Genesis grants a glimpse of the eventual possibility of arriving at an endgame and enjoying the light at the end of the tunnel. On that seventh day, God created redemption, the possibility of bringing the entire material world into the orbit of the Divine.[6]

By designating Shabbat as the first of the *mo'adim*, the appointed meeting times between people and God, the Torah empowers the individual to enter into a close relationship with God in time for the course of an entire day, every week. This sacred weekly event reveals the

---

4. William Shakespeare, *Macbeth*, act 5, scene 5.

5. Ibid.

6. See Rashi on Gen. 2:3, God created *menuḥa* (rest) on the seventh day. See also *Mussaf Rashi* ad loc.: God desired completion, *ḥemda*.

enormous implication of humans having been created in God's image and commanded to emulate God's characteristics.[7] Just as God rested on the Sabbath, thereby activating world redemption, so, too, must we rest on the Sabbath, thereby glimpsing the reality of world redemption.

If indeed the Sabbath day establishes our fellowship with God, even our partnership with God, we must then devote this seventh day to coming closer to our Partner-in-Heaven, to learning how to make our smaller worlds part of His greater world, how to prepare ourselves and our world for redemption. Then Shabbat truly becomes a time which touches eternity, a sacred day.

It doesn't happen on its own. The Torah tells us, "And the Children of Israel shall observe the Shabbat, to make the Shabbat for their generations an eternal covenant [or: a covenant with the world]" (Ex. 31:16). It is our responsibility to make Shabbat sacred. We must actively "make" Shabbat and "make Kiddush," actively sanctifying the Sabbath day along with the Creator of the universe.

THE FESTIVALS

The passage that marks the weekly Shabbat as a special, prototypical appointed time for human-divine encounter then goes on to discuss other sacred times – the yearly festivals: "These are the appointed times of the Lord, proclamations of holiness, which you shall proclaim at their appointed times" (Lev. 23:4). This general introduction is followed by a description of the Festival of Matzot, Passover (23:5–8). The next few verses (23:9–14) deal with the reaping of the first grain crop to ripen, the barley, and the subsequent Omer offering. This offering of the first grains, which are so basic to our physical sustenance, expresses the human encounter with the Universal Sustainer in the Land of Israel.

The Omer offering is followed by the seven-week Omer count which culminates in the Festival of the First Fruits, or Shavuot. The Shavuot offering of two Hallah loaves represents the ripening of the last of the grains – wheat, the staff of life – and symbolizes the completion and perfection of Israel's produce and God's bounty. The progression

---

7. See Sota 14a: "Just as He is compassionate, so must you be compassionate; Just as God clothes the naked, so must you clothe the naked."

from the barley, a rougher grain that was often used for animal fodder, to wheat, which was considered the finest grain and reserved for human consumption, illustrates the possibility of improvement and refinement in God's world. The Oral Law adds that Shavuot is likewise the day of the divine revelation at Sinai, when Israel encountered God as the Teacher of Torah and morality.

Beginning the Hebrew calendar of sacred days with the Sabbath day and the Festival of Freedom, Passover, intensifies the profound message of our having been created in the divine image; just as God is free, so must every human being be free. Our encounters with God on these days teach us our responsibility as God's partners to attempt to free every human being who is enslaved by any other human being, as well as the necessity of making ourselves free of negative character traits, of toxic human addictions. And the command for us to begin counting every day "from the morrow of the Sabbath" (rabbinically interpreted to mean the day following the first day of the Festival of Matzot), emphasizes the truth that it is only a free individual who is able to count time, who is empowered to make time count; a master removes this ability from his slave, and thereby robs him of his humanity, of his ability to encounter God and fulfill his divinely-mandated responsibility to perfect the world under the kingship of God.

The Festival of First Fruits, which marks the agricultural cycle from barley to wheat and celebrates the magnificent fruits for which Israel is praised, likewise expresses our partnership with God in working the land and providing human sustenance; such an occupation is a sacred endeavor and a meaningful encounter with the Divine.

The progression of the festivals defines our mission as a nation. It emphasizes the ethical and moral responsibilities of freedom, and allows us a glimpse into what free individuals can accomplish together with God: ending enslavement and exile, reaching a homeland, and establishing a successful agricultural society which provides a Sabbatical year of rest for the land and the farmers, as well as a respectable means of livelihood for the poor, the widowed or orphaned, and even for strangers.[8]

---

8. Through the mitzvot of *pe'ah, leket* etc., as demonstrated in the Book of Ruth.

contradictory verses are brought in need of a harmonizing interpreta-tion. The first verse reads, "To the Lord is the earth and all of its fullness" (Psalms 24:1), while the second verse states, "The heavens, the heavens belong to the Lord, and the earth He gave to humankind" (115:16). How does one reconcile these two ideas? To whom does the earth belong? The Talmud explains: "One verse applies before one offers a blessing, and the other applies after one offers a blessing." The conventional commentaries, including Rashi, explain that before one makes a bless-ing, the food belongs to God, and afterwards, the food belongs to the person who made the blessing. Indeed, it is the blessing which gives us the right to partake of God's world and requisition a specific aspect of it for our own personal use.

Rabbi Ahron Soloveichik, however, interprets the tension between the verses in a completely different way: According to him, a person who has not yet recited a blessing (or does not recite a blessing at all) sees two separate worlds or two separate realms: heaven, which belongs to God, and the earth, which belongs to humankind. Never do the two worlds meet. However, a person who is immersed in the world of blessings is able to perceive the sublime within the mundane, the godly within the earthly, the transcendent nature of God within the immanent universe. The food that he or she is about to eat becomes a bridge between this world and God and, through the blessing, a person is able to bring God down into this world. Therefore, after – and as a result of – blessing his food, an individual can truly feel that "the entire world belongs to God." Indeed, by means of a mundane apple or piece of bread he brings God into the material world.

Through this, one can understand Rabbi Joseph B. Soloveitchik's teaching that one of God's names is *HaMakom*, meaning "the Place" or "the Omnipresent in the Here and Now," since God yearns to be eter-nally present in this place, in this world. It is up to us, the inhabitants of this world, to make the entire world His Sanctuary. The verse recited by Ashkenazic Jewish visitors to a house of mourning is, "May the Omni-present (*HaMakom*) comfort you among the mourners of Zion and Jerusalem." It is a prayer for the future, a prayer that the time will come when the *Shekhina* will be ever-present, and even this world will be a place of consolation and salvation.

ROSH HASHANA: OUR CORONATION OF GOD

The sanctity of Rosh HaShana is mainly related to kingship, to our anointing God king of the world: "It is taught: Rabbi Yehuda said in the name of Rabbi Akiva...On Rosh HaShana, say before Me *Malkhuyot* (Kingship), *Zikhronot* (Remembrances), and *Shofarot* (Shofar Blasts) to crown Me over you. How? Through the shofar" (Rosh HaShana 16a). The sovereignty of God in the world is made explicit in the *Amida* prayer of Rosh HaShana in the blessing of *kedushat ha'yom,* the holiness of the day: "Blessed are You...King over all the earth..." This coronation is a fulfillment of the need to bring God into the world, to induce immediate, immanent divinity. The shofar was traditionally used in ancient Israel for coronation ceremonies (1 Kings 1:39). Hence, the Bible's reference to Rosh HaShana as "a day of sounding the shofar" – *Yom Terua* (Num. 29:1) – defines Rosh HaShana as the day of God's coronation as King of the world. The Hebrew *terua* would then refer to the exultant shouts which accompany and punctuate a coronation.

In contrast, a later discussion in Tractate Rosh HaShana (33b) interprets *Yom Terua* as a day of groaning or sobbing, based on the translation of *terua* as derived from the word *reu'ah,* which means feeble or decrepit. Indeed, the Talmud queries whether the *Yom Terua* calls for *ginuḥei ganaḥ,* the broken, groaning sighs known as the *shevarim* tones of the shofar or for *yelilei yalil,* the sobbing, wailing sounds known as the *terua* tones of the shofar – or, perhaps, for both "sighing" and "wailing" together. If so, how can we reconcile a day of weeping and sighing, as this passage interprets *Yom Terua,* with the concept of Rosh HaShana as the day of God's coronation?

The answer to this question is that as long as the presence of God is not felt in the world, as long as the world is far from having been perfected under the sovereignty of His Name, the world is indeed "a valley of tears." The Midrash is tragically succinct: "God's name is not complete and His throne is not complete...as long as Amalek is in the world."[12] In the words of Rabbi Simcha Bunim of Peshisha (1765–1827), "There is nothing more broken than a broken heart."[13] This vision of an

---

12. Exodus 17:16. Rashi ad loc. quotes *Midrash Tanḥuma, Ki Tetzeh* 11.
13. *Kol HaMevaser,* vol. 1, p. 287.

incomplete and broken world is documented by a startling verse in Isaiah, which all-too-honestly depicts the world created by God: "Producer of light and Creator of darkness, who makes peace and creates evil, I am the Lord, who makes all of these" (Is. 45:7). God created a world that contains evil as well as good, darkness as well as light, chaos as well as order. Our world is imperfect, incomplete, broken! This is the reason Rosh HaShana is a day of wailing, of weeping, of sighing – because of the chasm between our present reality and our anticipated vision, between what we have and what we still yearn for.

To unite our vision with reality, we must return to the initial biblical reference to the Sabbath:

> Then the heavens and the earth were completed, and all their array. God completed on the seventh day His work which He had made; and He rested on the seventh day from all His work which He had made. And God blessed the seventh day and made it holy, because on it He rested from all His work which God had created to make. (Gen. 2:1–3)

The meaning of the final phrase, "which God had created to make," is unclear, and it also seems superfluous. If these words were deleted, the passage would still make perfect sense. I would suggest that the phrase should be taken to mean, "He rested from all His work which God had created [leaving the rest for humankind] to make."[14] It is up to us to fill in the gap, it is up to us to complete the work God expects us to do. We must crown God as King of the World and perfect the world under His Name, so that He is known to all as the God of love and compassion, patience and loving-kindness (Ex. 34:6). This is the essence of Rosh HaShana.

The second paragraph of the *Aleinu* prayer that we recite as part of *Malkhuyot* on Rosh HaShana declares that we must "remove idolatry from the earth … perfect the world under the kingship of the Almighty, when all mortals will call upon Your Name and all the wicked of the earth will turn to You … Everyone will accept the yoke of Your Kingship

---

14. See Rabbi Menachem Mendel Kasher, *Torah Shelema*, ad loc.

and You will rule over them speedily, forever." The prophets prophesize that we will eventually succeed in this task,[15] and that all the nations will one day accept the teachings of our Torah. Hence, Rabbi Shimon ben Elazar teaches that ultimately all the gentiles will convert[16] and Maimonides[17] suggests that in the Messianic Age everyone will return to the true religion. The nations will come to the Third Temple to accept ethical monotheism, they will beat their swords into ploughshares, and the world will be redeemed.

It is this human empowerment and divine guarantee which caused the talmudic sages to add the triumphant *tekiya* sound of victory to the mournful *terua* sound of angst on Rosh HaShana – the *tekiya* echoes the redemptive sounding of the Jubilee year (Lev. 25:9). Furthermore, our sages mandate two exultant *tekiya* sounds to every broken *terua* sound, and insist that each individual *tekiya* be at least as long as each individual *terua*.[18] Our faith in our capacity to turn this vale of tears into a Garden of Eden is what makes Rosh HaShana a festival of joy and gives us the optimism to turn despair into directive as we continue to work towards the exultant crescendo-climax of our as-yet unfinished symphony.

SHABBAT, SANCTUARY, AND SANCTIFYING HUMAN BEINGS

God created time so that we, in historic time, will become a light unto the nations, will "meet" God in special moments of time – our festivals – and will eventually bring about that long-awaited time which will be the Day (or Epoch) "that is entirely Shabbat," when all of time will be spent in rendezvous with the Divine. Likewise, in regard to the dimension of place, we long to fulfill God's command to "make for Me a Sanctuary and I will dwell among them" (Ex. 25:8) – the world must become an extension of the Sanctuary! According to Rabbi Yehuda HaLevi's *Kuzari*, the Sanctuary symbolizes the world, which we must make worthy of the Divine Presence living in its midst. We

---

15. See e.g., Is. 2, Mic. 4, Zech. 7–9.
16. Berakhot 57b.
17. Maimonides, *Mishneh Torah*, Laws of Kings 12:1.
18. Mishna Rosh HaShana 4:10; Rosh HaShana 32b, and see *Tosafot* ad loc.

must transform the entire world into a sanctuary and we must elevate every day to the level of Shabbat – thus sanctifying the dimensions of space and time.

THERE IS NO SANCTITY WITHOUT SACRIFICE

It is the human obligation to sanctify space and time – and every act of sanctification requires sacrifice and commitment. According to Rabbi Isaac Luria ("the Holy Ari," 1534–1572), the great secret and foundation of the world's creation is *tzimtzum*, the diminution or contraction of God Himself, as it were. Reflect: if God is wholly goodness, and if the world and all of humanity are emanations of that divine goodness, from whence develops evil, darkness and emptiness?

This is probably the most significant question posed to the religionist: how and why does an imperfect world – a world which admits an Auschwitz – emanate from a Perfect God of Love?[19]

Rabbi Ḥaim Vital maintains that the Almighty created the world because "it was necessary for Him to be perfect in His actions and in the fulfillment of His Names," and since love and compassion require others to whom to express love and compassion, God created human beings, who would be that something "other" than Him.[20] That "other" had to be created with freedom of choice; if humans were totally controlled by God, were in actuality mere extensions of God, then divine love for humans would merely be self-love on the part of the Divine, it would be devoid of a true "other." So God created human beings with the ability to choose to do even that which God would not have wanted them to

---

19. The talmudic sages interpret even God's ineffable Name to mean that He is the God of unconditional love, both before and after we sin, the God of love who is always open to forgiveness. See Ex. 33:18, 34:6, Rosh HaShana 17b.

The very name YHVH, composed of the letters *yod, hei, vav,* and *hei,* may well mean "love": *hav* in Aramaic is the verb "to give," so the Hebrew letters *hei, vet,* and *hei* may be identified with giving or loving-kindness, since the most obvious expression of love is the desire to give to one's beloved. Although the Aramaic *hav* and the Hebrew *ahava* are spelled with the letter *vet* and YHVH is spelled with the letter *vav,* the *vav* and *vet* are homophones that may be interchanged: note, for example, that the Hebrew *ta'ava,* erotic desire, which is written with a *vav,* and *te'avon,* hungry appetite, which is written with a *vet,* are considered cognates.

20. *Sha'ar HaHakdamot,* sha'ar 1, hakdama 3.

do; God had to leave room in the world for humanity to be other and to choose other.[21]

This is the kabbalistic explanation for evil. God initially emanated a world which was an inextricable part of Himself. In that early creation, He filled all worlds and all times, He was the All in the all. Then, in an act of love and self-sacrifice, God restricted and contracted His Being to leave room in time and space for the other (i.e., human beings); the challenge is for us, the other, is to triumph over evil, and perfect this broken world, to reunite both time and space with the God who initially created them.

We must bring God into the world by extending the Sanctuary to encompass the world, and we must bring God into time by transforming every day into Shabbat. This will require great human effort and sacrifice. We, too, in imitation of God's ways, will be required to limit and contract our individual materialistic desires and needs in order to leave room for other people and for God. Sometimes, this may entail even the ultimate sacrifice of our lives and the lives of our children – for the sake of the continuity of our nation, our religion, and our mission as God's witnesses and a light unto the nations of the world. But God guarantees through His covenant and His prophets that we shall ultimately overcome the challenges and recreate a perfected world. This is the promise of the final triumphant *tekiya gedola* sounded on Rosh HaShana and at the close of Yom Kippur.

The shofar blasts herald the redemption of the world. In the Messianic Era, both time and space will be suffused and saturated with divine sanctity; there will be no suffering, no tragedies, no untimely deaths. At that time, God will be magnified, sanctified, and known to all (see Ezek. 38:23). At that time, God's name will be complete and the divine contraction will be expanded by the immanent Divine Presence. At that time, when God will be Omnipresent (*HaMakom*) and suffuse the world, every broken heart will be repaired and every mourning soul will be comforted. This is the significance of the Mourner's Kaddish and of the formula with which Ashkenazic Jews comfort mourners.

---

21. See Gen. 1:26, and the commentary of Seforno ad loc.

There is a fascinating dispute between two of the greatest figures of Ḥasidut – the Kotsker Rebbe and the Vorker Rebbe. The Vorker Rebbe said that he preferred the mitzva of sukka to the mitzva of the four species, because when a person holds the four species he is holding sanctity, but when he puts them down, the sanctity is gone. When a person sits in the sukka, however, he is being held by a sanctity he cannot put down; it surrounds him. The Kotsker responded that that was why he preferred the Sabbath over the mitzva of sukka. One can leave the sukka, and walk out of its sanctity, but one can never leave the Shabbat!

However, I would argue that it's not so clear-cut. The sanctity of Shabbat can be broken: when a person transgresses the Shabbat, when the peace of the Shabbat table is destroyed by an angry word or a malicious reference, then the individual *has* effectively walked out of the Shabbat. Sanctity is always dependent on the thoughts and deeds of people. "The Children of Israel must keep the Shabbat, making the Shabbat in every generation, as an everlasting covenant" (Ex. 31:16). We are required to "make the Shabbat," we must declare the sanctity of the Sabbath in our spoken Kiddush, in addition to God's declaration, and in addition to the natural astronomical advent of the Sabbath at sunset on Friday evening. Shabbat must be felt in our lives and in our deeds. We, by observing the Shabbat, actually create a unique twenty-five hour oasis – a sanctuary time, a blessed day that is different and distinct from every other day, and which serves as an inspirational model for the other days of the week.

A well-known midrash (*Tanḥuma*, Noah 13) describes how Noah partnered with Satan in planting the first vineyard. Satan killed a sheep and poured its blood on the earth, killed a lion and poured its blood on that same earth, killed a monkey and spilled its blood on that same earth, and then killed a pig and let its blood mingle with that of the others. From this blood-soaked soil, a grapevine sprouted. When a person drinks wine, he first becomes mild and sleepy like a sheep; when he continues drinking, he becomes as fierce as a lion; when he drinks still more, he frolics ridiculously as a monkey; and eventually, when he drinks to surfeit, he becomes repulsive and disgusting, like a pig.

At the end of Tractate Sanhedrin (71a), the Talmud queries why wine is red, and responds that under the influence of red wine, one may come to shed red blood; moreover, when a person recalls how he acted when drunk, he is ashamed, and his face flushes red.

In spite of all this, or perhaps because of it, we make Kiddush over wine every Shabbat; we seek to sanctify even the most mundane, to bring God into every aspect of our lives, uplifting the most material into the most spiritual. We make a special blessing on wine, "Blessed is He...who creates the fruit of the vine," rather than the expected "who creates the fruit of the tree," because of the intense level of human labor that is required to bring forth wine from the fruit of the vine. The wine symbolizes that with hard work, man is able to improve on nature; with hard work, a person can improve his own human nature and bring sanctity into every aspect of life. With sacrifice and commitment, humanity can perfect God's world, can bring the Divine into every realm, can sanctify every space and every day.

A TALMUDIC TALE PROVES THE SANCTITY OF IMMANENCE

In order to understand the concept of sanctity, it is important to study the talmudic story of Rabbi Shimon bar Yoḥai, one of the intellectual giants of the Talmud, who escaped Roman persecution by hiding in a cave with his son for thirteen years (Shabbat 33b–34a). The mystics maintain that during this period he was gifted with the divine revelation which produced the sacred Zohar.

According to one approach of the sages, "The Holy One, Blessed Be He, looked into the Torah and created the world" (Genesis Rabba 1:1) – that is, Torah (including the Oral Law) is none other than a transcendental literature that emanates from the sublime realm of the Divine. From this perspective, immersing oneself in Torah is essentially immersing oneself in non-physical, other-worldly engagements. Thus, involvement in Torah study came to be seen as a transcendent involvement, totally separate from this world.[22] Hence, the ḥaredi yeshiva world, in Israel as well as in the Diaspora, regards Torah study as completely incompatible with any secular study or pursuit. And, since the study

---

22. See *Nefesh HaḤayim* by Rabbi Ḥaim of Volozhin.

of Torah is sacred and outweighs any other pursuits (*talmud Torah keneged kulam*, Shabbat 127a), the essence of sanctity must be seen as the anti-thesis of worldly occupations.

Let us examine the approach of Rabbi Shimon bar Yoḥai:

> Rabbi Yehuda, Rabbi Yosi, and Rabbi Shimon were sitting and studying, and Yehuda a son of converts, was sitting near them. Rabbi Yehuda commenced [the discussion] by observing, "How fine are the works of this people [the Romans]! They have made market places, they have built bridges, they have erected bathhouses." Rabbi Yosi was silent. Rabbi Shimon bar Yoḥai answered and said, "All that they made they made for themselves; they built market places to set harlots in them; bathhouses, to unnecessarily pamper themselves; bridges, to levy tolls for themselves." Then Yehuda, the son of converts, went and related their conversation, which reached the ears of the government. [The Roman government] decreed: Yehuda, who exalted [us], shall be exalted, Yosi, who was silent, shall be exiled to Zippori. Shimon, who reviled [our efforts], must be executed.
>
> He [Rabbi Shimon bar Yoḥai] and his son went and hid themselves in the house of study, where his wife brought him bread and a jug of water for their meals. [But] when the decree became more severe he said to his son, "Women are of unstable temperament: she may be tortured and expose us." So they went and hid in a cave. A miracle occurred and a carob tree and water well were created for them. They would strip their garments and sit up to their necks in sand. (Shabbat 33b)

It is interesting to note how the cave is depicted as a grave of sorts – for they sat up to their necks, buried in sand. (We may recall, too, that the gravesite of our ancestors is a cave, the Cave of *Makhpela*.) In any case, they were cut off from the world, and it would seem that, for the author of this story, Torah isolated from the world is not a living Torah, but rather an impaired, estranged Torah; it is a living grave! The talmudic tale continues:

The whole day they studied; when it was time for prayers they dressed, covered themselves, prayed, and then took off their garments again, so that they would not wear out their garments. Thus they dwelt twelve years in the cave. Then Elijah came and stood at the entrance to the cave, exclaiming, "Who will inform the son of Yoḥai that the emperor is dead and his decree annulled?" So they emerged. Seeing a man plowing and sowing, they exclaimed in condemnation, "People such as he forsake eternal life and engage in temporal life!" Whatever they cast their eyes upon was immediately burnt up. Thereupon, a heavenly voice came forth and cried out, "Have you emerged to destroy My world? Return to your cave!" So they returned and dwelt there twelve months, after which they exclaimed, "The punishment of the wicked in Gehenna is only twelve months long."

Apparently, their cave became harder and harder to bear, despite the great amounts of Torah they learned within it. By this point, even Rabbi Shimon was experiencing their isolation as Gehenna, hell – the abyss that the wicked experience after death.

A heavenly voice then came forth and said, "Go forth from your cave!" Thus, they left the cave. Wherever Rabbi Elazar wounded, Rabbi Shimon healed. He [Rabbi Shimon] said to him, "My son! You and I are all this world needs [for total involvement in study. Let the rest of humanity work]!" On the eve of the Sabbath before sunset they saw an old man holding two bundles of myrtle and running at twilight. "What are these for?" they asked him. "They are in honor of the Sabbath," he replied. "But one should suffice you?" they asked him. [He replied] "One is for [the commandment to] 'Remember' and one for [the commandment to] 'Observe.' Said [Rabbi Shimon] to his son, "See how precious the commandments are to Israel!" Thus they were placated.

It is clear that the lesson Rabbi Shimon learns from the old man is most significant. But before we attempt to understand what Rabbi Shimon gleaned from the old man's response, we must first recall Rabbi Shimon's worldview prior to this encounter. There is a famous dispute between Rabbi Shimon and Rabbi Yishmael regarding the mitzva of Torah study (Berakhot 35a):

> It is taught: "And you shall gather in your grain" (Deut. 11:14). What is to be learned from these words? Since it says, "This book of the Torah shall not leave your mouth, you shall meditate therein by day and by night" (Josh. 1:8), one might think that this injunction is to be taken literally. Therefore, it says, "And you shall gather in your grain," which implies that you are to combine the study of Torah with a worldly occupation. This is the view of Rabbi Yishmael. Rabbi Shimon bar Yoḥai says: Is that possible? If a man plows in the plowing season, and sows in the sowing season, and reaps in the reaping season, and threshes in the threshing season, and winnows in the season of wind, what is to become of Torah study? Rather, when Israel performs the will of the Omnipresent, their work is performed by others, as it says, "And strangers [gentiles] shall stand and feed your flocks" (Is. 61:5). And when Israel does not perform the will of the Omnipresent [to study Torah full time], their work will be carried out by themselves, as it says, "And you shall gather in your grain" (ibid.). Nor is this all, but the work of others will also be done [by the Israelites].

It seems clear that, according to Rabbi Shimon, the ideal is indeed to literally learn Torah "all day and all night." And if we do, our material needs will be taken care of by "others."

It is interesting to note that in the subsequent talmudic passage, where the difference of opinion between Rabbi Shimon and Rabbi Yishmael is adjudicated, no one in the later generation of *Amora'im* agrees with the opinion of Rabbi Shimon – neither Abaye nor Rava nor Rabba.

> Said Abaye: Many have followed the advice of Rabbi Yishmael, and it has worked well; others have followed Rabbi Shimon bar Yoḥai and it has not worked well. Rabba said to the students in his academy: I would ask you not to appear before me [in the house

of study] during Nisan and Tishrei so that you will be able to do the necessary agricultural work, and not be anxious about your food supply during the rest of the year.

It would seem that Rabbi Shimon's approach was deemed to be unrealistic. Those who followed his conviction of total immersion in Torah study found themselves waiting in vain; "others" never appeared to do their work for them. Moreover, Rabbi Shimon's maximalist interpretation of meditating in Torah "all day and all night" (*yomam velayla*) contradicts the universally accepted maxim, "It is good to combine Torah study with a worldly occupation" (Ethics of the Fathers 2:2).

Even more importantly, Rabbi Shimon's strongly worded opinion in this passage seems to contradict another of Rabbi Shimon's own statements, which appears in Menaḥot 99b: "Rabbi Yoḥanan said in the name of Rabbi Shimon bar Yoḥai, If a person only recites the *Shema* prayer in the morning and the evening, he has fulfilled the commandment of 'This book of the Torah shall not depart your lips.' You shall meditate therein for *a portion* of the day and *a portion* of the night." And similarly, we read in the *Mekhilta*, on the verse, "Six days you shall labor and do all your work" (Ex. 20:9) – "Rabbi Shimon says, 'Work is so important that even if the High Priest, on Yom Kippur, would enter the Holy of Holies not as part of the service, he would receive the death penalty, whereas, when the Temple was being built, even unclean workers or people with defects were allowed to enter the Holy of Holies.'" Even more startlingly, in another version of the same *Mekhilta* passage just cited, we read: "Rabbi Shimon teaches that 'Six days you shall labor' – this is a positive commandment. It is incumbent upon a person to work during the week in order that it be recognizable that he is resting on the Sabbath."[23]

All these sources show the great value Rabbi Shimon places on work and worldly occupation! Clearly, Rabbi Shimon must have changed his mind at some point; but if so, can we find a clue as to when and why?

This contradiction can be resolved by reflecting upon the process Rabbi Shimon had undergone by the time he left the cave for a second

---

23. Amos Hakham, *Daat Mikra* to Exodus 20:8, p. 384. Cf. also *Mekhilta DeRashbi*, ibid., p. 149.

time. Earlier in his life, he saw Torah study and any other non-Torah involvement as being mutually contradictory, removing the scholar from his commitment to study Torah. He believed that, "If a man plows in the plowing season, and sows in the sowing season, and reaps in the reaping season, and threshes in the threshing season, and winnows in the season of wind, what is to become of Torah study?" However, once he reemerged from the cave,[24] he viewed Torah study in a different light.

For twelve years, Rabbi Shimon was immersed in the secrets of the Kabbala, together with his son. However, because he was completely isolated, in a sense he was dead to the world. As we have discussed, this withdrawal is problematic: humanity's challenge is to sanctify *this* world, the world we live in, and not to seek holiness through complete denial of the material world.

This was understood by Rabbi Akiva's students, who fought in the revolt of Bar Kokhba in order to free the Land of Israel and bring redemption to the world. They were not content to learn Torah and pray – rather, they took action! They died at the hands of the Sicarii – not by a form of whooping cough, as Rashi understands the talmudic term "*askera*," but rather by the sword, as Rabbi Ḥai Gaon describes: "The students of Rabbi Akiva died by *shemada*; they were murdered as a result of the harsh edicts of the Roman Emperor Hadrian, which were related to the revolt of Bar Kokhba."[25]

This is the moral of the old man running at sunset with two myrtle branches, one branch symbolizing the need to remember to prepare for Shabbat and the other symbolizing the need to observe the Shabbat. We have seen that Shabbat is a testimony to the creation of an incomplete world, a broken world. However, Shabbat is also a taste of the World to Come, an encounter between this incomplete world and the future world, perfect and redeemed. During the six days of the week we need to elevate the workaday and mundane so that the weekdays, too, serve as a foretaste of the World to Come, a time that is entirely Shabbat. Therefore,

---

24. The *Shulḥan Arukh* comments that Rabbi Shimon left the cave on the thirty-third day of the Omer count, a day which came to be marked as the festival of Lag BeOmer on the Hebrew calendar.

25. See Y. Taanit 4:6.

we "remember the Shabbat day" during the week, and prepare for our dream to "observe the Shabbat day" on Shabbat itself. In this way, we can live in both worlds at the same time; we can appreciate the disparity between where we are and where we yearn to be and prepare for a more glorious future at the same time. Preparing for Messianic times is in itself a holy pursuit; the effort to bring God into the world entails a higher level of sanctity than the passive realization that the Messiah is here. In halakhic terminology, *hekhsher mitzva* is also a mitzva.

How do we prepare for the Messiah during the week? By performing mitzvot in the material world, thereby elevating that which is worldly and physical. Through plowing and planting – by keeping the laws of tithing, *terumot* and *ma'asrot*, by not planting forbidden mixtures, by "not restraining the oxen when they plow," by leaving a corner of the field for the poor. In short, by observing the laws which are pertinent to every part of life: charity, the home, relations between neighbors, family purity, *kashrut*. Halakha sanctifies every aspect of life: commerce, community, eating, intimacy. We can reach sanctity through living in this world, not by escaping it, and by preparing every aspect of our lives in the not-yet-holy world for when we will merit the fully holy world. Even then, we will no doubt still struggle to rise higher and higher in sanctity (see Maimonides, *Mishneh Torah*, Laws of Kings 12:5).

This is precisely what Rabbi Shimon bar Yoḥai learned from the old man with the two myrtle twigs. He even said to his son, "See how precious the commandments are to Israel!" And then "they were placated," they understood the value of agriculture and other worldly pursuits. The commandments require us to engage with this world in order to prepare the way for a more perfect world.

If wine can be sanctified, there is nothing in the material world that cannot similarly be made holy.[26] As Rabbi Kook teaches: in this world there are only two categories, the holy and the not-yet holy. There is no unredeemable material, nothing that is wholly impure: "And God saw all that He had made and behold it was very good" (Gen. 1:31) – at

---

26. Note that the Hebrew word for material, *ḥomer*, is similar to the Aramaic word for wine, *ḥamar*.

least, in potential. Hence, we are entrusted with the task of sanctifying *everything* in this world.

The same applies to time. Every day is holy, for the same God who created Shabbat also created the six days leading up to it. As we say in our prayers, "who in His goodness renews the act of creation every single day." We must recognize the potential in every moment of every day, and make every moment holy and every place heavenly. This is the lesson the old man taught Rabbi Shimon: even a branch of myrtle, even the act of plowing or planting, is holy: for they are inseparable parts of remembering the Shabbat day to keep it holy, and observing the Shabbat day to keep it holy. They are all preparations for the period which is wholly Shabbat and for the world-Sanctuary, which will both enable us to host God within our midst.

THE MYRTLE, SYMBOL OF REDEMPTION

The myrtle is mentioned as one of the seven plants that will cause the wasteland to bloom in the time of the redemption: "I will put in the desert cedar and acacia, myrtle and olive, I will place in the wasteland cypress, fir and the box tree together" (Is. 41:19). There is a custom attributed to Rabbi Ḥaim Vital, a custom which I maintain in my home, to welcome Shabbat on Friday evening by making a blessing on two myrtle branches right before blessing the children, paralleling the blessings on the spices recited at Shabbat's departure at Havdala on Saturday night.

Myrtle is one of the four species we bind together on Sukkot; we then wave this bundle in every direction when we recite the *Hallel*, thanking God for our redemption. In the Book of Nehemiah we learn that myrtle was used in the actual construction of the sukka, which represents God's embrace: "Go out to the mountain and bring olive branches, oil tree branches, myrtle branches, date branches, and branches of a thick [or leafy] tree to build a sukka." (Neh. 8:15).

Queen Esther, who spent her years of growth and development in pagan, hedonistic Persia, nevertheless, at a critical moment, rejoined her Jewish past and secured a Jewish future for herself and her people. Appropriately, her Hebrew name is Hadassa, myrtle; her Jewishness bloomed in the pagan desert of Persia and she became a redeemer of her people.

According to the Talmud, all parts of the myrtle tree – its leaves, its branches, its fruit – taste the same, as was true of all trees in the beginning of creation, in the Garden of Eden.

Tractate Ketubbot 17a tells us, "They said that Rabbi Yehuda bar Ilai would take a cloth made of myrtle and dance before the bride, saying that the bride is beautiful and graceful." It is clear from the wedding blessings that every wedding has an aspect of redemption, of faith in the future of Israel, of "may there be heard in the cities of Judah, and in the streets of Jerusalem, the sounds of joy and gladness, the sounds of the bridegroom and bride." Again, the myrtle is associated with redemption.

In a similar vein, it is written in Tractate Rosh HaShana 23a that, "whoever learns Torah and teaches it in a place devoid of Torah scholars is like a beloved myrtle in the wilderness" – that is, the myrtle even blossoms in a wasteland. God must be brought into wherever His presence is lacking. As God commanded Abraham: "Walk before Me and be wholehearted" (Gen. 17:1), and in Isaiah's words, "A voice calls out in the desert, make way for the Lord, clear a path through the wilderness for our God" (Is. 40:3). A myrtle in the wilderness symbolizes the introduction of holiness into a not-yet-holy place. The myrtle is a symbol of the challenge – and the possibility – of bringing redemption to this world.

This is what Rabbi Shimon saw in the myrtle branches the old man was carrying on Shabbat eve. Sanctity can only radiate in all its glory *outside* of the cave, for only then can it reach and illuminate every corner of the world. We must not despair, but strive to sanctify even the most desolate and most godless of places.

THE POTENTIAL HOLINESS OF COINS, BATHS, AND MARKETPLACES

To truly understand the full meaning of sanctity, we must continue exploring the wondrous tale of Rabbi Shimon and what happened to him after he left the cave: "Since a miracle has occurred," said he, "let me go and fix something, for it is written, 'And Jacob came whole [to the city of Shekhem]'" (Gen. 33:18). The parallel is clear. Like Jacob, who struggled with Esau and triumphed, so did Rabbi Shimon struggle with Esau's descendant, Edom/Rome. He too triumphed and emerged whole:

As Rav interpreted, [Jacob was] whole in body, whole in finances, and whole in Torah. "And [Jacob] gave graciously [*va'yiḥan*] to the city." Rav said: He instituted coinage for them. Samuel said: He instituted markets for them. Rabbi Yoḥanan said: He instituted bathhouses for them. (Shabbat 33b)

Rabbi Shimon now understood that out of gratitude for God's salvation, he too must actively sanctify aspects of this world, as he learns from our ancestor Jacob. Is it not amazing that precisely those three aspects of Roman society which Rabbi Shimon had reviled at the beginning of our narrative, were the three things that Grandfather Jacob-Israel perfected for God! Coins, bathhouses, and marketplaces may be sources of evil and hedonistic materialism, or they may be the means to attain societal and economic wellbeing: thriving businesses can provide gainful occupation, and institutions of hygienic welfare can produce citizens with sound minds in sound bodies. The Romans developed these institutions to be hotbeds of corruption and immorality but, for Jacob, the very same institutions were a means to repair and perfect society. Rabbi Shimon had indeed been transformed; he no longer saw Torah in opposition to world but rather as the means to sanctifying the world. The story concludes:

Rabbi Shimon asked them [the leaders]: Is there something that needs fixing, something in need of repair? They replied: There is a place of questionable purity, which has been marked impure by priests, who avoid going there. He said: Are there people who can vouch for the fact that at one time it had been considered pure? One old man answered: Ben Zakkai used to gather lupines here [which must be kept pure, i.e., he testified that at one time the area had been considered pure]. According to this information, every hard place he [Rabbi Shimon] declared pure, and every soft place he declared impure [apparently, the hardness of the ground was a sign that no one had been buried there]. (Shabbat 33b–34a)

Rabbi Shimon found a large parcel of land which was avoided by priests because it was of questionable purity, because at least a portion of it had been used as a cemetery. Unfortunately, the entire area was now considered impure and rendered off-limits to priests, the teachers of Torah. Rabbi Shimon effectuated his *tikkun*, or repair, by declaring a goodly portion of the area pure and, therefore, permissible for priests.

Recall that the cave that Rabbi Shimon fled to in order to hide from the world was depicted as a graveyard of sorts, with Rabbi Shimon and his son buried up to their necks in the sand while they learned Torah. Later on, the cave is compared to Gehenna, hell. The symbolism here is striking: Torah that exists in a cave, isolated from world, is a cemetery, a gravesite. However, our Torah is a Torah of life, a Torah by which we must live and not die, a Torah which urges us to "choose life," a Torah which is "a tree of life for all who grasp it" (Prov. 3:18). It is a Torah which is meant for this world, the world of the living, a Torah which exhorts us to sanctify the mundane and bring God into everyday life. It is the Torah of the living God who wants us to live and not to die, the God whose greatest praise is that He makes the dead live again.

Hence, Rabbi Shimon's *tikkun*, of the place as well as of himself, was to bring the Torah of the priest to a place it had been prevented from going, a place which had been marked as beyond the realm of the living. Rabbi Shimon brought the God of life, through the Torah of life, into an area of death and impurity. This is the truest function of Torah.

THE ANNUAL FESTIVALS: THE SANCTITY OF TIME

Let us return to our discussion of the festivals and our questions with reference to the biblical passage in which they first appear together. The Jewish calendar begins with the month of Nisan, in which we celebrate the festival of Passover, and begin the counting of the Omer which leads to Shavuot. This time period commemorates the gestation and birth of a nation – physically, in our exodus from slavery to freedom, and spiritually and morally, in the revelation at Sinai. By linking the liberation from Egypt with the ethical laws of the Decalogue, the Torah defines the nation of Israel as a people who believe in freedom and the responsibilities of freedom. Freedom dare not be an excuse for lawlessness, for looting, rioting, and raping. Freedom under God is a freedom with responsibility – *ḥerut* with *aḥrayut*. But at this point, during the first three months of the calendar year, the responsibility is limited to the Jewish nation. Passover is a familial and national celebration, with a lamb for each household and the mandated exclusion of all uncircumcised males (Ex. 12:3, 6, 43–48). On Shavuot the Torah was given to the people of Israel, and to no others.

Rosh HaShana, the next festival, is at the beginning of the seventh month (Tishrei), and extends our responsibility out to the world. Rosh HaShana is a commemoration of the birthday of the world – albeit a broken, imperfect and incomplete world, a world symbolized by the *terua* sound of the shofar. Therefore, the Rosh HaShana liturgy highlights the *Aleinu* prayer, which exhorts the Jewish people to perfect the entire world under God's universal sovereignty, and transform the *terua* into a *tekiya*. Once our nation has developed and matured from its Passover and Shavuot origins, it must begin to accept the yoke of universal responsibility.

The progression is analogous to that of a baby who thinks that the entire world revolves around him and that he is the sole object of his parents' love. Rosh HaShana teaches that from the womb of the *Shekhina* emanate innumerable siblings of various colors and ethnic backgrounds, all born in the image of God, all possessing the DNA of the Divine Nature Association. Because we are created in the image of God, we are all free and inviolate, and we are all inextricably linked together as beloved children of the One universal parent.

Hence, we have two epicenters of the year: in the first holiday cycle, we move from the freedom of Passover to the revelation at Sinai to Israel, our homeland, where the first fruits were celebrated in the Holy Temple in Jerusalem. The counting of the Omer takes us from the offering of coarse barley to the offering of fine wheat, demonstrating our spiritual freedom to work with God in the physical world and continually refine it. These festivals define the Jewish nation, its homeland, its values, and its lifestyle.

The second epicenter occurs in the seventh month, Tishrei – which is parallel to the seventh day, Shabbat. The cycle begins with Rosh HaShana and continues with Yom Kippur, Sukkot, and Shemini Atzeret. This is the universalist epicenter of the year. On Rosh HaShana, the birthday of the world, Israel has a rendezvous with God which enables the entire nation to be present at the creation of the world, and which empowers them to engage with and teach the world. We are charged with uniting the world under the sovereignty of the Creator. Hence, Rosh HaShana is called a Shabbaton (Lev. 23:24), linking it to the universal Sabbath which begins the biblical passage about the festivals. The term Shabbaton is not used in conjunction with Passover and Shavuot, which are national festivals.

On Yom Kippur, the nation of Israel meets God not only in time, but also in space. In time, we commemorate the day when God defined Himself as a God of love and unconditional forgiveness, and confirmed His forgiveness of the sin of the Golden Calf by giving the second set of tablets. In space, we recall the Yom Kippur service in the Temple and pray for a universal sanctuary that will encompass all the nations of the world, as we repeat over and over in the day's liturgy: "For My House [i.e., Sanctuary] shall be called a house of prayer *for all nations*" (Is. 56:7). Yom Kippur is called a Shabbat Shabbaton (Lev. 23:32) – first, because it enables the human being to recreate himself through repentance and God's forgiveness, and second, because it broadens the sanctity of space as well as of time to all humanity.

SUKKOT: A FESTIVAL OF NATIONAL
AND UNIVERSAL SIGNIFICANCE

The festival of Sukkot contains two aspects, with dual significance. On the one hand, it is part of the trilogy of events that transformed a group of shepherds and slaves into a proud nation. This historicity connects the festival of Sukkot to Passover and Shavuot, and emphasizes, from a national point of view, that we have emerged triumphant despite the endless exiles and persecutions we have faced. The impermanence of the sukka symbolizes the precariousness of the House of Israel and how, despite the harsh and hostile environments that continually threaten the fragile sukka that is our lot, the nation has not only survived physically, but even spiritually, as a holy people. When describing this national aspect of Sukkot, similar to Passover and Shavuot, the Torah does not use the word Shabbaton.

The "nationalist" description of Sukkot is followed by a general summary of the annual cycle of festivals, and the three festivals of pilgrimage in particular: "These are the Lord's appointed festivals, which you are to proclaim as sacred assemblies" (Lev. 23:37). In each of these three festivals, we have had a special and sacred "meeting" with the Divine. On Passover, God chose us as His special firstborn child, and redeemed us from slavery. On Shavuot, God gave us His Torah, which we freely accepted. And on Sukkot, He confirmed that despite exiles and persecutions, we will survive, because God remains our national Protector.

But there is further significance to the festival of Sukkot. Sukkot is one of the triad of pilgrimage festivals but it is also related to Rosh HaShana and Yom Kippur, the special days of universal significance. Logically, given the sojourning in the desert that it commemorates, Sukkot would have been more suitably placed between Passover and Shavuot, after the Exodus from Egypt. Nevertheless, Sukkot is in Tishrei, only days after the High Holy Days. From this perspective, the sukka is a tribute to "the fallen tabernacle (sukka) of David," referring to the tabernacle-sanctuary that we pray will be rebuilt in the wake of Yom Kippur. The sukka symbolizes the ultimate dwelling place of God in the midst of the world; a house of prayer to all nations. Such a sanctuary does not require proud, strong walls for protection, because it represents the Temple in the period of world peace. It requires the presence of the Almighty, the sheltering shadow of divine love, and the *ushpizin* (the symbolic sukka guests) who conveyed His Torah teachings throughout the generations.

The biblical text then relates the second aspect of the festival of Sukkot, the commandment to take the four species, which symbolize God's bountiful gifts of heaven, earth, rain, and sustenance for all – but not without human input in working the land. As the Bible tells us, "On the fifteenth day of the seventh month, when you have gathered the crops of the land, celebrate the festival to the Lord for seven days; the first day is a Shabbaton, and the eighth day is a Shabbaton" (Lev. 23:39). Here, the ingathering of the crops is featured, for Sukkot occurs during the universal harvest time and the word Shabbaton reveals the universal, supra-national nature of the festival. Here, sanctity of time and sanctity of place intersect, for all gathering of crops – indeed, all raising of crops – is holy. The entire land is holy, and all the time spent in the field – planting, plowing, reaping, and threshing – is holy. This holiness is made manifest by the manner in which we work the land: allowing it to lie fallow every seventh year; not mixing different seeds together; not yoking an ox to an ass and forcing them to plow together; leaving the gleanings, the forgotten sheathes, and a corner of the field for the poor; granting living space and food to the landless Levites and the priest-teachers. The agricultural laws express our sacred partnership with God in nourishing humanity.

Hence, this second mention of Sukkot also specifies the four species: "Take for yourselves on the first day the fruit of a fine tree, palm fronds, the branch of a thick [or leafy] tree, and willows of the brook" – items that symbolize the universal fruits of Mother Earth. These plants also symbolize the universal need for rain, *geshem*; the universal need for the material world, *gashmiyut*; and the universal partnership expressed by the combination of rainfall from heaven with human agricultural ingenuity and hard labor. We must be grateful for, and deeply concerned about, the food supply for all of humankind.

Not only is the *land* of Israel connected to the world through the universal act of working the earth, but the *nation* of Israel must be connected to the world, extending the sanctity of Israel and its holiest city, Jerusalem, to all lands and cities of the world, by being a light unto the nations as witnesses of God and His compassionate righteousness, just morality, and peace. These universal festivals stress the interrelationship between all nations, especially important in today's global village. It is no coincidence that over the course of the Sukkot festival, Israel must bring seventy bulls as symbolic offerings on behalf of the seventy nations of the world.

Following these verses, the commandment to dwell in a sukka is repeated, with one important addition: "so your descendants will know that I had the Israelites live in booths when I brought them out of Egypt." The Exodus from Egypt was a public proclamation to the entire world that enslavement, tyranny, and totalitarianism are appalling sins. God alone rules over the whole world. We, the people of Israel, must always be ready to raise the banner of freedom as part of our blessing for all the families of the earth; God is the sole owner of heaven and earth, and under God every individual created in His image must be free and inviolate.

The eighth day of Shemini Atzeret is an additional gathering – the gathering of the entire world as one. This is the symbolism behind the single bull offering on this festival day; it is marked by prayers to the Universal Provider for rain and – as developed through the generations – a gala celebration of the Torah. It is on this day that we take the Torah to the streets, sing and dance with the Torah scrolls, and even invite gentile leaders to celebrate with us. On Simḥat Torah we conclude our yearly reading of the Pentateuch and begin once again the Book of Genesis and the story of creation. This is a fitting climax to the universalism of Rosh HaShana and Yom Kippur. On Simḥat Torah-Shemini Atzeret we bring God's Torah to the world!

And therefore, in the second passage, Sukkot is twice called a Shabbaton – once for the sukka-sanctuary and then again for the universal Torah, the Torah for the world.

WHAT IS SANCTITY?

Israel's mission is to bring God into this world, and cause Him to dwell within the dimension of time and history, thus bringing about redemption and the Messianic Era. From the very moment God elected Abraham, He charged him with this mission, saying: "I shall make you a great nation, and through you all the families of the earth will be blessed" (Gen. 12:3). Sanctity requires constant effort on the part of man in order to perfect the world in the name of God's sovereignty. This is the fundamental essence of the festivals, the fundamental mission of Judaism, and the fundamental definition of sanctity. We must join forces with God in order to create a world that is entirely Sanctuary, and a time that is entirely Shabbat.

> Thus says the Lord: Let not the wise man glory in his wisdom, and let not the strong man glory in his strength, let not the rich man glory in his riches. But only in this may one glorify himself and be glorified: [that he] understands and knows Me, for I am the Lord who does loving-kindness, moral justice, and compassionate righteousness on earth; for these are what I desire, declares the Lord. (Jer. 9:22–23)

The Boundaries of
Biblical Interpretation:
Are Biblical Personalities
Truly Human?

INTRODUCTION

One of the most challenging (as well as enjoyable) rabbinical functions I am expected to fulfill is the weekly sermon or *dvar Torah* on the Bible portion of the week. After fifty-plus years in the practical rabbinate, this has been broadened to include two columns on *Parashat HaShavua* each week (one for the *Jerusalem Post*, and the other a syndicated column which appears in some twenty-seven Anglo-Jewish newspapers, mostly in America) and a class in "The Art of Homiletics" for rabbinical students who are training to minister to Jewish communities throughout the world. As you can well imagine, as soon as I've delivered one week's sermon, I begin to think about what I shall say or write the next week. A worn copy of the Pentateuch and its major commentators has become my steady companion, and has even been accorded a place of honor on my night table, to provide for ready access if I find myself unable to sleep in the middle of the night.

"Well, that doesn't sound strange for a rabbi and interpreter of Jewish texts," you might say. "After all, what else might be the mainstay of your intellectual commitment and personal library, if not the Bible and its commentaries?!" But anyone even superficially acquainted with the traditional yeshiva course of study knows that it is the vast sea of the Talmud with its many commentaries and novellae – and not the Bible – which provides the main fare, with a side order of religious-legal codes for those studying for rabbinical ordination. Aside from the very early years of religious school study, the major intellectual enterprise of the yeshiva world is Talmud, and it is expected that Bible will be studied on one's own time, usually on the Sabbath when there are no formal classes anyway. In fairly typical fashion, my formal lessons in Bible were traded in for Talmud by the time I reached the grand old age of eight.

Given this educational background, as a novitiate rabbi I viewed the weekly *dvar Torah* – which was to be delivered before a much larger audience than any of the other classes I gave, and which is generally the major criterion by which a non-Israeli rabbi is judged – as a formidable challenge. I decided to tackle biblical study in as systematic a manner as I could devise; and so, each year, I set aside time to study the portion of the week with another Bible commentator, annotating certain key interpretations and basing every sermon that year on the commentator I was studying. Naturally, I began with Rashi, the eleventh-century commentator par excellence, and attempted to progress more or less chronologically. By my twelfth year in the rabbinate I had reached the almost-contemporary Rabbi Samson Raphael Hirsch, and I was beginning to feel more confident in facing the weekly challenge of the Torah sermon. More than that, the Bible had become my steady companion.

PLURALISM IN RABBINIC COMMENTARY

The world of Bible commentary revealed many secrets. First and foremost, the Bible – believed to contain the wisdom of the Divine – may be likened to a magnificent diamond, glistening with many brilliant colors, all at the same time. And although the different hues often appear to be contradictory, when you view the totality of the light emanating from the diamond, you begin to appreciate how complementary they really are. Thus the sages of the Talmud understood that there are many possible truths contained in each biblical statement, each adding its unique melody to the magnificent symphony of the whole, synthesizing, not in conflicting dissonance, but in holy dialectic:

> The School of Rabbi Ishmael taught, "As a hammer shatters a rock" (Jer. 23:29) – Just as a hammer splitting [a rock gives off] many sparks, so does the biblical verse give off many different interpretations. (Sanhedrin 34a)

Similarly, the code word for biblical commentary, which encompasses different approaches to the very same verse is PaRDeS (פרדס) or orchard. The acronym is comprised of *pshat*, the plain meaning of the text, *remez*, the symbolic meaning of the text, *drash*, the rabbinic explication of the text, and *sod*, the secret, mystical meaning of the text. The sum total of these add up to the "seventy faces of the Torah," symbolizing the myriad distinctive approaches to the meaning of the Bible, and to an understanding (however imperfect and incomplete) of the Divine.

Only on the basis of this axiom of multiple legitimate meanings of one biblical text can we understand how Rashi, for example, distinguishes between the plain meaning of the text and its rabbinic explication, usually favoring the plain meaning of the text while also citing the rabbinic interpretation (e.g., Rashi on Ex. 23:2). On occasion, Rashi even interprets what he believes to be the simple meaning of the text *in opposition* to its rabbinic explication (see e.g., Lev. 13:6). Nahmanides on this verse immediately notes that Rashi's interpretation is not in accord with the rabbinic explication.

The Rashbam, Rashi's grandson, explains in his introduction to *Parashat Mishpatim* that he "did not write his commentary to explain the laws, even though they are fundamental and preeminent…but rather to elucidate the plain meaning of the text…However, the law (ultimately) uproots the textual study (in practice)." Obviously, the Rashbam believes that the literal meaning of the text must not be ignored when studying the Bible academically, despite an occasional clash between *pshat* and *drash*.

Nahmanides, probably the most widely studied of the biblical commentaries after Rashi, unequivocally insists upon his right to interpret the text as he understands it, regardless of the rabbinic explication:

So (it states) in Genesis Rabba; but since Rashi overlooks the aggadic explications of the sages in other places and toils to elucidate the plain meaning of the text, he permits us to do the same, because there are seventy faces to the Torah, and many contradictory explications in the words of our sages. (Nahmanidies, *Commentary on the Torah*, Gen. 8:4)

Nahmanidies likewise writes in his Introduction to the Bible: "And they will see in our interpretations novel ideas (*hiddushim*) in the textual meanings." Nevertheless, Nahmanidies generally does distinguish between his original commentaries that elucidate the plain meaning of the text (*al derekh hapshat*) and the more accepted, traditional commentaries of our sages (*al derekh rabboteinu*), especially when practical halakha is at stake.

BIBLICAL TEXT VS. ACCEPTED HALAKHIC INTERPRETATION

So important was the right of the individual interpreter to comment on the text in accordance with his own understanding, that there are a significant number of instances in which commentaries interpreted a text in opposition to the normatively accepted halakhic practice. For example, the Rashbam in Exodus 21:6 translates the words "and he (the Canaanite slave) shall serve (his master) forever (*leolam*)" to mean "all of his lifetime," despite the fact that the sages of the Talmud interpret it to mean until the Jubilee year; he similarly interprets against the view of the rabbinic sages in verses 11 and 28 of that same in Exodus. Another example: Nahmanidies understands the word *onah* – one of the three obligations each husband has towards his wife, as specified in Exodus 21: 9, 10 – to mean a dwelling place, despite the fact that sages of the Talmud interpret the same word to mean sexual gratification. Similarly, Rabbi Yosef Bekhor Shor (of Orleans, an oft-cited disciple of Rabbenu Tam), when commenting on the biblical injunction to free a Hebrew servant on the seventh year (Ex. 21:2), interprets the verse to mean "on the Sabbatical year, when there is no necessity to work the fields," whereas the talmudic sages insist that it means the seventh year of his employ (see also his commentary to Ex. 21:29 and 22:3).

The Rabad of Posquieres even uses the *pshat* to support a halakhic opinion which was not only different from the accepted rabbinic interpretation but which made a profound difference in practical law (*halakha lema'aseh*). The Bible, in evaluating the status of a thief discovered having trespassed into one's basement, stipulated that, "if the sun is shining, he is not to be killed" (Ex. 22:2, 3). The Rabad, in his halakhic notes on Maimonides (*Mishneh Torah*, Laws of Stealing, chapter 9), writes as follows:

> I shall not be prevented from stating my opinion. Even though our sages have interpreted "if the sun is shining" to be taken as an allegory, that if the matter is clear to you as the shining sun that he is not after your life, only then are you not (to defend your property by) killing him... nevertheless the words cannot be removed from their literal meaning: by day, one is not permitted to kill the thief because a thief comes by day since (he does not expect anyone to be at home) and he can easily escape (if the necessity arises), and he doesn't anticipate spending a great deal of time on a big haul or confronting the owner of the house and killing him. But one who steals at night, since he knows that the owner of the house is at home, comes prepared to kill or be killed... and (I swear) by the life of my head that for anyone who understands (this explanation) is sufficient. (*Strictures of Rabad*, ibid.)

Similarly, Maimonides, in his *Guide for the Perplexed*, explains the verse "an eye for an eye" (Ex. 21:23) in accordance with the fundamental biblical notion "that it must be done to the perpetrator of the crime as he did to his fellow... he who causes someone else's limb to be lost must suffer the loss of his own limb." The rabbis of the Talmud, though, insisted upon monetary payment instead. Maimonides, however, is unfazed: "And do not be concerned or dissuaded from this notion because we mete out punishment through monetary payment (as the rabbinic halakha demands), since our intent now is to present the meaning of the verses, and not of the talmudic statements" (*Guide*, Part III, chapter 41).

The *Tosfot Yom Tov* (Rabbi Yom Tov Lipman Heller), in his classical commentary to Mishna Nazir 5:5, cites the interpretation of

Maimonides, which is not in accordance with the amoraic interpretation recorded in the Talmud. Nevertheless, the *Tosfot Yom Tov* praises Maimonides, and explains:

> And his interpretation is accepted, even though it is not in accordance with the talmudic interpretation, for as long as the interpretation does not affect halakhic practice, permission is given (the individual) to interpret (as he sees fit). I see no distinction between the interpretation of a mishna and the interpretation of a biblical verse, and (certainly) permission is granted to interpret a biblical verse (in a novel and individualistic fashion), as our eyes have seen in the novellae of the commentators after the talmudic period (who interpreted biblical verses differently from the talmudic sages); it is only necessary not to decide or interpret any legal sense in a manner which is in conflict with the wisdom of the talmudic sages.

This is also the view of Rabbi Shlomo Luria (the Maharshal) in his commentary to Sanhedrin 52a, as well as of the Gra (the great Gaon of Vilna). In his biblical commentary *Aderet Eliyahu*, the Gra cites the following on the beginning of *Parashat Mishpatim*:

> "And his master shall bring him near the door or the mezuza." The simple meaning of the text is that the mezuza is to be ritually fit (kosher), but the rabbinic talmudic law (which rules that the mezuza is not to be ritually fit) uproots the biblical text. And this is the greatness of the Oral Law, which is the Revealed Law to Moses from Sinai, and it is turned about like the material of the seal-maker…Therefore it is necessary that one know the plain meaning of the Torah, that one know the seal-maker.

Rabbi Menachem Kasher, the author of the *Torah Shelema*, explains these rather obscure words of the great Gaon of Vilna:

> Perhaps his intention is to make reference to the talmudic passage in Sanhedrin 38a which extols the virtues of the King of all Kings, Holy and Blessed Be He, since a human being mints several coins with

one stamp, and each one is similar to the other, but the Holy One, Blessed Be He mints every human being with the stamp of Adam the First, and not one is similar to his friend, as it is written "and it is turned about like the material of the seal-maker" (Job 38:14).

Perforce this is said concerning Torah, as our sages have said in the Jerusalem Talmud Sanhedrin, chapter 4, halakha 2: The Torah is expounded in forty-nine ways to decide purity and in forty-nine ways to decide impurity... and so the Torah is truth, and the seal of the Holy One, Blessed Be He is truth, and even though the seal which is revealed is one, that one has many facets, and herein lies its greatness... And therefore it is necessary to know the plain meaning of the text, and to know the seal-maker, the interpretation being that the plain words of the biblical text is referred to as the seal-maker, and herein lies the greatness of Torah: the seal-maker mints many forms, not one of which is similar to its friend, and so there are ninety-eight (legitimate) facets to Torah, and so it is necessary to know the plain meaning of the text (which has forged or minted them all).

The Gaon comes to posit a great principle: *It is necessary to know the literal meaning of the biblical text, even when the halakha uproots the plain interpretation.*[1]

THE IMPORTANCE OF THE LITERAL INTERPRETATION

What might the literal meaning of the text add to our understanding, even when it is superseded by halakha? I heard the following interpretation of "an eye for an eye" from my revered teacher, Rabbi Joseph B. Soloveitchik, *zt"l*.

We read the Written Torah every Shabbat so that every Jew who attends synagogue will hear the Five Books of Moses every year of his life. The Written Torah, therefore, educates the mind and the conscience of the individual; to this end, the Written Torah advocates "an eye for an eye," since the only way the perpetrator of such a crime can feel the enormity of his transgression is if his own eye is removed in turn.

---

1. Rabbi Menachem Kasher, *Torah Shelema*, additions to *Parashat Mishpatim*, p. 302, emphasis added.

However, the Oral Law must then mediate the Written Law to accord with practical life in the real world. In reality, taking out the eye of the perpetrator may not be a fair or useful punishment. Perhaps the eye of the victim was much weaker or stronger than the eye of the assailant, in which case the punishment is not exactly equivalent to the crime. Additionally, if the perpetrator's eye is removed, the victim cannot receive monetary compensation for his loss, because there is a legal principle which determines that one cannot receive two penalties for the same crime – and in most cases, the newly blinded victim would desperately require monetary compensation. It does not really help the victim for his assailant to be blinded too, even if a general concept of justice is demonstrated by the punishment. Hence, Rabbi Soloveitchik explained, the Bible teaches the lesson of the enormity of the crime by stating "an eye for an eye," while the Oral Law demands monetary compensation.

All of the above is predicated upon our desire to understand the truth of Torah and our understanding that the word of God contains multiple truths. With such an axiom, individual creativity in biblical interpretation – with an aim to endeavoring to understand as deeply as possible every aspect of the divine will – is not only permissible but desirable, as demonstrated by the fact that the greatest of the biblical commentators throughout the ages never hesitated to interpret the text in accordance with their individual – and often novel – understanding.

In the words of Rabbi Eliezer Ashkenazi (1513–1586), an ardent disciple of both Rabbi Yosef Karo and Rabbi Moshe Alsheikh, in his biblical commentary *Ma'asei Hashem*:[2]

> Concerning faith in (the contemporary) human being, it is said in *Parashat Nitzavim* (Deut. 29) "and not with you alone did I establish a covenant…but with those who are with us today and with those who are not here." Therefore, each and every one of us, our children and grandchildren, up until the end of all the generations who have entered the covenant, are duty bound to examine the secrets of the Torah and to straighten out our faith concerning it by accepting the truth from whoever says it…

---

2. *Parashat Balak* (Warsaw, 1871) p. 169.

neither ought we be concerned about the logic of others – even if they preceded us – preventing our own individual investigation. Much to the contrary...just as (our forebears) did not wish to indiscriminately accept the truth from those who preceded them, and that which they did not choose (to accept), they rejected, so is it fitting for us to do...Only on the basis of the gathering of many different opinions will the truth be tested. Thus, it is valuable to us to complete the views (of our predecessors) and to investigate (the meaning of the Bible) in accordance with our own mind's understanding. And even if in the course of investigation into the secrets of the Torah, through our love for it, we err (in our interpretation) it will not be accounted for us even as an unwitting sin because our intent was for the sake of heaven. But we shall be guilty if we desist from investigating the secrets of our Torah by declaring: the lions [the sages who preceded us] have already established supremacy, so let us accept their words as they are...Rather it is proper for us to investigate and analyze in accord with our own understanding and to write our interpretations for the good of those who come after us, whether they will agree or not. You must struggle to scale the heights and to understand our Torah...and do not be dismayed by the names of the great personalities when you find them in disagreement with your belief; you must investigate and choose, because for this purpose were you created, and wisdom was granted you from Above, and this will benefit you.

Rabbi Ashkenazi is herein expressing the supremacy of the authority of the text over the authority of any one individual interpreter, so that permission is given for anyone in each generation to attempt to interpret the text as he best understands it. To be sure, from a traditional perspective there are certain limitations even within this greatly widened area of acceptability. The interpreter must have the ability to properly deal with the text, and must be thoroughly conversant with the language in which it is written and the nuances of that language. He must not color his investigation with an attitude which strives to undermine the traditional consensual axioms regarding the text, such as the Wellhausen School of Biblical Criticism or christological interpretations which endeavor to confirm the truth of the Gospels on the basis of biblical explication. But other than these salient departures from traditional biblical thought, each generation has the right to interpret in accordance with its knowledge and perceptions, and the next generation of committed Jews – "history," as it were – will decide which interpretations are to be included in the corpus of accepted biblical commentary.

And so the Bible has the glorious and uncanny ability to speak to us with many voices – all at the same time! Perhaps most remarkable of all: not only does one hear through the words of the Bible the commanding voice of God, still impressing upon us His will of four thousand years ago at Sinai; not only do we experience the insights of the rabbinic sages of the Talmud, who informed the text with their unique insights and traditions; but I find that each week the Torah appears to be speaking directly to me, to my individual and communal concerns and commitments, in a manner which is always relevant and inspiring.

The Talmud calls the Bible *Mikra* , and this is usually interpreted as coming from the verb *kra* (קרא) to read, since the Written Torah is publicly read on Mondays, Thursdays, Sabbaths, and festivals. But Yisrael Eldad, in the introduction to his *Hegyonot BaMikra* (Reflections on the Bible), masterfully suggests that the term comes from the same root, *kra* (קרא), but it is to be interpreted as "to call." The Bible calls out to us, sometimes comforting and sometimes chiding, sometimes as if from the distant past and sometimes as if from the immediate present, but always with the imperative that we change our ways and reach for a higher level of morality and sanctity. This is the meaning of the public blessings the individual called to the Torah is commanded to recite: "Blessed art Thou, O Lord our God, King of the Universe, who has chosen us from all other nations and given us the Torah (past tense)," and "Blessed art Thou, who gives the Torah" (present tense).

It is precisely because the Torah is at one and the same time the oldest recorded document still directing human lives, as well as the most relevant and contemporary, that teaching and studying the Bible is such an important stepping-stone into the glories of our tradition. This multiplicity of possibilities extends into our attitudes concerning the commandments and even the personalities of our sacred Torah. What is the fundamental significance of the various biblical laws? Are the rules of *kashrut* chiefly a ritual linking the individual to his Creator, without any logical meaning or significance, or are they suffused with ethical and moral lessons concerning the ambiguity of eating meat, and aimed at sensitizing human thought and action to ideals of compassion and concern? Both are true, and the Bible student can accept the one, the other, both, or as many other meanings which speak to his soul. Each will discover his *pshuto shel mikra,* his plain meaning of the text, which takes on "renewed significance every day" (see Rosen's *Introduction to the Commentary of the Rashbam,* and his citation of Rashi's letter to his grandson).

THE NATURE OF BIBLICAL PERSONALITIES

How are we to view the matriarchs and patriarchs, the sons of Jacob who became the twelve tribes of Israel, the biblical leaders of our people such as Moses, Aaron and Miriam, David and Solomon? Are they to be seen as larger than life, midway between human and divine, or "closer to *malakhim* (angels) than to mortals" (*Jewish Observer,* March 1991, p. 51)? This latter opinion is certainly supported by the Zohar, the mystical interpretation of the Bible, which identifies the personalities of the Bible with the *sefirot* or emanations of the Divine. The Zohar describes Abraham as representing Ḥesed (Loving-kindness), Isaac as *Gevura* (Might), Jacob as *Tiferet* (Beauty), Joseph as *Yesod* (Foundation), and so on. This is likewise the view of the talmudic sage Rabbi Shmuel bar Naḥmani, who cites Rabbi Yonatan and declares: "Whoever suggests that David sinned (with Batsheva) is mistaken" (Shabbat 56a), and goes on to explain the context of David's action in order to greatly mitigate – if not obliterate – the seeming act of adultery that he committed. This was the approach of Rabbi Aaron Kotler, as quoted in the pages of the *Jewish Observer* (March 1991, p. 50). Certainly, many individuals find such an approach inspiring, and look to the perfection of the personalities of the Bible to spur them on to even greater spiritual heights.

But there is also a second approach, largely championed by Nahmanidies. For example, here is what Nahmanidies writes about Abraham, when he descends to Egypt in order to escape the grievous famine in the Land of Israel, and tells his wife Sarah to claim to be his sister, leading to her captivity in Pharaoh's harem:

And know that Abraham, our father, sinned a great sin unwittingly, in that he brought his righteous wife to (the brink of) the stumbling block of sin because of his fear lest he be killed; he should have had confidence in God that He would rescue him, his wife and his household... Likewise, his having left the land to which he had initially been commanded (to live) because of famine was a transgression, because (he should have realized that) God would save him from death by famine. (Nahmanidies, *Commentary on the Torah*, Gen. 12:10)

When the Torah informs us (in Gen. 16:4, 6) that once Hagar had conceived Abraham's seed, "her mistress became of little value in her eyes... and Sarai afflicted her and she (Hagar) fled from before her (Sarai)," Nahmanidies comments, "our mother sinned with this affliction, and likewise Abraham (sinned) in allowing her to do so. God heard her affliction and gave her a son who will be a wild-ass of a man, and (is destined to) afflict the seed of Abraham and Sarah with all types of afflictions" (Nahmanidies, *Commentary on the Torah*, Gen. 16:6).

To the best of my knowledge, in neither of these instances is there a midrashic precedent for Nahmanidies' interpretation that Abraham and Sarah had sinned. Moreover, their acts can certainly be justified, especially with respect to the second case, wherein the Bible itself explains Sarah's motivation and even justification. Nevertheless, Nahmanidies apparently believed that his understanding of the plain text suggested sin on the parts of Abraham and Sarah, and that it was his right – nay, duty – to express this novel interpretation. Even more to the point, he apparently did not fear that such interpretation would lessen the inspirational value of the Bible for the reader. To the contrary, Nahmanidies may well have believed that it is only when we can identify with the personalities of the Bible, when we see them as great human beings, but human beings nonetheless, who grapple with – and sometimes even fail in their effort to overcome – the very same problems and blandishments which assail our every step, that we can truly utilize them as models and learn from their experiences.

In a similar vein, Rabbi Samson Raphael Hirsch criticizes Isaac and Rebecca for having failed in the education of their children; after all, despite their vastly different and even antithetical natural proclivities, the two boys were placed in the very same educational system (*Commentary of R.S.R. Hirsch*, Gen. 25:27). Rabbi Hirsch also states that Moses' genealogy is emphasized by the biblical text in order to impress upon everyone that our Master Prophet is a human being and only a human being (*Commentary of R.S.R. Hirsch*, Ex. 6:14–30).

The famed Netziv, Rabbi Naftali Zvi Yehuda Berlin, dean of the Volozhin Yeshiva, points out and attempts to explain the lack of interpersonal communication between Isaac and Rebecca which led to the tragic breakup of their family and the undying enmity between brothers Jacob and Esau (*Haamek Davar*, Gen. 24:65).

Indeed, it is difficult to read the pages of the Bible in accordance with the "literal meaning of the text" and *not* come to the conclusion that our Torah pictures its heroes and heroines as complex human beings, rising to great spiritual heights and descending to jealous hatreds, prone to sin, but suffused with beliefs which enable them to rise above their weaknesses and accomplish great things – and thus be worthy of our veneration and emulation.

THE *AKEDA* REVISITED

In an article which appeared in the *Jewish Observer* (March 1991, pp. 48–51), written by the editor, Nissim Wolpin, and titled, "Approaching the Avos – Through Up-Reach or Drag-Down," I was severely taken to task for my treatment of the biblical personalities in several of my newspaper columns. I was charged with having suggested that Abraham ought to have argued with the Almighty for the life of Isaac before bringing him to be bound at the altar in the *Akeda* (and hence may have failed his final test); for raising the possibility that Sarah was opposed to the *Akeda* and, hence, left Abraham and Beer-Sheva for Hebron, where she subsequently died; and for picturing Joseph as a *baal teshuva* (a penitent), who cut off communications with his father for his first twenty-two years in Egypt, married the daughter of an idolatrous priest, and only as a result of Judah's persuasive argumentation and his own powerful memories of his father's house, returned to his family and his faith.

The *Akeda* is one of the most profound, complex, and difficult stories in the entire Bible. How can the God who commands us not to murder, who forbids the child-slaughtering practices of Moloch, and who promised Abraham that "in Isaac shall be called your seed," command Abraham to bring Isaac as a whole burnt offering? The command defies the logical understanding of biblical commentator and student alike.

Rashi suggests that Abraham misunderstood the divine command: "(God) did not say slaughter him, because the Holy One, Blessed Be He did not wish him (Abraham) to slaughter him (Isaac), but merely to bring him up to the mountain, to uplift him in dedication, and once he brought him up, he was to bring him down." The important point to note here is that, according to Rashi, God didn't want Isaac to be sacrificed, and Abraham initially misunderstood God's command.[3]

The *Sefat Emet*, written by Rabbi Yehuda Aryeh Leib of Gur, bases his interpretation on this very same understanding: God did not want Isaac slaughtered! He begins with another question, however: Why is the *Akeda* described as a manifestation of fear of God? Was not Abraham's service an expression of love of God, which ranks higher than fear of God? And if so, then why (at the end of the story) does the Bible state that Abraham now emerges merely as one who fears God? The *Sefat Emet* explains that one who loves God totally identifies with Him and His will, and in this instance – since it was not God's will to sacrifice Isaac – "Abraham's heart did not feel attachment and love…therefore he saw the place (*HaMakom* – or God) from afar (a result of fear of God, and not from near, which would have been a result of love of the Divine). Thus, (Abraham's divine) service now was only an expression of fear of God, in that he did not question God at all. He then requested that he not be tested again, in order that there not be any more distance between them (which happened as a result of the *Akeda*), because it is the way of Abraham (to serve out of) love."

The *Sefat Emet* clearly sees the entire *Akeda* story as expressing a lower relationship between God and Abraham, one in which Abraham doesn't penetrate God's true intent, one which expresses distance rather than closeness, and which results in silence rather than dialogue between Abraham and God.

---

3. Taanit 4a, Rashi s.v. כאשר לא צויתי.

Interestingly enough, a possible source for the *Sefat Emet* may have been Rabbi Yosef ibn Kaspi. In the fourteenth chapter of his biblical commentary *Gevia HaKesef* (see the edition translated and annotated by Rabbi Basil Herring, Ktav Publishing, 1990), he argues that the major message of the *Akeda* story is to impress upon the Jews, and especially upon the Jewish masses who are prone to extremism in their divine service, the divine abhorrence of child sacrifice. He proves his contention by pointing out that the more universal name for God (*Elohim*) is employed by the Torah text when Abraham is commanded to do the sacrifice, whereas the more Jewish (and loving) Tetragrammaton is used only when the command is rescinded; moreover, Abraham's name is repeated twice in the text when the Almighty tells him not to touch Isaac, in order to emphasize the preeminence of this second divine statement over the first, where Abraham's name is mentioned only once. The message is clear: the Abraham who stands ready to sacrifice is not as much in consonance with the ultimate divine will as is the Abraham who desists from sacrificing.

Even more to the point, the sages of the Talmud themselves place Abraham in a somewhat problematic context, together with Mesha the king of Moab and Yiftah – the latter two having wrongly sacrificed their children:

> It is written [in Jeremiah's prophecy concerning child sacrifice] "which I have not commanded, which I have not spoken, and which did not enter my mind." Which I have not commanded – that refers to the son of Mesha, king of Moab, of whom it is written: "And he took his firstborn son who was to rule after him and brought him as a whole burnt offering." Which I have not spoken – that refers to Yiftah. And which did not enter my mind – that refers to Isaac son of Abraham. (Taanit 4a)

To be sure, our tragic history of martyrdom has sadly enabled many generations of Jews to identify with Abraham, who was called on by God to sacrifice his beloved child, and in the cosmic perspective of biblical relevance, that may well have been one of the most significant reasons why the Almighty presents him with such an ambiguous and difficult command in the first place. Jewish history is heavy with tear-stained and blood-drenched periods wherein parents have been forced to stand silently by as their children have been slaughtered in front of their very eyes. Thus, the merit of the *Akeda* is poignantly invoked during the Rosh HaShana and *Seliḥot* prayers, one of the manifold symbols of the shofar is the evocation of Abraham and Isaac's merit, and every parent in Israel who sees his son off to the army hears the divine command: "Take your son, your only son, whom you love." Indeed, I have expressed these very interpretations in previous articles and, from this perspective, the command of the *Akeda* has given untold strength to countless generations who have been forced to watch their children cruelly slaughtered in sanctification of the divine name. Moreover, my commentary in question stressed Maimonides' admonition concerning the absolute truth of the prophetic message; when the Almighty commands, even if it runs counter to subjective reason or logic, it is the divine statement which carries final authority.

But nevertheless, the initial textual difficulty – that in the instance of the *Akeda* the Almighty appears to be contradicting Himself ("For in Isaac shall be called your seed" – Gen. 21:12) and His own morality ("One who sheds the blood of another shall have his blood shed, for the human was created in the image of the Divine" (9:6), as well as the fact that God Himself (or His angel) rescinds His initial command of sacrifice – leaves the door ajar for additional interpretations. In light of the possibility of a multiplicity of interpretations, and especially when we are dealing with a narrative aggadic text and not a legal halakhic one, I maintain the right to suggest an additional meaning.

Allow me to add the following personal note: There is no incident in the Torah with which I can identify more closely – and which has caused me as much personal anguish – as the *Akeda* story. I remember telling Bible stories to my children on Shabbat morning before shul and my young daughters crying out and begging me to stop because they could not bear to hear of God commanding a father to bring his child to slaughter. My daughter Batya once said, with tears in her eyes, "Abba, you can't be telling me the truth. Abraham is too good, too much of a *tzaddik*. He was so good to everyone; he opened his tent to everyone. How could he be so mean to his own child?"

My daughter's words ring in my ears each year when *Parashat Vayera* comes around, as the *Akeda* causes me to question my own experiences and priorities in raising my children. How often did I, as a busy communal rabbi involved in Jewish education and outreach, unwillingly and even unwittingly but nevertheless almost consistently, sacrifice my own children for my communal activities? When the family was growing up, how many evenings did I spend at home to help them with their homework, or just talk or play with them? How many Shabbatot did we have with only family around the table, and without many and sundry guests? And if that is the situation in my case, how much more so must it have been true regarding Abraham, founder of our faith, forger of Jewish souls, welcomer of all strangers, whose tent was always open?! Is it not possible that one of the messages that God was telling Abraham is that you dare not sacrifice your children – not even for Him?

When I made the difficult decision to leave America for Eretz Yisrael, and my mother barely spoke to me because she felt she was being abandoned, and my mother-in-law, only half in jest, tried to create an Association for the Prevention of Cruelty to Grandchildren, because I was subjecting her grandchildren to army service and mortal danger, once again the story of Abraham spoke to me in a most poignant and personal way. After all, did not God initially command Abraham, "Get thee forth from your land, your birthplace, your father's house" as the first test, and then, "Take your son, your only one, whom you love and get thee forth to Mt. Moriah," as the last test? Did God not require from Abraham that he sever his ties with both past and future, that, paradoxically, if the nation of Israel is to live and flourish, one must be ready to risk both one's parents and one's children?

Which is the true message of the *Akeda*? All of the above and even infinitely more, for the divine voice has the capacity to speak in manifold and seemingly contradictory ways to many people, in every generation, and even to the same person at different moments of his life.

Moreover, the Bible itself depicts Abraham successfully arguing with the Almighty before the imminent destruction of Sodom and Gomorrah, utilizing the ethical arguments that the righteous should not be destroyed with the wicked, and that the judge of the entire world dare not act unjustly. Moses is urged by the Almighty to argue against His decision to destroy the Jewish people after their sin with the Golden Calf – "Leave me alone and I will destroy them, argue with Me and I will save them" (Ex. 32:10) – and He does give in to the arguments of the leader of the Israelites. How much more justification would Abraham have required in order to argue against a command that God Himself is soon about to revoke? And if, indeed, it had not been God's will to have sacrificed Isaac, Sarah would have been correct had she refused to go along with the plan. Perhaps, to use the *Sefat Emet's* terminology, she was still in the category of loving God, and so she correctly understood that Isaac was not to be sacrificed.

JOSEPH REVISITED

In the tale of Joseph, one of the most difficult issues to comprehend is why Joseph did not contact his father, especially during the period when he was grand vizier of Egypt. It is likely that Joseph, while languishing in the pit into which his brothers had thrown him, realized that his father's favoritism had been responsible, albeit unwillingly, for his brothers' enmity, and Joseph may very well have resolved to cut all ties with his father's house. When we bear in mind the name Joseph gives his eldest son (Menashe – "for the Almighty has enabled me to forget all my toil and my father's house," Gen. 41:51), the wife he accepts from Pharaoh (the daughter of the Priest of On, according to the simple meaning of the text), the Egyptian language he constantly speaks (to the total exclusion of Hebrew), the Egyptian name and robe he accepts from Pharaoh, and the various ploys he uses on his brothers, I cannot but conclude that we have before us the magnificent story of an extraordinary person of remarkable moral stature who endeavored to escape what he had come to regard as a problematic upbringing, only to discover that no one can deny his ancestral roots, and that eventually everyone must come home again. Ultimately, Joseph becomes completely reconciled to his past, and even adjures his progeny not to leave him buried in Egypt, but to bring his remains with them when they return home to Israel. From this perspective, it is a most moving tale of *teshuva*, of return to one's roots, to one's father and one's home. It is fascinating that the Beta Yisrael Ethiopian tradition maintains that the meeting between Joseph and his father Jacob after twenty-two years of separation and despair took place on Yom Kippur, the Day of Atonement. Son returns to father, and children on earth return to their Father-in-Heaven, in a parallel dialectic which reflects both national exile and personal redemption, both alienation and rapprochement.

Was Joseph the righteous saint who never budged one iota from his initial piety in his father's house, despite the Egyptian blandishments? Or was Joseph the first penitent, who demonstrates how you can never really escape your origins and that it is never too late to come home? Here again, I believe that the Torah allows for both – and infinitely more – possibilities, as a hammer blow which gives off many sparks.

Interestingly enough, this last interpretation of Joseph's story came to me in a flash when I volunteered to lecture at the Ma'asiyahu Prison in Ramleh. I had planned on speaking to the Jewish prisoners about *Parashat Shemot*, the portion to be read in the synagogue the following Sabbath. More than one hundred prisoners attended the lecture, and they requested that I talk instead about Joseph. When I countered by explaining that the Joseph story was "old news," they reminded me that Joseph, too, had been imprisoned. For them, the story was still current. Throughout the next hour's session dedicated to Joseph, you could have heard a pin drop in the audience. The clear identification of these Jewish prisoners with the story of Joseph and his brothers – especially with the interpretation of *teshuva* that I felt I had revealed within it – was one of the most moving experiences of my life.

In conclusion to these thoughts on biblical interpretation, I would suggest that the interested reader study *Ḥamesh Drashot* by my rebbe and mentor, Rabbi Joseph B. Soloveitchik *zt"l* (translated from the original Yiddish into Hebrew by Rabbi David Telsner and also available in English under the title *The Rav Speaks*). These are *divrei Torah* (sermons) on the various portions of the week which Rabbi Soloveitchik delivered at a number of Mizraḥi conventions. The letters and articles of Rabbi Eliezer Shach, dean of the Ponovezh Yeshiva, were recently published, and it is fascinating (and for me, sad) to note what Rabbi Shach, leader of the *ḥaredi* (ultra-Orthodox) world, has to say about these biblical interpretations of Rabbi Soloveitchik, leader of the Modern Orthodox world.

Rabbi Soloveitchik, in his sermons at the Mizraḥi conventions, interpreted the biblical portions in a pointedly Zionistic and often personal fashion. He spoke of the eternal acquisition (*kinyan*) Abraham made both of the Land of Israel and of the God of Israel by walking the land and by sacrificing on it. He maintained that non-religious Jews acquired a portion of both the land and of God as a result of their sacrifices. He went on to note that at the time of the *Akeda*, Abraham had to separate himself from his family and friends who didn't comprehend his act of devotion. Joseph the Righteous was also isolated and alienated from his brothers because he felt that the old way of life had come to an end, that it had become necessary to prepare the way for the Egyptian exile. In similar fashion, continued Rabbi Soloveitchik, he and his fellow Zionists were censured by former friends and religious leaders in the *Aguda*, his brothers in Torah, because they felt that life in the European shtetl could not go on as usual, and that the *Yishuv* in Israel had to be prepared for the Jews escaping the European Holocaust.

Rabbi Shach severely criticizes Rabbi Soloveitchik's *divrei Torah* on two counts: he claims that Rabbi Soloveitchik's remarks were inappropriate since, Rabbi Shach explains, non-observant Jews have no portion in God; not only have they not acquired the land but they may well be responsible for its destruction, heaven forefend. He also criticizes Rabbi Soloveitchik for creating interpretations which were not previously stated by the sages of the Talmud:

> I wonder at the fact that so much time has passed, and (the rabbis of America) have not responded to his words, which contain things which are forbidden to hear and which are certainly forbidden to disseminate publicly for young people to learn from … for example, the fact that he (Rabbi Soloveitchik) imagines things and creates ideas from his mind which he places within the thoughts of the tribes who are the tribes of God … It is a complete distortion of the Torah view (*daat Torah*) to place some idea which he imagines in his mind within the thoughts of the tribes of God … and I, myself, wonder at the fact that (Rabbi Soloveitchik) forgot what any elementary Torah student knows, that the Land (of Israel) was destroyed because "they left My Torah, and did not observe My Commandments"; and certainly (because of those) who deny the Fundamental Principle! … Is this building the land or destroying it?

Who's an *Apikoros*?

O
f late, a spirit of zealotry or "Pinchasitis" seems to have overtaken the Orthodox Jewish community – a spirit that is sadly devoid of the covenant of peace which was ultimately bestowed upon the original Pinchas, biblical defender of the faith. On a broad variety of topics – conversion standards, the role of women, drafting yeshiva students, the election of a chief rabbi – vitriol abounds. Charges of heresy and wickedness have been leveled against various leaders of the more moderate Orthodox movements, within and without Israel.

Perhaps it would be salutary for those of us who seek a broader and more inclusive orthodoxy to attempt to define the term *apikoros*, or heretic, and explore the heretic's position vis-à-vis the Jewish community.

Those who conclude discussion with the pejorative "heretic" generally cite a well-known passage from Maimonides in support of their position. Maimonides, in his *Interpretation of the Mishna*, Tractate Sanhedrin, Introduction to Chapter Eleven, presents his well-known credo of thirteen principles of faith, and concludes:

> When an individual believes in all of these essentials [principles]...he enters into the category of Israel and it is incumbent to love him...But when there becomes weakened for an individual an article of these articles, behold, he is excluded from

the category and has denied an essential [article of faith]. He is called an apostate, an *apikoros* and a heretic, and it is incumbent upon us to hate and destroy him.

It is my contention that the basis for the Maimonidean doctrine of exclusion of the *apikoros* is virtually impossible to discover, that an operable definition of *apikoros* is virtually impossible to articulate, and that the present-day situation is such – as confirmed by halakhic authorities including Maimonides himself, the *Ḥazon Ish*, and Rabbi Kook – as to render the category of *apikoros* obsolete, inappropriate and ineffective.

The mishna which begins the eleventh chapter of Tractate Sanhedrin states:

> All of Israel has a share in the World to Come... And those who have no share in the World to Come (include) those who say there is no (concept) of the resurrection of the dead from the Torah, or that the Torah is not from heaven, or the *apikoros*. Rabbi Akiva says: "Even one who reads from the Apocrypha."

From the simple interpretation of the words of the mishna it is clear that the *apikoros* and his partners in denial may forfeit their share in the World to Come, but they are not excluded from the community of Israel in this world. Maimonides is consistent on this issue, for he also declares in *Mishneh Torah*: "Each one of the fourteen people we have enumerated (including *apikorsim*), even though they are (considered) of Israel, have no share in the World to Come."[1]

Most difficult of all, however, is arriving at the proper definition of the term *apikoros*. Maimonides teaches:

> These three are called *apikorsim*: one who denies prophecy and denies that any knowledge may reach the hearts of man from the Creator; one who denies the prophecy of Moses our Teacher; and one who declares that the Creator does not know the deeds of man.[2]

---

1. Maimonides, *Mishneh Torah, Hilkhot Teshuva* 3, 14.
2. Ibid., 3, 8.

In other words, Maimonides sees an *apikoros* as one who errs in ideological doctrine. The *Amora'im* of the Talmud, however, see an *apikoros* as one who errs in practical observance:

> *Apikoros*: Rav and Rabbi Ḥanina both say it is one who scorns a Torah scholar. Rabbi Yoḥanan and Rabbi Yehoshua ben Levi say it is one who scorns his friend in the presence of a Torah scholar.[3]

The Meiri attempts to explain (and thereby defend) Maimonides' "unorthodox" definition by suggesting that "through scorning a scholar one will come to scorn his words and wisdom, and will eventually deny all that we are required to believe."[4] Aside from this forced interpretation, he complicates matters by giving his own definition of an *apikoros* as anyone who habitually and willfully violates even one law of the Torah, a very broad definition which would render the majority of Jews in our times heretics. The overwhelming majority of the *Rishonim* uphold the amoraic definition,[5] and the *Kesef Mishneh* concludes his commentary on Maimonides saying, "We need a reason as to why our master deleted these (amoraic) views and wrote that which he wrote."[6] It is possible that Maimonides rejected the amoraic interpretations in favor of the philosophic category "epicurean" which is the linguistic origin of the term *apikoros*.[7] Nevertheless, the very definition of *apikoros* is open to argument; moreover, interpreting a mishnaic word not in accordance with the views cited by the Gemara is in itself sufficient to render one an *apikoros*, according to many modern-day zealots.

To further illustrate the explosive potential of the charge of heresy, the same Maimonides who initially posited that one who denies any of

---

3. Sanhedrin 99b.
4. Meiri, *Beit HaBeḥira* to Tractate Sanhedrin, p. 258.
5. The Arukh, Rashi on Sanhedrin 99b, and *Hagahot Maimoniot* on Maimonides, *Mishneh Torah, Hilkhot Teshuva* 3, 14.
6. *Kesef Mishneh* on Maimonides, ibid.
7. An interesting tannaitic proof to Maimonides' contention is the Mishna Avot 2:14. "Rabbi Elazar says: Be diligent in your study of Torah and know what to answer an *apikoros*." Apparently, the *apikoros* in this mishna is presenting philosophic contentions which must be countered.

the thirteen principles of faith may be excluded from the People of Israel, is himself vulnerable to attack. Belief in divine providence is one of the aforementioned thirteen principles, and an *apikoros* has been defined in *Mishneh Torah* as one who states that the Creator does not know the deeds of man. In his philosophic magnum opus, *Guide for the Perplexed*, Maimonides hedges on this notion, and insists that the degree of divine providence received by an individual depends upon his intellect, character, and achievement. The philosophic halakhist maintains that the prophets enjoy a special providence; the rabbis and wise men come next; and a person who is ignorant and disobedient is neglected by *hashgaha* and is treated like a lower animal, left to the governance of chance.[8]

In a similar vein, belief in the resurrection of the dead is another of the Maimonidean Principles of Faith. This doctrine is not mentioned in the *Guide*, and the picture of the World to Come which emerges from the *Mishneh Torah* is that of a place "without bodies or forms, but only the souls of the righteous."[9] The Rabad is clearly agitated by this description, and lashes out in his strictures:

> The words of this man in my eyes are close to those who say that there is no resurrection of the dead for the body, only for the soul, and by the life of my head this is not the view of our sages.[10]

In sum, therefore, the precise definition of *apikoros* is embroiled in controversy, and the very authority who originally suggested that the heretic be excluded from Israel comes close to being attacked for questionable doctrines.

Although we have concluded that defining an *apikoros* is virtually an impossible task, it is nevertheless instructive to learn how the Talmud and especially the latter halakhic authorities deal with those who are for some reason considered *apikorsim*. The Talmud teaches:

---

8. Maimonides, *Guide for the Perplexed*, Division III, chapters. 17, 18. Huzik, *A History of Medieval Jewish Philosophy*, p. 242.

9. Maimonides, *Mishneh Torah, Hilkhot Teshuva* 8, 2.

10. Rabad, *Strictures* on ibid. Maimonides subsequently wrote a "Letter on the Resurrection of the Dead" to clear up the controversy.

Rabbi Abbahu cited to Rabbi Yoḥanan: Idolators and shepherds of small cattle need not be brought up (from a pit) although they must not be cast down; but *minim*, informers and apostates may be cast down and may not be brought up.[11]

Although the category of *apikoros* is not included in this list of those who may be "cast down," most of the talmudic commentaries and halakhic codifiers include it.[12] However, the *Ḥazon Ish* adds a pathbreaking comment to this apparent mandate to destroy the *apikoros*:

> In our times when we do not see open miracles and when in these acts of punishment there is no heal of the breach, this law is not operable. The very opposite is the case; it is incumbent upon us to restore (the heretics) with chains of love and to place them in a ray of light to the greatest extent possible.[13]

The source for this seemingly radical statement of the *Ḥazon Ish* is none other than the revered sage Rabbi Tarfon. The Bible admonishes us to rebuke our wayward brother, and states that only after our rebuke has been rejected do we have we the right to hate him[14] – and even "cast him down" according to the talmudic dictum. Rabbi Tarfon declares that even in his generation (the second century of the common era), the transgressor could not be condemned, since there was no one qualified to give adequate instruction to the wayward:

---

11. Avoda Zara 26a, 26b. See Buchler, *Am HaAretz HaGalili*, p. 131 note 43, who points out that the Tosefta cited by the Talmud is dealing with the lost object of the *min* (which is to be cast down), and not the *min* himself.
12. Maimonides, *Mishneh Torah, Hilkhot Avodat Kokhavim* 10, 1 and *Hilkhot Rotzeaḥ* 4, 10, Rabbi Alfas and the Rosh to Avoda Zara 26b and *Shulḥan Arukh, Yoreh De'ah* 158, 2. The *Tur* does not mention *apikoros*. The *Mishneh Torah* and the *Yoreh De'ah* substitute *apikorsim* for *minim*, and Rabbi Alfas and the Rosh include both categories. One may possibly conjecture that the initial group mentions those who endanger the existence of Israel as a separate people viz. *minim* (Jewish priests of idolatry or Jews who became Christians), informers and apostates. The word *minim* may well have raised problems with the gentile censors of Jewish books, and so the term *apikorsim* was substituted.
13. *Ḥazon Ish* to *Shulḥan Arukh, Yoreh De'ah* 13, 16.
14. Lev. 19:17.

Rabbi Tarfon said: I wonder if there is in this generation any individual who can rebuke. If one says: Remove the flint from between your teeth, he (the transgressor) will say to him: Remove the beam from between your eyes.[15]

Hence, the Ḥazon Ish, following in the path of Rabbi Tarfon, would consider every transgressor as one who had not received proper chastisement.[16] In effect, we – the so-called religious representatives and teachers – must assume the brunt of the guilt, for the essential problem lies in our inability to properly direct and enlighten others. This, coupled with the "eclipse of the Divine" and the ineffectiveness of censure in our generation, causes the Ḥazon Ish to urge us to love and not hate, to teach and not reject, even the heretic. *A fortiori* we must exercise restraint and utilize well-reasoned critiques rather than hurl questionable epithets of paltry significance when dealing with the writings and institutions of respected representatives of Orthodoxy.

And yet, there is another aspect to this entire discussion. Many unabashedly non-Orthodox spokesmen, who literally trounce on many of our most hallowed precepts, are merely the products of their environments and educational institutions. Maimonides, the strictest interpreter of an isolationist policy against those who deny our basic beliefs, declares:

> Once it becomes publicly known that an individual has denied the validity of the Oral Law, behold he is considered like the rest of the heretics who deny the divinity of the Torah, and the slanderers and the rebels who are not in the category of Israel. This statement applies, however, only to one who initially denies the validity of the Oral Law in his mind… and goes after his paltry thoughts… like Zadok and Boethius and all of their followers. But the children of these followers, and their children's children, whose parents misled them – those who were born among the Karaites and were raised in their traditions – behold, they are as ones who were forced against their will… Therefore, it is proper

---

15. Arakhin 16b. I am indebted to Rabbi Moshe Besdin for having pointed out this source.
16. Ḥazon Ish to *Shulḥan Arukh, Yoreh Deʾah* 13, 28.

to bring them back in repentance and to encourage them with words of peace until they return to the complete power of Torah.[17]

Thus, Maimonides has reinterpreted the concept of *onuss* (one who has been forced to transgress against his will) to include the product of a non-Orthodox environment devoid of the opportunity to properly study and practice the tenets of traditional Judaism.[18] Certainly, this would include the overwhelming majority of those affiliated with Conservative and Reform congregations and even a great many of their leaders, who are increasingly coming up from the ranks of Conservative and Reform youth movements, summer camps, day schools, and rabbinic seminaries. Such individuals can hardly be dismissed with the term *apikoros* and excluded from the category of Israel, despite their professions of heterodox doctrines and observances. Indeed, we have seen many of them become more and more committed as they continued to study and develop. And many of us have much to learn from the honesty of their search and the sincerity of their convictions.[19]

But, it may be countered, Maimonides is speaking of those who can be classified as "children who were held captive by the gentiles." We are often confronted by supposed religious leaders from completely observant backgrounds who have received excellent yeshiva training and who are nevertheless perverting our tradition with their unorthodox teachings. Even in such an instance I would submit that if the individual is intellectually convinced of the correctness of his position based upon traditional sources, we are obligated to attempt to disprove his contentions, but we may not condemn him as an *apikoros*, exclude him from *Klal Yisrael*, or bar him from dialogue. Maimonides includes as one of the five he considers disbelievers (*minim*) "one who declares that there is one Master of the Universe, but that He is corporeal and of physical shape."[20]

---

17. Maimonides, *Mishneh Torah, Hilkhot Mamrim* 3, 2–3.
18. Cf. My article, "Reaching out to the Non-Committed," *Jewish Life*, October 1972.
19. "Stirrings in Reform Judaism," *Jewish Observer*, vol. 1, no. 8. I would urge the skeptical reader to visit the *Bet Kafe* which meets in the Brotherhood Synagogue in Manhattan, or the New York Havura and speak to the young participants about the genesis of their religious development and the present nature of their commitment.
20. Maimonides, *Mishneh Torah, Hilkhot Teshuva* 3, 7.

The Rabad argues: "Why does he consider such a person a disbeliever (*min*)? Many greater and better than he have held this opinion by reason of what they saw in the words of the *aggadot*, which are apt to confuse the intelligence."[21] Although the Rabad insists that the acceptance of a corporeal deity is incorrect, one cannot charge those who believe in such a deity with heresy as long as they base their doctrine on traditional texts; honest intellectual error is not to be confused with *apikorsut*.[22]

As a possible talmudic source for this view, there is a fascinating opinion in the Talmud which would remove all culpability from one who makes a false oath because of an intellectual misconception; in this view, the category of *onuss* (against one's will) becomes further extended to include honest errors of logic and understanding:

> The master says: "A man with respect to an oath," excluding (culpability for) an oath (taken) against one's will. What is an example of such a case? It is as in the incident of Rabbi Kahane and Rav Assi, who had stood before Rav. One took an oath that this was the statement which had been made by Rav and the other took an oath that that was the statement which had been made by Rav.
>
> When they (later) came before Rav, they established his statement in accordance with one of them. The other said to him: "I have therefore sworn falsely." (Rav) replied to him: "Your heart forced you."[23]

Hence, even according to the definition of Maimonides, we might make a logical distinction between those who deny a basic religious dogma as a result of the desire to behave in an unfettered fashion or to destroy the Jewish community (a willful *apikoros*, in effect), and those who deny as a result of intellectual conviction. Real intent can only be determined by God; our position vis-à-vis these individuals dare not be offhand rejection and isolation. Much the opposite: it is our obligation to articulate

21. Rabad, *Strictures* on ibid.
22. So explains Rabbi Joseph Albo, *Sefer HaIkkarim*, Book 1, chapter 2, translated by Husik, JPS 1946, p. 54.
23. Shevuot 26a.

our position as forcefully as possible and thereby convince them of the error of their thoughts. They are to be seen as intellectual *onussim*. And if we fail, the fault is with us rather than with them.

Rabbi Avraham Yitzḥak HaKohen Kook even suggests the category of an emotional *onuss*, an individual who is "forced" away from Judaism due to the overwhelming secular climate of the times. In one of his most far-reaching responsa, he comforts a father who is distraught over the apostasy of his son:

> Yes, my dear friend, I understand well the sadness of your heart. But if you should concur with the majority of the scholars that it is seemly at this time to reject utterly those children who have swerved from the paths of Torah and faith because of the tumultuous current of the age, I must explicitly and emphatically declare that this is not the method which God desires. Just as the (*Baalei*) *Tosafot* in Tractate Sanhedrin (26b) maintain that it is logical not to invalidate one suspected of sexual immorality from giving testimony because he is considered an *onuss* – since his instincts overwhelmed him – and the (*Baalei*) *Tosafot* in Tractate Gittin (41b) maintain that since a maidservant enticed him to immorality he is considered as having acted against his will, in a similar fashion (is to be judged) the "evil maidservant" that is the spirit of our times…who entices many of our youngsters with all of her wiles to commit adultery with her. They act completely against their will and far be it from us to judge a transgression which one is forced to commit (*onuss*) in the same manner as we judge a premeditated, willful transgression.

Rabbi Kook concludes that one who rejects aspects of Jewish tradition due to intellectual error or having been enticed by the hedonistic zeitgeist can be brought back to complete faith and repentance either through intellectual discourse or by providing a loving environment of concern and non-judgment.[24] The challenge then becomes ours, to articulate our position and forge our lifestyle in a manner which will inspire the errant to return; this can only be brought about if our doors are opened wide

---

24. Rabbi Avraham Yitzḥak HaKohen Kook, *Iggrot HaRayh*, vol. I, letter 138.

and our arms are outstretched in love and understanding. The utilization of the opprobrium *apikoros* to silence debate and exclude Jews from within our midst is not in accord with most halakhic opinions, from the Ḥazon Ish to Rabbi Kook to Rabbi Soloveitchik to the Lubavitcher Rebbe.

On the most pragmatic level, the use of epithets and the leveling of sanctions are counter-productive. In an open society whose leadership is university trained, such words and actions are tantamount to an admission of intolerant mindlessness at worst, and religious insecurity at best. Our standards must be taken from the Ḥazon Ish, who is apparently concerned with the effect of our tactics when he admonishes: "In these times…when in these acts of punishment there is no heal of the breach, the law is not operable."

Finally, the Orthodox Jewish community must own up to the fact that the real enemy is not the heretical Jew but the ignorant Jew; our battle must be waged not against *apikorsut* but against assimilation. The apocryphal story is told of the European shtetl Jew who would badger the rabbi with heretical questions for an hour after Havdala each Saturday night. "If this is your opinion, why do you persist on coming to shul every Sabbath?" ultimately asked the exasperated rabbi. Came the response: "An *apikoros* I am; a *goy* I'm not." Unfortunately, the contemporary Jewish scene consists of a majority of "Yiddishe *goyim*" who have no relationship whatsoever with any synagogue, not even for *Yizkor* services on Yom Kippur. Due to low birthrate and high assimilation rate, the non-Orthodox American Jewish community is literally disappearing. We dare not waste our precious resources and energy in the kind of intrareligious strife which will only encourage the assimilationist to justify his defection. We must galvanize all of our forces to create Torah institutions, to articulate Torah ideology, to produce Torah leaders, to build Torah communities.[25] If we but convey and not condemn, develop and not destroy, with God's help we shall not merely survive, we shall prevail.

---

25. This is the mission of the newly established Batei Ohr Torah – to articulate an open, loving, and non-judgmental Torah in Israel and throughout the world. The initiative has been described by one of the donors as "Chabad in a Brooks Brothers suit, with a conversion plan as well!"

Section 11

Women in Tanakh and Halakha

Women as Halakhic Scholars and Judges

WHAT IS THE REASON FOR THE HALAKHIC DISTINCTION BETWEEN MEN AND WOMEN?

Two of my greatest teachers, Rabbi Joseph B. Soloveitchik and the Rebbe of Lubavitch, Rabbi Menachem Mendel Schneerson, may their memories be a blessing, said that the greatest challenge facing Orthodoxy in their time was the role and status of women. Within the worlds of Modern Orthodoxy and religious Zionism, these issues continue to provoke vociferous debate.

It is an undisputed fact that Jewish law draws distinctions between men and women with regard to several issues, such as positive mitzvot which are time-bound, the obligation to study and disseminate Torah, and the place of women in synagogue ritual. The central question is: what is the reason for these halakhic distinctions? Is it because women are qualitatively different from men with regard to these issues – in which case the halakhic difference between them must remain forever – or does the difference arise from certain social conditions, such that if these conditions change, the halakha must address the new reality and rule anew based on the sources, defining proper behavior appropriate to the new situation?

ADVANCED TORAH STUDY FOR WOMEN

The best starting place for our investigation is the permissibility of Torah study for women, a point from which many of the other issues emanate. Maimonides, based on the mishna in Masekhet Sota 20a, rules as follows:

> A woman who studies Torah is rewarded, but not with the same reward as that given to a man, for she is not commanded [to study Torah] ... and although she is rewarded, the sages commanded that a man should not teach his daughter Torah, for the minds of most women are not suitable for study – they turn words of Torah into words of emptiness owing to their ignorance. Therefore, our sages taught, "Anyone who teaches his daughter Torah [is considered] as if he taught her foolishness." (Laws of Torah Study, chapter 1, law 13).

DO MEN AND WOMEN DIFFER QUALITATIVELY?

It is interesting that the mishnaic source of Maimonides cites a debate between Ben Azzai, who claims that a person is obligated to teach his daughter Torah, and Rabbi Eliezer, who maintains that if one teaches his daughter Torah it is as if he taught her foolishness; but the Gemara does not provide the reasons for each opinion. When Maimonides states that "the minds of most women are not suitable for study," is he stating a mental-intellectual-biological fact, or is he describing a sociological state of affairs in which girls stayed home, were not educated in any academic framework, and therefore lacked the skills necessary for textual study?

Rabbi Yisrael Meir Kagan, better known as the Ḥafetz Ḥaim, gave his approval to the establishment of the Bais Yaakov academy for girls, initiated by Sarah Schenirer in early twentieth-century Krakow, Poland. The Ḥafetz Ḥaim explained his ruling in his notes on Masekhet Sota (20a, ibid.) that since, "as a result of our many sins," girls are already studying language and arithmetic in a school setting, it is possible – and even desirable – that they be taught the simpler Hebrew subjects such as Ḥumash, *Pirkei Avot*, etc. It is therefore clear that the Ḥafetz Ḥaim understood the words of Maimonides as having been based on the social realities of the time, which denied women educational opportunities, rather than on a qualitative difference between the male and female intellect.

The Ḥafetz Ḥaim's approach opened the door for my rebbe and teacher, Rabbi Joseph B. Soloveitchik, to give a *shiur* in Gemara and its commentaries to young women at Stern College, because in his time (as in ours) women were studying literature, physics, and philosophy at university. This being the case, he concluded, in our day anyone who does NOT teach his daughter Torah is in effect teaching her foolishness!

The rabbis who still do not permit the teaching of the Oral Law to women apparently maintain that women are qualitatively different from men in their intellectual capacities.

A similar issue in the ritual realm is the exemption of women from the fulfillment of time-bound positive mitzvot that may only be performed at a specific time, as explained in Kiddushin 29a: "Any positive mitzva which is time-bound, men are obligated and women are exempt."

Rabbi David Avudraham, in his classic work on prayer, *Sefer Avudraham*, commenting on the words "who has not made me a woman," maintains that the exemption arises from the fact that the woman is subservient to her husband, and hence might not have the time to perform the time-bound positive mitzvot.[1] His opinion appears to be that this subservience is an integral part of the institution of marriage, and that household and familial duties define the woman's role. Rabbi Samson Raphael Hirsch (in his commentary on Lev. 23:43) suggests that the exemption is a result of the more naturally elevated spiritual status of the woman, who does not require the time-bound positive mitzvot to bring her to an awareness of God. According to both of these views, the halakha perceives the woman as qualitatively different from the man, whether it be in function (as a wife and mother) or in her higher spiritual capacity.

A different understanding is proposed by Rabbi Manoaḥ in his discussion of the requirement to recline as a symbol of existential freedom at the Pesaḥ Seder. His starting point is the halakha (Pesaḥim 108a) according to which a student who is at the Seder table of his Torah teacher does not recline because "the fear of one's teacher is like the fear of Heaven" – a result of the student having chosen to be subservient to his master-teacher. With regard to women, the Gemara rules that

---

1. Rabbi David ben Yosef Avudraham, *Sefer Avudraham*, originally published in fourteenth-century Lisbon. See 1963 edition, Jerusalem, p. 41.

"a woman who is at her husband's table does not need to recline, but if she is an important woman (*isha ḥashuva*) – she should recline" (ibid.).

Rabbi Manoaḥ, in his commentary on Maimonides' *Mishneh Torah,*[2] lists several ways of defining an "important woman." Based on the assumption that reclining is a mode of behavior befitting kings and free men that demonstrates their freedom, he writes that, "A woman is not required to recline since she is subservient to her husband, and the fear of him is upon her and she is not accustomed to reclining; but if she is an important woman – in other words, if she has no husband and she is the matron of the house – then she must recline." According to this understanding, similar to that of the Avudraham, the woman's subservience to her husband is an integral, definitive part of the husband-wife relationship, and therefore only a woman who is not married can be considered an "important woman."

Rabbi Manoaḥ then provides other definitions of an important woman, including one who is important because of her piety or Torah knowledge or the excellence of her handiwork (either before God or by the work of her hands), a God-fearing woman, or even a daughter of the great Torah teachers of the generation – indeed, any woman who embodies the praises attributed to the "Woman of Valor" in Proverbs is considered important.

Rabbi Manoaḥ goes on to explain what I believe to be the essence of his commentary. He states that women are not generally required to recline but the exemption does not stem from the woman's subservient status vis-à-vis her husband, but rather from the assumption that she is occupied with the preparation of the meal. The woman is exempt from reclining in much the same way as she is exempt from other time-bound positive mitzvot, on account of her other obligations to home and family. "However, an important woman who has manservants and maidservants [or other family members] to tend to the meal while she sits in her seat, is required to recline."

It is clear from the above that both a woman's exemption from time-bound positive mitzvot and her exemption from reclining at the

---

2. Laws of Ḥametz and Matza, chapter 7, law 8 (Fraenkel Edition, Commentary of Rabbi Manoaḥ, ad loc).

Seder table are a result of her being occupied with her domestic duties, such that she is not available either to recline or to fulfill those positive mitzvot whose performance is limited to a certain time. Further, the woman's involvement in domestic duties does not indicate subservient marital status. Rather, since the *ketubba* (marriage contract) obligates the man to finance the family, the woman is naturally obligated to take on the household duties in order to prevent resentment and discord in the home (see Ketubbot 58b, "Rav Yehuda in the name of Rav…"). It appears that if there are others – including the woman's husband and children – who share in the domestic chores, and this responsibility does not fall exclusively upon her, she is obligated, according to Rabbi Manoaḥ, both to recline and to fulfill time-bound positive mitzvot. This opinion, therefore, does *not* accept the assumption that there is a qualitative difference between the woman and the man with reference to time-bound mitzvot.

It seems apparent that the opinion of Rabbi Manoaḥ is the correct one. After all, we rule that women are permitted to fulfill positive mitzvot which are time-bound, and according to the *Baalei Tosafot* they may even recite a blessing with the words, "Who has commanded us to do this mitzva" when performing a time-bound mitzva (see Rosh HaShana 33a).[3]

Moreover, the Babylonian Talmud in Ketubbot 58b definitely states – and there are no dissenting opinions – that a woman may legally declare, "I need not be supported [by my husband] and I shall not do," i.e., I shall not take care of the house for my husband and I waive my right to receive sustenance from him. This demonstrates that although the role division between male breadwinner and female housekeeper was a comfortable arrangement for many generations, that setup is not an integral part of the marriage agreement, or the defining characteristic of the relationship between husband and wife. The situation depends to

---

3. This ruling regarding the recitation of a blessing by women performing time-bound commandments is generally followed in Ashkenazic communities but not in Sephardic ones. However, the *right* of a woman to perform time-bound commandments, when it is possible for her to do so, is agreed upon by all (see Maimonides, Laws of Tzitzit 3, 9.)

a great degree on the financial position of the household and/or on the subjective agreement reached by each couple independently as to their roles in the marital relationship.

FEMALE JUDGES

Can a woman serve as a teacher of halakha, an arbiter of halakha (*poseket*), or even as a judge? Let us first examine the question of whether women may serve as judges, a question dealt with at length in the sources. In examining the halakhic sources, several different approaches emerge.

Those Who Prohibit

It appears from the Bible that a woman can sit in judgment: "And Devora, a prophetess, wife of Lapidot, judged Israel at that time. She would sit under the palm tree of Devora, between Ramah and Beit-El in Mount Efraim, and the Children of Israel would ascend to her for judgment" (Judges 4:4–5).

Nevertheless, the Jerusalem Talmud rules in three places: "Behold, we have learned that a woman does not testify, therefore a woman also may not judge" (Yoma 6:1, Shevuot 4:1, and Sanhedrin 3:9).

In accordance with these opinions, the *Baalei Tosafot* in Yevamot 45b rule that, "A woman is not fit to judge, as we have learned that anyone who is fit to judge is also fit to give testimony, and we learn from the Jerusalem Talmud, in [Masekhet] Yoma that since a woman may not testify, she also may not judge." The *Baalei Tosafot* deal with the judicial precedent of Devora by suggesting that "Devora did not actually judge but rather would teach them [the correct way of] judgment." Hence, the *Baalei Tosafot* rule in chapter 1 of Bava Kama 16a: "A woman is unfit to testify and to judge."

Maimonides[4] rules thus: "A woman is not placed on the throne, as it is written, 'You shall make for yourself a king' – a king and not a queen, and likewise to all other positions of authority in Israel only a man should be appointed." It would seem that the position of judge is included in the term "positions of authority," as is evident from another

---

4. Laws of Kings, chapter 1, law 5.

ruling of Maimonides,[5] this one concerning converts: "A king should not be appointed from among the proselytes ... and [this applies] not only to the throne but to all positions of authority in Israel, and it goes without saying that a judge or prince should be only from Israel."

Maimonides derives the prohibition on women reigning as monarchs from Midrash *Sifrei*.[6] But from whence comes the prohibition on women assuming other authoritative positions? None of the commentators seem to know, not even Rabbi Moshe Feinstein.[7] Perhaps Maimonides ruled thus because of the subsequent prohibitions on a butcher, barber, bathhouse keeper, or tanner serving as a judge, not because any of these people are inherently invalid but because they are considered to have degrading professions which might prevent litigants from accepting their decisions.[8] It is possible that in his time litigants would not have accepted the rulings of women judges and this is why he ruled as he did. As we shall see below, some later commentators understood Maimonides differently.

Those Who Permit

Evidence for the existence of women judges can be seen in a midrash that elucidates two difficult words in Ecclesiastes: "I appointed *shidah* (male) and *shidot* (female)." The midrash explains that "this refers to male judges and female judges" (Ecclesiastes Rabba 2:8).

However, the best proof of the permissibility of female judges is from the biblical precedent of Devora (Judges 4:4–5), and no biblical verse may be removed from the simple meaning of the text.

The *Baalei Tosafot* deal with Devora's position as a judge in five places in the Talmud, and question the permissibility of women acting as judges. In one place, as we have seen, they reject the possibility of Devora actually having served as a judge, but in several other places the clear assumption is that she did serve as a judge and hence that women are fit to judge. In *Tosafot* Nidda 50a, commenting on the words "anyone

---

5. Ibid., law 4.
6. Deut. 17:8–11, ad loc.
7. *Iggrot Moshe, Yoreh De'ah*, Part 2, siman 44.
8. *Mishneh Torah*, Laws of Kings, chapter 1, law 6.

who is fit to judge is fit to testify," the question is asked as to how Devora could have judged if women were prohibited from testifying (in civil cases, as per Shevuot 30b). The *Baalei Tosafot* answer that the correlation between testimony and judgment applies only to males but not to females: any male who is fit to judge is also fit to testify, whereas a female who is fit to judge may nevertheless be unfit to testify.

The *Baalei Tosafot* on Bava Kama 15b, commenting on the words "who shall place," introduce another possibility: even if we say that under regular circumstances a woman may not judge, if the parties to the case accept the woman's authority as a judge, then she may render judgment.

There is a similar third source, in the Toṣafot on Gittin 88a, commenting on the words "and not before ignorant women." Here the *Baalei Tosafot* suggest that, "Perhaps she [Devora] did not judge but rather would teach them the laws; and perhaps they accepted her [as a judge over them] because of the *Shekhina*."

The same idea is to be found in a fourth source, the *Tosafot* to Shevuot 29b, commenting on the words "oaths of witnesses": "She [Devora] would teach them the laws but because she was a prophetess they accepted her [as a judge] over them."

In other words, in four places in the Talmud, the *Tosafot* permit a woman to serve as a judge either as a first preference – based on the precedent of Devora – or, at the very least, so long as the parties to the dispute accept her authority.

The *Sefer HaḤinukh* (mitzva 77) also emphasizes that if a judge is accepted by both litigants, she can be female, adding that it is not necessary for each party to independently accept the woman's authority as judge; it is sufficient that the heads of Israel or the elected officials accept her.

Despite the fact that the *Shulḥan Arukh*[9] writes that "a woman is unfit to judge," the *Sefer Halakha Pesuka*[10] unequivocally rules that "if

---

9. *Ḥoshen Mishpat*, siman 7 se'if 4.
10. Commentary on *Ḥoshen Mishpat*, siman 7 se'if 4. See new edition of *Sefer Halakha Pesuka* published by the Ariel Institute under the aegis of Rabbi Sha'ar Yashuv Cohen, chief rabbi of Haifa, and with the imprimatur of former Chief Rabbi of Israel Avrum Shapiro (Jerusalem, 1962).

the litigants accept a woman judge upon themselves, she is kosher [sic] to render judgment for them. And if the heads of the community accept a woman judge, and she is learned and expert in the laws of the Torah, their acceptance extends to the entire community (and a woman may be the judge for all members of the community, even without the personal acceptance of each litigant)."[11]

Netivot Mishpat goes so far as to say that even those who believe that a female judge may not use coercion, "if the judgment would stop one of the litigants from transgressing a Torah law, the female judge may use coercion."[12] After all, every Jew is required to prevent a fellow Jew from transgressing, if it is within his or her power to do so.

Hence, it would seem that in a society in which the secular world values, accepts, and respects female judges, the religious judicial establishment should welcome women as judges, as long as they have the requisite halakhic credentials. This could be especially significant in light of the difficulties women are having in receiving divorces from recalcitrant husbands.

Maimonides Reappraised

According to what we have already seen, Maimonides would seem to rule that a woman is unfit to serve as a judge, since judges are included in the category of "positions of authority in Israel." But this conclusion is not universally accepted among all the commentaries on Maimonides – in fact, not even among the majority of them. For example, according to

---

11. Footnote 98 of *Halakha Pesuka* quotes *Knesset HaGedola* as saying that "whomever the congregation accepts and whose appointment they find satisfactory [even a woman], is able to render decisions which require authority and coercion." This position is also accepted by Rabbi Ḥaim David HaLevy, former chief rabbi of Tel Aviv in his work *Aseh Lekha Rav*, Part 8:78, 79.

12. *Beurim*, siman 3, end of small se'if 4. The author, Rabbi Yaakov Lorberbaum (1770–1832), emphasizes that "even someone who has no connection to a religious court" can prevent transgression by coercion (ad loc.). Moreover, *Netivot Mishpat*, *Ḥiddushim* on *Shulḥan Arukh, Ḥoshen Mishpat*, Laws of Judges, siman 1, se'if 1, argues that judges have the right to coerce in any matter wherein transgressions occur frequently, "even if they are not expert, even if they are converts." And, I would logically add, even if they are women.

the Hida,[13] it would be improper to exclude a woman from judging because judges are not included in the category of "positions of authority." Apparently, his opinion is that it is the judges' knowledge, and not their position, which enables them to judge.

In the *Ein Mishpat*[14] we find a license for a woman to serve as a judge based on a careful analysis of the verse in the Book of Judges which describes Devora's activity:

> According to this it must be that a woman is fit to judge without coercion and without consideration [of this position] as a position of authority. This is the interpretation given to the verse in Judges: "And the Children of Israel would ascend to her for judgment" – in other words, they went up of their own accord, without any coercion, which means that they accepted her as a judge over them.

Rabbi Yitzḥak HaLevi Herzog, the Ashkenazic chief rabbi of Israel (1936–1959), innovatively suggests in his book, *A Constitution for Israel*, that the "position of authority" referred to by Maimonides relates specifically to a position which is handed down from generation to generation and for the duration of the person's life, as in the case of a king, and that a public servant, such as a judge, does not fall into this category. Rabbi Ben-Zion Ḥai Uziel, the Sephardic chief rabbi of Israel (1939–1954), maintains in his work *Mishpatei Uziel*[15] that even Maimonides would permit a woman to serve as a judge or in any other position of authority if she was elected to that position by a majority of the public, i.e., if the situation was one that could be categorized as "accepting upon themselves."

It is therefore clear that according to most commentators and halakhic authorities, a woman may serve as a judge if the majority of the public, the elected representatives of the city, the local council, or the parties to the dispute accept her authority as a judge over them.

---

13. *Birkat Yosef, Ḥoshen Mishpat,* siman 7 subpar. 11.
14. *Ot* 4, part of a collection of responsa on *Ḥoshen Mishpat.*
15. *Ḥoshen Mishpat,* siman 5.

WOMEN AS TORAH INSTRUCTORS AND DECISORS OF HALAKHA

It is interesting to note that the same halakhic authorities who only permit a woman to act as judge when all the parties to the case agree to accept her authority, all rule that a woman may *a priori* render halakhic decisions in all ritual areas. They express no doubts or reservations, nor do they impose any conditions or limitations. It seems to me that the reason for this is that instructors of halakha do not require any special appointment; they simply require sufficient knowledge.

Indeed, the *Shulḥan Arukh* states clearly that "any scholar who has reached the ability to render halakhic decisions and does not do so is preventing [the spread of] Torah and placing stumbling blocks before the multitudes."[16]

The Rema adds, "The rabbinical ordination which is customary in our time is a way of informing the nation that the ordained individual has attained the ability to give halakhic direction, and is giving instruction with the permission of his master who ordained him."[17]

There are precedents for accepting the halakhic teachings and decisions of women, even over the decisions of men. For example, the Tosefta brings an example of a debate regarding the ritual impurity of an oven in which the sages preferred the opinion of Beruria, the daughter of Rabbi Ḥanania ben Teradyon, over the opinion of his son.[18]

Rabbi Shlomo Luria, the Maharshal, relates in his responsa number 29 that his grandmother, Rebbetzin Miriam, regularly sat behind a curtain (for reasons of modesty) and taught halakha to outstanding male students.

The mother of the first Lubavitcher rebbe, Rabbi Shneur Zalman of Liadi, was said to have halakhic knowledge that exceeded that of most men, and she even adjudicated halakhic questions, according to the sixth Lubavitcher rebbe, Rabbi Yosef Yitzḥak Schneersohn.[19]

---

16. *Yoreh De'ah*, 242:14.
17. Ibid.
18. *Tosefta Kelim* 4, 17.
19. *Sefer HaZikhronot*, vol. 2, chapter 93, New York, 1971.

Another explanation for the freedom granted women to render halakhic decisions in ritual areas may be related to the laws of testimony. With regard to the laws of *Ḥoshen Mishpat*, which deal with financial matters, there is a general rule that anyone who is fit to testify is fit to judge. Since a woman is generally considered unfit to testify in financial matters, it is technically difficult to permit her to adjudicate such matters, as a first preference. But with regard to the laws of *Yoreh De'ah* – the laws concerning permitted and forbidden foods – since a woman is accepted as a reliable witness in these areas, she may also teach and even rule in matters of halakha in these areas.

Moreover, we derive the rule that "one witness is sufficiently reliable in matters of prohibition" from our reliance on the woman to count her days of ritual impurity and purification.[20] Therefore, the author of the *Sefer HaḤinukh* writes (mitzva 152): "Someone who is inebriated with wine should not enter the Sanctuary, and likewise one who is inebriated should not instruct ... And the prohibition of coming to the Sanctuary drunk during the Temple period applied to both males and females, and the avoidance of giving halakhic instruction [in such a state] applies to males in every place and in every era, as well as to a wise woman who is worthy of rendering halakhic instruction."

Likewise, we learn from the Hida's *Birkat Yosef*:[21] "Even though a woman is unfit to judge, nevertheless a wise woman may render halakhic decisions," and the practical halakha is brought in the *Pit'ḥei Teshuva*[22] and in the *Sefer Halakha Pesuka*:[23] "A woman may sit with the judges, to teach them the law in the cases brought before them in which she is knowledgeable, and she may teach halakha in matters of permissibility and prohibition."

It would seem that the only opinion that explicitly disagrees with this license for a woman to teach halakha is the author of the *Sha'arei Teshuva*.[24] Nevertheless, as we have seen, the great majority of authorities permit a woman to teach halakha and render halakhic decisions.

---

20. "'And she shall count for her' (Lev. 16:28) – i.e., for herself," Gittin 2b in the Tosfot that begins, "One witness is reliable for matters of prohibition."
21. *Ḥoshen Mishpat,* siman 7 subpar. 12
22. Ibid., subpar. 5.
23. Harry Fischel Institute, siman 7, ot 9.
24. *Oraḥ Ḥaim,* siman 461, subpar. 17.

Rabbi Eliyahu Bakshi-Doron, who was the chief Sephardic rabbi of Israel from 1993–2003, writes in his book *Binyan Av* (1:65): "A woman and a proselyte may serve as instructors of halakha, teachers of Torah, and decisors of halakhic rulings. All positions whose authority is determined by the abilities of those holding them, and where authority derives from one's knowledge and purity, may be filled by a woman or a proselyte."

In conclusion, let us take to heart the words of *Tana Devei Eliyahu*[25] concerning Devora the prophetess, the heroine of this article:

"And Devora, a prophetess, wife of Lapidot, judged Israel at that time." What was so special about Devora that made her [worthy of being] judge of Israel at that time, and a prophetess to them? Was not Pinḥas the son of Elazar alive at the time?! I hereby testify today before the heavens and the earth:

Whether an Israelite or a gentile,

Whether a man or a woman,

Whether a manservant or a maidservant –

Each has the divine spirit rest upon him in accordance with his own acts.

POSTSCRIPT

The discerning reader will note that I have not used the terms "Rabbi" or "Rabbah" in my discussion of a woman's acceptability for rendering halakhic decisions – and, of course, my choice of language was intentional.

I profoundly believe that qualified women may and must be empowered to actively participate in halakhic discourse on the highest of levels; Ohr Torah Stone has proudly given *morat hora'a* certification to two outstanding female students from our Manhigut Program who passed, with distinction, the same examination that the Chief Rabbinate of Israel gives to men seeking ordination (*smikha*). The two women, Idit Bar Tov and Anat Novoselsky, have recently published a booklet of halakhic responsa titled *Ma She'elatech Esther VaTe'as* (5774) which deals with issues of Sabbath and festivals, ritual family purity, and female

---

25. *Eliyahu Rabba*, chapter 9.

religio-legal leadership. The book has received much praise, and – at least to my knowledge – no negative reviews.

However, two of the main functions of a congregational rabbi, especially in smaller communities, are to lead the communal prayers and Torah reading. Indeed, the initial purpose of a synagogue was to establish a proper environment for the expression of these two rituals.

Since communal prayer and Torah reading are responsibilities which the Talmudic sages specifically placed upon the congregation of males, it is not halakhically permissible for women to discharge this obligation and to serve as Torah readers or cantorial representatives of congregations that include men. Hence, I do not believe that a woman can serve as the sole religious leader of a Jewish prayer community at the present time.

Nevertheless, there is a great necessity for women to serve in adjunct clerical positions, especially in the modern synagogue setting, which functions more as a house of Jewish assembly than as a house of communal prayer. I also believe that there are many more halakhically viable opportunities for women to actively participate in congregational prayer than is now considered de rigueur, and I hope to delineate these in a forthcoming article.

Women and the Torah Scroll

Is a woman permitted to touch, kiss, embrace, dance with, and read from a sacred Torah scroll? Conventional wisdom within the more observant sector of the Jewish community would most probably respond in the negative, especially regarding dancing with and reading from the Torah. And certainly a woman who is menstruating – or at least has not become purified by immersing herself in the *mikve* – must not be allowed to come in contact with an object as pure and sacred as a Torah scroll, as the following verses would seem to suggest:

> God spoke to Moses saying, "Speak to the Children of Israel, saying, when a woman conceives and gives birth to a male, she shall be ritually impure [and thereby forbidden from entering the Sanctuary] for a seven day period; just as during the days of her menstrual separation shall she be ritually impure." (Lev. 12:1, 2)

The over-arching conceptual scheme informing the concept of ritual impurity (*tuma*) is death. Impurity results from contact with a dead body or any object which suggests death, such as skin leprosy or menstrual blood, which signifies the loss of potential life. Hence, the common understanding would be that women – who must be presumed to

133

be in a state of ritual impurity – can neither dance with a Torah scroll on Simḥat Torah nor read from a Torah scroll, even in a congregation comprised only of other women. But is this actually the halakha?

The sages of the Talmud cite a *beraita* which teaches:

> Men with incontinent seminal discharges, lepers, and those who had relations with menstruating women [i.e., ritually impure individuals] are all permitted to read from the Torah, the Prophets and the Writings, to teach Mishna, Gemara, laws and legend... Rabbi Yehuda ben Beteira would often say: Words of Torah are not susceptible to ritual impurity, as the prophet (Jer. 23) cries out, "Is it not so that My words are like fire, says the Lord"; and, just as fire is not susceptible to ritual impurity, neither is Torah susceptible to ritual impurity. (Berakhot 22a)

It is important to note that this fundamental halakhic ruling – that the Torah is not susceptible to ritual impurity – is universally accepted by all of the religio-legal decisors. Maimonides, the great philosopher-legalist of the twelfth century, whose legal decisions have been widely respected throughout the generations, writes:[1]

> All of those who are ritually impure, even menstruating women and even gentiles, are permitted to hold a Torah scroll and to read from it, because words of Torah are not susceptible to ritual impurity. But this is only true if their hands are not dirtied or enmeshed with mud; if such is the case, they must first wash their hands and then they may touch [the Torah].

This position has been codified in the authoritative *Shulḥan Arukh* of Rabbi Yosef Karo, of sixteenth-century Safed, which states:

> All the ritually impure may read from the Torah, recite the *Shema* and the *Amida*... This is also permissible for someone who has had a seminal emission. And [all of these ritually impure

---

1. Maimonides, *Mishneh Torah*, Laws of the Torah Scroll 10, 8.

individuals may read from the Torah and participate in prayer] without ritual immersion in a *mikve*...and so has the custom spread throughout the world community of Israel. (*Shulḥan Arukh*, Laws of the Recitation of the *Shema* 88, 1)

A fascinating addendum to the collective halakhic agreement throughout the ages, which we have just documented, is the comment of the Rema (Rabbi Moshe Isserles), the sixteenth-century rabbi of Krakow, Poland, who is considered the most authoritative opinion for Ashkenazic Jewry:

> There are those who wrote that a woman who is actually in her days of menstruating blood is not to enter the synagogue or pray, or mention God's name or touch a Torah scroll (*Haga-hot Maimoniot 4*), and there are those who permit them to do everything [including mentioning God's name and touching a Torah scroll], and this latter view is the main one (Rashi, Laws of *Nidda*). However, he then goes on to cite the custom – not the law – in his community: But the custom in these countries [Poland] is in accordance with the former opinion [that a menstruating woman is not even to enter a synagogue]. (Mappa on *Shulḥan Arukh*, ibid.)

The *Mishna Berura* (Rabbi Yisrael Meir Kagan, the twentieth-century Lithuanian decisor also known as the Ḥafetz Ḥaim), adds the words of the Binyamin Ze'ev, siman 153, that it was the women's custom not to enter the synagogue because of their great respect for the objects of sanctity, but it was not halakhically forbidden for them to do so (ibid.).

I would argue that, to the best of my knowledge, it is certainly *not* the custom of our women – either in the congregations I have known in America or in Israel – to purposefully stay out of the synagogue during the days of their menstruation, so that we are left the with the halakhic permissibility for even menstruating women to grasp, embrace, and even read from a Torah scroll. Moreover, even the Rema himself concludes his halakhic addendum to Rabbi Yosef Karo with the following statement:

> And even in places where women accepted the custom of strin-
> gency [not to even enter a synagogue when menstruating], on
> the Days of Awe and similar times when the multitudes gather
> to come into the synagogue, it is permissible for [menstruat-
> ing] women to enter the synagogue like the rest of the women,
> because it would cause them great sadness to remain outside of
> the synagogue when everyone is gathered inside.

Since it is not our custom that menstruating women do not enter the
synagogue, and since even if such had been the custom, it would not
apply to Simḥat Torah (or even to a regular Sabbath morning in most
Orthodox synagogues) when the women's sections are filled, and when
many, if not most, women kiss the Torah scroll, there ought not be halakhic objection to women dancing with Torah scrolls on Simḥat Torah
behind a suitable divider (*meḥitza*) separating the sexes.

Despite what I have written, however, many legal authorities
may still object to permitting women to dance with Torah scrolls, or to
read from a Torah scroll at a prayer service consisting only of women,
because this has not been synagogue custom from time immemorial; it
is simply not our custom to do so.

I certainly respect the view which stands firmly against any obvious change in religious ritual. Fealty to past tradition strengthens our
present relationship with generations gone by, and protects us against
going down the "slippery slope" to lack of connection. Breaking from
tradition, even in a minor matter, can sometimes lead to a break from
tradition in a greater matter – one which might even involve a halakhic
infraction. Indeed, there is an understandable desire to retain even minor
details of traditional practice to preserve the sense of our eternal Jewish
continuity, to give the observant Jew the legitimate feeling that through
synagogue ritual he is participating in activities which were performed
precisely as he is performing them by his great-grandparents, and which
will be performed precisely as he is performing them by his great-
grandchildren. Hence, all things being equal, I am strongly opposed to
changing any time-honored custom of Israel, such as the second day of
the festival for Diaspora Jewry or eating *kitniyot* (legumes) on Passover
for Ashkenazic Jews.

The exception to this rule, however, is when the talmudic sages themselves tell us to be sensitive to moral demands incurred by changing times and mitigating circumstances. One example of this is the *prozbol* of the Sabbatical year, which enabled loans to remain in force when occupations went from agrarian to industrial, and people stopped lending money when they realized that their debts would be rescinded. Another example is the introduction of leniencies regarding the woman chained to an impossible marital situation, for whom the testimony of one witness, even a gentile, was deemed sufficient to free her from marital bonds (Gittin 2a, 2b).

In a similar fashion, when women desired to participate in Jewish ritual and to feel more actively involved in divine service, our sages responded to their requests. Hence, despite the fact that women had been excluded from "laying their hands" on the festival sacrifices brought to the Temple based on the verse "the sons [and not the daughters] of Israel shall lay their hands," the talmudic sages waived the prohibition because of their policy "to enable the women to achieve spiritual satisfaction (*nachat ruaḥ*) from serving their Creator" (Ḥagiga 16b). Embracing the Torah scroll would certainly help women feel that they too have a legitimate share in our greatest religious treasure.

Additionally, even though women were exempt from performing the positive commandments determined by time, our sages permitted women to perform them if they wished to do so, and many – like Rabbenu Tam – even permitted them to recite the blessing over the commandment they chose to perform (*Tosafot*, Rosh HaShana 33a), despite the serious prohibition against mentioning God's name in vain.

The sixteenth-century sage of Salonica, Rabbi Shmuel De Medina (Maharashdam), writes that the only time it is forbidden to change a custom is when doing so would lead to a sinful transgression – which is certainly not the case were women to carry Torah scrolls (Responsa *Oraḥ Ḥaim*, 35).

Finally, one can legitimately argue that even though women did not traditionally hold or read from a Torah scroll, the lack of a ritual does not constitute an established custom. In order for a custom to assume the force of law, it must be a positive act! Hence, when Rabbi Yosef Karo ruled that women may engage in the ritual slaughter of chickens or cattle if they are expertly trained, and one of the commentaries argued that he had never seen a woman ritually slaughter, the normative opinion insisted: "The fact that we might not have seen it done does not establish a custom against permitting a woman to slaughter" (*Shulḥan Arukh, Yoreh De'ah*, 1, 1, *Siftei Kohen* ad loc.). No custom can be established "in absentia."

Hence, it would seem that on Simḥat Torah and family occasions where all of one's crowd comes to shul, women can certainly come to the synagogue, grasp and kiss the sefer Torah, and when the opportunity permits – behind a proper *meḥitza* or in a separate all-female congregation – even read from the Torah.

In a generation wherein high-level Torah, Talmud, and halakha study for women is burgeoning at major institutions in America and Israel, is it any wonder that some women are also desirous of embracing the Torah and demonstrating their love of Torah by dancing with Torah scrolls on Simḥat Torah? If halakha says it is permissible, why remove from those women their religious satisfaction (*nachat ruaḥ*) on the day marked by Israel's rejoicing in the Torah?

The Blessing "Who Has Not Made Me a Woman"

THE PROBLEM

In almost any forum discussing the status of women in Judaism, one of the difficult questions that is raised – whether by learned women scholars or by women whose familiarity with Jewish texts and level of Torah observance is limited, sometimes even by men – concerns the blessing, "Who has not made me a woman (*shelo asani isha*)," which is recited by every observant man every morning. It is important to note that this issue is not an invention of our modern generation or a product of the feminist revolution. There is evidence dating back many centuries, testifying to the sense of discomfort aroused in many Jews with regard to this blessing. Examples include the following:

1. A siddur (prayer book) dating back to fourteen to fifteenth-century Provence, written in a Jewish-French dialect, in Hebrew letters. The cover is inscribed with the verse, "Our sister, may you become thousands of myriads," indicating that the siddur was meant for a woman's use. The first three morning blessings appear here as follows: "Who has not made me a gentile," "Who has not made me a maid-servant," and "Who has made me a woman (*she'asani isha*)."[1]

---

1. Based on Yosef Tabory, "The Benedictions of Self-Identity and the Changing Status of Women and of Orthodoxy," *Kenishta* 1 (2001), 107–138. My thanks to

2. A siddur written by Avraham Farissol in Italy, fifteenth century, which describes itself as a "complete siddur for the entire year, in accordance with the Italian custom." The dedication reads, "I, Avraham Farissol of Avignon, have written this complete siddur for the respected and honored matron, Lady…" (Mantova, 1490).[2] Here, the morning blessings include, "*For Your having made me a woman and not a man (she'asitani isha ve'lo ish).*"

3. Rabbi Barukh HaLevi Epstein, author of the *Torah Temima*, records the bitter resentment of his aunt, Rabbanit Reina Batya, the first wife of the Netziv, concerning the blessing, "Who has not made me a woman."[3]

> It pained my aunt bitterly, as she mentioned from time to time, that any hollow, ignorant man, however despised and lowly, almost not even understanding the meaning of the words, who would never dream of setting foot over the threshold of her house without respectfully asking her permission, humbly and with great modesty – that same person would nevertheless have no trouble uttering in her presence, clearly and proudly and full of self-importance, the blessing, "Who has not made me a woman"! Moreover… when he uttered this, she was then obligated to answer "Amen." Who could bear (so she would conclude with profound anguish) this stamp of disgrace and eternal shame upon women?

4. Avraham Berliner, a nineteenth-century scholar, addressed the issue of the blessing, "Who has not made me a gentile," and proposed an alternative formulation: "Who has made me an Israelite (*she'asani Yisrael*)." As an aside, he demonstrates sensitivity to the problematic nature of the blessing, "Who has not made me a woman."[4]

Dr. Gili Zivan for bringing this article to my attention, along with other related sources.

2. Cited in Tabory, ibid. The woman's name is not decipherable in the original manuscript.

3. Rabbi Barukh HaLevi Epstein, *Mekor Barukh* (New York, 5714), part IV, p. 1948.

4. Avraham Berliner, *Ketavim Nivharim* (Jerusalem, 5705), p. 21.

We must strongly recommend that all siddurim should feature the formula, "Who has made me an Israelite," as it appears in the siddurim from the Mantova Press (1558), Tinhingen (1560), Prague (1566)...The Vilna Gaon...Rabbi Yaakov Zvi Mecklenberg – all demand quite unequivocally that this formula be accepted. The proposed formula, thanking divine providence for placing my portion among the Children of Israel, who were chosen to fulfill a lofty purpose in the world, is expressed far better by this formula than it is by the original wording in its negative form.

If the proposed formula is accepted throughout the Jewish Diaspora, then two other blessings automatically fall away – "Who has not made me a woman" and "Who has not made me a slave." Thus we are exempted from having to try somehow or other to justify these two blessings. Likewise, there is no room for the latter versions of the blessing: "Who has not made me a gentile woman (*shelo asani goya*)" and "Who has made me in accordance with His will (*she'asani k'retzono*)."

The version of the blessing as adapted for women – "Who has made me in accordance with His will (*she'asani k'retzono*)" – is mentioned for the first time by Rabbi Yaakov ben Rabbi Asher, the Baal HaTurim (*Oraḥ Ḥaim*, siman 46), in the early fourteenth century. Many *poskim* have noted the fact that no such blessing is mentioned in the Talmud, and for this reason many of the later authorities ruled that women should not recite it – or, at least, that they should omit God's name and divinity (*A'donay Eloheinu*) when reciting the blessing.[5] The *Tur* himself ("Women have customarily recited the blessing") implies that the blessing is simply a custom that developed among women, with no source in the texts.[6] However, unlike other blessings which have no talmudic source and which were eventually removed from the siddur (including some which were, at earlier times, included in the morning blessings, such as "Who lifts up those who are lowly"), the blessing, "Who has made me in accordance with His will" remained. The institution of this

---

5. See, for example, *Pri Ḥadash*, siman 46; siddur Ya'avetz.
6. As noted by Rabbi Barukh HaLevi Epstein, ibid., n. 1.

blessing and its persistence throughout the generations may certainly be viewed as a critical reaction to the ancient blessing, "Who has not made me a woman."[7]

THE ORIGINAL SIGNIFICANCE OF THE BLESSING "WHO HAS NOT MADE ME A WOMAN"

Those who have difficulty with the blessing "Who has not made me a woman" generally believe that it reflects the lower status of women as perceived by those who set down its wording. There are, however, other interpretations by major Orthodox thinkers which attempt to explain the blessing in a manner more complimentary to womankind. For example: Rabbi Samson Raphael Hirsch, in his *Commentary on the Siddur*:[8]

> These blessings are not blessings of thanksgiving to God for not having made us gentiles, slaves, or women. [Rather] the blessing goads us to examine the role that God has placed upon us, by making us free Jewish men, so that we should proclaim a ceremonial promise to fulfill the obligations [mitzvot] of our role. Each of these three [Noahide gentiles, slaves, and women] requires [the fulfillment of] more numerous commandments than those imposed upon gentiles, who are not commanded at all. And if women are exempt from many of the commandments which men are obligated to perform, they [the women] know that their role as free Jewish women is not inferior, in terms of God's will and His satisfaction, to that of their male brethren.

Rabbi Eliyahu Munk in *The World of Prayer*:[9]

> The Jewish woman in particular – exempted by divine law from the fulfillment of many positive commandments – is especially

---

7. It should be noted that the earliest appearance of the blessing, "Who has made me in accordance with His will," from the fourteenth century, preceded only slightly the appearance of the alternative formulations mentioned above ("Who has made me a woman" and "Who has made me a woman and not a man").

8. Mossad HaRav Kook, Jerusalem, 1992.

9. Mossad HaRav Kook, Jerusalem, 1974, p. 36.

obligated to view this exemption...as an expression of divine faith in her independent moral importance. Jewish law is therefore based upon the assumption that women generally have greater inner willingness to devote themselves to their task, more enthusiastic faith as to their Jewish role, and the danger of the temptations that they encounter as they fulfill their role is smaller. Therefore, there is no need to apply to them all the many enactments meant to caution men.... The woman also symbolizes the angel who guards the spark of holiness, the embers of purity and morality in their supreme sense. It is in this spirit that the Jewish woman utters every morning the blessing, "Who has made me in accordance with His will" with absolutely positive emotion, with profound thanks, and with genuine joy.

It would be easier to agree with Rabbi Munk if both men and women were to recite the blessing, "Who has made me in accordance with His will." However, as we shall see below, the truth is that his explanation does not reflect the original significance of the blessing, "Who has not made me a woman" – which alone dates back to the Talmudic period – and, therefore, it is difficult to argue that, according to the view of the sages, the blessing "Who has made me in accordance with His will" raises woman to a level higher than that of man.

In fact, the intention of the sages in formulating the blessing, "Who has not made me a woman" – and, accordingly, their attitude towards women – is quite clear, if we look at the context in which it appears (Tosefta, Berakhot chapter 6, halakha 18):

> Rabbi Yehuda said: There are three blessings that a person is obligated to recite daily. "Blessed...who has not made me a gentile;" "Blessed...who has not made me an ignoramus;" and "Blessed... who has not made me a woman." A gentile – as it is written, "All of the nations are as nothing compared to Him, and are counted as nothingness and vanity" (Is. 40:17). An ignoramus – since an ignoramus does not fear sin. A woman – since women are not obligated concerning the commandments.

Hence, the following explanation, offered by the Avudraham, is better suited to the original meaning of the blessing:

> And the third [blessing], "Who has not made me [a woman]" is because she is not commanded with regard to time-bound positive commandments…. A man is like a laborer who enters his friend's field and plants there with his permission, while a woman is like one who enters without permission. Further-more, she is fearful of her husband, and is [therefore] unable to fulfill even those commandments that she is obligated to perform.[10]

There are some great Torah scholars who regard the blessing as a state-ment of a fundamental, metaphysical inferiority:

Rabbi Yehoshua ibn Shueib:

> Therefore we recite daily the blessings, "Who did not make me a gentile," and "Who did not make me a slave," and "Who did not make me a woman"…because the souls of Jews are holier than those of the [other] nations, and of the lowlier Canaanite slaves, and also of women – [for] even if they have a share in the commandments and are of Jewish seed, their souls are not like the souls of males.[11]

---

10. Rabbi David ben Yosef Avudraham, *Sefer Avudraham*, originally published in fourteenth-century Lisbon. See 1963 edition, Jerusalem, p. 41. And as he explains elsewhere (ibid., p. 25): "The reason why women are exempt from time-bound positive commandments is because a woman is subjugated to her husband, to perform his needs. If she were obligated concerning commandments that can only be performed at a certain time, it could happen that while performing a commandment her husband would order her to perform his own command. If she would [then continue to] perform the command of the Creator and set aside his [the husband's] orders, then woe to her because of her husband. If she would carry out his orders and set aside God's commandment, then woe to her because of her Creator. Therefore, God has exempted her from His commandments, so that she may be at peace with her husband."

11. Rabbi Yehoshua ibn Shueib, *Derashot al HaTorah* (Cracow, 5303), p. 48. Rabbi Shueib lived at the end of the fourteenth century.

Rabbi Avraham Yitzḥak HaKohen Kook:

> Souls are destined for their lives to be either active or passive –
> [either] inscribing life and existence in all of their richness, or
> being inscribed by them. This is the essential difference between
> the soul of a man – the active agent, engraver, conqueror, sub-
> duer – and the soul of the woman – inscribed, acted upon,
> engraved, conquered, subdued by the man.
>
> How many superior and fine attributes, what great joy and
> expansiveness there is in this good portion, of the soul being the
> soul of a man – active, creative, innovative... in accordance with
> his inner essence in the disposition of his holiness, which is higher
> than the soul of a woman, which is considered like "matter," as
> opposed to the soul of the man who is considered like "form."
> Great acknowledgment is due to the Creator of the soul, on the
> part of each and every man – "Who has not made me a woman."[12]

On the basis of these views, even so lofty a blessing as, "Who has made
me in accordance with His will" – which, on the face of it, certainly testifies to a sense of purpose on the highest religious level – is interpreted
differently by the voice of normative halakha. Rabbi Yaakov ben Rabbi
Asher, who is the first to mention the blessing, writes, "Women have
customarily recited the blessing, 'Who has made me in accordance with
His will,' and it is possible that this is customary in the manner of a person accepting a difficult decree."[13]

In fact, at one stage, an even more problematic version of the blessing was available to women. Rabbi Yosef ben Moshe (fifteenth century)
cites, in the name of his teacher, the author of the *Terumat HaDeshen*:

> He would follow this order [of blessings] with the congregation:
> "Who has given understanding to the rooster," "gentile," "slave,"
> and "woman." And he said that a woman says, instead of "Who
> has not made me a woman" – "Who has not made me a beast

---

12. Rabbi Avraham Yitzḥak HaKohen Kook, *Olat Re'iya* (Jerusalem, 5699), p. 71.
13. Rabbi Yaakov ben Asher, *Tur, Oraḥ Ḥaim*, siman 46:35.

(*shelo asa'ani behema*)." But I have heard from a woman [that] she says, instead of "Who has not made me a woman" – "Who has made me in accordance with His will." And it would appear to me that the *Gaon* [the *Terumat HaDeshen*], of blessed memory, did not acknowledge this since the *Gaon's* holy mother, from the Ostreich region – may God avenge their blood – would say, "Who has not made me a beast."[14]

Notwithstanding all of the above, and without any question of a doubt, it is always possible to imbue old forms with new meaning, as we see in the various interpretations and explanations given for the commandments over the course of many generations of Jewish philosophers.[15] There were certainly some among the early medieval commentators and halakhic authorities who viewed the exemption from time-bound commandments granted to women not as evidence of any fundamental, personal difference, but rather as nothing more than a statement of sociological fact.[16]

In our generation, women have far more free time than they did in earlier times and enjoy the advantage of many advanced frameworks for serious study of Jewish texts. A quiet revolution is being brought about by women who are committed to Torah study on an extremely high level. Many of these women also experience a sense of profound attachment to the fulfillment of the commandments, including time-bound positive commandments. Hence, it is not difficult to understand the sensitivity and even opposition that many women feel towards the blessing recited by men – "Who has not made me a woman."

---

14. Rabbi Yosef ben Moshe, *Lekket Yashar*, part 1, *Oraḥ Ḥaim*, p. 7.
15. See in this regard Yitzḥak Heineman, *Ta'amei HaMitzvot BeSifrut Yisrael*.
16. See, for example, Rabbi Manoaḥ on Maimonides, cited in the *Kesef Mishneh*, Laws of Ḥametz and Matza, chapter 7, law 8. He explains that the definition of an "important woman," obligated to lean at the Pesaḥ Seder, is one who has man-slaves and maid-slaves, such that she is not required to busy herself with serving the meal and other household matters. His assumption seems to be that if a woman is free, time-wise, to perform positive time-bound commandments, she would certainly be allowed to do so. According to Ashkenazic authorities, she should even recite the appropriate blessing (*birkat hamitzva*) before performing positive time-bound commandments.

"WHO HAS NOT MADE ME A GENTILE" VS.
"WHO HAS MADE ME AN ISRAELITE"

The question of whether the customary blessing "Who has not made me a gentile" could be replaced by a positive reformulation – "Who has made me an Israelite" – is of critical importance to our discussion, since if it were possible to adopt the latter version, then there would similarly be no need to recite either "Who has not made me a woman" or "Who has not made me a slave." According to Berliner (op. cit.), a man would simply recite the blessing, "Who has made me an Israelite" (*she'asani Yisrael*), while a woman would recite a female version of the same (*she'asani Yisraelit*), and that would suffice to acknowledge the existential identity of each.

Is there any basis for accepting the formula "Who has made me an Israelite" instead of "Who has not made me a gentile"? In the following two instances, the Tosefta and the Jerusalem Talmud record the formula, "Who has not made me a gentile":

> Rabbi Yehuda said: There are three blessings that a person must recite every day. [The first is] "Who has not made me a gentile." (Tosefta, Berakhot chapter 6, law 23)[17]

> Rabbi Yehuda said: There are three blessings that a person must recite every day. [The first is] "Blessed … who has not made me a gentile." (Y. Berakhot chapter 9, law 1)[18]

However, in the Babylonian Talmud (Vilna edition) the formula is, "Who has made me an Israelite":

---

17. It is interesting to note the formulations of the blessings from the Cairo Geniza, cited in the *Tosefta KePeshuta*, Berakhot p. 120: "Blessed are You … who has created me a human and not a beast, a man and not a woman, a Jew and not a gentile, circumcised and not uncircumcised, free and not a slave." Rabbi Lieberman notes (ad loc. nn. 70, 71) that this is a much later version, and should not be relied upon as an authoritative source.
18. It is almost certain that this formula was not amended in any way – certainly not under censorship orders.

Rabbi Meir used to say, "A person must recite three blessings every day and they are: 'Who has made me an Israelite,' 'Who did not make me a woman,' and 'Who did not make me an ignoramus.'" (Menaḥot 43b)

But clearly, as R.N.N. Rabinowitz, the author of the *Dikdukei Sofrim* notes, the correct version is "Who has not made me a gentile," since this is how the blessing appears in all of the manuscripts and in all of the early printings. The version "Who has made me an Israelite" appears for the first time in the Basel edition of the Babylonian Talmud, apparently owing to censorship. He writes, "If you find the version 'Who has made me an Israelite' as in the Rosh, and at the beginning of the *Sefer HaTanya*,[19] then it was changed owing to the censorship that was instituted in the year 5313."[20] Indeed, in the earliest edition of the Babylonian Talmud – the Venice edition of 5201 – the version of the blessing that appears is "Who has not made me a gentile."

The *Geonim* – the *Halakhot Gedolot*,[21] Rabbi Netronai Gaon,[22] and Rabbi Amram Gaon[23] – all record the formula "Who has not made me a gentile." Rabbi Ḥai Gaon[24] notes and cites the version of the Jerusalem Talmud – "Who has not made me a gentile." According to Rabbi Saadia Gaon,[25] the wording is *shelo samatani goy* ("for Your not having made me a gentile").

The great majority of the *Rishonim* (early medieval authorities) cite the version "Who has not made me a gentile." The Rif, at the end of Tractate Berakhot (44b in *Dappei HaRif*) cites the Gemara in Tractate Menaḥot 43b, maintaining the version "Who has not made me a gentile." Maimonides (Laws of Prayer, chapter 7, law 6) writes: "A person

---

19. Also referred to farther on as *Tanya Rabbati*.
20. Refoel Nosson Nota Rabinowitz, *Dikdukei Sofrim*, Munich, 5646, Part 15, p. 108.
21. Rabbi Shimon Kayara, end of "Laws of Blessings."
22. *Responsa of Rabbi Netronai Gaon*, Ofek Institute Publications, Jerusalem, 1994, p. 108.
23. *Seder Rav Amram Gaon* (Warsaw, 5625), p. 1.
24. *Teshuvot HaGeonim*, Sha'arei Teshuva, siman 327, attributed to Rabbi Ḥai Gaon.
25. *Siddur of Rabbi Saadia Gaon*, Mekitzei Nirdamim, Jerusalem, 5739, p. 89.

recites daily…'Who has not made me a gentile.'"[26] Rabbi Avraham, son of Maimonides,[27] claims that, according to his father, the blessing is to be recited whether a person actually sees a gentile or not, and likewise, with regard to the blessings concerning a slave and a woman – unlike the other morning blessings which are only to be recited when one becomes obligated by circumstances.[28]

The same standard version of the blessing is to be found in the siddurim of Rashi[29] and of Rabbi Shlomo of Worms,[30] in the Ritba,[31] *Ohel Mo'ed*,[32] Avudraham,[33] Rabbi Yeruḥam,[34] the *Tur*,[35] the Meiri,[36] and the Eshkol.[37] The Vitry Maḥzor[38] uses the wording, *shelo asani nokhri.* The Aguda[39] offers *shelo asani kuti.*

---

26. Likewise, in *Hagahot Maimoniot* (ad loc., ot 6), and also in the *Leḥem Mishneh*. The *Kesef Mishneh* (ad loc.) writes: "The Rif writes, at the end of Berakhot, citing the chapter on *tekhelet* in Menaḥot 43b: 'A person must recite three blessings every day: 'Who has not made me a gentile…'" This citation by the *Kesef Mishneh* demands some explanation, since it deviates from his usual practice of citing the source for Maimonides' ruling straight from the Gemara, if it is to be found there, and indeed, in this case, the source of the law is from Menaḥot. Perhaps we might suggest that the *Kesef Mishneh* knew of different versions in the Gemara in Menaḥot, and that it was for this reason that he preferred to cite the Rif, whose version was clear.

27. *Responsa of Rabbi Avraham son of the Rambam*, siman 83; cf. *Yad Peshuta* (ad loc.) concerning Maimonides.

28. Maimonides, Laws of Prayer, chapter 7, law 7.

29. Beginning of the siddur, Berlin, 1912.

30. *Shibbolei HaLekket*, siman 1, citing the responsum of Rabbi Netronai Gaon (mentioned above).

31. *Ḥiddushim al Masekhet Berakhot*, siman 72.

32. *Derekh Sheni*, netiv 8.

33. *Sefer Avudraham*, 1963 edition, Jerusalem, p. 41, citing the responsum of the Rema, ruling that a proselyte does not recite the blessing, "Who has not made me a gentile"; see below.

34. Netiv 3, part 1. Interestingly, in his version, the blessing "Who has not made me a slave" precedes "Who has not made me a gentile."

35. Siman 46 par. 4, in the *Tur HaShalem*. The version of the *Tur* cited by the Vilna Gaon (as cited below, n. 36) is, "Who has made me an Israelite"; likewise, Maharsha (Rabbi Shmuel Eliezer Edeles) in the *Biur HaTanya Rabbati*.

36. *Beit HaBeḥira*, Berakhot, siman 72.

37. Albeck edition, p. 10, and in the edition with the *Naḥal Eshkol*, p. 6.

38. Nierenberg Press, 5683, p. 57.

39. Berakhot, siman 72.

Among the *Rishonim*, only the Rosh[40] and the *Tanya Rabbati*[41] feature the version, "Who has made me an Israelite." As noted above, the *Dikdukei Sofrim* concludes that this is not the authoritative version.[42]

Among the *Aḥaronim* (later authorities), too, the accepted version is "Who has not made me a gentile." The *Beit Yosef* writes:[43]

> And we understand from (Rashi's) words that these blessings concern the obligation of the commandments. Since a gentile is not obligated with regard to the commandments at all...thus, we first bless, "Who has not made me a gentile"...and a proselyte does not recite "Who has not made me a gentile," insofar as his conception and birth were not conducted in holiness.[44]

Likewise, we find in the *Shulḥan Arukh*:[45] "One must recite every day the blessing, 'Who has not made me a gentile.'" The same version appears

---

40. Rosh, Berakhot 89, siman 24 (Vilna), and likewise in the *Kitzur Piskei HaRosh* (ad loc.).

41. Warsaw 5639, p. 9. See *Bi'urei Maharsha* (ad loc.).

42. The *Divrei Hamudot* (on the Rosh, ad loc.) likewise writes: "The essence of the version, 'Who has not made me a gentile' is like the two other blessings which are likewise formulated in the negative; furthermore, if one had recited the blessing, 'Who has made me an Israelite,' then he could not afterwards recite 'Who has not made me a slave.' Where we find written 'Who has made me an Israelite,' it would appear to have been introduced by printers who edited the books, this seems clear to me, since the old editions contain the formula, 'Who has not made me a gentile.'"
    Likewise, Rabbi Gedalia Felder, in his work *Peri Yeshurun* on the *Tanya Rabbati*, p. 86, asserts that the authentic version noted in the *Tanya Rabbati* is, "Who has not made me a gentile."
    According to the Vilna Gaon in his gloss on the *Shulḥan Arukh*, siman 46:8, the version that should properly be attributed to the Rosh and to the *Tur* is, "Who has made me an Israelite." Apparently, we may conclude from his words that to his view, this is the proper version that should be used. We shall discuss his view below.

43. *Oraḥ Ḥaim*, siman 46:4 in the *Tur HaShalem* (Makhon Yerushalayim).

44. The source of this law is the Avudraham. However, the *Taz* (*Oraḥ Ḥaim*, 46:4, note 5) comments, "Once he converts, he is a new person and, ipso facto, there is (at the time of conversion) a new making, as if the Almighty had created him now a new being." And so a proselyte does make the blessing "Who has not made me a gentile."

45. *Oraḥ Ḥaim*, siman 46:4. The same is to be found in the *Shulḥan Arukh HaShalem*, Makhon Yerushalayim edition. The *Hagahot VeHe'arot* (ad loc., ot 33) asserts that

in the *Shita Mekubetzet*,[46] Rabbi Yaakov Castro (Maharikash),[47] *Bah*,[48] *Pri Hadash*,[49] *Magen Avraham*,[50] *Taz*,[51] *Arukh HaShulhan*,[52] and the siddur of the Ari.

Concerning these words in the *Shulhan Arukh*, the Rema[53] adds, "Even a proselyte may recite this blessing, but he should not say 'Who has not made me a gentile' since he was originally a gentile.'" This strongly suggests that the version of the blessing in the *Shulhan Arukh* to which the Rema is referring is *not* the same version that appears in our printed editions, for otherwise his comment makes no sense: first he says that even a proselyte may recite "this blessing," but then he adds that he should *not* say, "Who has not made me a gentile"! Hence, it would seem that the version that the Rema refers to is, "Who has made me an Israelite,"[54] and it is in reference to this formula that he rules that a proselyte may recite the blessing, but should not say, "Who has not made me a gentile."[55]

---

this is the version found in the first edition of the *Shulhan Arukh*, but the Venice edition of 5327 features "Who has made me an Israelite." Likewise, in the Cracow edition of 5338, where the gloss of the Rema appeared for the first time, the wording is "Who has made me an Israelite."

46. Berakhot, siman 72.

47. *Erekh Lehem*, siman 46:4.

48. Siman 46:7, in the *Tur HaShalem*. See also below.

49. Siman 46:4.

50. Siman 46:9, "And one must say, '*shelo asani akum (goy)*.'"

51. Siman 46:4. The *Taz* gives a different explanation from the *Bah* as to why three different blessings are necessary rather than including them all under a single formula. He writes: "For they wished thereby to teach that a person should not make the mistake of evaluating some deficiency in the creation of man insofar as (God) has created gentiles, as well as in the creation of woman. For, in truth, it is necessary that gentiles, too, should be created, for proselytes will emerge from them."

52. Siman 46:10.

53. Gloss on the *Shulhan Arukh*, siman 46:4.

54. In the Cracow edition of the *Shulhan Arukh* (5338), which was the first edition to include the Rema's gloss, the blessing indeed appears as "Who has made me an Israelite." The *Magen Avraham* asserts that what the Rema meant to say is that a proselyte may say, "Who has made me a proselyte," but the *Bah* understands the Rema as we have explained above, as does the Hida in *Birkei Yosef* (Vienna, 1860).

55. The *Knesset HaGedola*, commenting on siman 46, writes: "A proselyte who was converted recites the blessing, 'Who has not made me a gentile'" – contrary to the ruling of the Rema.

The *Levush*[56] cites both versions of the blessing. The *Sefer Me'irat Enayim*[57] likewise notes the existence of both versions, and asserts that it is customary to recite "Who has not made me a gentile," but adds that they are essentially the same. The *Zekher Yehosef*[58] records both versions and maintains that "Who has made me an Israelite" (*she'asani Yisrael*) is the more accurate one.

The Vilna Gaon[59] writes, concerning the version in the *Shulḥan Arukh* "Who has not made me a gentile":

> So it appears in the Rif and Maimonides, as well as in the Tosefta and the Yerushalmi, but the version in our books is "Who has made me an Israelite," and thus it appears in the Rosh and the *Tur*.

It would seem from his words that he accepts the version, "Who has made me an Israelite" and this is the conclusion drawn by Rabbi Naftali Hertz HaLevi.[60] However, in his siddur,[61] the Vilna Gaon retains the version, "Who has not made me a gentile."

Rabbi Tzvi Yehuda Kook, in his gloss of his father's siddur, *Olat Re'iya* (end of part 2, note 11), cites most of the sources that we have mentioned, and concludes that the proper formula is "Who has not made me a gentile," noting that this arises also from his father's commentary throughout the body of his work.

Rabbi Shlomo Kluger[62] writes that the proper formula is "Who has not made me a gentile" and that anyone who changes it is liable to give an accounting. The *Peri Yeshurun*[63] similarly concludes that the majority opinion supports this version, and that any other version represents a change in the essence of the blessing.

---

56. *Levush HaTekhelet,* siman 46.
57. *Sefer Me'irat Enayim Gloss on the Shulḥan Arukh,* Makhon Yerushalayim edition, siman 46:4.
58. *Oraḥ Ḥaim,* siman 13.
59. *Bi'ur HaGra,* siman 46:8.
60. *Siddur HaGra BeNiglah U'VeNistar,* 5732, p. 2, *Likkutei HaGra,* ot 4.
61. Ibid., p. 10.
62. *HaElef Lekha Shlomo Responsa, Oraḥ Ḥaim,* siman 34. Rabbi Kluger addresses the question of a person changing the formula of the blessing to *shelo asani akum.*
63. p. 87.

a person who recites "Who has made me an Israelite" must go back and repeat the blessing with the proper formulation.

According to the other opinions concerning Maimonides' explanation, as well as according to the Ritba, it is not proper to change the existing formula; a person who does so acts wrongly, because he is changing the intentional wording of the sages from a negative formulation to a positive one, and is then also led to omit the two following blessings, thereby disregarding the intent of our sages in praise of obligatory commandments. In light of this, we must conclude that it is impossible to resolve the problem of the blessing, "Who has not made me a woman" by substituting the formula "Who has made me an Israelite" instead of the original blessing, "Who has not made me a gentile."

A PROPOSED SOLUTION

Although our sages warn against changing a set wording, the Gemara records instances of great scholars who did change a formula that had been instituted by Moshe himself – the phrase, "the great, powerful, and awesome God" (Deut. 10:17) – because they could not bring themselves to utter praise of God in terms that contradicted their own traumatic experiences.

> Rabbi Yehoshua ben Levi said: Why was [our judicial synod] referred to as the "Men of the Great Assembly"? Because they restored the [divine] crown to its pristine glory. Moses had originally declared "the great, powerful, and awesome God" (Deut. 10:17). Jeremiah came and declared, "The gentiles are reveling in His Temple; where is His awesomeness?" And he deleted [the word] "awesome" [from God's praises]. Daniel came and cried out, "The gentiles are subjugating His children; where is His power?" And he deleted [the word] "powerful."
>
> [The Men of the Great Assembly, who formulated our prayers] came and restored [God's praises] saying, "The very opposite is the truth! Herein lies the power behind God's power: that He overcomes His inclination [to cut down evil before it wreaks its damage] and shows patience to the wicked. And herein lies His awesomeness: were it not for the

awesomeness of the Holy One, Blessed Be He, how could
one lone nation withstand and survive the [powerful] nations
roundabout?"

But how, then, could [those prophets] have acted thus and
uprooted a Mosaic decree? Rabbi Elazar said: Since they knew
that God is truthful, they would not lie to Him.[73]

There are many men today who do not feel comfortable saying something that they do not believe and thanking God for not making them
women, "a lesser creation." Likewise, there are many women who cannot bring themselves to thank God for their identity in a way in which
they are being put down as inferior to men.

For the reasons set forth above, we cannot solve the problem
by substituting the blessing, "Who has made me an Israelite" for some
of the existing blessings. However, there is another solution. Everyone
would agree that a blessing in which we thank God for creating us in
accordance with His will is a very exalted blessing, as long as it does not
stand in contrast to a blessing which expresses greater appreciation for
the masculine gender.

Hence my suggestion: I would combine the blessings of "Who
has not made me a woman" with the blessing "Who has made me in
accordance with His will." The man would recite "Who has not made
me a woman, and has made me in accordance with His will (*shelo asani
isha ve'asani k'retzono*)," while a woman would recite "Who has made
me in accordance with His will, and has not made me a man (*she'asani
k'retzono velo asani ish*)."

This would still leave us with the three separate blessings, and the
original intention of the sages would be preserved. Since the addition
in each case accords with the view of the sages, it would not be classified as a "change in the formula of the blessing," according to most of
the halakhic authorities cited above. The proposed versions preserve
the formula as created by the sages, while at the same time allowing a
man the opportunity of thanking God for what he is, and allowing a
woman to thank God for what she is, each in accordance with his or her

---

73. Yoma 69b.

role and abilities, without either suffering any sense of discrimination. This would also realize the directive of the *Baḥ* (cited above), "[not] to shorten but rather to elaborate at length in thanksgiving and to recite a separate blessing for each and every kindness."

Nevertheless, I would not permit even so minor a change without the approval and approbation of several leading halakhic authorities. While an individual might make a private emendation to his or her prayer, any official change to the prayer book or public prayer – even as minor as the one I am suggesting – would require the endorsement of a major Orthodox rabbinical body.

Hafka'at Kiddushin:
Towards Solving the *Aguna* Problem in Our Time

The predicament of *agunot*, Jewish women whose husbands refuse them a halakhic divorce writ, or *get*, has been deeply exacerbated in our times by the increased mobility that allows errant husbands to escape easily, and by the decreased authority of the rabbinic courts that lack the power to enforce their rulings. The situation of these chained women calls out for a solution. I have written a book on this issue, *Yad La'isha* (Maggid Books, 2008, Jerusalem), that tackles the many halakhic difficulties involved and suggests a way out. Due to the pressing nature of this issue in our times, I feel that it is important to bring it up for discussion and debate whenever feasible. I would like to briefly describe my proposal here, and I refer interested readers to my full-length volume on the topic.

THE *AGUNA* PROBLEM TODAY

The very fact that a woman seeking divorce must receive a *get* from her husband places her at a disadvantage. Cases arise, we well know, in which husbands refuse to grant their wives *gittin*, and women remain *agunot* (chained to their marriages) for years. This problem became particularly acute following the period of the Emancipation, when civil marriage and civil divorce became widely available to Jews. In Western countries, even if a man marries a woman in a religious ceremony and in accordance with Jewish law, he may divorce her in a civil court and delay granting a *get* in order to "punish" or extort money from her, and rabbinical courts are largely helpless to do anything about it.

Even in Israel, where rabbinical courts have legal authority in areas of matrimonial law, the judges are not always able to deal effectively with a husband who absolutely refuses to grant his wife a divorce. It is true that the situation has been greatly alleviated of late, since the secular courts now impose sanctions on recalcitrant husbands who refuse to give their wives *gittin* after being ordered to do so by a religious court. These include removal of the husband's professional and driver's licenses and even incarceration. Still, there are some husbands who prefer lengthy jail sentences to granting their wives a divorce and, in that event, women have no recourse. Moreover, there are judges who are loathe to demand that the husband give a divorce – even though Jewish law allows them to – lest the divorce be considered, even by a minority opinion, an enforced *get*, which is biblically invalid.

It would appear, however, that a halakhic solution based on talmudic texts is available to us. It merely awaits our initiative to make full use of the latent possibilities. Surely, the Torah promises us "righteous laws," and if a legal solution exists, it is our responsibility to find the judge prepared to put it into practice within the framework of an eternal halakha that displays compassion to the *aguna*. The solution I am suggesting is that of *hafka'at kiddushin*, the cancellation of a marriage by a rabbinical court which would rule that the husband is taking unfair advantage of Jewish law, either by forcing his wife to remain married to him as a captive held against her will, or by extorting unfair demands in exchange for the *get*.

MARRIAGE AS AN INSTITUTION

In order to understand how a Jewish marriage can be dissolved when necessary, it is important to understand what Jewish marriage is. There are two fundamental ways to define the legal underpinnings of the institution of marriage:

1. Marriage is a contractual arrangement created by the two partners to the marriage. Only the two parties who created the marriage contract can terminate it.

2. Marriage may well be a contractual arrangement between the two parties, but since it creates a new legal entity with public ramifications, the formation of this "couple" status requires the formal ratification or validation of the state in which those two parties live, or of the local judicial authorities. Since the marriage is only effectuated, or rendered legal, by an extrinsic authority, it can only be terminated by the decision of some similar authority. This second option is the situation in most of the Western world.

Jewish tradition is generally believed to have adopted the first path: "If a man takes a woman" (Deut. 24:1) – the husband "takes" his partner as his wife by way of betrothal and marriage, as long as she is in agreement. Therefore, "he shall write her a bill of divorce, and give it in her hand"; in order to break the marital bond, the husband must give his wife a *get*, which she agrees to accept.

BETROTHAL: A RELATIONSHIP OF MUTUALITY

At the time of betrothal and marriage, both the bride and the groom perform mutual transactions and they assume mutual obligations. *Ḥatam Sofer* (Rabbi Moshe Sofer, *Ḥiddushei HaḤatam Sofer*, Bava Batra 47b) describes the transaction that is performed as *kinyan ḥalifin*, a transaction in which each of the two parties involved gives something and receives something else in return.

In the case of betrothal, the *Ḥatam Sofer* maintains that there is no buyer or seller, but rather *ḥalifin* (an exchange). The groom "sells" his virility and ability to provide financial support, giving over his person to his betrothed by assuming specified obligations, namely, sustenance, clothing, and cohabitation. In return, the bride "sells" herself, giving over her person by assuming the obligation of cohabitation by Torah law, and handing over her handiwork by rabbinic law. This is *ḥalifin*,[1] a mutual exchange.

---

1. Rabbi Moshe Sofer, *Ḥiddushei HaḤatam Sofer* to Bava Batra 47b. But see *Seridei Aish al HaShas*, no. 11, who disagrees with *Ḥatam Sofer*, arguing that betrothal cannot be

This mutuality notwithstanding, the active partner in the acts of betrothal and marriage, as well as in the act of divorce, is the husband. In betrothal, the rabbis specify that "*he* must give [the betrothal gift] and *he* must recite [the betrothal formula]" (see Kiddushin 5b); in marriage, it is the groom who brings the bride into *huppa*, or *his* house (*Shulḥan Arukh, Even HaEzer* 61:1); and in divorce, it is the husband who writes his wife a bill of divorce (the *get*), and places it in her hand. The husband's active role in these areas might stem from the fact that it is he who is regarded as the active partner in the sexual act, which is truly the exclusive and therefore defining aspect of marriage, or else from the fact that it is he alone who is obligated to have children.[2]

Nevertheless, Jewish law attempted, as much as possible, to reach a greater degree of mutuality between husband and wife even with regard to these ritual ceremonies. Thus, betrothal requires the woman's approval: "with her consent, yes [the betrothal is valid]; without her consent, no" (Kiddushin 2b).

Furthermore, Ḥazal enacted that the husband must write his wife a *ketubba* at the time of marriage. That document, which obligates the husband to pay his wife a considerable sum of money should he choose to divorce her, was instituted in order to prevent rash and hasty divorces (Ketubbot 10a).[3] In addition, although according to Torah law a woman

---

likened to *kinyan ḥalifin*: "The very fact that one can acquire a wife with a *peruta* proves that the [betrothal] money merely symbolizes the acquisition... And for this reason a wife cannot be acquired by way of *ḥalifin*, for a woman is not an object that can be bartered for another. Betrothal is a matter of prohibition and consecration, and the money symbolizes the acquisition. But *ḥalifin* is an act of trade, exchanging one thing for another. This would be a disgrace for a woman, as mentioned by Rashi."

I would suggest that the *Ḥatam Sofer* also understands that we are only dealing with an analogy to an acquisition, but not to an acquisition itself. This is clear from the *Baalei Tosafot* who make the point that a husband can never give his wife to another man, the kind of transfer he can always make with an object of acquisition. (Kiddushin 2b, s.v. she is prohibited). The *Ḥatam Sofer* only involves *ḥalifin* to stress the mutuality of the relationship.

2. Yevamot 65b, following the anonymous first *Tanna* of the Mishna: "A man is obligated to have children, but a woman is not," against Rabbi Yoḥanan ben Beroka; *Shulḥan Arukh, Even HaEzer* 1:13.

3. This is derived from the verse (Deut. 24:1), "And he shall write her a bill of divorce, and give it in her hand" (Rashbam, Bava Batra 48a, s.v. *vekhen ata omer*); or else from

may be divorced against her will, a millennium ago Rabbenu Gershom, "Light of the Exile," enacted that a woman can only be divorced if she accepts her *get* voluntarily, just as the Torah requires that the husband grant the divorce of his own free will (cited in Rema's strictures to *Even HaEzer* 119:6).[4]

THE PROBLEM OF THE *AGUNA*

The halakhic principle that the husband cannot be forced to divorce his wife against his will (Yevamot 113b, Gittin 49b) opens the door to the *aguna* problem should a woman seek a divorce and her husband refuse to grant her a *get*.[5] This problem is especially exacerbated when recalcitrant husbands acquire civil divorces – which enable them to remarry with state sanction – and then "hold up" their wives for a great deal of money in exchange for the religious divorce.

There are two aspects to this *aguna* problem: first, there is the tragic predicament and ordeal of the *aguna* herself (and, indeed, the entire community); second, there is a challenge to halakha as a reflection of "righteous laws." Leaving an *aguna* inextricably tied to a husband with whom she cannot live contradicts the Torah's imperative, "And you shall do that which is right and good" (Deut. 6:18). So, too, it stands in conflict with the obligation to walk in the ways of God (see Sota 14a; Maimonides, *Sefer HaMitzvot*, Positive Commandment 8), who is "merciful and gracious" (Ex. 34:6); moreover, the halakha itself declares that "its ways are ways of pleasantness" (Sukka 32b; Yevamot 87b).

---

the beginning of that very verse, "that she find no favor in his eyes" (Maimonides, *Hilkhot Gerushin* 1:2).

4. Following Rabbenu Gershom's enactment requiring the woman's free-will acceptance of her *get*, a man cannot divorce his wife against her will. But should a man seek a divorce and his wife refuse to accept her *get*, he has the option of obtaining a *heter me'ah rabbanim*, an allowance from a hundred rabbis permitting him to take a second wife, which is biblically valid.

5. See Nedarim 90a: "Originally [the sages] said: Three women are to be divorced [even against their husbands' will] and are to receive their *ketubba*... [One who says] "Heaven is between you and me" [Rashi: the husband is impotent]...The sages then revised [their views] and said that a woman must not be [so easily given the opportunity] to look at another man and destroy her relationship with her husband." See also Yevamot 65a, and *Tosafot, s.v. shebeno levena hi ne'emenet; Shulḥan Arukh, Even HaEzer* 154:7.

Clearly, it must be possible to find a solution to this complicated problem within the framework of halakha. And indeed, our talmudic authorities already viewed the *aguna* problem as one that requires non-conventional solutions and leniencies – "on behalf of the *aguna*, the sages ruled leniently" (Yevamot 88a). In dealing with this problem, Ḥazal, the *Geonim*, and the *Rishonim* suggested solutions and enacted legislation that reflect their concern for the honor of a woman who seeks a divorce from her husband.

EARLY MISHNAIC SOLUTIONS

The Mishna in Ketubbot 77a states that in certain cases the Jewish court may indeed compel the husband to divorce his wife in cases where he has a sickness or is involved in a profession that causes a foul odor to emanate from his body or breath, preventing mutually desirable physical intimacy. So, too, a man suffering from impotence may be compelled to divorce his wife.[6] In these cases, the court may apply pressure upon the husband to divorce his wife until he says that he agrees to the divorce (Arakhin 21a). In that way, the husband is viewed as though divorcing of his free will[7] and the problem of an imposed divorce does not arise.

The Jerusalem Talmud takes another path, that of prenuptial conditions which were customarily attached to the *ketubba* at the time

---

6. See Maimonides, *Hilkhot Gerushin* 2:20, who explains that the pressure that is to be applied to the recalcitrant husband of "beating him until he says 'I want to give the divorce'" is only done to enable him to reveal his true desire to be a part of the Jewish people and do as he is commanded, and it is merely his evil inclination that overtakes him and prevents him from doing the right thing. The words of Maimonides ring even truer today than they did in the eleventh and twelfth centuries: "Our wives dare not be treated by their husbands like captive women," like slaves or chattel, kept against their will! See also Rabbi Yitzhak HaLevi Herzog, *Heikhal Yitzhak* (pt. I, no. 1, note 32), who explains that wherever the Mishna or Talmud says that we force a divorce, it means that the sages legislated a coerced divorce for the benefit of Jewish women, relying on the assumption that if the rabbis order the husband to divorce his wife, the husband will agree to do so of his own free will, for there is a mitzva to obey the rabbis.

7. *Korban HaEdah* understands that this stipulation was written in a separate contract drawn up prior to the *ḥuppa*, whereas *Penei Moshe* explains that it was written into the *ketubba* itself.

of marriage in order to protect the woman's interests, such as a pre-nup in which the husband (or wife) agrees to a divorce, and even monetary compensation, if either of the two parties wishes the divorce:

> Rabbi Yosa said: Those who write,[8] "If he comes to hate" [his wife] or "If she comes to hate," [her husband, then the woman receives a divorce as well as financial compensation]; it is considered a monetary stipulation, and the stipulation is valid. (Ketubbot 5:8)

> It once happened ... Rabbi Mana said to them [the woman's relatives], "Bring her *ketubba*, so that we may read it." They brought her *ketubba*, and found written in it: If this woman marries this man, and does not wish the partnership[9] [i.e., if she seeks a divorce], she shall [receive a *get* and] collect half of her *ketubba*. (Ketubbot 7:6)

In our day, as well, various prenuptial agreements have been formulated in which the husband obligates himself to pay his wife a large sum of money or her maintenance in the event that he delays giving her a bill of divorce. Such agreements are intended to protect the woman and force the husband to grant her a divorce. The Rabbinical Council of America endorses the use of prenuptial agreements of this sort in the United States.[10] But this arrangement does not solve the *aguna* problem in all cases – e.g., when a wealthy husband is ready to pay for his wife's

---

8. See also Meiri, *Ketubbot*, p. 269, no. 4, who argues that the geonic decrees allowing for a forced divorce in the case of a woman who claims that she finds her husband repulsive were based on the normative practice of inserting such a stipulation into the marriage contract.

9. For the correct reading of this text, see my book, *Women and Jewish Divorce: The Rebellious Wife, the Aguna and the Right of Women to Initiate Divorce in Jewish Law. A Halakhic Solution* (Hoboken, 1989), p. 31, and p. 166, note 16.

10. See *Women and Jewish Divorce*, pp. 143–156, where I cite a responsum of Rabbi Betzalel Zolti, the former chief rabbi of Jerusalem, in which he accepts the idea of such a prenuptial agreement. See also Susan Metzger Weiss, "Sign at Your Own Risk: The RCA Prenuptial May Prejudice the Fairness of Your Future Divorce Settlement," *Cardozo Women's Law Journal* 6 (1999): 49–102, who surveys the various prenuptial agreements that have been proposed in recent years, and discourages the use of

maintenance, but refuses to divorce her, or if the two parties never signed such an agreement, or if the husband runs off to an unknown location.

MARRIAGE MADE IN ERROR

As will be explained below, the Talmud recognizes the possibility of *hafka'at kiddushin*, the annulment by a rabbinic court of a marriage hitherto considered legally valid, if one party was kept from knowing an essential piece of information regarding the other party before his or her acceptance of the betrothal. In such an instance, the marriage may be declared as having *never* been legally valid and a *get* would not be necessary. It is important to note, however, that four conditions must be met in order to declare a marriage invalid for having arisen in error, according to the responsa of Rabbi Moshe Feinstein:

1. The heretofore unknown blemish must have already existed at the time of the marriage.
2. The unknown factor only came to the other party's attention after the marriage had already taken place.
3. The previously unknown factor affects the essence of the marital bond (such as impotence), or is a major defect that makes it impossible to live with the affected partner (such as mental deficiency).
4. The unknown factor is a matter that would seriously vex most people[11] and deter them from marrying the affected partner had they known about the matter from the outset.

It was recently suggested that the criteria for error be expanded so that the discovery of a negative personality trait such as anger or miserliness could be recognized as a valid basis for a claim of a marriage made in error.[12] According to this suggestion, if a woman claims that she would

---

the RCA prenuptial in favor of other agreements (e.g., the one proposed by Rabbi J.D. Bleich) that she claims better protect the interests of Jewish women.

11. Rabbi Moshe Feinstein mentions this condition in *Even HaEzer*, pt. 1, no. 179, regarding a retroactive stipulation attached to *halitsa*.

12. This annulment procedure has been put into practice by *Beit Din LeBa'ayot Agunot*, or Court for the Problems of Chained Women, a special court established in the United

never have married her husband had she known earlier of his rage or miserliness, her marriage can be cancelled on the grounds that it had been based on false pretenses. It seems to me that the criteria established by Rabbi Feinstein cannot be expanded along these lines. Indeed, were it true that any negative personality trait can serve as grounds for arguing that a marriage had been created in error, the need for a *get* would never arise, for everyone appearing before a divorce court would maintain that, had he or she been previously aware of said trait, the marriage would never have taken place. There must have been a hidden objective physical or psychological problem in existence before the betrothal, which most people would consider a barrier to marriage, in order to invoke the principle of *ta'ut*, a marriage made in error.

TALMUDIC CASES OF *HAFKA'AT KIDDUSHIN*

Even though betrothal and marriage are regarded as contracts created by the two parties and thus terminated by them, a number of talmudic passages prove that, in certain circumstances, the rabbis authorized the cancellation of a marriage by a religious court without the husband's consent, and even against his will.

Five different passages in the Babylonian Talmud bring up *hafka'at kiddushin*. Two of the passages deal with *hafka'a* that takes place at the time of betrothal, whereas the other three address *hafka'a* after a period of time has lapsed.[13]

States in 1996 by Rabbi Emanuel Rackman and Rabbi Moshe Morgenstern to solve difficult cases involving *agunot*. Though fiercely criticized by most of the Orthodox establishment, this court has to date dissolved the marriages of hundreds of Jewish couples. The court was never really accepted, however, and it ceased functioning in about 2009.

13. The five cases are:

1. Gittin 33a – a man nullifies a *get* he has instructed to be given, but does so neither in the presence of the agent sent to give it nor in the presence of the woman who has not yet received it.

2. Gittin 73a – a dying man gives his wife a *get* and then lives. The *get* is invalid according to rabbinic law.

3. Ketubbot 3a – the conditions of the *get* were not fulfilled due to a force majeure (unforeseeable circumstance); the *get* is invalid according to the rabbis, but the betrothal is abrogated in order to free the woman.

It is clear in all the cases cited that the validity of Jewish marriages and divorces is dependent upon rabbinic authorization of the acts in question. The three cases involving *hafka'a* at the time of divorce invoke the principle that a man betroths his wife with the sanction of the rabbis. The repeating refrain is the principle that whoever betroths a woman betroths her with the understanding that his act has rabbinic approval. Hence, the rabbis have the authority to cancel the betrothal.

The two passages dealing with *hafka'a* at the time of the betrothal make no mention of the above principle. In its place, we find the notion that "he acted improperly, and so they [the rabbis] act improperly toward him." It is clear that when the *hafka'a* takes effect at the time of betrothal, a *get* is not required. In those cases where the *hafka'a* takes place at some later point, the *Rishonim* disagree as to whether a *get* is required. It must be stated at the outset, however, that in the three cases which have a *get*, the *get* was invalid according to rabbinic law. Indeed, in the first case, the problematic manner in which the husband administered the *get* is the very reason for the *hafka'a*! However, in these three instances, since the *get* was invalidated, the woman was still halakhically married to her present husband and not free to re-marry. The rabbis therefore abrogated the marriage in order to enable the women to be freed.

VIEWS OF THE *GEONIM* AND *RISHONIM*

The following points must be clarified when analyzing the views of the legal authorities to be cited below:

1. What is *hafka'at kiddushin*? What is the mechanism through which a marriage may be cancelled?
2. What is the result of *hafka'at kiddushin*? Is the marriage cancelled retroactively, or only starting from the time of cancellation?
3. Who is invested with the authority to cancel a marriage? Did such authority come to an end at the close of the talmudic period?
4. In which instances may a marriage be cancelled? Only in the cases mentioned explicitly in the Talmud, or in other cases as well?

---

4. Bava Batra 48b – a man forces a woman to become betrothed to him.
5. Yevamot 110a – a man snatches a young woman who had been married as a child.

5. Is there a distinction between *hakfa'a* at the time of betrothal and *hafka'a* at some later point, after the couple has actually lived together for some time as man and wife and perhaps even had children together?

Jerusalem Talmud

In the Jerusalem Talmud, there is only one incident of *hafka'at kiddushin* (Y. Gittin 4, 2), parallel to the first incident we brought from the Babylonian Talmud concerning the individual who nullified his *get* unbeknownst to his wife. The basis for the nullification is clear-cut: the right of the sages to uproot even a positive biblical commandment (as developed in Yevamot 90b) and therefore, even a biblically validated marriage, if the groom acted in an unseemly fashion.

Rashi

It seems that according to Rashi, *hafka'at kiddushin* is based on a set condition that is always and automatically attached to the betrothal.[14] Whenever a man betroths a woman, he conditions his betrothal on rabbinic approval. The rabbis as a whole act as silent partners in his betrothal, and the validity of the betrothal depends upon their consent. Even though Rashi doesn't mention the term *tenai* (condition) explicitly, this seems to be how he interprets the established betrothal formula, "You are hereby betrothed to me in accordance with the laws of Moses and Israel." The laws developed by our sages, the Oral Laws of Moses and of Israel, make our sages active participants in every betrothal.

It may be understood from Rashi's commentaries on the aforementioned talmudic passage that since *hafka'at kiddushin* is based on a conditional betrothal formula, and every betrothal is carried out only with the consent of Moses and Israel, a *get* is not needed to implement the *hafka'a*. According to this view, there is no need to say that the authority to cancel a marriage ended with the close of the talmudic period; the authority to cancel is built into the marriage formula in whichever era it is recited. Similarly, there is room to say that new enactments and

---

14. Rashi on Ketubbot 3a, Yevamot 110a.

practices may be instituted regarding marriage and divorce, and that *hafka'at kiddushin* is not limited to the cases mentioned in the Gemara. And furthermore, it may be argued that Rashi does not distinguish between *hafka'a* implemented at the time of betrothal and *hafka'a* implemented at some later point.[15]

Other Rishonim

While there may be a certain ambiguity in Rashi's position, because he does not use the term *tenai* (condition) outright, other *Rishonim* state clearly that *hafka'at kiddushin* is based on the condition of rabbinical consent. These include Rabbi Aharon HaLevi (Ketubbot 3a), Ritva (Ketubbot 3a), Rabbi Avraham ben HaRambam (*She'elot U'teshuvot Avraham* no.44), and Maharam of Rothenburg (*Mordekhai*, Kiddushin 3:522). These authorities would seem to accept *hafka'a*, at least theoretically.

On the other hand, there are *Rishonim* who raise objections against the principle of *hafka'at kiddushin* in general and, in particular, against Rashi's understanding that the *hafka'a* takes effect retroactively. After all, if a marriage can be cancelled retroactively because of unavoidable interference or cancellation of a *get*, then whenever a woman commits adultery – so that the woman is forbidden to her husband and lover, the adulterers are liable for the death penalty, and any child born from their relationship is a *mamzer* – all the husband has to do is send a retroactive *get* to his wife through an agent and then cancel the *get*, or attach to the *get* a condition that is likely to lead to unavoidable interference. Once this is done, the marriage will retroactively be cancelled, his wife will retroactively be considered a single woman, and she and her children will be saved from all the penalties of her adultery. This objection leads a number of *Rishonim* to a different understanding of *hafka'at kiddushin*.

---

15. However, *Shita Mekubbetset* (Rabbi Betzalel Ashkenazi) on Ketubbot 3a understands Rashi's position in a completely different manner, insisting that *hafka'a* can only be implemented after the time of the betrothal with a *get* that is valid, at the very least, by rabbinic decree.

Rashbam

Rashbam (*Shita Mekubetzet*) argues that the Gemara ought not to be understood to mean that a valid betrothal that has already been in effect can be cancelled retroactively. Rather, when a *get* is given, the marriage is terminated only from that time forward. The Rashbam argues that no person would want the rabbis to declare his sexual relations acts of prostitution! According to this view, the cancellation of a marriage after the couple has lived together even for a minimal period of time would be a halakhic impossibility.

Rabbenu Tam proposes an alternate solution to the difficulty raised above, and on the basis of his position, it is clear that he believes that the abrogation of a marriage can be retroactive. He explains that we are not concerned that the husband will take advantage of *hafka'at kiddushin* in order to protect his adulterous wife or to legitimize *mamzerim*, since *hafka'a* requires the decision of a court, and if the court sees that the husband is trying to protect his adulterous wife or permit *mamzerim*, it will not cancel his marriage. Rabbenu Tam rejects Rashbam's conclusion that once a man betroths a woman in the proper manner, the betrothal can only be terminated with a *get* that is valid by Torah law, but any *get*, even an invalid one, will do.

Other *Rishonim* agree with Rashbam that after a betrothal takes effect with rabbinic sanction, it cannot be cancelled without a *get*, but they argue, along with Rabbenu Tam, that the *get* need not be valid by Torah law. They, too, distinguish between *hafka'a* at the time of betrothal and *hafka'a* at some later point. For example, Ri MiGash to Ketubbot 3a states explicitly that a distinction must be made between the two types of *hafka'a*: when the husband betroths his wife in an improper manner, the woman leaves even without a *get* altogether; but, whenever he betroths her in a proper manner, and the marriage is later cancelled, the woman requires some sort of *get* (*get kol dehu*),[16] but not necessarily a *get* that is valid according to biblical standards. A similar distinction is put forward by Nahmanidies, Re'ah, and Rashba.

---

16. *Yad Peshuta, Hilkhot Ishut* 4:1; *Hilkhot Gerushin* 3:8.

Meiri

Rabbi Menaḥem HaMeiri (Ketubbot 3a) states explicitly that *hafka'at kiddushin* does not require a *get*: "When [the rabbis] said that they cancelled a betrothal, they applied the right to cancel not only in a case like this where there is a *get*, which is invalid, but also even in a case where there is no *get* at all." Meiri explains why in Ketubbot and Gittin a *get* is required, whereas in Yevamot and Bava Batra, a *get* is not required. "Here [in Ketubbot] the *hafka'a* stems from the doubt which arose regarding the *get*." The implication is that there is no essential difference between the *hafka'a* implemented at the time of betrothal and *hafka'a* implemented at some later point, *hafka'a* without a *get* being possible in both cases. Meiri's comment in Yevamot (89b) is particularly relevant to our discussion:

> We already explained in our commentary to the mishna that a court can only abrogate a Torah law in one of three ways: by declaring that the Torah law be abrogated in a passive manner; by declaring a person's property ownerless; or by proclaiming a temporary abrogation, thus constructing a fence safeguarding the Torah law. Any instance involving matrimonial law is not regarded as an abrogation, for a man betroths a woman with the understanding that he has rabbinic approval, and they have the authority to cancel a marriage.

Meiri implies that *hafka'at kiddushin* is not based on declaring the husband's property (and thereby the betrothal ring) ownerless or valueless. Rather, it is based on a specific authority of cancellation given to the rabbis in matters of marriage and divorce, and there is no reason to say that this authority does not operate today. Meiri's position may be based on the Jerusalem Talmud cited earlier, that the rabbis can even uproot a biblical command.

Ran

Nedarim 90b states:

> A woman who says to her husband that she is impure for him [for she has committed adultery] – according to the First Mishnaic Ruling [*Mishna Rishona*], she is believed and leaves the marriage

with her *ketubba* alimony agreement, but according to the Final Mishnaic Ruling [*Mishna Aharona*] she is not believed [as to the adultery] without real proof lest she cast her eyes on another man [and therefore is making up the story of adultery only in order to get out of her present marriage].

The Ran, in his commentary on this passage, asks how the woman can be permitted to her husband according to the Final Mishnaic Ruling. After all, Torah law forbids such a woman to continue to live with her husband, so how can the mere suspicion "lest she cast her eyes on another" rescind the biblical prohibition? The Ran responds, "To me that is not a question. Just as we say in several talmudic passages that anyone who betroths, betroths with the consent of the rabbinic sages, and the rabbinic sages can cancel the *kiddushin*, so too in this instance: any woman who says to her husband that she is an adulteress has her *kiddushin* annulled by the rabbinic sages retroactively – so that at the time she committed the transgression, she was a single woman. Because of this, she may be permitted to her husband and can also eat of his *truma* (if he is a priest) as we said in the Gemara." Hence, the Ran joins the list of *Rishonim* who maintain that the *get* is not a necessary factor in annulling a betrothal.

HISTORICAL CASES OF *HAFKA'A*

Over the generations there have been many attempts to apply the principle of *hafka'at kiddushin* to cases that were not mentioned explicitly in the Gemara. Most of the discussions relate to cases that became known as "secret marriages" or "deceptive marriages." By law, when a man gives a woman a ring or some other object of value in the presence of two witnesses, and says to her, "You are betrothed to me in accordance with the laws of Moses and Israel," they are man and wife. No additional ceremony is required. But in order to avert disputes between the parties and prevent any doubts as to the validity of the marriage, enactments were instituted in many communities (*takkanot kahal*) that introduced formality and publicity into the marriage ceremony. Among other things, these enactments required that the betrothal take place in the presence of ten people or before the community's rabbi or communal heads, that the betrothal have the parents' blessings, that a *ketubba* be written, and that the betrothal take place at the time of the *ḥuppa*. The question arose as to the validity of a marriage that took place in defiance of these enactments, "secretly" or "in a deceptive manner."

As far back as in the days of the *Geonim*, there was a difference of opinion as to whether the rabbis retained their authority to cancel a marriage after the close of the talmudic period. Rabbi Ḥai Gaon and Rabbi Yehuda Gaon are of the opinion that the authority to cancel a marriage did not end with the close of the Talmud, and that the possibility of canceling a marriage is not limited to the cases mentioned in the Gemara.

In contrast, Rabbi Yosef Karo writes (*She'elot U'teshuvot Beit Yosef*, no. 10) that he saw a responsum of one of the *Geonim* who argued "that we only say that the sages (of the Talmud) cancelled a marriage where they [actually] said so." It is obvious that according to that opinion, the authority to cancel a marriage terminated with the closing of the talmudic period.

At the end of the twelfth century, a disagreement arose between the rabbis of Worms and Speyer on the one hand, and the rabbis of Mainz on the other, as to whether *hafka'at kiddushin* could be implemented in a case where there was no prior enactment governing the matter. Ra'avan (*Sefer Ra'avan* p. 283) cites an incident that occurred in Cologne:

> A young man was trying to arrange a marriage with the parents of his prospective bride. In the meantime, another man of means came along, and the father of the bride agreed to accept the betrothal of the second suitor. They called for the community [to assemble for the betrothal] in accordance with the custom. When the second suitor stood up to go and betroth her, the relatives of the first suitor went ahead in a wily manner, and betrothed her to the first suitor in the presence of witnesses that they had prepared. When the [bride's] parents realized [what had happened], they said to her: "Throw away the betrothal [ring] in your hand," and she did so, and the second suitor betrothed her on that same occasion.

Rabbi Yaakov HaLevi of Worms and Rabbi Yitzḥak HaLevi of Speyer wished to cancel the first marriage without a *get*, on the basis of the Yevamot passage dealing with the snatching incident: "So, too, did the first suitor [act improperly when he] snatched her from the second suitor to whom she had been designated, and betrothed her. Let us cancel the betrothal." But the rabbis of Mainz, Rabbi Elyakim, Rabbi Yaakov HaLevi, and Ra'avan himself all rejected their arguments. "[Even] if the [talmudic] rabbis had the authority to cancel a marriage, we do not have the authority to do so." Ra'avan seems to imply that he would not implement *hafka'at kiddushin* in his time even to cases identical to those of the Gemara.[17]

Rashba in a *teshuva* (no. 1185) raises the matter of a betrothal conducted in the presence of witnesses who by rabbinic decree are disqualified from testifying: does such a betrothal require a *get*? He rejects Rif's argument that in such a case we should cancel the marriage on the basis of the principle that a man betroths a woman with the understanding that his act has rabbinic approval – and since they would never have approved of him marrying without proper legal witnesses, the marriage is invalid and no *get* is necessary. Rashba argues that this principle (of cancelling a marriage performed with witnesses who are rabbinically invalid) is not mentioned in the Talmud, specifically, so the marriage cannot be cancelled. He explained that, "In all these matters, you only have what the rabbis permitted explicitly."[18]

It would, however, be wrong to infer from what Rashba says that the rabbis lack the authority to *institute* new enactments that would allow for the cancellation of a marriage; the Rif and the Rashba would certainly allow for new enactments for cancellation, as did many of the *Geonim*.

Rabbenu Asher (Rosh) was asked (in *teshuva* 35:1) whether or not a court can legislate that if a man betroths a woman without her

---

17. As was already noted by *Seridei Aish*, pt. 3, no. 114. Rabbi Berkovits (op.cit. p. 152), on the other hand, tries to compare Ra'avan to *Tosafot*, arguing that even according to Ra'avan it would be possible to cancel a marriage at some later point after the time of betrothal, even without a *get*.

18. *Shiltei Gibborim* (Bava Batra 45a in Rif) raises the same question and offers the same solution, except that he focuses on the contradiction between Rashba and Maharik. But the same contradiction exists internally between the two responsa of Rashba.

parents' consent, the betrothal money is declared "ownerless" and the betrothal thus invalid. Rosh writes that in addition to this argument, the court can claim that "in every generation a man betroths a woman with the understanding that he has the approval of the sages of the generation who make enactments to serve as safeguards, and with the understanding that his betrothal will only be valid if it is conducted in accordance with their enactments." Thus, Rosh, too, allows for *hafka'at kiddushin* in accordance with contemporary rabbinic enactments.

The first sign of a change in attitude regarding *hafka'at kiddushin* – in which the theoretical principle is accepted, but the practical implementation is questioned – may be found in a responsum of Rivash (no. 799). Rivash was asked about a community that enacted a rule that a man may only betroth a woman with the knowledge of the community's trustees, in their presence, and in the presence of ten people. Betrothals conducted in any other manner were declared invalid, and the money (or its equivalent) given for the betrothal was declared ownerless. Rivash finds this acceptable, without invoking the principle that everyone who betroths, does so only with rabbinic approval; in this instance, the community's control over the money is enough to empower it over marriage. If, however, a man betroths a woman without money – say, by way of sexual intercourse – the principle that betrothals are conducted only with rabbinic approval would need to be invoked. At the end of the responsum, Rivash writes that, in theory, "if a man betroths a woman in violation of the community's enactment, his betrothal is invalid, and she does not require a *get*." However, "In practice I would lean towards stringency, and not rely on my opinion in the matter – on account of the severity of the issue of releasing a woman without a *get* – without the approval of all the sages of the different regions." Rivash does not reject the possibility of canceling a marriage that was conducted in violation of a communal enactment. But he hesitates to use the authority granted to the Torah scholars of every generation, as well as to the community, and requires the agreement of all the sages in the area in order to utilize that authority.

Rabbi Shimon ben Tzemaḥ Duran (*Tashbetz* 2:5) was asked about "a community that enacted that if someone betroths a woman without the knowledge of the city council and the communal elders, his betrothal is invalid." He rules that according to the letter of the law, every court and every community in every generation is authorized to cancel a marriage but, "even so, in matters of marriage we should be stringent."

A similar ruling is issued in another responsum (1:133): "Whatever I say on this matter is merely theoretical. For authorities have already been asked about this matter many times, and we do not find that they put this ruling into practice." And Tashbetz's grandson, Rabbi Shimon ben Rabbi Shlomo Duran (*Yakhin U'Boaz* 2:46), after distinguishing between *hafka'a* at the time of betrothal and *hafka'a* at some later point, and between the various different formulations of the communal enactments, adds:

> Even if the enactment would be formulated in this manner, it should not be acted upon. The great authorities have already testified as follows: "And so we have heard that the ruling was never put into actual practice." Now if the early authorities testify about the even earlier authorities that they never acted upon such an enactment...then how is it possible that we should do so?

Maharam Alashkar (Responsa no. 48) discussed a communal enactment declaring that a man may not betroth a woman in the presence of less than ten people or in the absence of the community's sage, and that any betrothal conducted in violation of this enactment would not be valid. He argued that according to Rabbi Ḥai, Rashba, Rosh, and Rivash, a community is permitted to enact such legislation. But he concluded that his personal support depended upon the agreement of the entire region and all or most of its rabbinical authorities. For a man does not betroth a woman with the understanding that he has the approval of a particular community, but rather with the understanding that he has the approval of all the communities in the region. Even though, in the case at hand, Maharam Alashkar required the issuance of a *get*, he agreed that in theory the rabbis of every generation have the authority to pass legislation allowing for a betrothal to be cancelled.

Rabbi Yosef Karo in his *Beit Yosef* (*Even HaEzer* 28) cites the three responsa of Rashba, as well as the responsa of Rivash, Rashbatz, and Maharik cited above, without commentary. As we have seen, these allow for the possibility of *hafka'a* when there is agreement on the part of the regional rabbinical authorities. The spirit of this responsa is to view *hafka'a* as a theoretical possibility that is best not applied practically by an individual religious court of a particular locality.

In the *Shulhan Arukh,* Rabbi Karo makes no mention of any of the issues raised in those responsa. The manner is also treated in two of Rabbi Karo's own responsa. In one place (*She'elot U'teshuvot Beit Yosef,* no. 6), he sharply attacks a ruling invalidating the betrothal of an individual who violated a communal enactment by acting without the presence of a court. Rabbi Karo accepts the view of Rivash that even if the enactment stipulated that the betrothal money would be declared ownerless, the woman may not be released without a *get.* This is all the more true when the communal enactment itself does not mention the consequence of invalidation of the betrothal. Elsewhere (no. 10), Rabbi Karo repeats his position and explains that "where they said [that the marriage is cancelled] they said so, and where they did not say [that the marriage is cancelled] they did not say so." In other words, *hafka'at kiddushin* is only implemented in those cases that are mentioned explicitly in the Gemara. Moreover, even if it is agreed that it is possible to cancel a marriage in other cases as well, "that only applies to them, and to the early generations who understood the reasons of things. But in these generations, who says that we have the authority to cancel marriages that are valid by Torah law."

Rabbi Moshe Isserles (Rema) writes in his gloss to the *Shulhan Arukh* (*Even HaEzer,* 28:21):

> If a community enacted among themselves that any betrothal not held in the presence of ten males is considered invalid, and then there was such a betrothal, we still remain concerned about the validity of the betrothal and the woman needs a *get.* Even if the community expressly stipulated that the betrothal will not be valid, and declared the groom's money ownerless – even so, one should be stringent in practice [and require a *get*].

Rema's position seems to be clear: A *get* is required, even if the enactment stipulates that the betrothal is invalid when done improperly. But there is still room for a certain doubt. The editor who notes Rema's sources traces Rema's ruling to the Maharik, but Maharik's ruling related to an enactment that did not explicitly mention *hafka'at kiddushin*. Thus, it is difficult to understand how his words can serve as a source for Rema's ruling. The editor might have made a mistake, and the true source of Rema's ruling may be Rivash. If so, just as Rivash said that he would join with other rabbinic authorities if they would agree to release the woman without a *get*, so, too, Rema might agree to such a proposition.[19]

THE CASE OF THE AUSTRIAN CAPTIVES: A PRECEDENT FOR OUR TIMES

Thus far, we have brought the Rema's ruling which appears in his gloss on the Code of Jewish Law, the Set Table (*Shulḥan Arukh*). Particularly interesting and important in the context of our discussion is the Rema's view, as expressed in *Darkhei Moshe* (7:13). Rema deals there with a lenient ruling (as cited by *Terumot HaDeshen* no. 241) issued on behalf of a group of Jewish women taken captive during a period of persecution in Austria, which allowed them to return to their husbands. (The operative law is that such women are generally assumed to have been violated during their captivity, and are therefore prohibited to return to their husbands; *Even HaEzer* 7:4.) Rema writes:

> It seems to me that the rabbinic authorities may have issued their lenient ruling not on the basis of the strict law, but because of the needs of the hour. For they saw that there was reason to be concerned about what women might do in the future. For if they knew that they would not be permitted to return to the husbands of their youth, in any case, they might sin willingly with their captors, and so [the rabbis] were lenient. And don't say, "From where do we know that we might be lenient in a case that involves a possible Torah prohibition?" It seems to me that they relied on that which they [had previously] said, that whoever betroths a woman betroths her with the understanding that he has rabbinic

---

19. A. H. Freiman, *Seder Kiddushin VeNissu'in* (Jerusalem, 1945), p. 345.

> approval, and the court is authorized to cancel his marriage, so
> they were like unmarried women, and even if they sinned, they
> were permitted to their husbands.

Obviously, according to no less an authority than Rema, today's rabbinic
authorities (that is to say, those living after the close of the talmudic era)
retain the authority to cancel a marriage that had once been valid – even
without a *get*, and even without an explicit enactment empowering them
to do so, in order to prevent grave discomfort to captive women and to
prevent them from possible transgression.

And indeed, the Rema's ruling was used as a precedent by contemporary *poskim*. Rabbi Mordecai Yaakov Breisch of Zurich permitted
female survivors of the Holocaust to re-marry, even though the where-
abouts of their former husbands could not be conclusively determined,
on the basis of the rabbinic power to cancel marriages (*Ḥelkat Yaakov,
Even HaEzer* 40, 49, 56)! It goes without saying that no *get* was involved
in these cases.

And on the theoretical plane, Rabbi Yehiel Yaakov Weinberg
(*Seridei Aish* 90) states: "But in any case we see that it is a position of
the Rema that even in our days it is possible to use this principle (of
annulling a marriage) under certain conditions. And even though the
permissibility granted in the Austrian decree only rescinded a biblical
negative prohibition (and not a capital offense)…nevertheless we do
see that the sages of Austria utilized this principle and that the Rema
concurred with their ruling."

Rabbi Yitzḥak HaLevi Herzog (*Teḥuka LeYisrael Al Pi HaTorah*,
Part 1, 82), likewise wrote: "In any case, we find here that it is his [the
Rema's] opinion that marriages were annulled long after the sealing
of the Talmud. According to this, it is necessary to say that also in our
time, rabbinic sages have the power to annul a marriage on the basis of
'all who betroth do so in accord with rabbinic approval,' and so the rabbis can annul the betrothal."

Rabbi Ovadia Yosef (*Torah Shebe'al Peh*, Part III, 100), after a
lengthy analysis of the words of the Rema concludes, "No matter what,
we learn from the sages of Austria that we may permit annulments
[of marriages] also in our times in cases of great necessity."

In his writings, Rabbi Avraham Yitzḥak HaKohen Kook initially says (*Ezrat Kohen*, 69) that only the sages of the Talmud had the right to invoke annulments, but he concludes his discussion:

> Nevertheless we do find that even in the later generations, our sages have utilized their power of annulment in times of great need, as is explained in the *Trumat HaDeshen* which is cited by the Rema. But that is merely a hint (*remez*) concerning the issue, because there the matter was decided by a gathering of the sages of the generation and for the sake of a case which touched a multitude of people. Nevertheless, it is not at all a closed matter – the idea that it is impossible to include the principle of cancellation of marriages after the time of the sages of the Talmud.

In other words, Rabbi Kook maintained that even in our times it might be possible for rabbis to annul marriages.

Even Rabbi Shlomo Zalman Auerbach leaves the door open for our utilization of this principle, when he writes, "the fact that we find sages who annulled marriages as is cited in the *Darkhei Moshe* and in other places, this occurred in time of persecution and great slaughter, in a matter which pertained to the multitudes; one should not utilize the principle of annulling marriages in order to save one single individual" (*Torah Shebe'al Peh*, Part 8, 45). It must be borne in mind that the present day situation of *mesuravot get* is causing more and more couples to choose to wed outside of halakhic nuptial canopies, and is truly adversely affecting "multitudes of women" and causing a tragic desecration of God's name and the Torah's supposed trademark of "righteous laws" (*mishpatim tzaddikim*).

Even though the tendency among the halakhic authorities always seemed to recognize the halakhic option of *hafka'at kiddushin* as being sound, they nevertheless discouraged the practical possibility of utilizing this approach, lest it weaken the sacred strength of marriage and divorce in Jewish life; and despite this concern, enactments including *hafka'at kiddushin* on the part of responsible Orthodox *batei din* continued to be passed into law until the beginning of the twentieth century. In a period of a little more than a hundred years (1804–1921), for example, no fewer than seven enactments allowing for the cancellation of marriages were instituted in various different countries – Italy, France, Algeria, and Egypt.[20]

Additionally, in the course of the last century, a number of attempts were made to resolve the *aguna* problem by attaching a condition to the betrothal and invoking the principle of *hafka'at kiddushin*. These attempts were based on the fifteenth-century enactment of Ri Berin, according to which a man with a heretic brother may betroth a woman, stipulating that if he dies without offspring, and she becomes subject to levirate marriage to her late husband's brother, the betrothal will not be valid (cited by Rema *Even HaEzer* 157:4).

In 1924, the rabbinic court in Constantinople published a work entitled "Conditional Marriage." The members of that court wished to attach a condition to all betrothals and marriages stating that if the husband left his wife for an extended period of time without her permission, or if he refused to accept a court ruling, or if he took ill with a mental or contagious disease – in all such cases the marriage would be retroactively cancelled, and the woman would not need a *get*. Besides attaching a condition to the betrothal, the Constantinople court suggested invoking the principle of *hafka'at kiddushin*. Most of the leading halakhic authorities rejected these proposals and the Constantinople enactments were never put into actual practice. (The situation in Constantinople was apparently different from that faced today; they were suggesting the abrogation of marriage in cases where there was no problematic abuse on the part of the husband).

In a theoretical discussion relating to present-day enactments to cancel marriages, Rabbi Yitzhak HaLevi Herzog writes as follows:[21]

---

20. Freiman, ibid., p. 337.
21. Rabbi Yitzhak HaLevi Herzog, *Tehuka LeYisrael Al Pi HaTorah*, vol. 1, p. 73. It should be noted that Rabbi Herzog emphasizes that whatever he writes on the topic should be understood as a theoretical discussion, and not be taken as a practical guideline. On p. 74, he writes: "But we have never heard, God forbid, that anybody ever acted on this matter. And when certain people rose up to act, wishing to establish a new practice, the great authorities of the generation fiercely objected and the matter was forgotten and never mentioned." In note 18 on that same page there is a reference to Rabbi Herzog's approbation to Rabbi Uziel's work: "But I must declare that I do

This might have halakhic ramifications even in our day, when the sages of the generation see that couples marry in civil courts ... and according to some opinions, as long as they live together afterwards openly as man and wife, she becomes his wife by Torah law, the sages of the generation should decree to uproot the marriage with the Torah authority invested in them .... Indeed, it could be [a situation] where the husband is obligated by Torah law to grant his wife a divorce, but he refuses to comply with the law, and the woman may have received a civil divorce in a non-Jewish court, but that does not help according to Torah law, and she remains an *aguna* forever. In such a case, the court has the authority to uproot the betrothal, or to rule according to the principle that a

---

not agree at all with the proposal in no. 45 regarding a conditional betrothal ... and while the author himself stresses that it is merely a proposal, nevertheless I find it necessary to make this declaration."

Elsewhere (pp. 82–83), Rabbi Herzog writes with greater caution: "As for *hafka'at kiddushin*, with attention paid to the words of Rashba, and the silence of the other authorities on this issue except for that which is stated explicitly in the Gemara, it would appear that we do not have that authority, even for a limited time. But in the future, if ordination is restored, and the Torah's authority is concentrated in Jerusalem with all or most of the fit communities and all the rabbis of Israel accepting her authority, the matter will require a decision ... And even so we have found an exception to the rule in our master Rema's *Darkhei Moshe, Even HaEzer* 7:13, where Rema cites in the name of *Terumat HaDeshen*, no. 241, with regard to women during the persecutions in Austria who were permitted [to return to their husbands] by the great halakhic authorities ... It seems to me that they relied on that which they said that whoever betroths a woman betroths her with the understanding that he has rabbinic approval, and the court has the authority to cancel a marriage ... I was later told that according to a responsum of an early *Gaon* they wanted to cancel a marriage, or they actually did so in a particular case. I must look for it, and if it happened like that, it is a great precedent, and we have the grounds to say that this authority was not removed from the sages of the generation even after the closing of the Talmud." In the next section he adds: "But this does not mean that we, orphans of orphans, should God forbid use this authority. Rather, when we merit the arrangement that I mentioned – the restoration of ordination, or even without that restoration, the establishment of a high court in Jerusalem with the agreement and acceptance of its authority on the part of a majority of the Torah-abiding residents in the Land of Israel, and a majority of the rabbis and fit communities in all the corners of the world – then it will be possible to consider such matters, a fixed order that will stand until the days of the Messiah."

man betroths a woman with the understanding that he has rabbinic approval. Even though Ḥazal did not cancel the marriage in such a case, that was because they were authorized to use physical force, or at least to impose a ban or excommunication, which is not the case in our day when these are forbidden.[22]

Rabbi Herzog is clearly opening the door for *hafka'at kiddushin* in our times.

CONCLUSION

We have seen that many *Rishonim* maintain that *hafka'at kiddushin*, even when implemented many years after the marriage, is based on an implied condition attached to the formula of the betrothal, "Behold you are sanctified unto me in accordance with the laws of Moses and Israel." The sages of each generation are partners to every betrothal, and so they have the right to abrogate the betrothal. Moreover, according to this opinion, even when the talmudic case-in-point involved a *get*, it was not the *get* that brought about the cancellation of the marriage, for in each instance the *get* was invalid by Torah law. Hence, there is reason to allow *hafka'a* many years after the betrothal even without a *get*. Moreover, according to this opinion, there is no reason to say that the authority to cancel a marriage ends with the close of the Talmud, for the mechanism of the *hafka'a* is built into the very same marriage formula that is in practice to this very day.

We have also seen that throughout the ages – during the days of the *Geonim*, the *Rishonim*, and the *Aharonim* – great sages of every generation have agreed to the possibility of abrogating a marriage whose husband was acting unfairly, including Rabbi Ḥai Gaon and Rabbi Yehuda Gaon, Rashi, Rabbi Aharon HaLevi, the Ritva, Rabbi

---

22. In general, there are many more references to enactments allowing for the cancellation of marriage than to cases in which *hafka'at kiddushin* was actually implemented. See also Freiman, *Seder Kiddushin VeNissu'in*, p. 343, where he cites testimony that in the seven years following the enactment passed in Egypt, nobody even attempted to betroth a woman in a manner not in accordance with the enactment, for everybody knew that the betrothal would be cancelled.

Avraham ben HaRamban, the Maharam of Rothenberg, Rabbenu Tam, and the Meiri.

To be sure, over time, the rabbinic authorities have hesitated more and more to invoke that authority, but they never gave it up altogether or doubted the possibility of executing it with a specific enactment of a regional *beit din*. *Hafka'at kiddushin* has always remained a legitimate solution to pressing halakhic problems. In times of need, and when no other halakhic solution was available to them, the rabbis invoked their authority to cancel marriages even without a *get*. Enactments allowing for the cancellation of a marriage never stopped, as we have seen in the enactments passed in Egypt less than a hundred years ago.

The authority to cancel a marriage was usually invoked to cancel betrothals that had been conducted in an improper manner in violation of explicit communal enactments that had been instituted to prevent "secret" or "deceptive" marriages. But the option of canceling a marriage even after a valid betrothal, and even without an explicit enactment, was never completely ruled out either in cases of extreme necessity, as we have seen in Rema's explanation of the lenient ruling issued regarding women who had been taken captive during a period of persecution. According to Rema, the lenient ruling allowing such women to return to their husbands is based on the assumption that today's rabbis have the authority to cancel a marriage – even without a *get* – and even though the couple had been living together as man and wife for many years. Rema justifies the ruling, emphasizing that it was issued because of "the needs of the hour." The rabbinic authorities ruled leniently because they were concerned that a more stringent approach would lead to sinful behavior in the future. These considerations are no less valid today than they were in the time of Rema.

It is my opinion that in difficult times like today, when many women are forced to live as *agunot* chained to their husbands, and recalcitrant husbands are taking advantage of their wives as well as abusing the halakha to hold up their wives for ransom and/or prevent them from marrying, there are certainly grounds to make use of the option of *hafka'at kiddushin* even without a *get*; this would release those women from their chains and from an almost certain life of sin. This is especially so when the problem of *agunot* causes such great human suffering and degradation of halakha. But this should be effectuated by a special *Beit Din* for *agunot* in Jerusalem with three judges of impeccable halakhic credentials who would render judgments, and rule on urgent issues of *mesuravot get* throughout the world.

TAKKANAT KAHAL BY MEANS OF THE KNESSET

Professor Berakhyahu Lifshitz, a widely recognized talmudic scholar and a professor of law at the Hebrew University, suggests a fascinating addition to this proposal. We have already seen how many halakhic decisions have been much more positive about abrogating a marriage if there were a specific regional enactment – *takkanat kahal* – that declared the betrothal money or ring to be ownerless, thus canceling the value of the betrothal gift and rendering the act of the betrothal null and void (Rashba, Nahmanidies, Rashi, Rivash, op.cit.). This is based upon the well-known talmudic principle of *hefker beit din hefker,* that a religious court has the power to nullify the value of one's possessions, as well as the geonic principle that a Jewish community has the power of the Great Jewish Court (*Responsa of Rabbi Ḥananya ben Rabbi Yehuda Gaon, Shaarei Zedek* Part 4, Gate 4, 16, and *Responsa of Rabbenu Gershom,* The Light of the Exile 67, Eidelberg Edition, based on Rosh HaShana 25a). Professor Lifshitz therefore suggests that the Israeli Knesset – the representative body of the legislating arm of the Israeli community – ought to enact a decree that if a recognized religious court of Israel orders a husband to give his wife a *get* and he refuses to do so for thirty days, his gift of betrothal shall be retroactively "*hefkerized*" or rendered valueless, and his wife will be free to remarry. It may even conceivably be argued that such an enactment would apply to couples living in the Diaspora as well, since every Jew has "four cubits in Israel" and the authentic Jewish community (*kahal*) is the community in Israel (Horayot 3b). At the very least, the Israeli Knesset certainly has the power of the elected town councils of the "seven good officials of the city" (*shiva tuvei ha'ir*) who enjoyed the authority to establish communal enactments throughout the Middle Ages. And in this manner, the Knesset would be strengthening the ability of the religious judges to enforce their judgments and to alleviate domestic injustices.

There is little need to worry that allowing for the dissolution of a marriage without a *get* would lead to a devaluation of the sanctity of the institution of marriage. The proposed enactment would only apply in the most extreme cases of a recalcitrant husband. Moreover, it is likely that the actual implementation of *hafka'at kiddushin* will be rare. The mere threat of *hafka'at kiddushin* – and with it the release of the woman from her marital chains – would deprive the husband of the strangling hold that he has over his wife, and should suffice to convince him to free her from the marriage with a valid *get*.

There are those who warn against this proposal by invoking the long-established tendency to be stringent in the area of *ishut*, or personal status, probably due both to the severity of the prohibition of *lo tin'af* (adultery) and to the potential for *mamzerut* (bastard offspring). However, one can well argue precisely to the contrary. Because of the fear of many women that they might end up as captives to recalcitrant husbands, more and more Israeli couples are opting to get married *shelo kedat Moshe VeYisrael* (not in accordance with the laws of Moses and Israel, in ceremonies outside the rabbinical traditions) – and even to merely live together without any kind of ceremony at all. Such conduct will more likely lead to *mamzerut* and adultery than a rare *hafka'at kiddushin*.

Additionally, it must be remembered that our talmudic sages understood this point when they ruled that "in order to prevent the situation of the *aguna*, our sages judge leniently" (Gittin 3a); because of this – despite the legal principle that any matter of personal status requires two religiously-observant male witnesses – a woman's testimony, one witness's testimony, hearsay testimony, and even the testimony of a gentile is acceptable in determining the death of a missing husband so that his wife may re-marry. Even in the case of forcing the husband to give a *get* desired only by the woman, the sages of the Talmud, the majority of *Rishonim*, and decisors up to and including contemporary times have been most lenient.

Moreover, it must be remembered that in our post-modern period of global mobility and individual autonomy, the ability of any Jewish court to enforce their decisions vis-à-vis the husband has been sorely weakened. In the words of Rabbi Herzog, "in those instances when the husband could be forced to divorce his wife, our sages were not lenient in terms of annulling the marriage. There was no necessity for it; the [judges] had the power to compel with force and to declare sanctions which were adhered to. This is not true in our times."

Finally, the possibility of a rabbinic court with the power to abrogate marriages would release women from the unilateral power of husbands in the area of divorce, an act which would at long last remove the tears of *agunot* from within our midst, remove the desecration of God's name from our Torah and its laws, and restore the mutuality of marriage as so meaningfully described by the *Ḥatam Sofer* in the beginning of this article ("Betrothal: A Relationship of Mutuality," Note 1). We must pay close attention to the commentary of the Maharsha (1555–1631, Poland) at the end of the Tractate Yevamot:

> Rabbi Elazar said in the name of Rabbi Ḥanina: Torah scholars increase peace in the world, as the verse states, "And all of your children shall be taught of the Lord, and great shall be the peace of your children" – read not *banayikh* [your children], but rather *bonayikh* [your builders – Torah scholars are the true builders of peace].

The Marasha explains that Tractate Yevamot concludes with these words because that particular Talmud tone contains many strange laws that appear to contradict and uproot that which is stated explicitly in the Torah. Rabbi Elazar teaches that these laws were not taught in order to uproot the Torah, but rather to increase peace in the world, the peace that is engendered by healthy family life. The parallel Gemara in Berakhot then cites the verse, "Abundant peace have they who love Your Torah" – these laws bring abundant peace to the world, allowing a woman to free herself from her husband so that she not remain forever tied to him, as the verse about Torah states: "Her ways are ways of pleasantness, and her pathways peace." A woman without a husband cannot live in peace. The Gemara ends with the verse, "The Lord will give strength to His people." And so the Maharsha concludes: "May God give the leaders of His people, the Torah scholars of every generation, the courage and boldness to be lenient in these matters, for only then will 'the Lord bless His people with peace.'"

ADDENDUM

Rabbi Michael Broide initiated a tri-partite prenuptial agreement which includes a *get al tnai* (a conditional divorce) as a condition for the betrothal. Although many authorities would argue that with the first act of marital intercourse all conditions are nullified – and so the *get* is invalid – many more *Rishonim* would agree to an abrogation of the betrothal if there is a *get kol dehu*, even an invalid *get*. I would suggest appending this prenuptial agreement to every *ketubba* issued by the Religious Ministry in Israel.

Section III
Israel and the World

The Significance of Israel's Return to Zion: *Tikkun Olam*

INTRODUCTION: MY FIRST LESSON IN ZIONISM

The most profound tragedy of horrors as well as the most uplifting confirmation of our faith were both experienced by the Jewish people within the very same decade of the last century: the shame of humanity which either cooperated with, or silently permitted, the decimation of the Jewish people and the diabolical atrocities of the Holocaust, and then – only three years after the suicide of Hitler – the newfound hope for humanity with the rebirth of the State of Israel confirmed by a vote of the United Nations.

To suggest that the Holocaust was the necessary price the Jews had to pay for their return to their homeland after almost two thousand years of destruction, exile, and persecution, borders on the blasphemous; but to overlook the inextricable juxtaposition of these two nationally defining events – the first bringing us down to the hellish depths of despair and the second raising us up to the dizzying heights of redemption – would be blinding oneself to the commanding voice of Jewish history. And so I begin this essay with my first lesson in Zionism, which emerged from the ashes of Auschwitz.

It was the Shabbat of the weekly portion *Ki Tavo*, toward the end of the summer of 1952. I had known that the Rebbe of Sanz-Klausenburg had taken over the Beth Moses Hospital (the place where I was born), where he had built a very large beit midrash-*beit knesset* (study hall-synagogue), as well as a printing press to teach his disciples a trade, and I wanted to pray with the Hasidim that Shabbat morning. I also wanted to wear my new bar mitzva suit, which had very recently arrived from the tailor.

I had to conduct a long, hard negotiation with my mother, who was reluctant for me to take such a long walk alone in what was not a very wholesome neighborhood, and was also adamantly opposed to my wearing the bar mitzva suit close to a year before my bar mitzva (which was scheduled for the following year's portion of *Emor*). At length, my mother relented, but not until I promised not to get into any altercations with toughs who might start up, and not to partake of any Kiddush if there was one.

When I arrived at the beit midrash, I was amazed by the sea of black and white swaying figures that greeted my eyes, all newly immigrant Holocaust survivors. It was said about the Rebbe that, although his wife and thirteen children had been murdered, he had not sat *shiva* for any of them; he preached that those still alive must be saved with exit visas before one could be allowed the luxury of mourning for the dead. The Rebbe himself was among the last to leave Europe, insisting that the captain does not leave the sinking ship before its passengers. I took a seat directly behind the Rebbe, who stood at his lectern facing the eastern wall and the Holy Ark, with his back to the congregation. The prayer was the most intense I had ever experienced, with no talking whatsoever, and chance individuals even bursting out in tears during varying parts of the service, apparently in response to a sudden association with a painful memory.

Then the Torah reader began to chant the weekly portion. When he came to the passage known as "the Chastisement" (*Tokheḥa:* the curses that would befall the Israelites), which he began to read (in accordance with time-honored custom), in a whisper and very quickly, a sound suddenly came from the place of the Rebbe; he said only one word: *hecher*, louder.

The Torah reader immediately stopped reading, and seemed to hesitate for a few moments. I could almost hear him pondering. Did the Rebbe actually say "louder"? Would the Rebbe go against the custom of Israel in all congregations to chant the curses rapidly and in a barely audible voice? The reader apparently decided that he had been mistaken in what he thought the Rebbe had said, and continued reading in a whisper.

The Rebbe turned around to face the congregation, banged on the lectern, his eyes blazing: "*Ich hob gezogt hecher,* I said louder," he shouted out. "Let the Master of the Universe hear! We have nothing to be afraid of. We have already received all of the curses – and more. Let the Almighty hear, and let Him understand that the time has come to send the blessings!"

I was trembling, my body bathed in sweat. Many people around me were silently sobbing. The Rebbe turned back to his lectern, facing the wall. The Torah reader continued to chant the curses loudly, and distinctively, and in a much slower cadence.

At the end of the additional prayers, after *Aleinu,* the Rebbe once again turned to his congregation, but this time with his eyes conveying deep love, "*Mein tayere shvestern un brider,* my beloved sisters and brothers, the blessings will come, but not from America. Indeed, God has promised the blessings after the curses, and He has already begun to fulfill His promise by bringing us home to Israel. May more blessings await us, but they will only come from Israel. Let us pack our bags for the last time. Our community is setting out for Kiryat Sanz, in Netanya, Israel."[1]

THE CONFIRMATION OF GOD'S COVENANT

As the founding patriarch of the Hebrew nation, Abraham enters world history with the "Covenant between the Pieces" (Gen. 15:1–21) in which God guarantees to Abraham the seed of eternal continuity and the inheritance of the land from the Nile to the Euphrates. This is the covenant of the Jewish *nation* emanating from Abraham's loins and Sarah's womb; a nation is, after all, that which develops from a family "writ large," expanding into tribes that become geographically defined by clear borders. Generally, such a nation is forged by common historical experiences that are commemorated in days of celebration characterized by unique

---

1. I have published this memoir elsewhere, most notably in my book, *Listening to God* (Maggid Books, 2010). In this essay, the last words of the Rebbe appear a bit differently from the way they were recorded in other places. I believe that this version is more in consonance with my recollection as well as with the message I am trying to impart.

foods and customs, and which have a compelling purpose and narrative that is transmitted from generation to generation. The Passover holiday, which stresses Jewish freedom from Egyptian bondage, is a powerful example of the Hebrew narrative.

The precursor to the Covenant between the Pieces is found three chapters earlier, at the very moment that God elects Abraham, a moment that is also centered on a specific, yet unspecified, land:

> The Lord said to Abram: "Go for yourself out of your (present) land (Ur of the Chaldees), out of your familial birthplace, and out of your father's house to the land that I will show you. I shall make of you a great nation; I shall bless you and make your name great and you shall be a blessing. I shall bless those who bless you, those who curse you I shall curse and all the families of the earth shall be blessed through you." (Gen. 12:1–3)

Alongside the crucial importance of establishing Abraham's seed as a great nation on its own land, there is a divine charge, universal in import: "All the families of the earth shall be blessed through you." We can understand this reference by looking at Genesis 18:18, 19, wherein God reveals the reason for Abraham's election:

> And Abraham is surely to become a great and mighty nation, and all the nations of the earth shall be blessed through him. For this reason, have I loved (chosen, appointed) him, because he commands his children, and his household after him to keep the way of the Lord by doing compassionate righteousness and moral justice (*tzedaka u'mishpat*), in order that the Lord might bring upon Abraham that which He had spoken concerning him (to make him a great nation).

IS GOD'S COVENANT CONDITIONAL?

It appears that God's covenantal promise is a two-way street, a contractual agreement between two parties, God and Israel. In his pathbreaking work *Created Equal*,[2] Joshua Berman analyzes the covenants between God

---

2. Joshua Berman, *Created Equal*, Oxford University Press, 2008.

and Israel in the light of parallels with late Bronze Age Hittite suzerainty treaties. He concludes that the Bible expresses an "egalitarian theology" in which honor between suzerain and vassal is bestowed bilaterally if not with full mutuality. In imposing upon Israel the status of late Bronze Age vassalage, the Bible establishes a paradigm for the human-divine encounter that placed all of the nation Israel on an unprecedented pedestal; not only could Israel honor God, but God could honor Israel. The whole of Israel attains the status of subordinate king – with benefits and obligations – entering into a treaty with Sovereign King, God.[3]

Since our patriarch Jacob-Israel was the grandson of Abraham and Sarah (according to the biblical narrative), the Bible insists that the Children of Israel will never be destroyed and that nation Israel will eventually inherit the land of Canaan. These gifts, however, seem to be predicated upon Israel's dedication to compassionate righteousness (*tzedaka*) and moral justice (*mishpat*) and upon Israel's blessing the nations of the world with the moral imperatives that produce "compassionate righteousness and moral justice" throughout the world, i.e., ethical monotheism. Israel's mission is to become a "sacred nation and kingship of priest-teachers to all of humanity (Ex. 19:5–6, Seforno ad loc.).

Is, then, Israel's covenant with God conditional? Yes and no. Our ability to conquer the Land[4] and maintain Jewish habitation upon it *is* conditional upon proper comportment. Given the reason for which God elected Abraham, it is logical that God's purpose in making of Abraham's seed a nation-state upon their own land is that they may become a nation among other nations, obligated to grapple with the national challenges of peace and war, economic struggles, how to treat minorities and foreigners, how to deal with criminals and drug addicts, as well as the universal challenges of ecology and international relations. Guided by the Torah teaching (chiefly of the Ten Commandments) that was revealed to Israel in the Sinai desert shortly after their freedom from Egyptian bondage, Israel must serve as a beacon and light for all the nations (Is. 42:6, 49:6).

---

3. Ibid., chapters 1 And 2. See also Saul Olyan, "Honor, Shame and Covenant Relations in Ancient Israel and its Environment," JBL 115 (1996), 210.
4. In this chapter, I capitalize "Land" to indicate the specific noun, the biblical Land of Israel.

Israel will maintain its privilege to the Land only if the Jewish people are worthy of fulfilling its divine mission to demonstrate and teach compassionate righteousness and moral justice (Deut. 8:16–20).

However, from a theological perspective, just as God is eternal, so must His covenants be eternal and not subject to abrogation. Hence, despite the fact that the Israelites will be exiled from the Land if (when) they lose their moral worthiness, and will become persecuted strangers in foreign countries, a situation which will cause Israel to cease being an active player on the world scene, *nevertheless* God guarantees the eventual restoration of Israel to their homeland, the eventual return to their calling, the eventual resumption of their historic destiny (Gen. 15:12–21; Deut. 4:26–31).

This is the symbolism of the three animals in the drama of the Abrahamic National Covenant (Gen. 15): the heifer, the goat, and the ram, symbolizing the powerful nations of the world, and the two birds, symbolizing Israel.[5] The animals were bisected and each piece was placed facing its counterpart. Abraham, representing the future Hebrew people, walked between the severed parts, and a smoky furnace and a torch of fire, representing the *Shekhina* or Divine Presence, also passed between the parts. These actions symbolize the mutuality of the covenant: God and Israel, each with their own respective commitment, each dependent on the other for mutual fulfillment. Yet, this also symbolizes Israel's eternal life and relationship to the Land, since each animal (i.e., nation with ascendancy over Israel) will ultimately be vanquished – bisected – and only the birds, symbolizing Israel, will remain alive and intact.

The paradox that the Bible reveals and that I wish to analyze is that while some of Abraham's seed will be eternal and continuous, its relationship to the Land will be eternal but interrupted, dependent upon its moral worthiness. Abraham's seed will remain alive, but will not emerge from its exiles unscathed: Persecutions and assimilation will deplete its population, yet ultimately, the Jewish people will return to *tzedaka u'mishpat* and then to their Promised Land in perpetuity. God will forgive His repentant nation, their hearts will be purified, and their scattered compatriots will return home. The eternity and irrevocability of the covenant will be vindicated in historical time, when Israel will indeed be, and will remain, worthy.

---

5. See commentary of Rashi, ad loc.

the first Jerusalem Temple in 586 BCE. The subsequent Babylonian exile lasted only fifty years, after which Cyrus of Persia gave the Jews permission to return to Judea and rebuild the Temple. Although most Jews opted to remain in Babylon, the Jewish nation had been bereft of their land for only five decades and of the Temple for only seven decades – a mere blink in historical time. Hence, the chastisement of Leviticus includes the promise of God's remembrance and Israel's return in the very same passage that catalogues their sufferings.

The second chastisement, in Deuteronomy, refers to the second exile, begun at the hands of Rome in 70 CE. In the Roman exile, the Jews were scattered to the "four corners of the earth," and that exile lasted nearly two thousand years until the Jewish return to the "born-again" State of Israel in 1948. The Deuteronomy chastisement makes no mention of comfort or return, since the return would take millennia; Jews would be bereft of their Temple and homeland for many more years than they had had them.

Yet, two chapters later, in Deuteronomy 30:1–10, we do read of Jewish return, a near historical impossibility after two millennia:

> It will be that when all these things come upon you – the blessings and the curses that I have set before you – you shall cause yourself to return to your hearts within the midst of all the nations where the Lord your God has dispersed you. And you shall return unto the Lord your God and listen to His voice, in accordance with everything I command you this day, you and your children, with all your heart and all your soul. Then the Lord your God will return your exiles (captives in foreign lands) and have compassion upon you. He will return and He will gather you in from all the nations to where the Lord your God has scattered you. If your dispersed will be at the end of the heavens, from there will the Lord your God gather you in and from there He will take you. The Lord your God will bring you to the Land that your forefathers possessed and you shall inherit it. He will do good to you and make you more numerous than your forebears. The Lord your God will circumcise your heart and the heart of your seed to love the Lord your God with all your heart and with all your soul, that you may live.

CONTEMPORARY HISTORY AND THE DOUBLE
INITIATIVE OF THE JEWISH PEOPLE

There are two important aspects of the return promised by God in this passage. The return is a double one, a physical return to the Land of Israel "from within the midst of all the nations where the Lord your God has dispersed you," and a spiritual return to God and divine commandments. The context dictates that the spiritual return should be particularly to the universal laws emphasized by the Third Covenant. Critically, these physical and spiritual returns are to be initiated by Israel, and only after humans have taken the initiative, will God aid in their conclusion.[9] Only after Israel begins returning to the Land, will God restore its exiles, and only after Israel returns to God's voice, will God circumcise (i.e., purify) Israel's hearts (Jer. 31:30–33).

Nahmanides referred to this passage as "the portion of repentance," the source of God's commandment to Israel to repent. Another medievalist, Maimonides, saw these verses as God's *guarantee* that Israel will repent. This is crucial, because for Maimonides there could be no redemption without repentance, and like all the biblical prophets, Maimonides understood redemption to mean universal redemption,[10] i.e., the time when through the seed of Abraham all the families of the earth will be blessed with freedom, morality, and peace.

As if in response to biblical demands, two unique events have occurred in recent Jewish history: 1) the Zionist movement towards the end of the nineteenth century, which signaled for the first time since the abortive 135 CE Bar Kokhba rebellion against Rome the Jewish initiative to return to the Bible's covenantal land without waiting passively for God or the Messiah to take the Jewish people there, and 2) the widespread movement of *teshuva*, the return or repentance movement in which alienated Jews are finding their way back to God.[11]

Until the early twentieth century, repentance was understood to apply nearly exclusively to religious Jews who had lapsed in their

---

9. This accords with the talmudic adage, "one who begins to purify himself will be aided from On High" (Yoma 38b).

10. *Mishneh Torah*, Laws of Kings 12, 1; Laws of Repentance 7, 5.

11. The famous religious journey of Franz Rosenzweig in early twentieth-century Germany is a primary initial example of this growing phenomenon.

observance of one or another of the commandments. But the recent phenomenon of "born-again" Jews making a total change in their religious orientation (à la Franz Rosenzweig and, of course, the entire *baal teshuva* phenomenon), as well as the many thousands of Crypto-Jews in South America, "hidden" Jews in Eastern Europe and Germany, and the newly revealed tribes of Africa coming out of the "closet" and rediscovering their Jewish roots, are all products of our very special period of return.

THE CONFIRMATION OF THE COVENANT

I submit that the deepest significance of the Jewish return to Zion is its confirmation of the eternality of our covenant and the truth of the promises of our sacred Scriptures. In the words of Paul Johnson,[12] "the creation of Israel was the quintessential event of the last century, and the only one that can fairly be called a miracle." This miracle has also brought in its wake the ingathering of Jewish exiles, from the forgotten tribe of Dan in Ethiopia to the lost tribe of Menashe from India, to the Jews of Persia, and Kaifeng, China, to the most recent return of the more than one million Jews of the former Soviet Union (FSU), who were hitherto "lost Jews" (see Is. 11:11).[13]

This profound miracle illustrates the "dry bones" vision of Ezekiel, where he watched as the Lord put sinews and flesh upon dry bones in a valley in Babylon, coated them with skin, placed His Spirit within them, and enabled them to come to life and to acquire renewed faith and vigor as they walked upon the soil of Israel reborn (Ezek. 36). These are the dry bones of the muselmann prisoners of Auschwitz, who rose from their graves of the not-yet-dead and not-yet-quite-alive to miraculously fight in Israel's War of Independence and participate in Israel's miraculous rebirth.

---

12. *Commentary* magazine, May 1998.
13. The words of Isaiah 11:11–12 are resonant with this return: "It shall be on that day that the Lord will once again extend His hand, to acquire the remnants of His people, from Assyria and from Egypt and from Pathros and from Ethiopia (Cush) and from Persia (Elam) and from Babylon (Shinar, Iraq) and from Hamath and from the isles of the sea. He will raise a banner for the nations and assemble the castaways of Israel; and He will gather the scattered ones of Judah from the four corners of the earth."

THE RESPONSIBILITY OF THE
JEWISH RETURN TO ZION[14]

The perseverance of the people of Israel during the past two thousand years – despite being bereft of its historic homeland and central Sanctuary, the two most tangible expressions of the Covenant of Abraham and the Covenant at Sinai – can only be explained by the ability of rabbinic Judaism's comprehensive religio-legal system (*halakha*) to adapt to the cataclysmic changes wrought by the destruction of the Second Temple and the subsequent exile. It was the foresight of Rabban Yoḥanan ben Zakkai and the rabbinic scholars of Yavneh in the first century CE who set the stage for the transition from a Land-and-Temple-centered priestly aristocracy to a rabbinically-directed study hall and synagogue-centered democratic "nomocracy." This system worked remarkably well until the European Emancipation at the end of the eighteenth century. Similarly, our own post-Holocaust generation of survival, return, and renewal demands no less a creative adaptation than the one achieved by the revolutionary generation of Yavneh.

Using the prophetic "Return and Repentance" promise of Deuteronomy 30 as our guide, I would like to outline the most salient religious and national challenges and opportunities facing halakhic leadership in our return to Zion. To be sure, those voices opposed to change will argue that any significant deviation from our religio-legal practice will perforce lead to the weakening – and perhaps even to the obliteration – of the continuity of our time-honored tradition; nevertheless, it was a very carefully-crafted dialectic between continuity and change that expressed the genius of the generation of Yavneh. The leadership at that time was mindful of the tension which existed even in biblical times between the priest, whose task was to retain the continuity of the ritual from generation to generation, and the prophet, whose task was to bring the living God of Compassionate Righteousness into the contemporary ritual of his time.

---

14. Two recent important articles that express much of my thoughts on this vital subject: "Halakha's Moment of Truth" by Evelyn Gordon and Hadassah Levy (*Azure*, no. 43, Winter 5771/2011) and "Let us Not Be Among Those who Refuse Redemption" (*Al Nihyeh Sarvanei Geula*), by Yoav Sorek, *Akadamot*, vol. 20, pp. 71–88.

Indeed, the Bible itself expresses this tension within the two commanding verses of religio-legal decision making: "Ask your father and he will tell you, your grandfather, and he will say unto you" (Deut. 32:7), that is to say, conduct your ritual lives precisely in the manner of your parents and grandparents; and, conversely, "When you are in a quandary as to how to make a judgment, you must go up to the judge in that time (the religio-legal authority who is sensitive to the changes in various historical periods and understands the zeitgeist of that particular time), and in accordance with the Torah which he will teach you shall you conduct yourself" (17:8–11). The rabbinic sages of the Talmud even apply this last verse to a situation in which the contemporary judge is a person of lesser knowledge and authority than was the judge of the earlier period.

Surely, the period in which we are now privileged to live, which has experienced the two cataclysmic changes of the Holocaust and our return to Israel, deserves – and desperately requires – the invocation of this latter verse.

The leadership of Yavneh succeeded in retaining the eternal sanctity and values of the Bible while hermeneutically reinterpreting the meaning of its words to cover a panoply of new conditions and issues. Similarly, our return to Zion requires that we adopt the talmudic attitudes which pioneered a marriage contract that provided women with divorce alimony and their husbands' life insurance two thousand years ago, but change the completely out-moded language and monetary amount – stipulations which are woefully inadequate in our contemporary society; the new *ketubba* must craft the proper formula which will express the talmudic dictum: "in order to free women chained to intolerable marital situations our sages always found leniencies in the law."[15] In the ritual sphere we must find halakhically permissible ways to "provide spiritual satisfaction to women" (Ḥagiga 16b), and as a sovereign host nation for the first time in two thousand years, we must seriously consider our policies towards minorities (Christians as well as Moslems) and non-Jews clamoring for Israeli citizenship, in accord with the biblical mandate: "You must love the stranger for you were strangers in the land of Egypt" (Deut. 10:19).

---

15. See the article in Section II on *Hafka'at Kiddushin*.

OUR LITERAL RETURN TO THE LAND

Biblical Judaism was Land-oriented, seeing the Land as providing the nutrition and natural resources necessary for the wellbeing of its resident people of Israel (Deut. 8:7–10). Thus, many biblical laws are dependent upon living on the Land: the festivals are rooted in the harvesting of the produce of the Land, and national ecology for protecting our resources – both natural and human – is mandated through the Sabbatical laws requiring the Land to lie fallow every seven years, granting every landowner a Sabbatical year for spiritual and intellectual refreshment. The taxation methods by which wealthier, land-owning gentry discharged their obligations towards the non-landed religious functionaries of the Temple and the Torah educators of the nation was via tithes that every farmer was obligated to contribute from his harvest. Biblical Judaism worked out an effective way for the noblesse oblige to fulfill its responsibility to the poor without a welfare system promoting indolence and an exaggerated sense of entitlement. A portion of every privately-owned field was required to be set aside for the poor, who were responsible to plant, till, and harvest it before they could then take their "earned" produce for themselves. Moreover, the poor were entitled to keep any grains falling from the arms or carts of the harvesters, as well as the grain left on the threshing floor after the harvest.[16] All the social classes went to the fields to work, with everyone earning his daily bread, even if he or she was officially "jobless."

This economic system is described in the Book of Ruth (2:1–17), and demonstrates how even an impoverished Moabite stranger could support herself and her mother-in-law. Moreover, Ruth was able to move from class to class and eventually marry Boaz, the wealthy landowner. Applying this value system today, it is crucial that we find a similarly effective method of this kind of self-help for the poor in contemporary industrial and technological society.

The biblical Sabbatical year required land to lie fallow as an ecological value, which we could express today in numerous other ways of "greening" our communities. But this "Sabbath of years" had two additional societal and human values: It reminded every farmer that

---

16. Lev. 23:22.

neither the Land nor its produce ultimately belonged to him, for every seventh year God, the Owner of the universe, commanded each citizen that he had to learn to "let go" of his material possessions and allow any passerby to avail himself of the produce that grew spontaneously on his property. Anyone with a backyard or a garden today can continue to learn this lesson, even in our sophisticated industrial society.

Second, the Sabbatical year that parallels the Sabbath day is an effective way for every person to devote one year in seven to religious study, academic degrees, self improvement, additional time with family, intensive therapy, or exploring other professional or residential options. Unfortunately, in modern Israel this idea has degenerated into finding more ways to circumvent the biblical command regarding agriculture, e.g., selling the topsoil of Israeli land to Arabs, or growing hydroponics. A methodology of preserving the original values of the Sabbatical year, by encouraging farmland development and agricultural produce in modern-day Israel, and seeking to enhance the general quality of life by creatively introducing mandatory sabbaticals in staggered fashion for the working population, ought to be a high priority for an economically-oriented legal and religious Israeli think tank. Further still, we should recapture the biblical ethical ideal by designing a mechanism for rescinding personal loans that cripple individuals without undermining the national economy.

RETURNING TO OUR NATIONAL HERITAGE

Returning to our national homeland presents Jews with four areas of major responsibilities which require further study, but which are important to at least briefly outline:

Assuming responsibility for the Jewish nation as a diverse people

If the covenantal obligation of the Jewish nation is to transmit "compassionate righteousness and moral justice," and if Jews are charged by divine commandment to be a sacred nation and a kingdom of priest-teachers to the world, then the elected leadership and religious authorities of the Jewish state must take a unique covenantal responsibility for every one of Israel's Jewish citizens.

At Sinai, God was not interested only in the elitist "study hall" Jew who studies in isolation, but in the entire Jewish nation, with whom He sealed His Covenant.[17] So also in the Jewish state. While in Israel, no Jew can become invisible: He is an indelible part of the nation, and an inextricable part of a united bond imbued with a divine Jewish mission of representing the historic Jewish people-hood to the world.[18] If so, Israeli religious and government leaders including the chief rabbis, have a responsibility to be concerned with all Jews in Israel, rather than with a narrow segment of society. Our government must promote a core curriculum for every Jewish citizen of the state which will educate him/her as to the values of our Jewish civilization, the ethics which we must impart to ourselves and to the world, and the traditions which expressed these ideals for the last four thousand years.

Establishing religious freedom and broad Judaic education

While statehood is an expression of the covenantal narrative, religious laws must not be imposed upon Jews in Israel. Religious coercion is an oxymoron, and imposed religious law is *ipso facto* denuded of any religious significance. Any attempt to legislate religious practice will prove to be counterproductive.[19]

The covenantal Jewish narrative, imbedded in the Hebrew calendar and our national literature, should not be relegated to what is wrongly called "the Jewish religion." It is more properly seen as the civilization of Judaism that encompasses the totality of Jewish expression and covenantal mission. The Jewish covenantal narrative including the Sabbath,

---

17. Berakhot 32a pictures God commanding Moses to "go and descend" from the supernal space atop Sinai (Ex. 20) to tend to his flock that is acting perversely and worshipping the Golden Calf. God directs Moses: "Descend from your greatness! I only granted you greatness because of Israel. Now that Israel has sinned, what need have I of you?"

18. See Sota 37b, where the talmudic sages understood the Third Covenant discussed previously, which was sealed as the Hebrews entered Israel, as the Covenant of Responsibility (Heb. *arevut*, a play on *arava*, the word used to describe the plains of Moab where they were camped).

19. This has been stated often by my teacher and religious authority, Rabbi Joseph B. Soloveitchik.

the festivals of Freedom (Passover), Revelation (Shavuot) and Redemption (Sukkot), Ḥanukka and Purim, Jewish mourning commemoration (Tisha B'Av), as well as the High Holy Days of Rosh HaShana and Yom Kippur – all of these must be significant parts of the Israeli calendar and cultural experience.

Moreover, the Bible – particularly its fundamental moral and social concepts of humans created in God's image, freedom from tyranny, an objective moral code, the Sabbatical year and the ideal of human perfectibility – as well as the Talmud, Jewish philosophy, and ethical teachings, constitute our national literature and should be standard curriculum throughout the Israeli school system.

Assuming responsibility for non-halakhic Jews in Israel

Jewish religious leaders must take responsibility for the more than 300,000 Israelis (mostly immigrants from the former Soviet Union) who do not fulfill the classic legal criteria of Jewish identity. By joining the nation of Israel, these people have chosen to join our "covenants of fate and destiny."[20] Israeli leadership should consider their choice to live in Israel and their willingness to die for the Jewish state as members of the Israel Defense Forces (IDF) as significant (although not exclusive) aspects of their "acceptance of the commandments."[21] Indeed, living in Israel was

---

20. See Rabbi Joseph B. Soloveitchik, "The Voice of my Beloved Knocketh" in *Theological and Halakhic Responses on the Holocaust*, Ktav/RCA, Hoboken, NJ, 1993. This applies also to accepting those gentiles in Israel who seek to formally convert to Judaism through rabbinic courts. An inclusivistic rabbinate would be able to include those with strong Jewish identities – those who were attracted to the Jewish nationhood although not as strongly to the Jewish religion – to even convert to Judaism by emphasizing Jewish values and traditions – Sabbath, festivals, *kashrut* – rather than details of our prayer ritual. The challenge the rabbinate faces is its ability to unite all Jews under a broad umbrella via a wide concept of Jewish civilization rather than a narrow understanding of Jewish religion. This humanistic approach to Jewish law and the policies of Israeli rabbinic leaders must also extend to the implementation of marriage and divorce in Israel. All this can be achieved within the boundaries of Jewish law. The interface between the Israeli nationality and the Jewish religion awaits further analysis.
21. This halakhic position has been extensively explored in Rabbi Ḥaim Amsalem's monumental work, *Zera Yisrael* (Jerusalem, 2010) pp. 298–300.

probably the first commitment of conversion by Ruth to Naomi on her way back to the Land of Israel: "For where you go, I will go; where you lodge, I will lodge; your nation is my nation, and your God is my God" (Ruth 1:15). To be sure, they must be exposed and expected to live in accordance with the practices and values of Jewish civilization previously described.

Two new opportunities: Just warfare and justice for the stranger
Finally, the recent Jewish return to our national homeland offers two historic opportunities for renewing and rethinking two areas of Judaism that had been previously left to the dustbins of history during our exile. First, for good or for ill, Jews have returned to the necessity of engaging in defensive warfare. Rabbinical authorities ought to declare that participating in the defense of the Jewish people by serving in the IDF is a moral and religious obligation that devolves upon all Israelis, with only limited exceptions. The responsibility of national defense should be borne equitably and justly by all. Individual and national survival are not merely political ideals, but also religious responsibilities. Rabbis, military experts and ethicists need to advance new legal and moral standards for legitimate contemporary warfare, including targeted assassinations, aerial bombardment, house-to-house searches, forms of self-protection against unarmed enemies, and the legitimacy of negotiating with terrorist regimes for the sake of freeing Israeli captives.

Second, Israelis and Israeli law must treat the minorities living in the Jewish state as Jews have hoped the host countries of our exile would have done for us. During exile we were the stranger – the ultimate Other, outcasts struggling for basic human rights and safe havens. We now have the opportunity to breathe life into the ancient biblical concept of *ger toshav*, the non-Jewish resident alien in Jewish society. We must grant them recognition, citizenship with full rights, and acceptance of their differences consistent with the biblical mandate that we "love the stranger because we were strangers in the land of Egypt" (Lev. 19:34). Israelis have the responsibility to ensure that gentiles living in Israel find means of supporting themselves, and to enable them to feel that they live among Jews as siblings (Lev. 25:35–36).[22] Israel must assume

---

22. See Rashi ad loc., *ger* or *toshav*, and Maimonides, Laws of Prohibited Relations 14, 7.

responsibility to sustain and heal them when they are in danger.[23] Such a legislative policy regarding the minorities in Israel would indeed be a light unto the nations of the world.

ABRAHAM AND ISRAEL: THE NATION OF PRIEST-TEACHERS ENGAGES THE WORLD

As we have seen, the first Hebrew and patriarch of Israel, Abraham, entered the religious world as an iconoclast, a smasher of pagan idols and a visionary of ethical monotheism. God charged him to be the source by which "all the families of the earth shall be blessed" (Gen. 12:3), and the teacher of God's path of "compassionate righteousness and moral justice" to the entire world (Gen. 18:18–19). Abraham's mandate is passed on to his progeny, the nation of Israel, directly before the revelation at Sinai:

> "You shall be unto Me a kingdom of priest-teachers" (Ex. 19:6) – to understand and to teach the entire human species, to call upon everyone in the name of the Lord to serve Him with one accord, as it is said (Is. 61:6), "And you, the priest-teachers of the Lord, shall call out," and as it is said (Is. 2:3), "From Zion shall come forth Torah and the word of the Lord from Jerusalem (to all the nations)." (Seforno, ad loc.)

It goes without saying that we cannot begin to teach the gentile nations unless they wish to learn from us and desire to emulate our covenantal ethical ways. Hence, the Jewish people must become a holy nation. Talmudic authorities taught that the revelation at Sinai was initially meant for the world; they queried as to why the revelation was given in the desert, in a no-man's-land, and responded that whoever wishes to accept it (among the nations of the world) may come and do so."[24]

---

23. See Nahmanides, gloss on Maimonides' *Book of Commandments*, Positive Commandment 16, who maintains that we must even desecrate the Sabbath to help non-Jewish residents when they are in danger. Indeed, the resident alien is referred to as our "brother" within the Bible.

24. *Mekhilta, Yitro*, Matan Torah, *Parasha* 1.

Rabbinic tradition similarly taught that when God will appear a second time before all living beings in the eschaton, God's universal laws of morality will be accepted by everyone.[25]

The prophets clearly articulated the Jewish mission of teaching ethics and monotheism to the world, the covenantal mission as God's agents: "You are My witnesses, says the Lord, My servant whom I have chosen" (Is. 43:10); "I shall make you for a covenantal nation (*brit am*), a light unto the nations" (42:6). This "chosenness" is not a privilege; it is a divinely mandated *responsibility*.[26] The prophet Amos stresses that, "Only you have I known out of all the families of the earth; therefore, I shall visit upon you all of your iniquities (Amos 3:2)."

---

25. See the *Mussaf Kedusha* prayer in the Shabbat liturgy, which declares that God will reveal His will a second time "before the eyes of every living being" and the *Aleinu* prayer citing the words of Zachariah, that, "On that day (the eschaton) God will be one and His Name will be one." (Zach. 14:9)

    See also Maimonides' *Book of Commandments* (Positive Commandment 3), where Maimonides derives from the verse, "And the souls that they made in Haran" (Gen.12:5) that it is incumbent upon the Jews to make God beloved to all of humanity; he also strongly implies that we must expose the gentile world to the commandments of God, to the wonders of God's creations and to the actions of God in history. In his magnum opus *Mishneh Torah*, Maimonides goes so far as to say that we must even coerce the nations of the world to accept the seven moral Noahide laws, the laws of universal morality. See too Isaiah 2 and Micah 4; Isaiah seems to imply that all of the Torah is ultimately to be shared with the gentile world, whereas Micah would suggest ritual pluralism ("everyone will call upon God in his name" which means there can be different names for God and different methods of serving Him) but ethical absolutism, with everyone worshipping a God of peace and morality.

    See too Maimonides, *Mishneh Torah*, Laws of Kings (12:1) where he states that at the end of the days, "everyone will return to the true religion," which I believe refers to Judaism. In truth, there is a difference of opinion in the Talmud as to whether, at the end of the days, everyone will convert to Judaism or whether there will be no conversion at that time but there will be universal morality (Berakhot 57b, Avoda Zara 3b). What is interesting to note is that no authority I know would suggest any kind of forced conversion to Jewish ritual, and all of the sources I know believe that there is a place in the World to Come for the morally righteous, whatever their religious persuasion may be.

26. Our responsibility to engage the world is magnificently analyzed by Rabbi Lord Jonathan Sacks in his book *To Heal a Fractured World: The Ethics of Responsibility* (Schocken Books, NY, 2005).

Thus, as we have seen, the Jewish people are fated to absorb the brunt of the punishment when it fails in its mission to the nations (Is. 53). But the Jewish prophetic dream is for the Temple to be a "house of prayer for all nations" (56), a beacon for all peoples, "who will desire to learn God's ways and follow His teachings," a center from whence "the Torah will come forth from Zion and the word of the Lord from Jerusalem, so that nation will not lift up sword against nation and humanity will not learn war anymore" (Is. 2:3; Mic. 4: 2–4). While Micah states that "each person will call out in the name of his God" (Mic. 4:5), a declaration on behalf of religious pluralism, it is clear that in the realm of ethics, the seven Noahide laws will be absolute. Everyone, all of humanity, will agree and commit to the inviolability of human life, the rejection of war, the goal of peace. If Jews as a covenantal people do not succeed in teaching the world absolute morality, then in today's global village of nuclear proliferation, there will not be freedom and peace but only curses and destruction.

Indeed, many of our sages were converts or came from families of converts.[27] Perhaps the most obvious example of the Jewish desire to gain converts to Judaism from among the Romans is the well-known mishna in Ethics of the Fathers (Avot 1:12): "Hillel says, 'Be among the disciples of Aaron: love peace, pursue peace, love all humans (*beriyot*) and bring them close to Torah.'" According to Josephus, Jews influenced many gentiles throughout the Roman Empire, who refrained from eating non-kosher animal meat, who rested on the Sabbath and who fasted on Yom Kippur. "Just as our God fills the entire world, so His Torah has spread to encompass all human seed."[28] Yet, alas, due to Jewish internal strife (*sinat ḥinam*), the petty political conflicts and the personal grudges that expanded every disagreement into an international confrontation, Jews failed to become a holy nation worthy of emulation.[29]

There was also a more practical reason why, after the destruction of the Second Temple and especially after the loss of Beitar and

---

27. E.g., Shmaya and Avtalyon, Rabbi Meir, Rabbi Akiva, Onkelos, Ben Bag Bag, Ben Heh Heh.
28. *Contra Apionem*, 2.
29. Gittin 57. See too Netziv, *Haamek Davar*, Introduction to Genesis.

the death of Bar Kokhba, Jews put an end to aggressive conversion activities. Without a nation-state that creates its own legal system of civil rights and individual human freedoms, without the possibility of initiating unique societal structures, educational opportunities, economic policies and ethical standards of waging wars, conducting international affairs, dealing with minorities, and supporting the indigent and physically and emotionally challenged, the Jewish covenantal people cannot possibly bring to the world a formula which would inspire the nations to learn from us.

Specifically, without the power of a nation-state and an army providing protection and security, without international standing that provides an international Jewish voice to oppose totalitarian powers seeking world domination and to fight those espousing terrorism, the Jewish people could not begin to be leaders in the world arena. The most Jews in a Diaspora situation can hope for is that more powerful nations like the United States will allow us to "do our own thing," and not interfere with our internal life-cycle and calendar-mandated traditions.

RABBAN YOḤANAN BEN ZAKKAI VS. RABBI AKIVA

While the Temple was being destroyed by the Romans in 70 CE, Rabban Yoḥanan ben Zakkai asked Emperor Vespasian to grant him the small village of Yavneh and its rabbinic sages. While most of the sages were still waging battle against the Romans, Yoḥanan ben Zakkai decided that the Jews had no chance of victory against Rome, that we were engaging in a suicidal act of folly, and that, therefore, the biblical imperative from Leviticus 18:5, "You shall live by these My laws" (and not die by them) was to be the normative guiding principle. He conceded national sovereignty and the Temple for an opportunity for the Jewish people to live with Torah and the Sanhedrin under the protection of Rome.

Sixty-five years later, Rabbi Akiva said about the pragmatic Rabban Yoḥanan ben Zakkai, revered teacher of both of his (Rabbi Akiva's) teachers, Rabbi Eliezer ben Hyrcanus and Rabbi Yehoshua ben Hanania, that "God turns sages backwards and makes of their wisdom foolishness" (Is. 44:25). For Rabbi Akiva, a Judaism without a Holy Temple in the holy city of Jerusalem, a Judaism without a vision of teaching the world compassionate righteousness and moral justice, a Judaism without a mission of spreading the truth that every human being is created in the image of the Divine and is thereby free and inviolable, a Judaism without the message of a world of peace and security, is a Judaism bereft of God's word, a Judaism emptied of its soul, and a Judaism denuded of its central purpose.

And so Rabbi Akiva, strengthened by the religious warrior he believed to be the long-awaited Messiah, Bar Kokhba, waged a rebellion against Rome (132 CE). His guiding verse was, "Hear, Oh Israel, the Lord who is now our (Judean) God must become the United Lord (of the Universe)" and his commanding mandate was, "Better be killed than relinquish our Jewish mission."

After three and one-half years of battle, during which time Jerusalem was liberated by the Judeans and it almost seemed that their national sovereignty might be restored after all, General Julius Severus finally quelled the rebellion, demolishing fifty fortresses, destroying 985 villages, and killing 580,000 people in addition to those who died of hunger, disease, and fire. The Judeans' last stand took place at the fortress of Beitar in the Judean Desert, which fell on the 9th day of Av "in the fourth year of the liberation of Israel," wherein every last Judean was massacred and Bar Kokhba himself was slain.[30]

The rebellion failed, and a trauma for Judaism ensued. In the generation in exile after the rebellion, the rabbis formulated a doctrine of the "three oaths" taken by the Jewish people and the gentile nations: Jews would not rebel against the gentile nations by seeking national sovereignty; Jews would not "storm the ramparts to Jerusalem," i.e., not go to war against the power controlling the Land of Israel; and, in response, the nations would not persecute the Jewish people excessively.[31] With this policy, the Jews tragically left active covenantal history, along with the dream of redemption and bringing blessing to the world, and were forced to devote all of their energies to survival. The once proud Jewish nation had tragically become a scattered and dispersed people pushed from pillar to post in search of safe haven. The gentile nations who continually oppressed us and barred our return to

---

30. *Encyclopedia Judaica,* Jerusalem 1971 Keter, vol.4, Bar Kokhba, esp. p. 235.
31. Ketubbot 111a (based on Song of Songs Rabba).

our homeland became "the enemy." A prominent talmudic personality, Rabbi Shimon bar Yoḥai, taught: "It is a known law of nature that Esau (Rome and/or Christianity) hates Jacob."[32] Based on this reality of a hostile Roman and Christian world, Jews built higher and higher walls of separation between "us" and "them" – between their internal, rich but defenseless Jewish world, and the external, threatening gentile nations. The twin dangers seeking to blot out the memory of Israel from the earth were assimilation and anti-Semitism; we were forced to reject gentile culture and any meaningful social interaction with gentiles if we were to have any hope for survival.

THE SHOAH

The Holocaust during the Second World War was the final and ultimate game-changer. The third oath was no longer operable in any form or fashion; the nations proved by their actions (and non-actions) that even after the Jews surrendered their national sovereignty, they still had no right to live; there was no room at all in the world for Jews and their teaching of biblical morality, including the ideas that all humans are created in the divine image, have the right to freedom, and deserve to be treated with compassionate righteousness and moral justice. So, they murdered us actively by sending Jews to the gas chambers, and passively by silently watching the systematic genocide of our people. The only silver lining to be found was in the exceptional instances of righteous gentiles who risked their lives to save Jews, and the active fighting of the Allied Forces against the evil Nazi empire. The majority of the world was indifferent to the obliteration of the Jewish people.

From Auschwitz emerged the new reality of a world that had rejected the third oath, a world that had certainly persecuted us excessively, subjugated us unto death, a world that did not allow us even to live isolated on the sidelines of history. What emerged from Auschwitz was the Jewish understanding that *ein breira* – we have no choice. Rabban Yoḥanan ben Zakkai's option of living under foreign rulers who would allow us our unique Torah lifestyle was no longer an operative possibility. The only way

---

32. Gen. 33:4. Rashi ad loc., Genesis Rabba ad loc. Rabbi Shimon bar Yoḥai, was an implacable opponent of Roman culture, see Shabbat 33.

for Israel "to be" was for Israel to return to its original mission, to dare to return to national sovereignty in Jerusalem, to attempt to realize its calling to bring the nations of the world to compassionate righteousness, moral justice, and ethical monotheism, as in the vision of Rabbi Akiva.

My revered teacher, Rabbi Joseph B. Soloveitchik, distinguished between two different modes of individual and national life: at times, people and nations behave as *objects*, passively forced to accept what external fate brings upon them; at other times, they must become *subjects*, voluntarily daring to shape their own destinies.[33] For close to two thousand years of exile, the Jewish nation was an object, forced to accept paltry handouts of favors and to suffer the persecutions foisted upon them by the nations in whose midst they lived as strangers; their only refuge was their internal world of traditional celebrations of past triumphs, and their transcendent world of prayers to God.

Then came Hitler, who tragically taught us that Jews can no longer afford such a luxury. Either we become subjects as a nation-state on the world scene and attempt to fulfill our destiny as God's witnesses, or else we, as well as the Lord, will be obliterated in a nuclear explosion perpetrated by the heirs of Amalek. We have but one choice: Either become a sacred and powerful nation of priest-teachers to humanity or cease to exist altogether.

And we have learned another lesson from the Holocaust. While Lord Acton claimed that "power corrupts, and absolute power corrupts absolutely," we have learned that powerlessness is what corrupts most of all. The victim comes to believe the sub-human canards ascribed to him and, at the least, loses the energy and the ability to even dream about our biblical values of freedom for every human being, about our responsibility to attempt to perfect our imperfect world.

More than a decade ago, my wife and I saw a play entitled, *Edge of Night*. Its sub-plot involved a survivor of Auschwitz who had become

---

33. *"Kol Dodi Dofek,"* *Besod Hayaḥid Vehayaḥad* Pinḥas Peli, ed. (Orot, Jerusalem, 1976). He contrasted the Covenant of Fate, which God made with us in Egypt ("I shall take you for Me as a nation, [Ex. 6:7]), with the covenant God made at Sinai, which was a Covenant of Destiny. He links the Covenant at Sinai with the Third Covenant in Deuteronomy, seeing both of these as Covenants of Destiny, p. 368.

a wealthy and highly regarded businessman-philanthropist and a leader of the Jewish community of Melbourne, and who was very impressed with his own accomplishments. His son-in-law chooses the occasion of a large, extended-family Pesaḥ Seder to publicly confront his father-in-law with documents and pictures proving that he had been a hated Kapo – a Jew who assisted Nazis in Auschwitz. The arrogant father-in-law crumbled before our eyes: "Yes, it is true. That was/is me," he whispered, with tears rolling down his cheeks. "But there were no heroes in Auschwitz. There were only two types of prisoners: those who survived and those who didn't. Let none of you ever ask a survivor how he survived. It's none of your damn business, you who never knew the hell in which we were forced to use any means to remain alive."

ISRAEL BECOMES AN *EDAH*

After Auschwitz we chose to become subjects once again, significant players on the world scene as a proud nation-state, much the way we had been before, in the period of the biblical prophets. In the words of Rabbi Soloveitchik:

> Although a mortal human being may come into the world and leave the world as an "object," in between he has the challenge, and opportunity, to don the garb of creative Adam, to assume the Crown of Kingship and become God's partner in the perfection of the world; even more importantly, the Jewish nation can either act as a collective with its (only) goal that of protecting its (own) existence, or as a witness-congregation (*edah*) in which we fulfill our Abrahamic obligation to be God's witnesses and a beacon of light to the world.[34]

From this perspective, the Zionist dream is for Jews not merely to be a nation like all other nations, with Jewish criminals, prostitutes, and drug pushers. We have returned to history and this enables us to return to our historic mission to be "a light and beacon to the nations," "a kingdom of priest-teachers" to humanity, the purveyors of the blessings of ethical

---

34. Ibid., *Besod Hayaḥid Vehayaḥad*, pp. 337–338.

monotheism, of compassionate righteousness and moral justice from Zion to all the families of the earth.[35]

CHRISTIANS AS PARTNERS

This new reality must also bring about changes in our national psyche. We must cease seeing all gentiles as the evil descendants of Amalek. Today, we must begin to recognize the potential gentile Yitros (Jethros) who wish to be inspired by divine teachings.[36] We need to recognize the sea-change that has occurred in Christian teaching about Jews and Judaism since the Second Vatican Council's *Nostra Aetate* in 1965, and begin viewing many Christians as partners in bringing God's message of ethics, morality, and peace to three potential audiences: to those dissatisfied by an atheistic and materialistic understanding of the world, to those frightened by fanatic jihadists, and to those searching for an alternate spiritual approach to life.[37] We must remember that Judaism is a world religion which can bring blessing to all the families of the earth.

Indeed, even Maimonides, who was unalterably opposed to Christian theology, nevertheless admits that Christians picked up the mission of spreading God's word after the Jewish people found it impossible to do so and were even prohibited from doing so by the Hadrianic persecutions:

---

35. This definition of Zionism has enormous ramifications regarding how we view ourselves and how we determine religious and state policy. Many national decisions we take will reverberate throughout the world; and we must take responsibility for this global influence. In order for us to be a Kingdom of Priests and be credible witnesses to the world, decisions such as policies for organ transplants, treatment of foreign workers, and negotiating with terrorist regimes require that Israel develop creative applications to its religious and civil law and that its religio-legal discussions give proper consideration to the talmudic prescriptions of "for the sake of paths of peace" and "for the sake of perfection of the world" (Mishna Gittin, chapter 5).

36. Moses' father-in-law who befriended Moses and his people. Note that the Bible juxtaposes these two prototypical gentiles; cf. Amalek in Ex. 17:8–16 and Yitro in Ex. 18; Amalek is the gentile enemy who must be destroyed (either by physical annihilation or spiritual conversion) and Yitro is the gentile from whom we can learn and whom we can influence. Both passages follow each other directly!

37. See also the chapter in this book titled "Confrontation Revisited: Jewish-Christian Dialogue Today."

It is beyond the human mind to fathom the designs of the Creator, for our ways are not His ways and our thoughts are not His thoughts. All these matters relating to Jesus of Nazareth and the Ishmaelite who came after him, only serve to pave the way for King Messiah, and to prepare the entire world to worship together as one, as it is written, "For then will I turn to the peoples a pure language, that they may all call upon the name of the Lord to serve Him with one accord" (Zeph. 3:9). Thus, the Messianic hope, the Torah, and the commandments have become familiar topics of conversation among inhabitants of the far isles and (was brought) to many peoples uncircumcised of heart and flesh.[38]

Today, when most respected Christian theologians and churches reject replacement theology and the charge of deicide, and when a large portion of the Evangelical world is demonstrating its allegiance to the State of Israel, it behooves Jews to partner with Christians as children of Abraham – while not forgetting the essential theological and lifestyle differences between Christians and Jews – in bringing God's path of compassionate righteousness, moral justice, and universal peace to a world on the precipice of nuclear destruction.[39]

To be sure, the precondition for this is that we Jews must redouble our efforts to become a sacred nation, especially with regard to our interpersonal relations. Without doing so, we will forfeit the possibility – and the right – to be priest-teachers to the world. This means even greater fealty to Jewish law, while we remain mindful that we must readjust priorities and outlooks. There was a price that we paid for having largely forgotten our universal missions; our legal structure has taken an inward and problematic turn as a result of our long exile and isolation.

---

38. Maimonides, *Mishneh Torah*, Laws of Kings 11, 4 (unexpurgated version of Kafih).
39. See my "Covenant and Conversion: The United Mission to Redeem the World," and Eugene Korn, "The People Israel, Christianity and the Covenantal Responsibility to History," in *Covenant and Hope*, Robert W. Jenson and Eugene B. Korn eds. (Eerdmans, 2012), 99–128 and 145–172 respectively.

Allow me to suggest an analogy.[40] Our covenants with God were made in the context of Israel relating to humanity, with the expectation that all the world would be our arena, that our task would be to bring "blessings to all the families of the earth." As we have seen, the Third Covenant has the universal laws translated into the seventy languages of the nations of the world (Deut. 27:8; Sota 32a). In the Middle Ages, Maimonides understood this universal mandate by concluding his *magnum opus*, *Mishneh Torah*, with a description of the Messianic Age of peace and harmony throughout the world. It is apparent from this grand vision that for Maimonides, the entire purpose of Judaism is to bring about an improved and perfected human society throughout the world (*tikkun olam*).

As I indicated, however, after the rebellion against Rome, after our disillusionment with any possibility of immediate return to national sovereignty, the world fast became a frightening place for the displaced Jews; the gentile nations all became our enemies, threatening to destroy us together with our faith. So we formed a protective "hut" in which to take refuge, an exilic sukka which would service us year-round; yes, its "protective" walls were flimsy, wind-tossed and almost "virtual," its roof was made of vulnerable vegetation which couldn't even shade us from the hot sun or shelter us from a teeming rain, but from its open spaces we could still see the stars of salvation, and the traditional symbolic guests (*ushpizin*) would constantly remind us of our eternal values and our ultimate faith in redemption.

It must be admitted that the sukka-refuge served us well until this last period. As the Yiddish folk-song *A Sukkele* describes it, when the daughter enters the frail structure to tell her father that the sukka seems to be collapsing, she is told: "Don't be foolish, don't be upset, have no anxiety about the future. For two thousand years, our sukka has stood firm and secure!"

Indeed, we built stronger and higher fences around our hut, and even neglected to put in windows so that "they" couldn't see in and "we" couldn't see out. Jews feared that if there was too much communication

---

40. See above, p. 208 n. 14.

between us, the gentile nations might succeed in destroying us through physical annihilation or spiritual assimilation. At most, we ventured out of our huts to find work and whatever else we needed for material subsistence. And, in truth, those who did enter the outside world generally did assimilate.

It was, perhaps, inevitable that with time the most observant among us began to believe that our covenant with God was meant to apply only to the "hut" from its very beginning, that our religious obligation was to influence only those who lived inside of the hut. We forgot that the real meaning of the sukka was not the frail hut in the desert, but rather the cloud of God's glory, the desert sanctuary, which was meant to be a house of prayer for all nations and enable the Divine Presence to become manifest in our world.

We thought that only by living an isolated life would we be able to preserve our faith, our religious narrative, and our survival. Many of the most fervent Jews even reinterpreted the Torah's universalistic teachings and Jewish religious tradition to apply only to the stalwarts of the hut: that we need only to love other Jews and be concerned for their welfare, that the hut is the only universe in which God dwells and in which He is interested. The laws referring to the outside world and the necessity of sanctifying the earth and its material, economic, and political aspects were reinterpreted, theorized, and etherealized; the study of Torah in the hut became not a prescription for life, but a substitute for it, a mystical and theoretical Torah with little to do with the material, social, and historical realities of life and the world around us.[41] Indeed, we forget that the sukka hut of our desert *galut* was meant to morph into the Sukkat David (Temple) in Jerusalem and stretch out from there to encompass the entire world. The *haredim* among us see the hut of the desert as the ideal, and have blinded their eyes to the realities and possibilities of a Jewish state.

Today, the Jewish people have become empowered to leave their little hut and return to Zion, to history, and to the worldwide arena. This development is a great miracle from God, and a return to

---

41. The tragic irony of this interpretation may be seen in the words of the prophet Zechariah 14:16, who sees all nations eventually coming up to Jerusalem to celebrate Sukkot.

the original biblical covenantal ideal. We now are privileged to live under conditions under which we can begin to realize the Torah's pre-scribed path towards human redemption, the true goal of Zionism. It is a time of great challenge and opportunity. We pray that we will not be found lacking.

POSTSCRIPT: CENTRAL PARK WEST BANK
AND A PROMISE FULFILLED

I first came to Efrat, Israel in 1983 with a great deal of excitement. I had been the rabbi of Lincoln Square Synagogue in Manhattan, NY for nineteen years, and the community watched me leave with mixed feelings. Most of the leadership of the synagogue was certain that I'd be back in a year. I told the leaders that I was leaving the synagogue for *aliya* but they insisted that I was taking a year's leave of absence, and were careful to hire an interim rabbi for one year only. They pre-sented me with a *sefer Torah* (Torah scroll), which I brought with me when I came to Israel. That Torah has since been in almost every one of the thirty-seven synagogues in Efrat until each congregation received its own, after which I would loan it to the next newest syna-gogue. Soon I hope to be able to bring the *sefer Torah* back to my own, where I have an ark waiting for it – yet I'd rather see Efrat synagogues continue to multiply.

The time of my *aliya* was romantic and exciting – until I actu-ally arrived in Efrat and reality set in. The streets weren't paved, there were no private telephones – only one public telephone that generally didn't work – and during that first rough winter we were often without heat or electricity, or both. Additionally, within a few months I real-ized that I had no clear means of earning a livelihood for my wife and four children. The Efrat rabbinate was to be an elected position, and to qualify to teach I would have to pass special exams on all of Tal-mud and rabbinic response administered by the Chief Rabbinate. The only salary I received was to be the rabbi of the *beit sefer*, the elemen-tary school that had only two grades. That job paid only one-third of a modest full-time salary. During that first year I continued to be paid by Lincoln Square Synagogue for the one year leave of absence, but the year was quickly passing.

My family was young then, and I would wake up in the night in a cold sweat, thinking that I had made a terrible mistake. It was difficult for me to admit this even to my wife. We had sold our apartment in New York against the advice of the real estate experts, who told us to rent it because Manhattan real estate was on the threshold of a boom – precisely because we didn't want a convenient escape hatch for a return to America. So I was left with no satisfactory job in sight in Israel, and no place to return to in New York.

At that time we rented a modest apartment in Efrat, but we began to build a home in Efrat when we still lived in New York. The contractor had promised me that it wouldn't cost more than $100,000, which I could barely manage, but upon arrival in Israel we received a bill for $120,000 for the skeleton alone. The contractor then told me that the completion of the house would cost $300,000. There was no way that I could afford such a price, and while I had made certain that the families I brought to Efrat were protected by legal counsel, I had never gotten a lawyer for myself. I began to panic, beset by apparently insurmountable problems. My wife Vicki was much more steadfast in her commitment to *aliya* than I was. She said that even if she had to wash floors we had come to Israel to stay! If Efrat didn't work out, there would be someplace else that would, and I needn't worry. But I was still concerned and felt my responsibility for my family deeply.

In the midst of all these difficult thoughts came a knock on the door of our apartment. It was Yoni Ben-Ari, who was in charge of security of the young Efrat. "*Kevod HaRav*" ("Honored Rabbi"), he said, "take this Uzi. You have guard duty between two and six o'clock tomorrow morning." My wife whispered to my older children, "If Abba is protecting us, maybe we should spend the night in Jerusalem!"

Yoni understood from my wife's comment and by the way I looked at the Uzi that I didn't know what to do with it. "You don't know how to shoot an Uzi?" he asked. "Listen Yoni, I don't think I've ever killed a mosquito in my life. How should I know how to shoot an Uzi?" I responded. He took me out to what passes for a forest in Efrat, an area of trees that I affectionately call "Central Park West Bank," and in short order I learned how to fire the gun.

I had guard duty from 2:00 a.m. to 6:00 a.m. My partner was Yussi, a fine young man from Holland who still lives in Efrat with his family. We walked the outer periphery of inhabited Efrat, at that time in about fifteen minutes. He spoke a flawless Hebrew, and he had come to many of the classes that I began to teach as soon as I moved in. We walked in the stillness of the night, completing a full circle every quarter of an hour. He asked me about my life prior to *aliya*, and I, of course, described being the rabbi in Lincoln Square, and the head of a number of *yeshivot*. I described it nostalgically, even lovingly and yearningly – perhaps all the more so because I was beginning to think that maybe I'd made a mistake by burning my bridges behind me.

When I asked him about his life before *aliya*, he answered:

"Believe it or not, I was a Christian. I went to church every Sunday with my parents and brother. But on June 7, 1967, when I was a young high school boy, nineteen years ago, I read something that changed my life. It was on the front page of the Dutch daily newspaper, the magnificent story of the amazing Israeli victory in the Six Day War. From that moment on, I became invested and involved – body and soul – in the State of Israel. I responded viscerally to the victory, to the salvation from enemy danger and destruction, to the gutsiness of a nation that emerged from the ashes of the Holocaust to recreate itself. When I had to write a senior paper for graduation from high school, I wrote on the burgeoning State of Israel. There was a compulsory draft in Holland, and everyone who was in the Dutch army is expected to talk to a clergyman of some kind. I found myself filling out the form with the request to talk to a rabbi, and I began learning how to read Hebrew.

"At home, one weekend, I was learning the Hebrew text of Grace after Meals. The rabbi had given me a prayer book, and as I was trying to make out the words, I saw my mother mouthing the words in Hebrew. Shocked, I asked how she knew this prayer. She smiled and explained that before the war she had worked as an *au pair* for a religious Jewish family. This seemingly inconsequential piece of information strengthened my resolve to learn even more about Judaism.

"When the Yom Kippur War came, I volunteered to help on the farms. The kibbutz members were all fighting on the front lines, and the fruits and vegetables needed to be gathered and harvested. Three Christian friends and I were sent to a secular kibbutz in the Galilee. I was sparked and excited. I fell in love with the land, and I fell in love with the people. Since I have an ear for languages, I picked up Hebrew easily. I read a great deal about Jewish history, Jewish philosophy, and Judaism. I decided then that I wanted to keep kosher and keep the Sabbath. Someone from the kibbutz suggested that I go to a special *ulpan*, a school for converts. There was one in Kfar Etzion, a kibbutz right near what was to become Efrat. So I went there and joined the school for converts.

"After an intensive period of study, I was assigned a date to go to the ritual bath, the *mikve*, to immerse and to convert. The time had come then to tell my parents, since conversion was a momentous decision for a nineteen-year-old to make by himself. I called home and told my parents that I had an important matter to discuss with them. I announced that I wanted to convert to Judaism and live my life in Israel.

"My mother broke out in a cold sweat and fainted. After she revived, she told me, 'You don't have to convert. You are Jewish because I'm Jewish. I am the daughter of the *ḥazan,* the cantor, of the main synagogue in the town where my parents were murdered in front of my eyes. Before the Nazis shot my father dead, he cried out *Shema Yisrael Adonai Eloheinu Adonai Eḥad* (Hear O Israel, the Lord Our God the Lord is One), but to no avail. While being transported in the crowded, fetid cattle car to Thereienstadt, I felt that if one Holocaust was occurring, a second was even more likely, and I did not want my grandchildren or my great-grandchildren to suffer as I was suffering. I took an oath that if I ever go out of the hellhole, it would be as a Christian and not as a Jew.

"'I got out, I don't know how or why. I had no one to answer to because all of my relatives had been murdered in the Holocaust, so I became a Christian. Until now, the only person who knew my Jewish background was your father. But if you wish to rejoin the religion of my parents and their parents, may the God in whom I can no longer believe, bless you and keep you.'"

At that moment, during guard duty in the young city of Efrat in the stillness of the night, all I could think of was the four thousand year old promise that Moses gave to the Jewish people in God's name: Yes, you will be exiled. Yes, you will be persecuted. Yes, "you will be scattered to the ends of the heavens, for there the Lord your God will gather you, and from there will He take you up…and return you to the land of the your fathers" (Deut. 30:4–5).

The promise is being fulfilled now in our generation. Gone were all my questions. I understood that Israel was not only my destination, but was the destiny of my family and my people. I understood as deeply as anyone could understand that despite the unpaved streets, the lack of heat or electricity, the financial insecurity, I had come home.

My faith was strengthened in that momentous night of guard duty. As the prophets promised, the fulfillment of God's covenant, the security of the Jewish people, the final perfection of the world and world peace, will emanate from Israel and Jerusalem. The *coup de gras* came more recently when I performed the marriage ceremony of Avishai, Yussi's oldest son, a member of Israel's Air Force. As the young war hero stood before me, in army uniform and ritual fringes waving in the wind, I pictured Avishai's cantorial grandfather, looking down from his heavenly abode, smiling and declaring, "This is indeed the time of the coming of the Messiah."

If we've come this far since the Holocaust in realizing Moses' prophecy, we will surely come to the next stage and realize the vision of our prophets, that "From Zion shall come forth Torah and the word of the Lord from Jerusalem…. Nation will not lift up sword against nation and humanity will not learn war anymore" (Is. 2, Mic. 4).

Judaism and Democracy

INTRODUCTION

Conventional wisdom, especially among the religious and political right wing in Israel, has it that "Jewish democracy" is an oxymoron. Democracy, after all, is the rule of the people, whereas Judaism, as the expression of the will of the Divine, is properly defined as theocracy, or the rule of God.[1] I would argue that the very opposite is the case: that it is Judaism – the Bible, the Talmud and the Codes – that bequeathed to the world the foundation stones of democracy, the fundamental freedom of the individual to choose how to live his life, and by whom to be governed. Judaism bequeaths to man the ultimate existential freedom of having been created in the divine image and likeness; it negates the moral and religious sanction of any human being becoming a means for another's end, and of a totalitarian regime enslaving its citizens.

Our starting point for establishing this thesis will be the biblical account of the creation of the human being and of the Exodus from Egypt, and their ramifications. Thereafter, we shall show that Maimonides, the great religio-legal authority of the twelfth century, posits the voice of the people as the decisive, authoritative stamp of approval – paralleling and even outvoting the commanding voice of God in two central aspects of Jewish public life: the appointment of a ruler-king, and the revival of

---

1. Josephus was the first to use the term "theocracy" to describe the concept of government in Israel, in *Contra Apionem*, statement 2 (Hebrew edition, Tel Aviv 5699, p. 74).

the Great Jewish Court (Sanhedrin). Finally, turning our attention to historical precedent, we shall see that the overwhelming majority of European and occidental Jewish communities alike ordered their governance on the basis of representative democracy, as prescribed by the accepted Code of Jewish Law (*Shulḥan Arukh*).

IN THE DIVINE IMAGE: HUMAN FREEDOM
AS AN INALIENABLE RIGHT

The Torah opens with the divine creation of the world and – as the pinnacle of the genesis of life – the creation of the human being, on the sixth primordial day (epoch): "And God said, 'Let us make the human being in our image, like our likeness; and God created the human being in His image, in the image of God He created him, male and female He created them" (Gen. 1:26–27). What precisely is the definition of that "divine image" and "divine likeness" which clearly separates the human being qualitatively – in essence and not merely in relative sophistication – from the various living creatures which had been created earlier?

The Seforno (Rabbi Ovadia Seforno, 1475–1550, Italy) maintains that "in the divine image" indicates a separate intellectual endowment and eternal essence (similar to what we call the human "soul"), whereas "like our likeness" means that in the realm of his/her actions, the human being will resemble in part the Divine, and in part the "heavenly family" (angels, spiritual forces):

> On the one hand, humanity will act out of knowledge and cognition, but the "heavenly family" does not have the power of free choice, and in that sense humans may not be compared to [the heavenly family]; in that partial manner the human being may be compared to the Almighty, may He be blessed, who operates out of free choice. But the choice of the Almighty is always for the good, which is not the case regarding human freedom of choice... Hence the Bible states "*like* our likeness" rather than "*in* our likeness."[2]

---

2. Seforno on Gen. 1:26. See also Seforno on Lev. 13:47: "The human mind is called '*tzelem Elohim*' and the (human) power of choice is called '*demut Elohim*,' since the human being – alone among all other creations – is capable of freedom of choice."

The Seforno offers a magnificent insight into the essence of the human being, differentiating man from God as well as from His heavenly hosts. The human capacity to freely choose either good or evil distinguishes us from the "heavenly hosts" – creatures having no power of free choice whatsoever. They are functional rather than moral creations, bound to obey the divine will. God, on the other hand, can only (as it were) choose the good, which is the divine essence. Only the human being truly has the freedom to go either way, even to choose a path which God would not want him to choose – i.e., evil – because that very freedom of choice is what ultimately defines the essential human character in all of its majestic and malevolent uniqueness. That fundamental freedom of choice, which is the essential definition of humanity, dare not be denied by any mortal ruler, unless it be to secure the wellbeing and inviolability of other human beings. Hence, the right to choose one's governance becomes fundamental to one's biblically endowed humanity.

EXODUS

This perspective sheds new light on the critical message of the Exodus from Egypt – a seminal experience in the history of Israel which reverberates within every one of our sacred days as well as many of our regular ritual objects and activities.[3] The Exodus did not occur solely for God to "acquire" Israel as His special and exclusive possession, His first-born, His personal vineyard. Had this been the intent, God could have merely uplifted the Hebrews from Egypt "on the wings of eagles," much as a later generation of Israelis air-lifted the Beta Yisrael Jews of Ethiopia to Israel. In the biblical account, the miraculous deliverance of the nation of Israel is only half of the story; the other half describes the treatment meted out to Egypt, over the course of the ten plagues and especially at the Reed Sea. The message conveyed by this divine retribution, carried out before the eyes of the entire world, was one that encompassed all of humanity:

> The nations heard and they were frightened, trembling seized the residents of Philistine; the lords of Edom became

---

3. See Nahmanidies at the end of *Parashat Bo* (Ex. 13:16).

discombobulated, the strongmen of Moab were seized with shudders, all the inhabitants of Canaan melted down. May fright and fear fall upon them at the greatness of Your (divine) arm, may they become silent as stone... May the Lord rule forever. (Ex. 15:14–18)

Clearly, God's intent was to demonstrate not only to Israel but to the world – and especially to future world leaders – that the Lord of the Universe is the only Lord; that human rulers are also subservient to the one Lord, the God who demands freedom for every human being created in His image; and that the Lord of all beings will not allow totalitarian and enslaving despots to continue their immoral tyrannical control with impunity.

This understanding explains why the twice-repeated Decalogue, as well as our liturgical Friday evening Kiddush, offer what seem to be two disparate reasons for our observance of the Sabbath day: a remembrance of the creation of the world (Ex. 20:8–11, "For in six days the Lord made the heavens and the earth... and rested on the seventh day"), and a remembrance of the Exodus from Egypt (Deut. 5: 12–15, "in order that your gentile servant and hand-maiden may rest like you. And remember that you were a servant in the land of Egypt, and that the Lord your God brought you out from there").

Maimonides suggests that this dual basis for Shabbat reflects two axioms about God which the Jewish faith community must accept: 1) that God created the universe; 2) that He continues to actively guide world history, as demonstrated by the Exodus. Based on the discussion above, we may posit that the two concepts are even more profoundly interconnected. The Exodus from Egypt is a corollary which emanates *of necessity* from the creation of the human being in the divine image. If indeed the human being resembles God in his free choice, then he dare not be controlled or compromised by any mortal despot or earthly leader.[4]

---

4. See Y. Stavisky, "On Democracy in Judaism," *BeSedei Ḥemed* 39, 5–6 (5756) pp. 55–61, arguing that freedom of choice, and freedom in general, is cardinal to Judaism. Similarly, Rabbi Yaakov Ariel, "Freedom of Choice," in *From the Tents of Torah*, Kefar Darom, 5758, pp. 106–108.

THE COVENANT AT SINAI

The covenant between God and Israel, forged at the revelation at Sinai at the very dawn of our nationhood, defining Israel as a people set apart, a holy and moral nation, and giving content to our historic mission as a kingdom of priest-teachers to the world, is biblically described as a contractual two-way street, requiring the acceptance by the nation as the *condicio sine qua non* for our chosenness by God. Indeed, it is only after the Israelites declare that "everything which the Lord has spoken we shall do and we shall obey" does Moses sprinkle blood upon the nation, announcing, "Behold, the blood of the covenant which the Lord has made with you over these words" (Ex. 24:7–8), and that God summons Moses to the top of the mountain where He will give him the tablets of stone, the teaching (Torah) and the commandments (24:12).

Apparently, the consent of the nation – rather than the will of the Divine – is the real source of Israel's obligation to maintain the law. In this context it is worth noting that at various points in the future, whenever the nation enters a new phase of its history – as happened at the plains of Moab just prior to their entry into the Promised Land (Deut. 27), at the conclusion of the conquest and division of the land at the end of the Book of Joshua (Josh. 24), and when the nation returns to Judea after the Babylonian exile (Neh. 8) – the Bible calls for a renewed acceptance of the covenant on the part of the nation. And, at least according to Maimonides, the commandment of *hak'hel*, the gathering of the entire nation once every seven years, on the festival of Sukkot following the Sabbatical year, is fundamentally a re-affirmation by the nation of the covenant at Sinai.[5]

Joshua A. Berman, in a groundbreaking article "God's Alliance with Men" (*Azure*, Summer 5766/2006, pp. 79–113), goes one step further. He describes how, in ancient Mesopotamia and Ugarit, the earthly king – self-appointed by virtue of his prowess – "mimicked"

---

5. *Mishneh Torah*, Laws of Ḥagiga, chapter 3, esp. law 6; see also Rabbi Elḥanan Samet, *Studies in the Portions of the Week*, second series, Maliot Press, Deut. pp. 449–450.

the Heavenly King, enjoying supreme authority and power. This was not so in Israel. According to the plain biblical text, it is the nation – not God – who is responsible for appointing a king (Deut. 17:14–15). Saul, the first monarch, is anointed king against the backdrop of God's assurance to the prophet Samuel, "It is not you (Samuel) whom they have rejected; it is Me (God) they have rejected as King" (1 Sam. 8:4–22), i.e., when they, the nation, insisted upon appointing a monarch.

Even more to the point, Berman demonstrates that the model for our biblical covenant with God is the late Bronze Age suzerainty treaty, whereby the sovereign enters into a treaty with a subordinate sovereign, who freely accepts moral and legal obligation for the favor bestowed upon him by the greater sovereign. The difference between God's covenant with Israel and the suzerainty treaty is that in our case, it is not the king of Israel but rather the entire nation of Israel, every individual citizen, who assumes the role of the subordinate sovereign. (In Ugarit, the subordinate, chosen vassal for the treaty enjoys a favored status called "*sglt*" or *segulat*).

Berman's remarkable contribution to our understanding of democracy and freedom in the Bible is his demonstration of how the biblical notion of covenant empowers each individual within the Israelite polity to view himself as being accorded the status of king – subordinate only to the Divine King of the universe. This freely-given fealty of moral and ritual obligation is undertaken out of gratitude for God's beneficence in liberating and delivering Israel from Egypt; in return for this fealty, Israel will be forever protected by the Divine King. (The parallels are instructive. In Hittite treaties, for example, it was the subordinate king who was obligated to "come before the Majesty and look upon the face of His Majesty" in fealty; in Israel, every Israelite is required to present himself before God three times a year. See Ex. 23:17, 34:23; Deut. 16:16.)[6]

---

6. See also Ḥaim Hirschenson, *Malki BaKodesh*, Part III 5683, pp. 80–81, and Shimon Federbush, *Rule of Kingship in Israel*, Second Expanded Edition, Jerusalem 5633, pp. 33–34.

GOVERNMENTAL OR PUBLIC LEADERS
REQUIRE MAJORITY ACCEPTANCE

The Talmud (Berakhot 55a) cites an authoritative teaching of Rabbi Yitzhak which, although derived from the professional appointment of the architect-artisan of the desert Sanctuary, is formulated in much more general terms, applying to all positions of public office:

> A *parnas* (leader or custodian) may not be appointed to lead the congregation without the consent of the congregation, as it is written, "Look, you, the Lord has summoned by name Bezalel" (Ex. 35:30).
>
> The Holy One, Blessed Be He, said to Moses: Moses, is Bezalel worthy enough for you?
>
> (Moses) said to Him: Master of the Universe, if he is worthy enough for You, he is certainly worthy enough for me!
>
> (God) said to (Moses): Nevertheless, go and ask the same question of the Israelites.
>
> (Moses) went and said to the Israelites: Is Bezalel worthy enough for you?
>
> They said to (Moses): If he is worthy enough for the Holy One, Blessed Be He, and for you, is he not certainly worthy enough for us?!

Even though this particular appointment was a professional (artistic) rather than a governmental one, the standard of national acceptance – the consent of *vox populi* – seems to be considered necessary for an important public position. Hence, concerning the appointment of the seventy elders, whom God asked Moses to gather together for the nation (Num. 11:16), it was necessary that the nation ratify the selection made by their prophet and leader: "And God said to Moses: 'Gather for Me seventy men of the elders of Israel, whom you know to be elders and officers of the nation' – (meaning) you must know whether they will be clearly chosen before the nation." You – the nation – must ultimately make the choice by your ratification.[7]

---

7. *Sifrei Devei Rav, Behaalotekha* 92; see also Rabbi Shlomo Goren, "Democratic Elections in the Light of Halakha," *HaMa'alot LeShlomo - A Memorial to Rabbi Shlomo Goren*, Dr. Yitzhak Alfasi (ed.), 5756, p. 85. See also the discussion of *smikha* below.

MAIMONIDES AND THE RESUSCITATION OF *SMIKHA*:
A DEMOCRATIC ELECTION

Linked to the aforementioned necessity of public approbation for the original "seventy elders" – the first Great Sanhedrin of Israel – is the remarkably novel approach (*ḥiddush*) of Maimonides with regard to the resumption of the historical tradition of ordination (*smikha*), which he believed would be necessary in the period of national redemption, and which he predicates upon special elections:

> It seems to me that when there will be agreement by all the sages and their students to elevate one of their members to be above them and to establish him as their chief rabbi (*rosh*) – a procedure which must take place in the Land of Israel as we have explained – that individual will establish for himself an academy (*yeshiva*) and will thereby be (officially) ordained (*samukh*); afterwards he will (have the authority to) ordain anyone as he sees fit.
>
> If we do not posit such a procedure, the reestablishment of the Great Sanhedrin will forever be an impossibility, because at the very least each of its members must be officially ordained (*samukh*). And the Holy One, Blessed Be He, testifies that (the Great Sanhedrin) will be revived, as it is written (Is. 1:26): "And I shall restore your judges as they were at the beginning, and your counselors as they were originally, for only after that shall you (Jerusalem) be worthy of being called the City of Righteousness."
>
> And this will unquestionably occur when God will prepare the hearts of the people and they will increase their merits and their desire for God and for His Torah and shall magnify their righteousness before the coming of the Messiah.[8]

In another discussion of this issue,[9] Maimonides amends the nature of the electorate. While in his *Commentary on the Mishna* on Sanhedrin,

---

8. Maimonides, *Commentary on the Mishna*, Sanhedrin 1, 3.
9. Ibid., Bekhorot 4, 3.

as we have seen, he defines the electorate as "all the sages and their students," here, in his *Commentary on the Mishna* on Bekhorot, he writes as follows:

> We have already explained in the beginning of Sanhedrin that no one may be considered an authentic member of the (Great) *Beit Din* unless he had been properly ordained in the Land of Israel, whether he was ordained by one who had been ordained (in the chain of ordinations going back to God's ordination of Moses), *or whether the residents of the Land of Israel (benei Eretz Yisrael) agreed to appoint him Dean of the Yeshiva;* this is (possible) because the residents of the Land of Israel are the ones who are called a "congregation" (*kahal*) and the Holy One refers to them as the "entire congregation" (*kol hakahal*) even if they were only ten men. They (the leaders of Israel) do not seek other additional (candidates) who are in the Diaspora, as we have explained in Tractate Horayot.

Hence, the residents living in the Land of Israel vote on the chief authority (yeshiva dean, Sanhedrin prince), and that individual *ipso facto* is considered to have been ordained with the traditional ordination.[10]

---

10. Maimonides, in his *Mishneh Torah* Laws of Sanhedrin 4, 11 (published a little more than two decades after his *Commentary on the Mishna*) offers a slightly different formulation:

    > It appears to me that if all of the sages (*ḥakhamim*) who are (living) in Eretz Israel agree to appoint judges and to properly ordain them, they become properly ordained; they are authorized to judge those issues which entail levying fines and they are qualified to ordain others... And if there was present there (in Israel) at that time, one ordained individual who had been ordained by one who (himself) had been properly ordained, he does not require the consent of the entire electorate; he may judge and levy fines for everyone since he has been properly ordained by the Court. But the matter requires adjudication.

    It seems to me that the differences in Maimonides' definition of the electorate – "all the sages and their students," "the residents of the Land of Israel," "the sages who are (living) in Israel" – stems from the fact that those who lived in Israel in his day were all halakhic sages. Clearly, however, his bottom line position is that those who live in Israel vote on the one Dean of the Academy, the *primus inter pares* judge, who

As Maimonides takes pains to indicate, this entire possibility of the renewal of ordination by a public election is his own innovative thesis (*ḥiddush*): "It seems to me…; The matter appears to me…." Might it be possible for us to discover some Scriptural basis for this radical and perhaps even genius suggestion?

Our quest is hampered by the fact that at the root of the original ordination in Moses' generation – the actual authoritative source for it – was none other than the Almighty Himself. As the Torah records it (Num. 11:16–17):

> God said to Moses, "Assemble seventy of Israel's elders – the ones you know to be the people's elders and leaders. Bring them to the Communion Tent and let them stand there with you. When I bring down My essence and speak with you there, I will cause some of the (divine) Spirit which I gave over (from Myself) to you to emanate, and I shall place it upon them. They will then bear with you the burden of the nation; you will not have to bear it alone."

The Talmud (Sanhedrin 17a) supports the above interpretation of the term *veatzalti* (translated here as, "I shall cause to emanate").

---

will then be the authoritative reviver of the original ordination which the Almighty bestowed upon Moses.

See also Rabbi Fishman-Maimon, *The Renewal of Ordination in our Renewed State*, Jerusalem 1951, citing the dispute which erupted in sixteenth-century Safed and spread throughout the Jewish world over the election of Rabbi Yaakov Bei Rav and the ordination he bestowed upon Rabbi Yosef Karo, author of the *Shulḥan Arukh*. Rabbi Levi ibn Habib of Jerusalem denied the validity of the ordination, first because Maimonides himself seems to have back-tracked from his clearly-stated position of ordination via vote in his *Mishneh Torah*, with his qualifier, "But the matter requires adjudication," and second, because he felt that Safed should not trump Jerusalem by recreating the Sanhedrin in the city of the "Holy Ari" (Rabbi Isaac Luria) rather than within the city of King David, forerunner of the Messiah. Rabbi Maimon proves, on the basis of a photocopy of a handwritten note by Maimonides himself to a passage from his *Guide for the Perplexed* (which he authored towards the end of his life), that shortly before his death, Maimonides still maintained the possibility of renewing ordination by general election.

The Talmud says: "And I shall cause some of the (divine) spirit…to emanate" – (meaning) the Divine Presence shall dwell upon them.

Nahmanides, in his *Commentary on the Torah* (ad loc.), specifically explains:

> And those who translate from foreign languages say that *atzilut* connotes the emanation of some power from the divine powers which spread out upon the created being…it is an expression of extension…and it says further concerning extension, that the Giver continues to be with him (the recipient) as part of that (emanation) which was given, and it remains with him (the recipient).

In the same vein, Rashi adds the following analogy to explain the phrase in question:

> And I will cause some of the (divine) Spirit which I gave over (from Myself) to you to emanate, and I shall place it upon them" (ad loc.). To what may Moses be compared at that time? To a candle which is placed near a candelabrum; all of the lights of the candelabrum are kindled from the one candle, yet no light at all is missing from the candle. (*Sifrei*, ad loc.)

Hence, it is the divine power which remains the source of all of the ordinations!

The same idea is continued in Moses' ordination of Joshua (Num. 27:15–20):

> And Moses spoke to the Lord, saying, "Let the Lord God of spiritual powers over all flesh appoint an individual over the witness-community (*edah*)" …And the Lord said to Moses, "Take for yourself Joshua the son of Nun, an individual with divine spirit within him, and ordain him with your hand upon him… And you shall give from your majestic splendor (*hod*) upon him, in order that the entire witness-community of the Children of Israel may hear."

Rashi explains the phrase, "And you shall give from your majestic splendor (*hod*) upon him": "This refers to the radiance emanating from his (Moses') facial skin" (ad loc. 20). He also notes that Moses gives "*from* (i.e., some of)" his majestic splendor – not all of it: "Moses' face was like the sun; Joshua's face was like the moon." The *Siftei Ḥakhamim* comments:

> Some understand this as an allusion to the fact that the sun takes its light from the Holy One, Blessed Be He, while the moon takes its light from the sun. Similarly, Moses received the radiance emanating from his facial skin from the Holy One, Blessed Be He, while Joshua took his from Moses.

And so our query is even stronger than before! How can we possibly reactivate a divine spiritual gift by means of a public election?

I believe that the key to a proper understanding of Maimonides' novel proposal for the national resumption of ordination by means of an election by the majority of the citizenry of Israel is to be found in the biblical identity between the witness-congregation of Israel and the Great Sanhedrin:

> If the entire witness-congregation of Israel shall sin inadvertently as a result of a matter (of traditional law) having been hidden from the eyes of the congregation (*kahal*), and they violate one of the prohibitory commandments of the Lord, incurring guilt, then when the violation that they have committed becomes known, the congregation (*kahal*) must bring a young bull as a sin offering, presenting it before the Communion Tent.
>
> And the elders of the witness-congregation (*edah*) shall lay their hands (*samkhu – smikhat yadayim*) on the bull's head before the Lord, and the bull shall be slaughtered before the Lord. (Lev. 4:13–16)

Throughout this biblical passage, the Hebrew words for the elders of the witness-congregation (*edah*) and the gathered congregation (*kahal*) are used as synonyms for the Great Sanhedrin, the seventy-one judges who make the highest judicial decisions. This is how Rashi understands these terms, based on the Midrash (Torat Kohanim 4, 241). And, since *kahal*, the gathered congregation, refers only to the congregation in the Land of Israel (Horayot 3a), the electorate for the resumption of the initial ordination consists only of those in Israel – just as the traditional ordination can only be given in Israel.

We find the same identity between witness-congregation and Sanhedrin in the talmudic interpretation (Yoma 73b) of the biblical verse describing Moses' ordination of Joshua (Num. 27:22–23):

> And Moses did (to Joshua) that which the Lord commanded him: He took Joshua and he placed him in front of Elazar the Priest and in front of the entire witness-congregation. He then laid his hands upon him.
>
> Rabbi Abahu declares…"the entire witness-congregation refers to the Sanhedrin."

Hence, the witness-congregation (*edah*) as well as the gathered congregation (*kahal*) are midrashically identified with the Sanhedrin. In more theological terms, this may be understood to mean that just as the will of the Divine is believed to be expressed through the decisions of the Sanhedrin, so, too, the will of the Divine is expressed through the decisions of the Jewish community in Israel – the only Jewish community with historical continuity extending from the Cave of the Couples in Hebron to the Third Temple in Jerusalem. And from this perspective it is fascinating to note that within the mystical *sefirot* of Kabbala, the tenth and final emanation is – at one and the same time – *Malkhut* (Kingship), *Shekhina* (Divine Presence), and *Knesset Yisrael* (the historic nation of Israel). This certainly opens the door to a clear identity between God and the community of historic Israel: the will of Israel becomes *ipso facto* the will of God. And so if, in prior generations, there was faith in the divine rights of kings, the Jewish perspective may well be recognition of the divine right of the democratic decisions of the Israelites!

MAIMONIDES AND THE DEMOCRATIC ELECTIONS OF KINGS

From a biblical perspective, the very acceptance of a monarch in Israel required the consent of the nation – or at least the majority of the nation.[11] The text is fairly ambiguous in its introductory formulation (Deut. 17:14–21):

> When you come to the land that the Lord your God is giving you, so that you have occupied it and settled it, and you will say, "We would like to appoint a king, just like the nations roundabout," you ought then appoint a king from among your brethren.

Whether the verses are describing an optional potential situation ("*if* you will say etc.") or a mandatory obligation ("then you *must* say etc.") is subject to dispute among the commentaries.[12] If the Torah seems tentative as to whether a monarchy is necessary – or, indeed, the optimal system of government – it is definitive about the fact that monarchic power is not absolute, but is rather to be limited by God's commandments. Indeed, the king is also to be limited with regard to the usual materialistic accoutrements of power such as horses, women, and wealth, and cannot take a step (literally) without having a copy of the Torah with him, at all times (ibid.).

Furthermore, the Torah is also definite about the need for the people's assent: the people must want the king. Not only the establishment of a monarchy, but even the very identity of the king, requires the consent of the people. The absence of such public approbation caused the prophet Samuel to anoint King Saul – the first king of Israel – twice (1 Sam. 11:14, Rashi ad loc., "the first time, there were those who opposed;

---

11. The principle that "a majority is always considered sufficient when the entire quantity is required" (*rubo kekulo*) is normative halakha. In fact, the Talmud (Avoda Zara 36b) provides a biblical source for this principle from Malachi 3:9, "the entire nation."

12. Those who see the establishment of a monarchy as mandatory include Maimonides (*Mishneh Torah*, Laws of Kings 1, 1), Nahmanides ad loc., *Derashot HaRan II*. Those who view it as a voluntary possibility include Rabbi Saadia Gaon, Ibn Ezra, Seforno, and Don Yitzḥak Abrabanel (ad loc.). See also Judges 8:22, where Gideon the Judge refuses the people's request that he become their ruler and create a monarchic dynasty with the theological argument, "I shall not rule over you, and my son shall not rule over you; God must rule over you." See too the discussion of the pros and cons of a monarchy in Sanhedrin 20b.

the second time, there was unanimous consent), and caused David to be anointed three times (see Radak to II Sam. 2:4; 5:3).[13]

Maimonides begins his *Mishneh Torah* Laws of Kings (1:1–3) with the following clearly-defined framework:

> Three commandments were commanded to Israel at the time of their entry into the (Promised) Land: to appoint for themselves a king...to destroy the seed of Amalek...and to construct a Holy Temple...They are permitted to initially establish a king only at the behest of the High Court of Seventy Elders and at the behest of a prophet.

We have already seen that the members of the Sanhedrin themselves must be acceptable to the nation by biblical mandate,[14] so that it is fairly evident that the six names chosen from each tribe to comprise the Great Sanhedrin (as suggested by Sanhedrin 17a) were elected by the tribes, and perhaps had even been previously tested in positions of tribal authority.[15]

Hence, the publicly elected judges of the Sanhedrin had the democratic right to vote upon the king of Israel. To take this a step further, as we attempted to demonstrate in the previous section, in the absence of a Sanhedrin the *vox populi* rightfully assumes the authority to decide upon those matters which were previously within the Sanhedrin's purview, and therefore could naturally assume the right to elect a king or prime minister.

The consistency of Maimonides' position concerning the voice of the people as a fitting substitute for the decision of the Sanhedrin is again evident in the case of the choosing of a monarch. In his "Interpretations

---

13. See the discussions in the Jerusalem Talmud (Rosh HaShana 1, 1; Horayot 3, 2 and *Midrash Shmuel*, Buber, 26, 5) concerning the status of King David during the time of Absalom's rebellion, as well as Responsa *Avnei Nezer, Yoreh De'ah*, siman 312; *Tzitz Eliezer*, Part 12, siman 64. See also the talmudic treatment of King David's discussion with Abigail, Megilla 14b.

14. Section V, note 6 (above).

15. See *Midrash Yalkut Shimoni* on Num. 11:16, chapter 736, and Rabbi Goren, ibid., p. 87.

to the Mishna" on Tractate Keritot (chapter 1, mishna 1), he writes as
follows:

> The biblical text (Deut. 17:20) teaches that kingship is an inheri-
> tance to the sons. But if there should arise a disagreement or argu-
> ment among the scions of David as to which one of them will
> reign – this one or that one – and afterwards there is agreement
> by all on one of them, or the majority of the nation is drawn to
> endorse one candidate (by popular election), or the Sanhedrin
> appoints one, or a prophet or a High Priest chooses – by which-
> ever manner is found to be most appropriate to resume the mon-
> archy in the hands of one (individual) – that individual is to be
> anointed by the special anointing oil.

Based on this, Rabbenu David ben Zimra, a universally accepted decisor
and chief rabbi of Egypt in the sixteenth century, writes in his Commentary to the *Mishneh Torah* of Maimonides, "an (authoritative) king is one
who rules either by the appointment of a prophet or one who has been
accepted by all of Israel" (Ridbaz, Commentary to Laws of Kings 3, 8).

Rabbi Avraham Yitzḥak HaKohen Kook, first chief rabbi of Israel
and one of the most significant philosophers and foremost decisors of
Jewish law in the twentieth century, strongly confirms democratic elections as a legitimate procedure for appointing a ruler who would thereby
assume the status of monarch:

> If Israel establishes a king (by electoral consent of the nation,
> even) without (divine guidance through) a prophet, he neverthe-
> less has the status of king with regard to all the laws of kingship....
> And aside from that, it would seem that at a time when there is no
> king, since the laws of kingship are involved in whatever is neces-
> sary for the general state of the nation, the meritorious author-
> ity of these laws (of kingship) are returned to the nation entire.
>
> And it seems especially true that any judge who rises (to
> rule) in Israel has the status of a king regarding several of the laws of
> kingship, and especially whatever is necessary for the leadership of
> the entire (nation). (*Mishpat Kohen*, Responsum 144, chapters 1–15)

The Tosefta (Bava Metzia 11, 23) set down the basic principle in this regard in the early tannaitic period:

> The residents of a city may force one another (by majority vote) to build a synagogue, to acquire a Torah scroll and a set of the Prophetic Writings. The residents of the city may determine the proper market price, the weights and measures, and the pay for laborers.

The city was run by "Seven Good People of the City" who were elected by a majority of the residents and – if the process was not too unwieldy – would generally make their decisions on the basis of a vote of the majority of the townspeople. The Code of Jewish Law (*Ḥoshen Mishpat* 2, 1) goes so far as to award this city council a status equivalent to that of the Great Court in Jerusalem:

> And so is the custom everywhere: the Good People of their City are like the Great Court (*Beit Din HaGadol*): they may levy floggings, punishments (such as fines), and whatever property they declare ownerless becomes ownerless, in accordance with the custom.

Hence, this city council, elected by a democratic majority, is authorized not only to legislate laws for the wellbeing of the city and its townspeople, but also to enforce their decisions by means of corporal punishments (flogging), incarceration, and confiscation of property and/or funds from problematic citizens. As far as the electorate is concerned, every

---

90, pp. 283–290); Prof. Eliav Schochetman, "*Hakarat HaHalakha Be'ḥukkei Medinat Yisrael*," *Shenaton HaMishpat HaIvri* 16–17 (5750–5751), pp. 417–500; Prof. David Elazar, "*HaKehilla MeReshita Ve'ad Sof Haldan HaModerni*," *Am VaEda – HaMassoret HaMedinit HaYehudit VeHashlakhoteiha LeYameinu*, Jerusalem 5751, pp. 183–185; Prof. Aviezer Ravitzky, "*Mishpat HaMelekh: Hagut Politit Be'shalhei Yemei HaBenayim*," *Al Daat HaMakom*, Jerusalem 5751, pp. 105–128; Prof. Yaakov Blidstein, *Ekronot Mediniim BeMishnat HaRambam*, Ramat Gan 5753, p. 115; Rabbi Dr. D. Guttenmacher, "*Pesika Hilkhatit Tzibburit U'Mussag HaDemokratia*," *Higayon* 3 (5756).

tax-paying resident has the right to vote; the general view of the decisors is that the minority dissenters may be forced to go along with the majority (*Ḥoshen Mishpat* 163:1 esp. Rema).[20]

---

20. Rabbenu Tam insists that the individual may not be forced to go along with the majority unless he committed himself to do so at the outset (Bava Kama 8b). See also Mordecai to Bava Kama, siman 179; Responsa of Rabbi Meir of Rothenberg, Part IV (Prague edition), siman 968; *Talmudic Encyclopedia*, entry "Tovei HaIr," vol. 19, pp. 72–99; Rabbi Yisrael Spitzansky, *HaTakkanot BeYisrael*, vol. IV, Introduction, pp. 17–24.

However, the overwhelming view is that the minority may be forced to go along with the majority. Certainly, if the democratic majority automatically operates with the power of the Great Court, then the minority must concede to it. This is the view of the Rashba (Responsa, Part V, siman 126):

"Wherever an enactment is authorized with the agreement of the residents of the city, for any matter which has the agreement of the majority and was enacted and agreed upon by majority consent, there is no need to be concerned about a minority opinion; the majority of each city vis-à-vis the minority is like the Great Court vis-à-vis individual laws of the Jewish people: once the Great Court decreed, their decree stands and any violator must be punished."

It must be emphasized that the Rashba is speaking about an enactment which enjoys the support of the majority and which treats every citizen fairly before the law. See Rashba part V, siman 178.

The Rosh (Rabbenu Asher) agrees (Responsa, Rule 6, siman 5):

Know than any matter which has the majority behind it falls under the biblical category of "the majority must decide"... and the minority must fulfill whatever is agreed upon by the majority. If this were not to be the case, no congregation would ever be able to decide anything, since the minority could always overturn their decisions.

Rabbenu Gershon Meor HaGola upholds the authority for an enactment of the congregation on the basis of a majority vote on the principle that "whatever a *beit din* declares ownerless, is ownerless" (either from Ezra 10:8, where Ezra, the ministers, and the elders confiscated the property of any Israelite who refused to send away his gentile wife, or from Joshua 19:51 where the Land of Israel was divided and apportioned by Joshua and the heads of the tribes; see Yevamot 89b). He writes (Responsum 67, Heidelberg Edition p. 157): "And if you will ask, When do we correctly invoke the principle that 'Whatever a court declares ownerless, is ownerless'? For that applies only when we are dealing with an important court like that of Shammai and Hillel, but nowadays that is not the case, and we dare not invoke such a rule. (But the answer is that) it is impossible to say such a thing. The Talmud states (Rosh HaShana 25a), "Even the simplest lightweight who is appointed judge (*parnas*) over the congregation (by a majority vote) is like a giant of the giants (Yiftaḥ in his generation is like Samuel in his generation). Hence the conduct of the congregations (with their "Seven Good People of the City") is proper; their decrees are decrees and their actions are actions."

The first chief rabbi of the State of Israel, Rabbi Dr. Yitzḥak HaLevi Herzog, understood that the new Jewish state required a democratic form of government with Knesset members elected by the people. He awarded Israel's democratic system his halakhic imprimatur based on the precedent of the medieval system of the "Seven Good People of the City."[21]

Rabbi Shaul Yisraeli likewise pointed to the "Seven Good People of the City" as a precedent for our democratic form of government. He added the idea that the "residents of the city" discussed in the Talmud and the Codes comprise a partnership of city ownership, with the "Seven Good People" whom they elect serving as their representatives. This city council, or national Knesset, if you will, become the elected agents of the population of the city, invested with the power to make decisions on behalf of the people, who elected them as their agents – since an agent appointed by an individual is considered to represent the individual himself.[22]

There are many issues which remain to be clarified if we seek to broaden the parameters of this study. To what extent is it necessary that the elected representatives, corresponding to the "Seven Good People," be God-fearing and Torah-observant Jews? If the model is the Great Court, electing a secular Jew might be problematic, whereas if the relationship is viewed as a partnership, religiosity would probably not be a factor. We have not explored here the fascinating possibilities offered by the model of Rabbenu Nissim of Gerona (*Derashiot HaRan, derasha* 11), who raises the idea of a secular structure of government for the social betterment of society, separate from and alongside of the

---

The Maharam of Rothenburg (Responsa, siman 230) writes, "Just like the great decisors of the generation always and everywhere had the authority to declare property ownerless, in order to legislate for the communal good and enact enactments, so too the Good People of the City have that same authority, since all (i.e., the majority of) the residents of the city rely upon them."

21. See his articles, "Theocracy and Democracy" and "The Authority of Torah in the State of Israel" in his book *A Constitution for Israel in Accordance with the Torah* (ed. A. Warhaftig), Jerusalem 5749, vol. 1.

22. The concept that "the agent of an individual assumes the rights of that individual" is normative halakha (Mishna Berakhot 5:5; Kiddushin 41b).

religious structure for ritual issues. Nor have we dealt with the question of non-Jews in the State of Israel and how to provide them, too, with a share in governance and a sense of true partnership in decision-making. Here again there are precedents in the biblical concept of *ger toshav* – a category which certainly deserves a lengthy study in itself. Suffice it to say that in this article I have attempted, at the very least, to show that a government of the people, by the people, and for the people is not at all foreign to Jewish thought.

The Torah of Mother Rebecca: *Yeshivot Hesder*

T he epoch of the patriarchs and matriarchs, at the matrix of our nation's origins, is one of the most fascinating in all of Jewish history. All the more amazing is how tales of flesh and blood creatures – husbands and wives, parents and children, brothers and sisters – have engaged our interest for thousands of years, stimulating the intellect as well as the imagination. No matter how often we read these stories, there are always new insights to be gained – not only into the lives of the very human patriarchs and matriarchs, but into our own lives as well.

In this article, I would like to concentrate on the central matriarch, Rebecca, who is central not merely because she was chronologically centered between Sarah, Rachel, and Leah, but because her life, her decisions, and her insights guide us to this day in our return to Israel, the national Jewish homeland.

What makes Rebecca unique?

Rebecca's arranged marriage is the most traditional one related in the Book of Genesis – Abraham is introduced by the Bible together with his wife Sarah, and Jacob conducts an unconventional courtship based on love at first sight – but paradoxically, Rebecca proves to be the most untraditional of wives; she circumvents the will of her husband,

Isaac, in order to ensure that their younger son Jacob, instead of the older Esau, receives the birthright.

Rebecca's actions provide the precedent for women throughout the ages to challenge their husbands – or any other figure of authority. In this sense, she is a modern woman whose defiance is not only exonerated by the Torah but blessed, since her actions become the model of the matriarch as visionary.

At first glance, it seems strange and blatantly unethical that Rebecca sends her son Jacob into her husband Isaac's tent with the specific purpose of acquiring the blessing under false pretenses. Is it ethical to deceive one's husband, and to use one's son as the tool of deception? Is this the Jewish way? Anyone who reads this text must ask himself this question. Indeed, there are those who use these events as a pretext for rejecting all of Judaism, or at least for rejecting the patriarchs and matriarchs as viable role models.

Rebecca's behavior raises practical questions, too: Did she really believe that Jacob could get away with this ruse? What is the value of a blessing received under false pretense? And of what use is a birthright to someone who is dead? Knowing her son Esau as she did, surely Rebecca could have anticipated that if Jacob succeeded in deceiving his father, Esau would find out and respond the only way he knew how – with violence. In the best scenario, Jacob would be forced to become a fugitive. In the worst, he would be murdered. If Rebecca was truly a visionary, how could she have willingly put her son in this dangerous position?

Let us review the ancient biblical narrative, and hopefully a portrait of Rebecca will emerge which will answer these questions as well as address some contemporary issues.

The Torah records that the founder of our faith, Abraham, mourned for his beloved Sarah and purchased a burial place for her in Hebron (the Cave of Machpela). Abraham then commanded his trusted servant, identified by the Midrash as Eliezer, to find a wife for his son and heir Isaac, but with one condition: "Swear by the Lord…that you shall not take a wife for my son from the daughters of the Canaanites, among whom I dwell. Rather you shall go to my country, and to my kindred" (Gen. 24:3–4).

Although Abraham would live another forty-five years after Sarah's death, even taking another wife and having more children, the Torah is only concerned with one aspect of the last stage of Abraham's life – the mission he assigned to Eliezer, to find Isaac a suitable wife from a proper family. There is no doubt that Abraham profoundly appreciated the importance of a good wife. From the Torah, it seems that following Sarah's death, Abraham's role in world leadership came to an abrupt end.

What it boils down to is that everything the founder of ethical monotheism lived for would be for naught if he didn't find the right match for Isaac. In a sense, this challenge was the most important one of Abraham's life. Abraham turned for assistance to Eliezer, his trusted servant. Eliezer was the perfect person for the job, as exemplified by the fact that on the journey to Haran his own personal name is never used. Instead, he is referred to as the *eved* – servant, or *ish* – man, an indication that he subjugated his individual identity to one single task: fulfilling his master Abraham's will to find a mate for Isaac.

Upon Eliezer's departure, the text tells us: "The servant took ten camels of the camels of his master, and departed, for all the goods of his master were in his hands" (Gen. 24:10). The master commentator Rashi explains that the phrase "all the goods of his master were in his hands" indicates that Eliezer had a "blank check" from Abraham to do whatever was necessary to bring back the right woman. This clearly indicates how important the marriage was to Abraham. Thus, even before Rebecca appears on the scene, the reader is aware of how much rides on Eliezer's choice.

The phrase "all the goods of his master were in his hands" can also be interpreted literally, meaning that whatever Abraham had discovered, whatever Torah he had learned and disseminated, was now in the hands of Eliezer. Eliezer's choice would either guarantee or destroy the future of Abraham's creed. Apparently, Eliezer was far more than a servant; he was an important personage (*ish*) completely devoid of self-interest. In a way, Eliezer might have had the clearest sense of who would be the right woman for Isaac since his vision was objective, while a father's vision might be clouded by subjectivity.

We have much to learn from Eliezer's criterion for a bride. He believed, as he probably learned from Abraham, that

ḥesed – loving-kindness – is the most important quality in a person:
"Oh God … be with me today and grant a favor to my master Abraham.
I am standing here by the well, and the daughters of the townsmen are
coming out to draw water. If I say to a girl, 'Tip over your jug and let me
have a drink,' and she replies, 'Drink, and I will also water your camels,'
she will be the one whom You have designated for Your servant Isaac"
(Gen. 24:12–14).

The Torah records that even before Eliezer finished speaking,
Rebecca, a member of the family from which Eliezer was meant to choose
a bride, appeared at the well. The Torah also records that Rebecca was
beautiful. Many marriages begin (and therefore also end) with physical
charm and the right family connections, but Eliezer introduced the most
crucial element into the equation, which is character.

In verse 17 of chapter 24 we read that "the servant ran to meet her"
(*vayaratz ha'eved likrata*) and asked for a drink of water, just as he had
arranged with God. Rebecca replied, "Drink, my lord," a phrase which
should raise our antennae because there is all the reason to believe that
Rebecca would recognize a servant when she saw one; nevertheless, she
addressed Abraham's servant as "lord" – either because she immediately
recognized his inherent character, or as further indication of her compassion. And she rushed to give him to drink.

Only after Eliezer finished drinking did Rebecca offer to draw
fresh water for his camels. The commentators explain that Rebecca drew
fresh water for the camels so as not to give the beasts to drink from the
same water Eliezer drank, which might be disrespectful. The biblical
prose reinforces this distinction by using different verbs for virtually the
same action performed by Rebecca. The verb used to describe Rebecca's
act of offering her pitcher to Eliezer is *lehashkot* (to give drink), but the
verb used when Rebecca waters the camels is *lish'ov* (to draw water).
Sensitive Rebecca showed concern for the camels, but was careful to
distinguish between brute beast and human being.

When Eliezer saw how quickly his criterion was met, "the man
took a golden earring of half a shekel's weight and two gold bracelets
weighing ten gold shekels" (Gen. 24:22). Rashi interprets the permu-
tation of the numbers here as a hint to the Two Tablets and the Ten
Commandments. In other words, in the act of righteousness performed

by Rebecca, we find a foreshadowing of the Torah itself. And it turns out – as we shall see – that one of the major reasons why the Jewish people emerge as a nation able to receive the Torah is as a result of Rebecca's compassionate character, indomitable will and vision.

In fact, Rebecca's life is Torah. Since Abraham and Sarah were not yet Jewish when they got married, Rebecca and Isaac actually had the first Jewish marriage in history, and specific rules of conduct for Jewish weddings were learned from their betrothal – for example, the woman's right to accept or reject a match.

The specific characteristics of an ideal Jewish wife emerge from the following verse: "And Isaac brought her into his mother Sarah's tent, and took Rebecca and she became his wife, and he loved her, and Isaac was comforted after his mother's death" (Gen. 24:67). Note the order: first Isaac and Rebecca were married, and afterwards he loved her. This is critical. Love before marriage has more to do with sexual anticipation than a feeling forged from years of living together and working toward common goals. Isaac and Rebecca are examples of the love which expresses the value of time over the power of chemistry. Their lives demonstrate that in a true and ideal relationship, love will grow and not dim with the passage of time.

The verse concludes by telling us that Rebecca brought Isaac consolation for the loss of his mother. Rashi cites the Midrash that as long as Sarah was alive, three miraculous phenomena were apparent in her tent: a candle remained lit from Friday eve to Friday eve, there was a special blessing in the dough, and a cloud was "tied" to the tent. When Sarah died, all three phenomena ceased...until Rebecca came into Isaac's life.

These three miracles are linked to the three commandments specifically given to the Jewish woman. The lit candle presages the mitzva of *hadlakat nerot*, in which the Jewish woman ushers in the Sabbath by kindling lights – the lights of warmth and love, the lights of harmony and sanctity, the light of *shalom bayit* – a peaceful home.

The second phenomenon which Rebecca's presence revived was the blessing in the dough. Since baking was usually the woman's responsibility, she was generally also responsible for fulfilling the commandment of Hallah – the removal of a certain amount of dough for the *kohen*, the priest. This mitzva serves as a reminder that our bread is not our own, but rather belongs to God, who commands us to share our material possessions with those who are less fortunate. Just as the candles symbolize *shalom bayit*, the Hallah symbolizes opening one's home to strangers to share one's bread. With the arrival of Rebecca, Sarah's tent was once again open to all.

The cloud attached to the tent symbolizes the presence of God, for later on, during the Israelites' travels in the desert, God's presence was attested to by an accompanying cloud. How did God's presence return to Sarah's tent? In the form of the laws of *taharat ha'mishpaḥa*, or family purity. When God is brought into the bedroom and His presence attends the most intimate moments between husband and wife, then love and progeny are blessed with divine purity.

These three wondrous traits – peacefulness, hospitality, and purity – returned to Sarah's tent when Rebecca came to live there as Isaac's wife. But the comfort Isaac felt did not last. The marriage, like that of Isaac's parents, was not immediately blessed with children. "And Isaac entreated the Lord together with his wife, for she was barren and God granted his plea, and Rebecca his wife became pregnant" (Gen. 25:21).

The blessing of pregnancy, however, brought with it an unexpected source of pain. "And the children struggled together within her, and she said, 'If it be so, why do I live?'" (Gen. 25:22). The Hebrew word describing the struggle is *va'yitrotzetzu*. Rashi points out that its root suggests running, and quotes the midrashic interpretation that whenever Rebecca passed a house of study (beit midrash) Jacob wanted to run out, but when she passed a house of idolatry, Esau wanted to run out.

Rebecca then had a prophetic vision. God told her, "there are two nations in your womb, and two peoples shall be separated from inside you, and the one people shall be stronger than the other people, and the elder shall serve the younger" (Gen. 25:23). Up until this point, Rebecca had feared that the struggle inside her womb meant that she was carrying a conflicted soul, violently torn between two opposing ways of life. Rather than bear such an unfortunate child, she preferred death. But when she found out that she was bearing twins and that the struggle was between two distinct beings rather than within one tortured soul, she was comforted. Despite the pain, Rebecca understood that God had granted her an awesome responsibility, that of raising two distinct nations.

The midrash cited above not only describes the essential difference between the two brothers, it also foreshadows the difference in how their parents perceived them: "And the boys grew, and Esau was a cunning hunter, a man of the field, and Jacob was a whole-hearted man, dwelling in tents. Isaac loved Esau because he relished hunted game, but Rebecca loved Jacob" (Gen. 25:27–28).

The Hebrew phrase for "relished hunted game" is *ki tzayid be'fiv*, which literally means "because the hunt was in his mouth." Although this phrase is a euphemism for "enjoying meat," it could also mean – in a literal sense – that "he trapped with his mouth." In other words, Esau was slick and smooth, ensnaring with the gift of the gab. And Isaac, perhaps somewhat naively, fell victim to Esau's smooth line.

Opposites attract. Perhaps an ethereal, spiritual Isaac, generally shy and even passive – after all, he was led to the sacrificial binding, a wife was chosen for him, and the blessings were soon to be wrested from him – was naturally drawn toward his aggressive and dynamic son. Having survived the *Akeda*, an act of supreme sacrifice for God, Isaac may have appreciated Esau's physical strength and prowess.

Rebecca, however, was wiser; Esau couldn't fool her. She had carried Jacob and Esau for nine months, and she knew in her gut who was who. Rebecca also had previous experience with the superficial hypocrisies of her brother Laban, whose home she had shared until her marriage. Rebecca's knowledge, born from the pain of her early upbringing, the insight of her pregnancy, and her divine prophecy that "the elder shall serve the younger," made her far more perceptive than Isaac regarding the twins.

Although Isaac may have been old and slowly going blind, more interested in certain creature comforts than in trying to see through Esau's wiles, nonetheless the text indicates quite clearly that Esau violated an important commandment upheld by the pre-Sinaitic children of Abraham, forbidding marriage to a member of the seven nations of Canaan. This precept led to the marriage between Isaac and Rebecca, as Abraham insisted that Eliezer search for a suitable wife for Isaac only from among Abraham's own kin. Nevertheless, the Bible records: "When

Esau was forty years old, he took to wife Judith the daughter of Be'eri the Hittite, and Basemath the daughter of Elon the Hittite. And they were a bitterness of spirit unto Isaac and Rebecca" (Gen. 26:34–5).

Immediately following this, in the very next verse, despite Esau's transgressions, we are told that Isaac called Esau and said to him, "Behold now, I am old … now therefore take … your weapons … and go out to the field and hunt me game; make me a delicacy such as I love and bring it to me that I may eat, that my soul may bless you before I die" (Gen. 27:2–4). When Rebecca heard Isaac's words to Esau, she sprang into action in an effort to get Jacob blessed before his brother. She personally prepared the tasty morsels that Isaac had requested, she provided Jacob with Esau's clothes, covered his smooth flesh with hairy goat skins, and commanded her reluctant son to pretend to be someone he was not.

At first, the reader may sympathize with Rebecca's desire to make sure that the blessing went to the son who deserved it most. Esau's violation of Abraham's command was catastrophic, and therefore Isaac's intention to give him the blessing was incomprehensible. Esau had also demonstrated that he did not value the birthright – by selling it to Jacob for a pot of lentils. In that same incident, he had shown himself to be a rough and impulsive character, unsuited to the task of fathering the Jewish people.

Nonetheless, Rebecca clearly engaged in an act of deception, intentionally providing the means for Jacob to wrest from his blind father the blessing meant for Esau.

Isaac was suspicious. He recognized the voice as Jacob's but was confused by the hand which felt like Esau's. Isaac even asked, "Are you he, my son Esau?" In the end, however, Isaac ate of the meal Jacob brought him, drank the proffered wine and, drawing his son close, blessed him with the "dew of the heavens and the fat of the earth" (Gen. 27:28).

As Jacob departed, Esau arrived, bearing fresh game. But it was too late. Apparently, blessings are not mere words uttered mechanically. Once blessed, Jacob became the sole possessor of his blessing. Esau cried out from the depths of his heart and beseeched his father for one leftover blessing, which Isaac haltingly produced. But Esau was not appeased by what was clearly a second-rate and insignificant blessing. Leaving the tent, Esau resolved to kill Jacob upon the death of their father. When Rebecca heard of her elder son's intention, she sent Jacob away to her family in Haran.

Although we can sympathize with Rebecca's intent, it is difficult to condone her method of deception. And in a way, her method doesn't make sense. Both parents, the text informs us, were bitter about Esau's marriages with Hittite women. If Rebecca was astonished by Isaac's short memory and his seeming willingness to let things ride, why didn't she choose to do the obvious? Why didn't she talk to her husband? Couldn't she have used her powers of persuasion to remind Isaac that Esau was still Esau, a wild and unruly hunter, married to idolatrous women, who had sold his birthright for a bowl of soup?

Another question: Didn't Rebecca realize that in a short while Esau would return from the hunt, discover his usurpation, and seek revenge against Jacob? The consequences of the act were inevitable, yet Rebecca still went through with her subterfuge. Didn't she care what might happen to Jacob? Why didn't she at least try to talk to her husband?

I'd like to offer two explanations which offer us two plausible, yet different, scenarios. The first was suggested by the Netziv (Rabbi Naftali Tzvi Yehuda Berlin, 1816–1893), in his commentary *Haamek Davar*.

The Netziv believed that there was a deep communication gap between Isaac and Rebecca. The lack of a common language between Isaac and Rebecca can be traced to the fact that they emerged from two different worlds. When they first met, the Torah says, "Isaac went out to meditate in the field toward evening. He raised his eyes and saw camels approaching. When Rebecca looked up and saw Isaac, she fell from the camel" (Gen. 24:63–64).

The Talmud in Tractate Berakhot (26b) says this meditation was in fact the creation of the *minḥa* (afternoon) prayer. Perhaps the reason why the Torah tells us that Rebecca fell from the camel is because she had never before seen a person quite like Isaac. After all, Isaac was brought up in the home of Abraham, the great visionary of ethical monotheism, and he had willingly experienced the *Akeda* on Mt. Moriah, an act of near-sacrifice of self to the Creator of the World. What a far cry was the home of Isaac from that of Rebecca, brought up in a den of deceivers and charlatans – Bethuel and Laban. Isaac, the man of faith par excellence, went out into the fields not to graze sheep but to communicate with the Divine.

"Who is this man coming toward us in the field?" Rebecca asked Eliezer. He answered, "That is my master." Rebecca immediately took her veil and covered her face. Why? According to the Netziv, Rebecca, who was still quite young, felt unworthy, and on a far lower level of spirituality than Isaac. She had never before seen a personality so spiritual, so dedicated to God, and what she saw so astonished her that she fell off her camel. The Netziv says that Rebecca never quite recovered from the shock of this first encounter. From that moment on, she always felt inadequate to confront or disagree with her saintly husband. The veil, psychologically speaking, never left her face in Isaac's presence.

In addition to Rebecca's sense of inadequacy, Isaac was plagued with his own set of deep inner traumas, which didn't help their ability to communicate. Undoubtedly, they had a good marriage – the text even tells us that the Philistine king actually came upon them while they were "playing," a biblical euphemism for sexual intimacy. But the intimacy of the bedroom was apparently not always translated into the intimacy of the living room.

Isaac never fully recovered from the experience of the *Akeda*. He carried it with him for the rest of his life, and it affected all of his relationships, including his marriage. After the *Akeda* Isaac seems to have lost the power of speech. We are told by the Bible that following the *Akeda*, Abraham returned (*vayashav Abraham*) from Moriah. The verb used is singular and no mention is made of Isaac. The implication seems to be that a part of Isaac never descended from the mountain top – the social aspect of his personality which he was never to recover. One can imagine that it would be difficult, if not impossible, to deal normally with people after having seen the face of a demanding God, "the terror of Isaac" (Gen. 31:42).

Apropos this explanation, an incident which occurred during the early years of my rabbinate made a very deep impression on me. I was called to the side of an elderly congregant who had just lost his wife. He wept uncontrollably and refused any words of comfort. He said again and again, "But, rabbi, you don't understand...." So it went before and after the funeral, and into the evening. The man refused to even drink a cup of coffee, constantly repeating, "You don't understand!" Almost in exasperation, I asked him, "What don't I understand?" Between sobs, he said, "We were Holocaust survivors, my wife and I. After all we'd been through, it was very difficult for us to express our feelings. We were married for over forty years, and I never told her that I loved her. Now it's too late."

The *Akeda* may have been a similarly horrific and silencing experience for Isaac. The Netziv's interpretation that suggests a heavy silence between the two parents would certainly explain why Rebecca urged Jacob to pretend he was Esau. Since Rebecca felt inadequate to disagree with her husband, she believed that trying to convince Isaac of Jacob's worthiness would be to no avail.

But this reading tends to downplay the significance of Esau's intermarriage, and the resulting "bitterness" of his parents. Although Isaac and Rebecca may not have been voluble talkers, after Esau's wives appeared in their lives, it strains credibility to suggest that they never spoke about the issue. Past traumas aside, it is the fate of their son – and the destiny of their nation – which hangs in the balance.

Another possibility is that they did speak, but disagreed. If they did speak, what could they have said to each other which yielded the deception described in chapter 27 of Genesis? The following imagined dialogue attempts to illuminate an additional reason why Rebecca may have resorted to subterfuge, a reason which has nothing to do with the problem of personal communication.

Rebecca: After what Esau did, the blessing must go to Jacob.

Isaac: Jacob? Impossible. He's too much like me, just sitting and learning all day. Look, I know what it means to be passive, and he's passive. But in the future, our descendants will need some aggressive leadership!

Rebecca: So you're suggesting the blessing go to Esau just because Jacob's not aggressive?

Isaac: There's no choice. Esau is strong and shrewd. You think I don't know the tricks he plays on me with those so-called religious questions about tithing salt, pretending to be so righteous? But he knows how to influence people. That's important.

Rebecca: I hate to admit it, but our son Esau is a selfish, lazy, good-for-nothing.

Isaac: He may be selfish, but he's not lazy.

Rebecca: And his marriages? Are you going to defend those too? I saw your face when he brought those Hittite women home. Those intermarriages defy God's will.

Isaac: I'm not defending him. But I'm looking at the total picture, and some of his faults can also be seen in a positive light. After all, Esau's shrewdness can also be called diplomacy – and diplomacy is a very useful survival skill.

Rebecca: Esau would be a disaster. He's not a model for the Jewish nation. Everything about him is immediate gratification – "I want my meal, now! And if I don't get it, I'll sell my birthright!" The Jewish nation is going to have a long history, with many ups and downs, and if their leaders are short-sighted they will lose heart and lose hope. The Jewish people are going to need the inner strength to wait, to suffer, to develop, and to wait some more. Only Jacob's children will stand a chance because they'll have patience carved into their souls.

Isaac: I admit you have a point. The truth is I'm planning to divide the blessings into two parts, the physical blessing and the spiritual blessing. The physical blessing I'll give to Esau, because he will know what to do with it. He understands granaries and business and banking systems. Let him get the "dew of the heaven and the fat of the earth." He'll know how to wheel and deal and even fight, if need be, to protect what is his. And Jacob can have the spiritual blessing, the birthright, the blessing of Abraham, the leadership of Israel, the dream of becoming a light unto the nations. That's his department.

Rebecca: My husband, you are wrong. I know it in my heart. Jacob must get everything. You cannot divide the spiritual from the physical. If Jacob is meant to direct the spiritual future of the Jewish people, then he has to have the physical powers as well, so he'll have the means to change the world. Without a physical basis, the spiritual will not be able to develop. And because the physical must be sanctified, it can only go to Jacob. The truth is there is no such thing as the spiritual and the physical. There is only the holy and the not-yet-holy. The physical must be sanctified; who will do it if not Jacob?

Isaac: But he's a tent dweller. How can we place such enormous responsibility on his narrow, weak shoulders? He wouldn't know what to do with a material blessing. Can he be an artisan, a craftsman, a businessman? Can he wage war, if need be? He'll never know how to use his hands like Esau. It would be a waste to give him that blessing!

And so the matriarch and patriarch argued, day after day and night after night, neither one able to convince the other...until the moment when Rebecca overheard Isaac's plan to bless Esau when he returned from the field with his game.

There was no time to waste – Rebecca was forced to take radical action, to prove once and for all that Jacob could do the job despite his bookish manner and unworldly ways. She advised Jacob to dress in animal skins to demonstrate that, if necessary, the smooth-skinned Jacob could be transformed into the rough-skinned Esau. "Isaac, I'm going to show you," she thought to herself, "that he can dress like Esau, use the hands of Esau, and even utilize Esau's machinations in order to get what is rightfully his."

Rebecca risked the danger of Esau's revenge because she had to prove Jacob's capabilities to Isaac. And she knew she would succeed because of the prophecy given to her by God that "the elder shall serve the younger." Abraham was called to sacrifice Isaac on Mt. Moriah and, in a narrower sense, our mother Rebecca was called upon to sacrifice the future of Esau for the future of Jacob. Knowing that only one of her two sons could become Israel, Rebecca was forced to choose the most worthy one.

When the real Esau showed up with his pot of game, Isaac was seized with a fit of violent trembling. "Who... where... is the one who trapped game and brought it to me? I ate it all before you came, and I have blessed him; yea, he shall be blessed (*gam barukh yihiyeh*)" (Gen. 27:33).

Considering that someone had just deceived him, one has to wonder why Isaac added the phrase, "he shall be blessed" – when he could just as easily have said, "he shall be cursed!" I believe it is because, at that moment, Isaac realized that Rebecca was right all along; that, when necessary, bespectacled Jacob would be capable of putting down his Talmud and picking up an Uzi. "He shall be blessed," Isaac declared because he recognized that Rebecca, his wise and prophetic wife, had been right; you cannot divorce the physical from the spiritual. Jacob would need every tool possible at his disposal – including those more natural to Esau – in order to make this imperfect world a little better.

Ever since the Jewish people took on the responsibility of defending the nation physically in addition to keeping its spiritual legacy alive, we have been blessed with the "dew of the heavens and the fat of the earth," but we have also been forced to use the hands of Esau in order to maintain these blessings.

The challenge of Rebecca has become the challenge of every Jewish mother in modern Israel who must take her son, her "Jacob," and dress him in the skins of Esau, the hunter-soldier, in order to ensure our Jewish future. What is the army of Israel if not the sons of Jacob wearing the skins of Esau?

Even though it goes against the Jew's nature, even though it's not the image we have of ourselves, we are able to live this way because of Rebecca's strength and vision, her willingness to choose truth rather than acquiesce to her husband, her insistence that the spiritual and physical dare not be divided but that the birthright and blessing are one.

In effect, it was the prophecy of Rebecca which determined the continued survival of the Jewish people. All the matriarchs were confronted with aspects of evil – Sarah saw through Ishmael, the son of Hagar; Rachel and Leah saw through their father Laban; but Rebecca managed to see through her own son Esau, one of the toughest experiences a mother can face.

Rebecca's actions represent the willingness to sacrifice everything in order to guarantee the synthesis between the spiritual and the material. In her attempt to convince Jacob to utilize the hands of Esau in order to achieve what he truly deserves, she is willing to pay for her conviction with the highest possible price: "Let any curse be on me, my son" (Gen. 27:13), she says to convince him, and she acts with sensitivity and strength, with devotion and defiance, with compassion and courage.

For nearly two thousand years the entire nation of Israel lived like Jacob the tent dweller, possessor of the spiritual blessing but not the physical one. But when the first tremors of Zionism began to wake the slumbering bones of the Jewish people, we awakened not only to the spiritual legacy of Israel, but also to the physical one formed from cement, plaster, and stone. Even a tent dweller must know how to build a tent which will not fall down at the first sign of a winter storm.

THE VOICE OF JACOB WITH THE HANDS OF ESAU: YESHIVA STUDENTS AND THE DRAFT

Long before the modern world ever heard of draft deferments, the Torah was already weighing the possibility of military exemptions. In Deuteronomy 20:5–7 we read that "the man who built a new house but has not yet lived in it…who planted a vineyard but has not yet redeemed its first vintage…who betrothed a woman but has not yet taken her in marriage" has his conscription deferred. The explanation given is that it would not be right, should the soldier die on the battlefield, for a stranger to reap the fruits of his labors. In addition to men in these three situations, the Bible also exempts those who are "afraid and tender-hearted" (Deut. 20:8). "Afraid lest he be killed and tender-hearted lest he kill," the Malbim explains, opening the door to a unique brand of Jewish pacifism.

Our tradition likewise recognizes two basic categories of war: voluntary (*milḥemet reshut*) and obligatory (*milḥemet mitzva*). In a voluntary war we attack offensively in order to pre-empt an enemy from attacking us as soon as they become strong enough to do so.[1] Military campaigns to expand national territory are also considered voluntary wars. In ancient Israel, both these types of voluntary war required the approval of the Sanhedrin as well as the imprimatur of a prophet.

In contrast, an obligatory war is a war waged in self-defense against an army poised to destroy us.[2] Every war that Israel has fought since the establishment of the state belongs in this category. In the case of modern-day Israel, a small nation-state surrounded by enemies that requires an enforced standing army to ensure its survival, it is clear that all military training in preparation for war is likewise to be considered an aspect of obligatory war (Y. Sota 8, 10).

The magnanimous spirit of the biblical deferments cited above are clarified in the mishna recorded in Sota 44b. There we learn that those exemptions only apply to a voluntary war, and not to an obligatory one. In language which could not be more vivid, our sages declare that if Israel is under threat of attack, "even a groom must leave his bridal chamber and even a bride must leave her nuptial canopy" in order to protect our land and its citizenry. No exceptions for anyone! This is an authoritative law, later codified in Maimonides' Laws of Kings (7:4). The great hasidic authority, Rabbi Isaac of Karlin, wrote in his well-known talmudic commentary *Keren Orah* that "in an obligatory war everyone goes to battle, and so even Torah scholars must be freed from their studies" (Commentary to Sota, ad loc.).

In sharp exception to the above, there is a so-called ultra-Orthodox sector in Israel which insists that yeshiva students be exempt from military conscription under all circumstances. They base their argument on three sources:

The first source is the *Mishneh Torah*, Laws of the Sabbatical year and Jubilee, in which Maimonides concludes with praise for the tribe

---

1. This is *milḥemet mena*, as explained in Y. Sota.
2. Wars against Amalek and the seven indigenous nations of Canaan are also obligatory but are no longer considered possible, since the Talmud concludes that Sennacherib, king of ancient Assyria, confounded all of these nations to the extent that they can no longer be identified.

of Levi and explains why they were excluded from any inheritance in the Land of Israel. He explains that the Levites were uniquely sanctified because they dedicated their lives to teaching the righteous precepts of Torah to the Jewish people. Consequently, they cast off from themselves all accountings of financial remunerations or obligations. "They do not conduct war like the rest of Israel, they do not inherit the land, they do not succeed from the strength of their own labor, they are the soldiers of the Lord." Maimonides then writes that in addition to the biological offspring of the house of Levi, "any individual from the inhabitants of the world whose spirit so moves him" to dedicate himself to the work of the Divine becomes sanctified as well, and may be accorded the same dispensations as the sacred tribe of Levi. This description would certainly seem to include the yeshiva students of our generation, who might therefore not be required "to conduct war like the rest of Israel."

Second, in Bava Batra 7b, the amoraic text discusses the mishnaic principle that a city council can force local residents to pay a tax for the purpose of constructing a defensive wall around their community. The sages maintain that Torah scholars ought to be exempt from paying such taxes because "Torah scholars do not need to be guarded." This passage would, at least on the surface, lend credence to the notion that Torah study is at least as powerful a means of protection as is a standing army. Indeed, the Talmud cites a verse from Psalms: "'I count them as being more numerous than the sand…' – Just as the sand provides a bulwark against the sea, so the righteous deeds of the scholars provide a bulwark against the enemy" (ibid.).

The third source used to buttress the argument for exempting yeshiva students is *Sifrei* on Numbers, *Parashat Matot*, 157. *Sifrei* comments on the biblical text enjoining universal military conscription: "With the exclusion of the tribe of Levi" (*lehotzi shevet Levi*). In other words, the tribe of Levi was exempt from serving in the army!

Let us analyze these prooftexts in opposite order. There is an alternate manuscript version of the midrash quoted above which reads, "with the inclusion of the tribe of Levi" (*lehavi shevet Levi*). This is the reading preferred by Rashi when he insists that the tribe of Levi went out to battle against Midian – even though that particular battle could not even be classified as an obligatory war in the classical sense (Num. 31:4).

Moreover, in Kiddushin 21b the text queries whether the military laws concerning *yefat to'ar* apply to priests from the tribe of Levi. The Bible describes a situation in which a soldier may, in the heat of battle and/or in the strange environment of foreign shores, become attracted to a woman of another nation and religion whom he considers alluring (*yefat to'ar* literally means "of beautiful appearance"). Under certain circumstances, after following a prescribed course of action including a waiting period and conversion, they are permitted to marry. However, a priest or *kohen* ordinarily has marital restrictions above and beyond the average Israelite; he cannot, for example, marry a divorcee or a convert. The question raised by the Talmud here is whether the special laws that enable a soldier to marry a *yefat to'ar* hold true for a priest as well. The question clearly assumes that the priests of the tribe of Levi went out to war!

The second text cited is also a flawed proof. It is true that the sages of the Talmud ruled that the righteous deeds of Torah scholars guard them against attack, therefore exempting them from sharing in the cost of defensive walls. But the *Baalei Tosafot* (ad loc.) as well as the *Hazon Ish* on Bava Batra (5:18) limit this exemption to defense against robberies, to monetary protection. All of these accepted authorities insist that if the town was erecting a wall for the protection of human lives, even Torah scholars would be expected to contribute. After all, we dare not rely upon miracles when life is at stake. And, of course, they are obligated by the commandment of *lo ta'amod al dam re'ekha* – the prohibition against standing idly by while another Jew's blood is spilled.

The talmudic passage in Bava Batra 7b also contains a fascinating difference of opinion between Rabbi Yohanan and Resh Lakish regarding the source of the city's protection: Is it provided by the Torah study or by the good deeds of the Torah scholars? In an earlier generation, this question was seemingly resolved in favor of righteous deeds during a riveting repartee between two scholars imprisoned during the Hadrianic persecutions (Avoda Zara 17b). Rabbi Hanina ben Teradyon, who was charged with one crime, informed his colleague Rabbi Elazar ben Parta who was charged with five crimes, that he – Rabbi Elazar – would be saved while Rabbi Hanina himself would be martyred. Why? Rabbi Hanina explained, "Because you occupied yourself with the study of

Torah as well as the performance of good deeds, whereas I occupied myself only with the study of Torah. And it has been taught: He who only studies Torah is compared to someone who has no God" (ibid.).

I would submit that in the present Israeli climate of thirty-fifty days per year of reserve duty, when small business owners must simply put a lock on their shops and somehow absorb the loss of clientele, and when young husbands must leave wives and fledgling families, what greater "good deed" can there be than lessening this pressure and sharing in this national obligation?

This leaves us with the first textual argument from Maimonides' *Mishneh Torah*, which seemingly awards "Levite status" to those who dedicate themselves to studying and teaching Torah. It must be stressed that this passage is homiletic in nature; its context is theological and ethical rather than legal-halakhic. In his Laws of Kings, which includes the laws of warfare, Maimonides makes no mention of exemptions from military conscription for Torah scholars or Levites – although he does mention the exemptions listed earlier for men who have just become engaged, built a house or planted a vineyard, as well as the tender-hearted.

Furthermore, when Maimonides writes that "the Levites do not conduct war like the rest of the nation," is he granting total exemption from military service? The noted halakhic authority and dean of Yeshivat Har Etzion, Rabbi Aharon Lichtenstein, suggests that since the precise language of the text does not stipulate total exemption but rather implies a difference in the form or style of military service, perhaps Maimonides is mandating special units with unique conditions, much like the *yeshivot hesder* which combine Torah studies with military service over a five-year period.

The real significance of the words of Maimonides for our times is explained by the Radbaz (Rabbenu David ben Zimra, sixteenth-century halakhic authority, chief rabbi of Egypt and eminent interpreter of Maimonides). The Radbaz emphasizes Maimonides' insistence that the "voluntary Levites" cast off from themselves all financial accountings and depend solely on God's bounty for their support. It is clear, says the Radbaz, that "they would never cast themselves *upon the community* for their material subsistence" [emphasis added]. This is very much in consonance with Maimonides' fundamental position that Torah may never be used as a means for personal benefit or privilege, "as a plough with which to dig," and that no Torah scholar should accept payment for his Torah teaching or judging – and certainly not for his Torah learning!

Maimonides was exceedingly sensitive to the possibility that a potential sanctification of God's name could easily turn into a desecration of God's name if the public were to perceive Torah scholars as gaining financial advantage from their Torah study or contributing less to the common good than the rest of the Jewish people. Along these lines, Rabbi Yoel ben Nun, noted rabbi, biblical scholar, and educator, has suggested that any Torah student who claims army exemption ought to be required to sign a contract prohibiting him from owning any property in Israel – in order to fulfill the minimum of the Levite commitments.

In summary, careful investigation of rabbinic literature provides no precedent whatsoever for exempting Torah scholars from military duty. Joshua, the successor to Moses who conquered the land of Canaan for the Israelites and who is described by the talmudic sages as having been the greatest Torah luminary of his generation (Menaḥot 99b), is given a special blessing by the Almighty that, despite his military commitments as leader-in-battle, nevertheless "the book of Torah shall not depart from your mouth, you shall meditate upon it by day and by night" (Josh. 1:8). In other words, God promises that Joshua will succeed both militarily and scholastically at the same time!

Skipping many centuries to the end of the mishnaic period, the Talmud records that twenty-four thousand disciples of Rabbi Akiva died in the period between Passover and Shavuot (or between Passover and Lag BaOmer, according to other textual readings). The *Geonim* maintain that the students were killed during the Bar Kokhba rebellion, a battle which was encouraged – and perhaps even initiated – by their master and rebbe, Rabbi Akiva.[3] Again, we find that yeshiva students were in the

---

3. Although the Talmud, in Yevamot 62b, does record a later tradition in the name of Rabbi Naḥman that Rabbi Akiva's disciples died of *askera*, often translated as "whooping cough" or "diphtheria," I would suggest that this hapax legomenon actually comes from the Greek *sikarii*, which means "sword"; this definition of the word confirms the explanation of the *Geonim* and is also consonant with our historical understanding of the period.

thick of the battle in what seems to have been a remarkable precedent for today's *yeshivot hesder*.

In addition to their textual arguments, those opposed to drafting yeshiva students like to remind others that the Jewish people are fighting two simultaneous wars: the external, physical enemy at the border and the internal, spiritual enemy of assimilation. In the face of this internal threat, nothing is more cardinal for the preservation of the Jewish people than Torah learning.

We need not go any further than the Books of Judges and Kings to see that military strength without the moral and ethical values of Torah only leads to corruption and destruction. In modern times, the material and social successes of the Diaspora Jewish community have resulted in unprecedented rates of intermarriage, lessening our numbers by more than fifty percent. Especially after the tragedy of the Holocaust, which included the wholesale slaughter of one-third of our nation and perhaps eighty percent of our religious and intellectual leadership, we are duty-bound to make up for our loss and swell the depleted ranks of Torah scholars once again.

This argument is a very powerful one. Unquestionably, all of Jewry must be thankful to the *haredi* (ultra-Orthodox) world for demonstrating the eternal strength of Torah, for leading the way in recreating Torah centers in America and Israel, and for reminding all of us of the central and critical role commitment to Torah study must play in the rebirth of our nation.

We must, however, be mindful of a parallel situation which almost makes the loss in this regard greater than the gain. With the breakdown of communist and socialist ideologies, as well as the realization of the emptiness of a life spent solely in pursuit of material gain, secular Israel finds itself at a crossroads and is searching for authentic meaning and significance, for Jewish identity and destiny.

However, since the five wars Israel has fought in the last five decades have affected virtually every family in Israel with death or disability, the resentment against those who avail themselves of a wholesale military exemption prevents the majority of our citizenry from investigating or even respecting the religious lifestyle. Torah-observant Jews (and despite *yeshivot hesder, mekhinot,* and the sacrifices and leadership of the national-religious sector *vis-a-vis* the IDF, all observant Jews are painted with the same brush) appear to be a special privileged class, protected by government-by-coalition, straining both the pockets and the patience of the majority of Israel's citizens.

Toward the end of the biblical Book of Numbers, it is related that the tribes of Gad and Reuven and half the tribe of Menashe were so taken with the grazing potential of the land east of the Jordan River that they requested permission to remain there. Moses strongly rebuked them, saying, "Shall your brethren go to war, and you shall sit here?" (Num. 32:61). The greatest of our prophets insisted that these Israelites had to join the other tribes in battle until the entire land was conquered. Only "then may you return, and you shall come out pure in the eyes of God and of Israel." Indeed, it is from this last phrase that the talmudic sages derive the principle of *mar'it ayin* (lit., "the appearance to the eye"). The lesson: What we do is important, but how our actions appear to the rest of the Jewish people is of equal importance.

How does the wholesale draft exemption of yeshiva students appear to the rest of Israel? Their perception is that the secular send their children to the front, and the religious send their children to the back, where they are protected by a wall of holy books. The danger lies not only in the weakening of our nation by an internal, heart-wrenching tear, but also in the desecration of God's name that results from a negative assessment of Torah and its adherents.

The religious Zionist sector has also been deeply disappointed by their religious compatriots. A few years ago, a well-known university professor and scholar, who is also a religiously observant Jew, lost his son, a soldier in the IDF, in battle. At the military funeral, he delivered a eulogy in which he said that he was sure his cries were piercing the heavens, but that he was less certain about the nearby neighborhood of Bayit VeGan, where so many young men, studying in yeshivot, were not affected by the wars. After the *shiva*, he thought of a compromise with the ultra-Orthodox world; he petitioned the heads of the foremost ultra-Orthodox yeshivot to at least intone the prayer for the welfare of the IDF each Sabbath morning – since, after all, they believe in the efficacy of prayer and perhaps the greater volume of prayer might prevent more sacrifice. Unfortunately, he was met with a polite but firm rebuff.

I can certainly understand that the ultra-Orthodox fear to subject their youth to the secular and even licentious atmosphere of most army units. However, their religious leadership must take into account the negative ramifications that across-the-board yeshiva exemption has for the majority of our citizens. I therefore urge that the present situation be modified: First, objective examinations ought to be given to yeshiva students in order to provide long-term deferments to the top ten percent. This would insure the preservation of Torah leadership. Second, the IDF should establish special all-male *ḥaredi* units which would train and serve together and receive regular Torah classes.[4] These unique units would cater to the dietary needs of the *ḥaredi* soldiers and provide a proper environment for them. Third, special units ought to be formed for non-military national service, especially in the area of *ḥevra kaddisha* (religious burial services) work, for those who feel they cannot be engaged in actual warfare.

We must do everything possible to unify our fractured nation, and a national draft that doesn't automatically exempt one sector of the population would go a long way toward healing the tragic rift which divides us.

In the past century, the Jewish people have had no choice but to don the skins and wield the weaponry of Esau in order to secure a physical haven. It is our dream that finally, in our times, in the Land of Israel, we will succeed in building a sanctuary that combines the dew of the heavens with the fat of the land, a sanctuary in which the material and spiritual are united in the service of God, a sanctuary imbued with the light of Rebecca which will spread from Zion and Jerusalem to the entire world.

POSTSCRIPT

Since the notion of *yeshivat hesder* was inspired by our matriarch Rebecca, why not a *yeshivat hesder* for women? After all, from a halakhic perspective, if we are dealing with obligatory wars (*milkhamot mitzva*) – and all

---

4. Since the writing of the article, the Naḥal Ḥaredi has been established – an army unit that caters to the needs of ultra-Orthodox soldiers. Unfortunately, currently only a very small minority of the *ḥaredi* population has enlisted.

wars fought in Israel are obligatory wars – the Mishna clearly states, "For an obligatory war everyone goes out, even a groom from his marriage chamber and a bride from her nuptial canopy" (Sota 8, 6).

I am proud to say that Ohr Torah Stone established the first *yeshivat hesder* for women in 1998, in which young women combined study in Midreshet Lindenbaum with service in the Educational Corps, the Intelligence Corps, and the Air Force. We now have close to 100 women officers in the IDF, sanctifying God's name daily. In our wake, several more women's *hesder* programs have developed.

Covenant and Conversion: Our United Mission to Redeem the World

The word "hope" in English has a positive and optimistic connotation, as in "hope for the best." However, it does not suggest certitude of outcome. Much the opposite: I don't *hope* to graduate if I have passed all my exams and fulfilled all the requirements; I *know* that I shall graduate. On the other hand, I do *hope* to participate in my grandson's wedding, although he might not yet have chosen his fiancée.

In Hebrew, however, the word for hope, *tikva*, contains the added nuance of *faith*, the anticipation of a blessed event that I know will occur because it has been guaranteed by God. This is the force behind Israel's national anthem, "Hatikva," which glories in the fact that "our hope (faith) was never lost, our two thousand-year-old hope (and faith)... to be a free nation in the land of Zion and Jerusalem." Indeed, it was this belief that faith can turn anticipated hope into cognitive certainty that kept the Jewish people alive as a committed, separate ethnic entity despite their two millennia of homeless peregrinations, persecutions, and pogroms.

Probably the best source for the identity of hope and faith is
Psalm 27:

> To David: The Lord is my light and my salvation; whom must
> I fear? The Lord is the stronghold of my life, whom must I be
> afraid of? Although evildoers are near me, about to consume
> my flesh, and my enemies and foes are arrayed against me, they
> will falter and they will fall... Have hope (*kavei,* faith) in the
> Lord, be strong and make your heart courageous, and have hope
> (*kavei,* faith) in the Lord.

When hope turns into faith because the outcome of your salvation
is guaranteed by God, then you truly have nothing to fear – for your
faith in God's word leads to belief that His guarantees will eventually
be delivered.[1] Here, the two topics of this theological project come
together magnificently: Hope and Covenant as well as Responsibility and Mission. Our optimistic hope for (or faith in) the realization
of God's covenantal promise to Abraham that "through you all the
families of the earth shall be blessed" (Gen. 12:3) and that at the "end
of the days, when the Temple Mount shall be established on the top
of the mountains... all of the nations shall rush there... nation will
not lift up sword against nation and humanity will not learn war
anymore" (Is. 2:2–4) reinforces our responsibility to convert the
world to the ideals of peace on earth as a result of universal moral
principles (i.e., the seven Noahide laws) that emanate from "the
word of God from Jerusalem" and will move the process of messianic
redemption forward.

In this essay, I will attempt to define the Jewish role in these
endeavors, particularly our obligation to "convert the gentiles," bearing
in mind that we must define precisely both what we mean by "convert"
and who is included in the category of "gentiles." I will then explain how
Jews and Christians must join hands both in hope and covenant, as well
as in terms of responsibility and mission.

---

1. Martin Buber, *Two Types of Faith* (Syracuse University Press, December 2003).

REASONS FOR DESPAIR

I began this article discussing the concept of hope, but reading the newspapers or watching daily news programs is sufficient for one to logically conclude that the belief that we are moving towards a perfect human society, a messianic and redemptive end-game, is sheer naiveté and unworthy of a rational human being.

Look at our world. Barely seven decades after the Holocaust, the United Nations that was created with the hope of insuring world peace, time and time again gives a respected and well-publicized forum to the former president of Iran, Mahmoud Ahmadinejad, for him to spew his hateful anti-Zionist and anti-Jewish venom. The United Nations refuses to enforce stringent economic sanctions that might prevent Iran's mission to develop nuclear weapons of destruction. North Korea flexes its nuclear muscles while thumbing its nose at the United States to a largely stunned but silent world. All of this is the backdrop to widespread and violent Islamist extremism, and to terrorist suicide bombers preaching jihad and death to any infidel who refuses to endorse their brand of religious extremism. This extremism is not only taking over the Moslem world, but also threatens to engulf Europe and the West. The wars being waged by extremist Islam are religious wars, the result of a misguided and diabolical interpretation of Islam, which is not monotheistic but satanic because it has exchanged the God of love, life, and peace for the unholy Satan of power, death, and jihad.

If the threat of nuclear self-destruction were not sufficient, global warming and the havoc we have wrought by polluting the air we breathe by our disregard for ecological concerns in the name of "progress" will probably finish off any life that manages to survive the next world war. Indeed, Freud's id, expressing the dark, death-desiring and destructive dimension of the human personality, appears to be far more powerful than the "portion of God from on high, the image of God"[2] aspect of the human being that could lead us to salvation and world peace.

From this perspective, Europe's negative population growth, as well as the banner of gay parades and advocacy of alternative marital unions, is perhaps the logical response to a world marching directly

---

2. Gen. 9:6, Job 31:2.

toward doomsday, rather than belief in a Messianic Era of human perfection – an ideal that is a unique gift that Jews bequeathed to Western civilization.[3]

THE JEWISH MESSIAH AND FAITH IN HUMANITY

In defense of optimism and hope, I would like to analyze a curious aspect of biblical Judaism, a teaching that is *prima fascia* quite strange. King David of the tribe of Judah – the progenitor of the Messiah according to the Jewish tradition – can only lay claim to a very problematic lineage. His paternal ancestors, including his noble great-grandfather Boaz, were the result of an act of incest between Judah and his daughter-in-law, Tamar, who posed as a harlot in order to have a child. Yet Judah is father of the tribe from whom the Prince of Peace will one day emerge (Gen. 38–39:10, Ruth 4:18–22).

On David's maternal side was a disputed convert to Judaism, Ruth. She was a Moabite princess, and although the Bible forbade Moabite converts into the Jewish people (Deut. 23:4), the religious court of Boaz ruled, nevertheless, that the prohibition applied only to male Moabites, not to females. Moreover, Moab, Ruth's direct ancestor, was the result of incest between Lot and his elder daughter (Gen. 19:30–38). Apparently, Ruth, great-grandmother of the progenitor of the Messiah, stemmed from a very questionable past! What is Judaism expressing by having the Messiah emanate from incestuous acts?

The rabbinical sages of the Midrash maintained that this messianic ancestry was purposely designed, their proof-text being the strange usage of the word *zera* (seed), rather than *ben* (child or son), in reference to Boaz and Lot. When Boaz marries Ruth in the Book of Ruth, the Israelites bless the couple at the gates of the city of Efrat, saying, "May your house become like the House of Peretz, whom Tamar bore to Judah, from the seed (*zera*) which the Lord gave you from this young woman (*na'arah*)" (Ruth 4:12).

---

3. See Matthew Arnold, "Hebraism and Hellenism," in his *Culture and Anarchy* (London, 1869); Leo Strauss, "Jerusalem and Athens" reprinted in *Jewish Philosophy and the Crisis of Modernity* (SUNY: Albany 1997) pp. 377–405, and Thomas Cahill, *Gifts of the Jews* (Random House: New York, 1999).

It is uncharacteristic for the text to refer to Ruth – a widow for at least a decade – as a young woman (*na'arah*), and the reference to Lot's act of incest with his daughter seems like a strange blessing. Based on the verse in Ruth, the rabbis interpret the verse in Genesis 19:31 that reads: "And the elder daughter said to the younger…'Come, let us give wine to our father to drink, and let us lie with him, so that we may enable our father to give life to (his) seed (*zera*).'" The rabbis said, "This (*zera* in the Book of Ruth) is part of the same *zera* that came from a strange other place, (i.e., from Lot). From these seeds came King Messiah."[4]

POSSIBILITY FOR CHANGE AS A SOURCE OF OPTIMISM

I understand this Jewish tradition to be teaching that despite the appearance that the belief in human perfectibility appears to belong in the realm of the absurd, the notion that good may emerge from evil, that exalted and majestic sanctity can grow from the dregs of immoral sexuality, is built into the Jewish concept of the Messiah. Just as the daughter of the cruel and flagrantly inhospitable Moab could be the loving, kind, and gracious Ruth, a generation of despair and disrepair can rehabilitate itself and bring a redeeming Messiah.[5]

My spiritual teacher, the most important Orthodox talmudist and philosopher of the twentieth century, Rabbi Joseph B. Soloveitchik, read this very message and more into the midrash, insisting that this is precisely the lesson that Lot's daughter attempted to impress upon her younger sister in Genesis 19:31: "The elder sister said to the younger, 'Our father is old and there is no man throughout the land to come upon us (impregnate us) in the manner of all societies.'" Another midrash[6] suggests that "these sisters believed the entire world had been destroyed as in the days of the great flood," since the earthquake that destroyed Sodom and Gomorrah seemed to them to have consumed the entire

---

4. Rabbi Tanḥuma in the name of Rabbi Yosi ben Pazi, *Midrash Rut Zuta*, Buber, 4, 12.
5. This may be the source for the unusual Jewish custom of eating dairy foods on the festival of Shavuot when Jews publicly read the Book of Ruth. Despite the fact that Jewish law prescribes meat for Sabbath and festival meals, Jews eat milk products coming from animals to show that Jewish law recognizes how derivatives can differ from their source. Ruth can come from Moab and the Messiah can emerge from messiness.
6. Midrash Genesis Rabba (Vilna, Parsha 51, 8).

world. Hence, taught Rabbi Soloveitchik, the elder sister suggested that each in turn seduce their father so that they could begin to repopulate the universe.

The younger sister demurs, expressing disgust at the act of incest; but more importantly, she sees no point in attempting to restart the universe. After all, God had attempted to establish a more perfect world, first in Eden with Adam and Eve, then again with Noah and the Covenant of the Rainbow (Gen. 9), and for a third time with Abraham. Each experiment ended in failure for a humanity that sank repeatedly into depravity. It would be absurd – and in this case of proposed incest, immoral – to start humanity once more.

At this point, the elder sister would not be silenced, contended Rabbi Soloveitchik. She argued that God would never have created the human being in the divine image if evil were to be destined to emerge triumphant and if human civilization would destroy itself. No, she insisted, we must have faith in the possibility of repentance, of change, of human perfectibility. Because belief in the Messiah is predicated fundamentally upon faith in the possibility of human change throughout the world, upon an era in which all "spears will be turned into ploughshares and humanity will not learn war anymore," it is appropriate that the seed of the sexual relationship between Lot and his elder daughter was the sacred seed that ultimately led to messianic lineage.

GOD'S COVENANTS WITH THE WORLD

From a biblical perspective, hope *for* and faith *in* the advent of a perfected world of peace and security is not dependent upon God alone. Not only must humanity undergo a fundamental change, individual by individual, but there must be human catalysts who inspire them to want to change and who educate them in how to change. A Yiddish adage has it, "humans must act, if God is to activate." The interface between hope (faith) in the divine promise and human responsibility to actively be engaged in making it happen is expressed in the biblical term "covenant," a two-way contractual, immutable relationship between God and human beings.[7]

---

7. See Joshua Berman, "God's Alliance with Man," *Azure*, Summer 5766/2006.

The first of God's biblical covenants was with Noah (and derivatively with all humanity), in which God promises never again to destroy the world by flood. He stipulates at the same time that humanity must not destroy itself by violence. The rainbow is God's symbol of the divine side of the agreement (Gen 9:9). The prohibitions against eating a limb or the blood of a living animal, against suicide and murder – and, according to the talmudic sages, the remaining moral Noahide laws (prohibitions against theft, sexual licentiousness, idol worship and blasphemy, and the obligation to establish courts of law) – as well as the requirement to procreate, are the responsibilities of all humanity (Gen. 9:4–7).

God's first two covenants with the Hebrews

The Bible teaches that ten generations after Noah, when humanity had again descended into violence and immorality, God made a strategic decision to choose a nation to consecrate as His special agents to the world. God therefore elected Abram, commanding him to leave behind his land and birthplace of idolatry to become a great nation through whom "all the families of the earth shall be blessed" (Gen. 12:1–3). God then entered into two covenants with Abram and his descendants. In the first, God promises Abraham (Hebrew for "father of a multitude of nations") seed and a homeland (Gen. 15) – the necessary appurtenances of a nation, which is a family writ large. The Bible strikingly explains the purpose for which Abraham was elected:

> Abraham will surely become a great and holy nation, and through him shall be blessed all the nations of the earth. I have loved, recognized and singled him out [all three verbs are legitimate translations for the Hebrew root y-d-a] because he shall command his children and his household after him to keep the way of the Lord, doing compassionate righteousness (*tzedaka*) and justice (*mishpat*), in order that the Lord might bring upon Abraham what He said about him. (Gen. 18:18–19)

In other words, we can hope for and have faith in the eternal nationhood of Israel, that Jewish seed will never be destroyed, and that the Jewish people will be united with their homeland, as long as the children of

Abraham fulfill their responsibility to imbue all future generations with compassionate righteousness and justice.

The second covenant is with the Israelite nation on Mt. Sinai, wherein God added to Jewish national identity a distinct religious identity, the Ten Commandments (Ex. 20) and, according to normative Jewish tradition, the entire legal structure of 613 commandments that serves as the Jewish national constitution (Ex. 21–24; Lev. 25, 1:2). These laws serve to unite Jews wherever they may live on the globe, and provide moral, ethical, and ritual boundaries even when Jews are temporarily bereft of their homeland (Ex. 19:4–6). In other words, Jews have every right to hope for, and have faith in, their development as a unique and eternal religion connecting to God in a special way and even affecting the entire world.[8] However, the Jewish people has the responsibility to observe the laws if it expects them to work! Compassionate righteousness and justice are not sufficient; becoming a sacred nation requires at least the Ten Commandments, and the 613 Mosaic commandments given at Sinai, according to Jewish tradition.[9]

The Third Covenant

God entered into a covenant of nationality with Abraham and into a covenant of religion with the newly formed People of Israel soon after they were freed from Egypt. The powerful message in this exquisite timing – revelation at Sinai having occurred seven weeks after the Exodus – is that freedom requires ethical and moral responsibility.

It is generally not recognized that there is yet a Third Covenant,[10] commanded by God to the Jewish people entering the Land of Israel. This Third Covenant consists of twelve, not ten, commandments. It does not seem to include the other commands in the four chapters following the Decalogue (Ex. 21–24) or the other biblical commands throughout the Pentateuch, although it does reiterate other moral and universal

---

8. See commentary of Rabbi Ovadia Seforno on *Mamlekhet Kohanim*, Ex. 19:6.

9. "All 613 commandments are under the rubric of the Ten Commandments," Midrash Numbers Rabba 13:16, cited by Rashi, Ex. 24:12.

10. See also a discussion of the Third Covenant in "The Significance of Israel's Return to Zion: *Tikkun Olam*," which appears in this volume.

biblical teachings. This covenant was written on stones taken from the riverbed of the Jordan River, which were revealed when the river split in order to allow the Israelites to pass through on their way into the Promised Land (Josh. 3:4–18). The Bible stresses that the covenant is to be "well clarified" (*be'er hetev*), which rabbinic tradition interprets as the commandment to translate it into the seventy languages of all the nations of the world.[11]

The Bible also delineates the punishments that will befall the Israelites if they disregard this covenant. At the conclusion of the litany, the Bible states, "These are the words of the covenant which the Lord commanded Moses to seal with the Children of Israel in the land of Moab, aside from (in addition to) the covenant which He sealed with them at Horeb" (Deut. 28:69), emphasizing the unique nature of this Third Covenant.

What is the message of this third, additional covenant, especially since our other two covenants have already designated us as an eternal nation and an eternal religion? I submit that this is the Covenant of Universal Redemption, which can only come about if the nations of the world accept fundamental biblical morality. It is the covenant that squarely places upon the Jewish people the responsibility to teach the moral truths of the Bible to the world.

This explains why this covenant is sealed only when the Jewish people are about to enter the Land of Israel: Only a people which has its own homeland and is a nation among nations that must deal with problems of peace and war, economic and social gaps within society, poverty, crime, and minorities, can ever hope to influence and inspire other nations to accept an ethic of compassionate righteousness, justice, and peace. In this way, the Third Covenant links together in an indelible bind the two previous covenants of ethnic nationality and religious morality.

It is important to note that the laws delineated in this Third Covenant are all directed to *ish*, the Hebrew generic term for "person" – as opposed to "Jews." They are universal in import:

---

11. Sota 37b, cited by Rashi in his commentary to Deut. 27:8.

> Cursed is the person (*ish*) who degrades his father or mother.
>
> Cursed is the person who perverts the judgment of the widow and the orphan.
>
> Cursed is the person who puts a stumbling block before the blind.
>
> Cursed is the person who receives a bribe to slay an innocent person. (Deut. 27:15–26)

This also explains why the Sabbath and circumcision are not mentioned in this Third Covenant, although circumcision is an important aspect of the First Covenant and the Sabbath is an important component of the Decalogue and Sinai Covenant. Despite the fact that the first "curse" applies to "the person who will make a graven or molten image, an abomination to the Lord," recall that one of the seven Noahide commandments of morality was the prohibition against idolatry. Noahides are not obligated to believe in God, but they are prohibited from engaging in the cruel and immoral acts that idolaters performed in the names of the idols. Indeed, according to some rabbinic opinions, idolatry is defined by immoral acts rather than theological error.[12] It is interesting to note that virtually in every place that the Pentateuch deplores idolatry and forbids idol worship, it adds the reason "lest we learn from their practices" (Ex. 23:24; Deut. 7:5–11; 12:3–4, 30, 31; 18:9–13; 20:17–18).

This universal message of the Third Covenant may likewise be why, immediately after the content of the Third Covenant is delineated, the Bible records, "Not with you (Israelites) alone do I seal this covenant and this imprecation, but with whoever is here, standing with us today before the Lord our God, and also with whoever is not here with us today" (Deut. 29:13–14). The meaning of these words seem to be the inclusion of the gentiles as well as the Israelites: the gentiles who are not with us today will one day stand with us in acceptance of the fundamental laws of morality.

---

12. See Jacob Katz, *Exclusiveness and Tolerance* (Shocken: New York, 1962) chapter 10, and Moshe Halbertal and Avishai Margolit, *Idolatry* (Harvard University Press, 1992), pp. 204–209.

This is also why the sages of the Talmud saw fit to interpret the biblical *be'er hetev* (well-clarified) to mean "translated into seventy languages of the world." Were these moral laws only meant for Jews, there would be no need to translate them into the languages of the gentiles or to position them on the twelve stones placed in Gilgal, at the point of entry and exit into Israel near the two great mountains of Gerizim and Eybal (Deut. 27: 1–9). This locus of the twelve stones was Israel's gateway to the world, to where and from where Israelites and gentiles would come and go, read, and reflect upon whatever was displayed on those stones.

WHICH TORAH IS TO BE TAUGHT TO THE GENTILES?

It is difficult to know precisely which text was to be written on the stones, as the verse declares, "and you shall write upon the stones all the words of this Torah (teaching), well clarified" (Deut. 27:8). I have assumed it refers to the "Torah" of the Third Covenant, the twelve moral laws on the twelve stones that are delineated in verses 15–26 – six blessings expressed by six tribes on Mt. Gerizim and six curses expressed by six other tribes on Mt. Eybal (27:9–26).

The medieval biblical exegete Isaac Abrabanel interpreted "all the words of this Torah" to mean some parts of Deuteronomy, which can refer to the verses of "Cursed be," as I maintain. Another medieval commentator, Abraham Ibn Ezra believes that "a number (or the number) of commandments… like warnings" were written on the stones. He may well be referring to the twelve imprecations (*azharot*, warnings), as well.[13]

However, Maimonides (ad loc.) suggests that all 613 commandments were written on the stones, and the Aramaic Targumim,[14] together with the majority of the biblical commentaries, claim that the entire Pentateuch was somehow inscribed – with seventy translations – on those twelve stones. In truth, and perhaps in support of this latter view, the Book of Joshua records, "and (Joshua) inscribed there on stone a copy of the Torah of Moses" (8:32). However, I would argue that these

---

13. See their respective commentaries on the Bible, ad loc.
14. The traditional Aramaic translations of the original Hebrew biblical text.

Hebrew words may also be taken to mean the Deuteronomy of Moses or even a part thereof.

If I am correct in interpreting this Third Covenant to be a covenant for all the nations of the world, the implications of this debate are serious indeed. Are Jews responsible to teach gentiles only the seven Noahide laws and these twelve moral imprecations, or is the Jewish people duty bound to teach the world all 613 commandments and to convert them to Judaism? I will analyze this question in greater depth before concluding this study. I add here that there are actually three possibilities:

1. Jews are responsible to teach gentiles only the universal laws of Noah and the twelve imprecations.
2. It would be salutary – but not necessary – for gentiles to learn and practice all 613 commandments, and hence Jews ought to expose them to the entire Torah but are not obligated to convert them.
3. Jews are obligated to teach gentiles and even attempt to convert them. However, Jews are only to coerce gentiles regarding acceptance of the Noahide laws.

CONVERSION AND THE JEWISH RESPONSIBILITY TO THE WORLD

We have seen that at the moment of the election of Abraham, God explicitly proclaimed, "Through you (Abraham), shall all the families of the earth be blessed" (Gen. 12–13). God repeats this universal directive immediately after the binding (and near-sacrifice) of Isaac at the place of the future Temple Mount stating that, "through your seed all the nations of the earth shall be blessed" (22:14–18). God ordains this same mission for Isaac (26:4), and then for Jacob: "And your seed shall be as the dust of the earth, and you shall spread out significantly westward, eastward, northward, and southward, and all the families of the earth shall be blessed by you and by your seed" (28:14). Hence, from the inception of our faith, Jews were ordained to be a blessing to the world, apparently by virtue of teaching the gentiles the message of Abrahamic ethical monotheism and to fulfill the biblical mandate to be "a kingdom of priest-teachers" (Ex. 19:6).

The Third Covenant reflects a third creation, the redemption of the world, "the last for which the first was made," the very goal of the initial creation. This is the new covenant in which God will place His Torah within us, will inscribe it onto our hearts. The Torah will not be foreign to us but will emanate from the portion of the divine within each and every human being, so "no one will have to teach about God, for everyone will know Him, all of humanity together" (Jer. 31:30–33). At that time "no one will injure or destroy in all My holy mountain, for the earth will be filled with the knowledge of the Lord as the waters cover the sea bed" (Is. 11:9).

This Third Covenant reflects the truth that the Jewish people are "God's witnesses"[15] and affirms the Jewish covenantal responsibility to bear witness before all of humanity. The Midrash defines the Jewish obligation in a specific way.

> The Bible teaches, "A person is considered a sinner if he hears a false oath, and he is a witness – either because he saw or knows [the truth] – if he does not give testimony, he must bear the guilt (Lev. 5:1)." "He is a witness" – this refers to Israel, as it is said, "You are My witnesses, says the Lord" (Is. 43:12). "Either because he saw" – as it says, "You (Israel) have been shown in order to know that the Lord He is God" (Deut. 4:39). "And if he does not give testimony, he must bear the guilt" – if you (Israel) do not declare My Lordship to the nations of the world, I shall exact punishment from you.[16]

Another midrash[17] emphasizes that the Torah was revealed in the desert rather than in the Land of Israel to express the truth that the revelation at Sinai was intended for all peoples, not just for Jews:

> "They encamped in the wilderness" (Ex. 19:2). The Torah was given in a free place (*demos, parresia*). For had the Torah been

---

15. "You are My witnesses," says the Lord, "and I am God" (Is. 43:12).
16. Leviticus Rabba 6.
17. *Mekhilta DeRabbi Yishmael, Baḥodesh* 1 (Lauterbach ed.) p. 198.

given in the Land of Israel, the Israelites could have said to the nations of the world, "You have no share in it." But now that it was given in the wilderness publicly and openly, in a place that is free for all, everyone wishing to accept it could come and accept it.[18]

THE THIRD COVENANT IS READ PUBLICLY
BEFORE ROSH HASHANA

The Talmud records a striking and frightening prescription concerning when certain biblical texts are read in the synagogue:

> Rabbi Shimon ben Elazar says: Ezra (the Scribe) enacted for the Israelites that they publicly read the curses of the Book of Leviticus before Shavuot (The Feast of Pentacost, *atzeret*) and the curses of the Book of Deuteronomy before Rosh HaShana."
> (Megilla 31b)

The two biblical texts known as "the curses" are Leviticus 26:14–46, and Deuteronomy 28:15–69. Each of these begins with the exile of the Israelites from the Land of Israel, leading the medieval rabbinic authority Nahmanides to maintain that the Leviticus curses refer to the Babylonian exile after the destruction of the First Temple (586 BCE), while the Deuteronomy curses refer to the exile after Rome's destruction of the Second Temple in 70 CE.

Ezra the Scribe worked out the schedule for Jews to read specific biblical portions each week in synagogue, and he prescribed that they read the Leviticus punishments before the reading of the Sinai Covenant and Ten Commandments on the Pentecost festival that commemorates revelation of the Torah at Sinai – despite the fact that the Sinai Decalogue occurred chronologically well before the Leviticus punishments in the Bible. However, Jewish tradition decided that Jews not read the Deuteronomy curses as Ezra ordained, but two Sabbaths before and reserved the latter portion of Deuteronomy 29, 30 for the Sabbath immediately before Rosh HaShana, the Jewish new year.

---

18. Marc Hirshman, *Torah for the Entire World* (Kibbutz HaMeuḥad: Tel Aviv 1999), especially chapter 7.

Why does Jewish practice today depart from Ezra's prescribed reading sequence? I maintain that the biblical portion of *Nitzavim* (Deut. 29:9) is a direct continuation of the Third Covenant in the previous portion:

> You are standing today, all of you, before the Lord, your God, from the heads of your tribes…to the drawer of your water, for you to pass into the covenant of the Lord your god and into His imprecation… Not with you alone do I seal this covenant…but with whoever is here…and with whoever is not here with Me today. (Deut. 29:9–14)

As I have interpreted, these last words refer to the gentile community, which was not yet standing together with the Israelites when they were poised to enter the Land of Israel close to four thousand years ago. Yet, the Third Covenant was meant to include them, as far as the moral laws of the twelve imprecations.[19]

It is thus understandable why the talmudic sages prescribed the Third Covenant be read before Rosh HaShana, since it is the most universal Jewish holiday. The New Year's liturgy maintains that Rosh HaShana is the day "on which the world was conceived, when the

---

19. My revered teacher, Rabbi Joseph B. Soloveitchik, offered another reason why *Nitzavim* is a continuation of *Ki Tavo*; the curses of *Ki Tavo* conclude with a promise of return, just as was the case in *Beḥukkotai*, yet not immediately. Jews must wait for the following biblical portion of *Nitzavim*. It is there (Deut. 30:4, 5) that God promises, "Even if you are scattered to the end of the heavens, from there the Lord your God will bring you to the land that your ancestors possessed and you shall possess it." Why is the promise not immediate? Because God tells us that in the instance of the second destruction, Jewish return will depend upon our repentance, and so the exhortation to repent and its historical occurrence must precede the promise to return (Deut. 30:1–10). "Return" involves a physical return to the Land of Israel as well as spiritual return to God's biblical teachings. Indeed, the two unique and revolutionary Jewish movements of this past century are 1) Zionism, a return to Israel initiated by the people rather than a passive waiting for a reluctant Messiah, and 2) the Baal Teshuva (repentants) movement, bringing alienated Jews "home" to their traditional roots in a radical change of persona, à la Franz Rosenzweig. See Nahum Glatzer, *Franz Rosenzweig: His Life and Thought* (Hackett Publishing, 1998).

first human being was formed in God's womb." On that date, Jews blow the shofar (trumpet) of world redemption to anticipate the day "when all the inhabitants and dwellers of the earth will see the banner of God hoisted upon the mountains and will hear the sounds of the shofar," as Isaiah 18:3 insisted. Indeed, the central prayer of the day is the *Aleinu* prayer, in which Jews are called "to perfect the world in the Kingship of the Almighty, when all children of flesh will call upon Your Name and all the wicked of the earth will turn towards You... when everyone will accept the yoke of Your Kingship and You will rule over them forever."

Ten days later, on Yom Kippur, the Fast of Universal Forgiveness, Jews repeatedly recite God's own prayer that, "My House (i.e., the Temple) shall be called a house of prayer for all peoples" (Is. 56:7). And the universal Kingship of God is described by the High Holy Days liturgy as the time when, "all created beings will fear You and all creatures will bow down before You; everyone will unite in one bond to carry out Your will with a full heart."

The Third Covenant and the High Holy Days liturgy both emphasize the Jewish responsibility for the world, and thus the two experiences are conjoined. It is now not only clear why the curses are publicly read before Rosh HaShana, and why the Third Covenant is known as the covenant of the responsibility (*brit arevut*).[20] The Hebrew term, *arev*, denotes a co-signer, i.e., one who assumes legal responsibility for paying a loan when the debtor defaults. This Third Covenant, exhorting the Jewish people to teach ethical monotheism to the world, is crucially important for a free world to survive. In our global village, where one extremist madman can set off a nuclear war and destroy humanity, without the universal acceptance of "Thou shall not murder an innocent person," no person is safe or secure. Each one of us – humanity in its entirety – is responsible for the other, co-signers for each other. We dare not "ask for whom the bell tolls"; it tolls for all of us together!

The Jewish covenantal mission is to teach the world ethical monotheism, as the term kingdom of priest-teachers (Ex.19:6) suggests. If the Jewish people fail to fulfill this responsibility its onus is grave indeed.

---

20. Sota 37b.

The Jewish people will suffer the consequences for the sins of the nations of the world. The nations will hate us because we gave them a divine moral order, but which they chose to dismiss. It is easier to shoot the messenger rather than refute the message. Hence, we will become the first victims of hateful arrows and will be "the suffering servants," casualties of human immorality (Is. 53). This may be why the covenant was sealed in the plains of Moab. The celebrated convert to Judaism, Ruth, hailed from Moab and, according to the Bible, she was destined to be the progenitor of the Messiah, the standard bearer for Judaism that fulfills its mission with world redemption.

IS THERE A JEWISH OBLIGATION TO CONVERT?

Conventional wisdom is that Judaism is not a proselytizing religion and that we do not encourage – and perhaps that we are even legally mandated to discourage – proselytes to Judaism. I have argued that there is an undisputable Jewish obligation that Jews have largely abandoned since the Hadrianic persecutions in 135 CE: It is to actively proselytize gentiles to accept the seven Noahide laws of morality or the twelve imprecations of the Third Covenant. Maimonides' formulation of this obligation leaves no room for doubt:

> Moses our Master did not bequeath the Torah and the commandments to anyone except to Israel, as it is written, "Moses commanded to us the Torah, a heritage for the Congregation of Jacob" (Deut. 33:4) as well as to those of the nations of the world who wish to convert, as it is written: "The Congregation (of Israel) shall have the same statute for you and for the convert who lives among you" (Num. 15:15). But one who doesn't wish to convert is not to be forced to accept the Torah and its commandments. Similarly, Moses our Master commanded Israel *to force* everyone to accept all of the commandments commanded to Noah.[21]

A beneficent social order is dependent on the acceptance of the fundamental principles of morality and that no human being is safe when

---

21. *Mishneh Torah*, Laws of Kings 8:10.

another individual rejects these fundamental laws. Hence, we have the right to coerce, if necessary, people to accept these universal laws of morality. Moreover, according to Maimonides, once an individual accepts this ethical system and acknowledges its divine authority and, hence, its permanent validity, he is worthy of salvation and has a share in the World to Come.[22]

TWO TYPES OF COMMANDMENTS AND THE COMMANDMENT TO CONVERT

Is there a specific commandment for Jews to convert gentiles to Judaism? Since a life of commitment to the seven Noahide commandments is sufficient for non-Jews to secure a place in the World to Come, it is clear to me that there is no *obligatory* commandment (*mitzva ḥiyuvit*) upon a Jew to convert a gentile to all the Jewish commandments. There is, however, a type of commandment known as a *fulfillment* commandment (*mitzva kiyumit*). One is not obligated to act on this commandment, but if one chooses to do so of their own free choice, one then indeed fulfills a divinely desirable act. For example, no one is obligated to become a physician; if one does, however, and saves a person's life, he fulfills the divinely desirable act of saving lives. I maintain, therefore, that if the gentile *chooses* to convert, even though it is not necessary, he would then be fulfilling such a divinely desirable act. This is an important position, if only to ensure a welcoming attitude towards gentiles who display interest in becoming Jews.

The Talmud[23] ordains that when a would-be convert is circumcised for the sake of conversion, the Jew who oversees the act intones the blessing, "Blessed art Thou O Lord King of the Universe who has sanctified us with His commandments and has *commanded us to circumcise the converts* and to extract from them the blood of the covenant." The assumption of the Talmud may be that there is a

---

22. Ibid., 8:11. For the scholarly discussion of this important passage and its implications, see Eugene Korn, "Gentiles, the World to Come and Judaism," *Modern Judaism*, October 1994.
23. Shabbat 137b.

Within the talmudic literature, the sage Hillel went so far as to entice gentiles with study stipends to teach them Torah and to ease them into conversion. The Talmud (Shabbat 31) also records how Hillel converted virtually anyone who expressed a desire to do so, no matter what conditions the would-be convert demanded, confident that in subsequent lessons Hillel could disabuse them of their conditions. The Talmud likewise records traditions that the rabbis Shmaya and Avtalyon, Onkelos, Ben Bag Bag, and Ben Heh Heh were all proselytes, and that Rabbi Akiva and Rabbi Meir were born into families of proselytes. The Tosefta (Pesaḥim 7:9) recounts that when a large group of Roman legions converted the day before Passover, that very night they ate the Passover sacrifice at the Seder, in accordance with the view of the Academy of Shammai.

Rabbi Yehuda HaNasi expounded on Song of Songs 1:15, "There is a type of dove which, when it's being fed, gives off a certain fragrance which attracts its friends to come to its dove-cote. A similar phenomenon occurs with Israel. At the time when the Elder sits and expounds Torah (to his disciples), many proselytes convert at that very time."[31]

Finally, the blessing of the daily statutory prayer (*Amida*) which praises God for being a "support and security for the righteous," opens with the words: "Upon the righteous, upon the pious, upon the elders of your nation the House of Israel, upon the remnants of their scribes and *upon the righteous proselytes* may You rouse Your mercies, O Lord our God." It is likely that had conversion not been widespread, proselytes would not have been mentioned![32]

CONVERSION TO JUDAISM OR TO THE NOAHIDE LAWS?

Do the Bible and Talmud advocate converting the world to full Judaism, or merely to bring as many people as possible into the Third Covenant and the Noahide covenant with its seven fundamentals of morality? This

---

31. Song of Songs Rabba 1:15.
32. See further Rosh HaShana 31b, Berakhot 27b, and Mishna Yadayim 4:4, which all deal with questions of proselytes after the destruction of the Temple, when they could not bring their "conversion" sacrifice.

question may be seen as a difference of opinion between the prophets
Isaiah and Micah. Isaiah has a magnificent vision of the end of the days:

> When the mountain of the Temple of the Lord will be firmly
> established…and all the nations will stream to it, the multitude
> of nations will go and say, "Come let us go up…to the Temple
> of the God of Jacob, and he (Jacob) will teach us of his ways and
> we will walk in his paths." For from Zion shall come forth the
> Torah and the word of the Lord from Jerusalem…. They shall
> beat their swords into plowshares and their spears into pruning
> hooks; nation will not lift sword against nation and humanity
> will not learn war anymore. (Is. 2:1–5)

These words may be taken to mean that everyone will convert to the
complete Jewish tradition, that from Zion the entire Torah will come
forth, and the "word of the Lord will extend from Jerusalem" to the world.

Micah 4:5 repeats this prophecy, yet he adds the following significant phrase: "For all the peoples will go forth, *each person in the
name of his God,* but we shall go forth with the name of the Lord our
God forever and ever." This suggests a pluralistic view, an acceptance of
other faith communities with different names for God and other ritual
customs, as long as those communities accept the basic moral principles
of the Noahide laws, eschew war and bloodshed, and are committed to
the God of Peace.

As the foremost legal authority and philosopher in Jewish history,
Maimonides' views on this question are critical to Jewish theology. As we
have seen, Maimonides requires coercing humanity – if necessary – to
accept the seven Noahide laws, but he does not require Jews to convert
moral gentiles to Judaism and its 613 commandments. He accepts every
human being as a child of God and salvific in his/her own right as long
as they accept the seven Noahide laws.

Maimonides maintains, however, that in the Messianic Age, when
true peace will reign and every individual will strive to know God to
the greatest extent possible, "everyone will return to the true religion"
(*dat ha'emet*). The meaning of this term, *dat ha'emet,* – and by implication whether Maimonides considers universal conversion to Judaism a

theological ideal for today – is still unresolved. Scholars disagree whether Maimonides believes that gentiles (a) will accept all Jewish beliefs and commandments; (b) will fully accept only the Noahide commandments; or (c) will accept the Noahide commandments and belief in the God of creation and revelation. In other words, scholars disagree as to whether Maimonides believes that gentiles and Jews will remain separate and distinct religious bodies in the eschaton.[33]

It is in *Mishneh Torah*, Laws of Kings, chapter 12:1 that Maimonides mentions *dat ha'emet*. The expression in question seems to refer to commandments beyond the seven Noahide laws and additional to belief in monotheism:

> Let it not enter your mind that in the days of the Messiah any aspect of the regular order of the world will be abolished or some innovation will be introduced into nature; rather, the world follows its accustomed course. The verse in Isaiah, "The wolf shall dwell with the lamb, the leopard lie down with the kid," is an allegory and metaphor. Its meaning is that Israel will dwell in security with the wicked nations of the earth which are allegorically represented as wolves and leopards, as it says (Jer. 5:6): "The wolf of the desert ravages them; a leopard lies in wait by their towns." *Those nations will all adopt the true religion (dat ha'emet).* They will neither rob nor destroy; rather they will eat permitted foods in peace and quiet together with Israelites, as it says, "the lion, like the ox, shall eat straw."

One can argue that Maimonides maintained here that in the Messianic Age, everyone – Jew and gentile alike – will keep Jewish dietary laws,

---

33. Menachem Kellner contends (a) that Maimonides believes gentiles will convert to Judaism; Chaim Rapoport, believes (b) that Maimonides' texts indicate only that they will accept the Noahide laws. See Kellner, "Maimonides 'True Religion': For Jews or All Humanity?" and Rapoport, "*Dat Ha'emet* in Maimonides' *Mishneh Torah*" in *Meorot* 7:1, Tishrei 5769, found at www.yctorah.org. Gerald Blidstein claims that Maimonides requires acceptance of Noahide laws and fundamental belief in God. See Blidstein, *Political Concepts in Maimonidean Halakha* (Bar Ilan University: 1983) p. 98, Note 27 and p. 227.

and by implication all other Sinaitic commandments. There are textual variants that support alternative interpretations.[34]

Other writings of Maimonides stress the salutary quality of a gentile performing the commandments, even to the extent of his identification of *dat ha'emet* with conversion. In his "Epistle to Obadiah the Proselyte,"[35] Maimonides describes a convert as "a person who left his father, his native land, his nation's realm (parallel to Abraham of Gen. 12) and, having gained inner understanding, came to join this nation (Israel) ... and recognized and knew that their (Israel's) religion is a true and righteous religion (*dat emet vatzedek*). He came to recognize all this and sought after God, traversing the holy path and entering beneath the wings of the Divine Presence, embracing the dust at the feet of Moses our Teacher."[36]

In *Guide for the Perplexed* (II:31) Maimonides refers to the Sabbath as a day when all humanity will rest, "ultimately as a universal day devoted to matters of the spiritual intellect. In his Responsa,[37] Maimonides declares that "it is permissible for Jews to teach Torah and commandments to Christians (but not to Moslems, since Christians accept the sanctity of our Scripture) in order to draw them closer to our truth, and he adds that, "a Jew is permitted to circumcise a gentile if the gentile wishes to remove his foreskin, since a gentile receives reward for every commandment he performs" (section 148). To put it another way, Maimonides encouraged us to "bear witness" before gentiles, but did not believe that there is an obligation to convert gentiles.

---

34. Rapoport, ibid., p. 5, offers an alternative interpretation in the name of the Lubavitcher Rebbe, based on the textual version that includes the word "*keYisrael*" ("like Israel" or "like Israelites") instead of "with" Israel. I respectively disagree. "*KeYisrael*" indicates to me that Maimonides pictured a period when the differences in behavior between Jews and gentiles will largely disappear.

35. *Responsa of Maimonides*, ed. Freiman, (Tel Aviv, 5694, 1933–34) Section 369.

36. Note the reference to Moses with regard to the convert, and not to Abraham. Maimonides described Abraham's discovery of monotheism as *derekh ha'emet*, because Abraham did not grasp and accept all of the commandments (*Mishneh Torah*, Laws of Idolatry 1, 10). *Dat ha'emet*, the religion of truth, is apparently reserved for Moses and those converts who accept all the commandments.

37. Book I:149 (Blau edition).

Does this mean that Maimonides posited that in the eschaton all gentiles will accept the 613 commandments of the Torah and formally convert to Judaism? In his discussions of the eschaton, Maimonides never explicitly mentions conversion. Gerald Blidstein insists, however, that in Maimonides' vision, gentiles will eventually accept more than the seven Noahide laws or the twelve commandments of the Third Covenant.[38]

Whether or not the gentiles will formally convert to Judaism in the eschaton is a difference of opinion within the Talmud (Berakhot 57b):

> One who sees a place from which idolatry was uprooted recites, "Blessed (be God) who has uprooted idolatry from our land: and as it has been uprooted from this place, so may it be uprooted from all places in Israel, and may You return the hearts of their worshippers to worship You." But outside the Land of Israel there is no need to say, "Return the hearts of their worshippers to worship You," for the majority there are gentiles. Rabbi Shimon ben Elazar says: "Even outside the Land of Israel one must say that, for (all the gentiles) are destined to convert, as it is written: 'Then will I turn to the peoples a pure language, that they may all call upon the name of the Lord to serve Him with one consent.'" (Zeph. 3:9)

The question of whether the Diaspora prayer should or should not include the request, "return the hearts of their worshippers to worship You," hinges on whether or not Jewish theology maintains that eventually all gentiles will convert. The sages believe they will not, so the prayer in the Diaspora is superfluous; Rabbi Shimon ben Elazar believes they will, and so the prayer must be recited. Rabbi Shimon ben Elazar uses as his proof-text our citation from Zephaniah. Maimonides decides the law in accordance with Rabbi Shimon ben Elazar, i.e., that we do recite the line in question in the Diaspora, suggesting that everyone will eventually formally convert.[39]

---

38. See Blidstein, op.cit, pp. 228–235, who cites the sources mentioned here.
39. *Mishneh Torah*, Laws of Blessings 10:9. This is significant, since Maimonides here departs from the normal legal protocol, deciding with the individual opinion of Rabbi Shimon and against the majority.

To buttress the view that all gentiles will convert to Mosaic Judaism in the Messianic Age, despite the fact that the Talmud teaches that proselytes were neither accepted in the days of the kings David and Solomon, nor will they be accepted in messianic times (Yevamot 24b), Maimonides cites only the prohibition during the periods of the kings David and Solomon.[40] He pointedly omits the Messianic Era, apparently because he believes that gentiles will then convert and that they must be accepted for redemption to arrive.

Maimonides' position seems clear. He believed that Jews are enjoined to coerce, if necessary, gentiles to accept the seven Noahide laws of the Third Covenant because that acceptance is crucial for civilization to endure. We are not obligated to convert gentiles, and we surely do not coerce their conversion. When one's acceptance of Noahide moral principles is coupled with belief in a transcendent, commanding God, this person has a share in the World to Come (salvation) and is to be respected and loved as a child of God created in the divine image. We are, however, permitted – and perhaps even encouraged – to teach gentiles the Torah and its commandments, an act that Maimonides saw as part of the commandment for Jews to love God. Finally, Maimonides contended that in the eschaton all will convert because it will be rationally and morally compelling for them to do so.

There is historical confirmation of a gentile community that accepted universal natural law and monotheism, chose which of the ritual laws they desired to keep, generally prayed in the synagogue, but that did not formally convert. These "quasi or associate" Jews were nonetheless highly respected by the official Jewish community during the Second Commonwealth. Called *yirei Hashem* or *yirei Shamayim* (God-fearing persons), they were involved in sundry Jewish practices but never converted:

> They accepted without doubt faith in one God and the interpersonal commandments, but as far as the commandments between humans and God, they differed greatly from each other

40. *Mishneh Torah*, Laws of Forbidden Sexual Relations 13:15.

in practice. Many of them even attended synagogue – but they did not, and nor did they intend to, convert.[41]

Permit me a personal insight, one that is critical to the ground rules of Christian-Jewish dialogue: I believe it is quite legitimate for any particular faith community to maintain that its revelation is the perfect one, and that ultimately (in the eschaton) all the others will convert to that faith. However, it is crucial that the members of each respective faith community respect the members of other faith communities as inviolable children of God even when they do not convert, as long as they subscribe to the ethical Noahide commandments.

IN DEFENSE OF RELIGIOUS PLURALISM
AND ETHICAL ABSOLUTISM

Maimonides adopted the Aristotelian monistic conception that led him to insist on absolute monotheism. This caused him to reject Trinitarian Christianity as idolatry for both Christians and Jews.[42] However, Maimonides' view is not the only Jewish perspective, neither from a study of the Bible nor from an investigation into the views of other rabbinical authorities and decisors of Jewish law, both early and late.[43]

Nearly every time the Bible forbids idolatry, it is in the context of *immoral behavior*:

"Do not bow down to their gods and do not serve them; you must not do actions which are like their (the idolaters) actions" (Ex. 23:24).

---

41. Saul Lieberman, *Greek and Hellenism in Jewish Palestine* (Bialik Institute: Jerusalem, 1962) pp. 59–68. Lieberman entitles this section of his book, "Semi-Converts, Semi-Gentiles." See also Ps. 115:13,118:4, 135:20, which make positive reference to them as a separate and venerated group.

42. Commentary on Mishna, Avoda Zara 1:3–4 and *Mishneh Torah*, Laws of Idolatry 9, 4.

43. See Eugene Korn's masterful study, "Rethinking Christianity, Rabbinic Positions and Possibilities," in *Jewish Theology and World Religions* (Littman Library of Jewish Civilization, 2012), from which this catalogue of early and late rabbinic authorities is taken. See also Moshe Halbertal and Avishai Margalit, *Idolatry*, op. cit., and Jacob Katz, *Exclusiveness and Tolerance*, op. cit (chapter 10).

> Guard yourself...lest you seek out their gods...Do not do that
> to the Lord your God, because every abomination to the Lord,
> which He hated, they do to their gods; they even burn their sons
> and their daughters in fire to their gods." (Deut. 12:30–31)

> Do not learn to act like the abominations of those nations; let
> there not be found amongst you someone who passes his son or
> his daughter into fire." (18:9–10)

> You shall surely destroy the Hittite and the Amorite; the Canaan-
> ite and the Perizite...in order that they not teach you to do in
> accordance with all their abominations which they did to their
> gods." (20:17–18)

The unmistakable concern of the Bible is correct behavior. This points
to the profound difference between the Jewish outlook and the philosophical worldviews of Plato and Aristotle: Whereas the philosophers
were mostly interested in correct thought (as is clear from Plato's
"Theatitus"), Judaism is primarily interested with moral action.[44]
God chose Abraham because he was committed to teach succeeding
generations *tzedaka u'mishpat*, "compassionate righteousness and justice" (Gen. 18:19) – rather than because he discovered or would teach
pure monotheism![45] Perhaps the most important biblical verse that
expresses emphasis on proper action as the cardinal principle of biblical faith is found in Jeremiah. Jews read this verse publicly on the 9th
of Av, the fast day when they mourn the destruction of the Temple
that Jeremiah foresaw:

> So does God say, "Let the wise man not be praised for his wis-
> dom, let the strong man not be praised for his strength, let the

---

44. The fact that the Septuagint translates Torah as *nomos* (law in Greek) and that the
    Talmud concludes its argument as to what is superior, study or action, with the
    directive: "Great is study because it leads to action" (Kiddushin 40b) buttresses
    this contention.

45. Although Maimonides portrays Abraham as philosopher, *Mishneh Torah*, Laws of
    Idolatry 1:4.

rich man not be praised for his riches. Only in this regard shall one be praised: Be wise and know Me, for I am the Lord who does loving-kindness, moral justice and righteous compassion in the land, because these are what I desire, says the Lord." (Jer. 9:22–23)

Note well the prophet's words: proper knowledge of God is derived not from intellectual cognition, but from compassionate and moral conduct.[46] From this perspective, although Maimonides defines idolatry exclusively in theological and metaphysical terms,[47] Rabbi Menaḥem HaMeiri defined idolatry in terms of the "disgusting immoral acts of the idolaters, whose paganism kept their adherents from accepting the moral norms of the Noahide laws or of the Third Covenant."[48]

In addition to these two end positions, there are two intermediate positions held by the overwhelming majority of halakhic decisors. The first is based upon the talmudic statement (Ḥullin 13b) that "gentiles outside of the Land of Israel are not idolators but only follow the traditions of their fathers." This was the normative ruling held by all medieval rabbinic authorities living in Christian Ashkenaz, including Rashi and Rabbi Asher ben Yeḥiel, as well as by Rabbi Yosef Karo in Turkey and Sefat. They consider Trinitarian Christianity to be illegitimate theology, but ruled that Christians are not idolators.

The second of these intermediate positions maintains that while Christianity is illegitimate for a Jew, it is not so for gentiles. The

---

46. This idea is also strikingly noted by the Talmud in a conversation between Rabbi Ḥanina ben Teradyon and Rabbi Elazar ben Parta during the Hadrianic persecutions. The former says that he will be executed by the Romans and his colleague will be saved, since his colleague has both Torah knowledge and good works, whereas he has only Torah knowledge. The Gemara adds in the name of Rabbi Ḥuna that someone who has only Torah knowledge but is devoid of good works is similar to someone who has no God! (Avoda Zara 17b)

47. Significantly, Maimonides ends his philosophic work *Guide for the Perplexed* explaining the importance of Jeremiah's verse for Jewish theology. He maintained that when one attains a correct knowledge of God, he will then naturally act like God, performing loving-kindness (*ḥesed*), justice (*mishpat*) and righteousness (*tzedek*).

48. *Beit HaBeḥira*, Sanhedrin 57a, and Avoda Zara 20a. See also Jacob Katz, op. cit., chapter 10, and Moshe Halbertal, *Bein Torah LeḤakhma* (Jerusalem 2000), chapter 3, and *Idolatry*, op. cit., pp. 204–209.

Decalogue in the Book of Exodus forbade idolatry for Jews after idolatry had already been forbidden to all humanity in Genesis in the form of the seven Noahide laws of morality. Jewish exegetes inferred that apparently there was a specific addition to the prohibition in Exodus meant for the Jews alone, and this is the requirement of absolute monotheism.[49] As long as a religion worships the God Who is the Creator of the heavens and the earth as the ultimate moral authority of the universe, it is not idolatrous for its adherents, even if it appends other elements to the Creator – as is the case with Trinitarian Christians. This is the Jewish legal opinion of the majority of late rabbinic authorities (*Aharonim*).[50]

Beyond this, Rabbi Moshe Rivkis (17th century, Lithuania) argued that Jews should pray for the welfare of our Christian brethren since they believe in the creation of the world and in the Exodus from Egypt, and their intention is directed towards the Creator of heaven and earth.[51] Rabbi Jacob Emden (18th century, Germany) similarly praised Christians for having eradicated idolatry from the West and instilling a moral faith in consonance with the seven Noahide laws. Christians are instruments for the fulfillment of the prophecy that the knowledge of God will spread throughout the earth.[52]

A talmudic source for this last position can be found in the final mishna of chapter eight of the Tractate Berakhot, where the Jerusalem Talmud states that one should respond Amen to a gentile who blesses or praises God. The same passage cites Rabbi Tanḥum as maintaining that "one must respond Amen to a gentile who makes a blessing in the name of the Lord, as it is written, 'Blessed shall You be by all the nations.'"[53]

---

49. Rabbi Joseph Saul Nathanson, *Sho'el U'Meishiv* 1:26 and 51.
50. These include Rabbis Moshe Isserles (Rema, 16th century, Poland), Shabtai HaKohen (*Shakh*, 17th century, Bohemia), Rabbi Moshe Rivkis (Be'er HaGolah, 17th century, Lithuania), Jacob Emden (Ya'avetz, 18th century, Germany), and David Zvi Hoffman (19th century, Germany). See Korn, "Rethinking Christianity..." op. cit. regarding this list of rabbinic authorities.
51. Gloss on *Shulḥan Arukh, Ḥoshen Mishpat*, Section 425:5.
52. Commentary on Ethics of the Fathers 4:13. See Eugene Korn, "The People Israel, Christianity and the Covenantal Responsibility to History," for a fuller treatment of Rabbis Rivkis and Emden.
53. Rabbi Moshe Isserles established the normative ruling that one answers Amen to a gentile blessing when it is heard directly from the mouth of the gentile (gloss to

I further suggest that Meiri's view – that idolatry is defined by ethical and moral abominations in the name of religion than with incorrect theological concepts – is strongly supported by the fact that a gentile (*ger toshav*) who is permitted to live in the Land of Israel under Jewish religious sovereignty is only required to conform to proper moral behavior. He need not believe in one God and it is sufficient that he merely not practice idolatry.

The case for religious pluralism alongside ethical and moral absolutism is strengthened by the nature of the Noahide covenant, effectuated between God and the new humanity that descended from Noah and his sons after the rest of the world was destroyed:

> And the Lord said, "This is the sign (symbol) of the covenant which I am giving between Me and between you and between all living beings who are with you forever: I am giving My bow into the cloud, and it shall serve as the sign of the covenant between Me and the earth." (Gen. 9:12–13)

The rainbow is the symbol of the covenant, signaling both the end of the rain and the divine promise never to send another destructive flood upon the world again. The famous medieval Jewish commentator, Nahmanides, adds (ad loc.) content to this symbolism: In ancient times, when two nations were at war with each other using bows and arrows, when one side held up an inverted bow it was a sign of surrender and peace. God's inverted bow symbolized God's commitment to never again go to war against humanity. Thus, the rainbow is a divine sign to the world that God will never again attempt to destroy life on earth.

This may explain why God's sign of the rainbow is immediately preceded by God's moral demands upon humanity, i.e., no drinking the blood or eating the flesh of a living animal, no suicide, and no murder:

Shulḥan Arukh Oraḥ Ḥaim 215.2). *Mishna Berura* (ibid., 12) explains that when the gentile uses the same term for God that a Jew uses, he does not intend the blessing to be for an idol; *Biyur Halakha* adds that the Jew need not hear the blessing from the mouth of the gentile, and this became the later normative law as decided by Rabbi Elijah of Vilna (the Vilna Gaon).

"One who sheds human blood shall have his blood shed by humans, since God made the human being in His image" (Gen. 9:4–6), which is the basis of the seven Noahide moral laws. The rainbow is a half circle, still an incomplete symbol. In effect, God said that He will never destroy humanity again. But having created humanity with free choice, God cannot guarantee that humanity will not destroy itself. The future of humanity can only depend upon the universal human acceptance of "Thou shall not murder."

Rabbi Samson Raphael Hirsch provides additional content to the rainbow's symbolism: Gazing upon a rainbow, one sees seven dazzling colors: red, orange, yellow, green, blue, indigo, and violet. Yet, in reality there is but one color, white. When the rays of the sun shed their light upon the cloud, the white of the cloud refracts into the seven colors of the red, orange, yellow, green, blue, indigo, and violet. So it is also with human beings: Humanity seems separated into different peoples, with different skin pigmentations from black, to brown, to yellow, to white. In reality, however, we are all descendants of one human being, created in the image of the One Unique God. We all emerge from the divine womb and are all endowed with a portion of divine eternity.

Allow me to add to his symbolism. Can we not argue that, although we use different names, symbolic images, rituals, customs, and incantations by which we call and worship the Deity, everyone is speaking and praying to the same divine force who created and guides our world? Allah is another name for the One God (*El* or *Elohim*), the Trinity is mysteriously considered a unity by Christians, and all the physical representations of the Buddha are meant to express the All in the All that is the god of the Far East. Is it not possible that the real meaning of the credo of Judaism, the *Shema*, is: "Hear O Israel, the Lord (who is known by our different names of different forces and powers), *Eloheinu*, is (in reality the) One (YHVH of the entire cosmos)." Just as the white of the cloud is refracted into different colors, so the One God of love may be called by different names and different powers, but these all coalesce in the mind of the one praying and in the reality of the situation into the one all-encompassing Lord of the universe.

If this is the case, as long as humans are moral, they can call God by any name or names they wish since their true intent is the God of the universe. They may even be secular humanists, as long as they do not engage in the abominations of idol worship. The ultimate religious concern is that humans not destroy the world, and this can only be predicated upon the universal acceptance of ethical absolutes, compassionate righteousness and justice, the inviolability of the human being, and his/her right to live in freedom, peace, and security.

EPILOGUE

Our generation lives in an age of miracles. In addition to the return of the Jewish people to their covenantal home in the Land of Israel and the ingathering of the remnants of the Jewish people from the "lost" tribe of Dan in Ethiopia to the "lost" tribe of Menashe from India, there is the miracle of the rapprochement between Christianity and Judaism after nearly two thousand years of bitter enmity and Christian persecution of Jews.

Christianity sees itself as being grafted onto the Jewish covenant, God's covenant with Abraham. This is legitimate from a biblical and Jewish perspective since Abraham, by his very name, is a patriarch of a multitude of nations. Christianity worships Abraham's God of compassionate righteousness and justice, and traditional Christianity surely accepts the seven Noahide laws as given by God. The return of the younger faith to its maternal roots was eased by leading theologians from most churches recognizing the permanent legitimacy of the Jewish covenant with God and the possibility of Jewish salvation on the merit of that covenant. The partnership between the daughter and mother religions is particularly important today in the face of the existential threat of Islamist extremism against which all who are committed to a hopeful future must battle – including moderate Muslims. The Bible records a loving reconciliation between Isaac and Ishmael, coming together in bringing their father to his eternal resting place (Gen. 25:9).[54] The God of Abraham as the God of love, compassion, and peace is the antithesis of Satan, who instructs violence against all those who do not accept his cruel prescription for world domination.

---

54. See commentary of Rashi ad loc.

Yet our relationship goes beyond our mutual faiths in a God of love and our mutual struggle against religious violence. I have tried to show that Israel came onto the world scene, from the dawn of Abraham, with a mission to the world, a responsibility to teach the compelling message of a God of love and morality. Until the Hadrianic persecutions, Jews attempted to fulfill that mission. With Hadrian, the Jewish people were forced to leave history. Jews were exiled from the state of historic actors, and perforce became insularly concerned with ethnic survival. We forgot – or were forced to forget – our world mission.

Thankfully, Christians took up this mission. Traditional rabbis like Maimonides and Jacob Emden understood that Christians brought the concepts of divine commandments, morality, Messiah, and the God of love to the furthest corners of human civilization. Faithful Jews must be grateful for this.

Now that the Jewish people have returned to their homeland and to empirical history and now that Christians again recognize the legitimacy of the Jewish covenant, Jews and Christians must march together to bring the faith of morality and peace to a desperate but thirsting world. We dare not rest until we succeed and see "justice roll like the waters, and compassionate righteousness as a mighty stream" (Amos 5:24). This is our united mission, far more important than the legitimate and the to-be-respected differences that divide us. And if the moderate, religiously pluralistic Moslems join us, we will all not only survive as free people created in the divine image. We will redeem ourselves and the entire world.

Confrontation Revisited: Jewish-Christian Dialogue Today

My revered teacher and mentor, Rabbi Joseph B. Soloveitchik, published an essay entitled "Confrontation," dealing with the subject of Jewish-Christian dialogue; it appeared in the Spring 1964 edition of *Tradition* magazine, the official journal of the (Orthodox) Rabbinical Council of America. What follows is an analysis of and commentary on my mentor's masterful study forty-six years later, including some noteworthy encounters with Christians over the years, and a discussion of the changes which have occurred within Christian doctrine since 1964. My contention is that Rabbi Soloveitchik fundamentally *permits* theological dialogue with Christians, albeit under certain carefully-crafted guidelines, and that, under those guidelines, such dialogue is essential and critical to defending the interests of the Jewish people today.

INTRODUCTION

Professor David Flusser and a Protestant nun

My first involvement in Christian studies took place at the Hebrew University of Jerusalem in 1960–61, when I had the privilege of attending a course on the Greek text of the Gospels given by the renowned

Professor David Flusser, the foremost international scholar of the "Inter-Testamental" period. A deeply observant Jew, a talmudic scholar, and a historian-theologian of early Christianity, Flusser brought to bear all of the talmudic parallels to Jesus' teachings. The course – which covered most of the gospel according to Matthew in Greek – exposed me for the first time to the Jewish life that Jesus led.

Since the requirement for the course was fluency in ancient Greek, only four students enrolled; an Israeli Egged bus driver, an autodidact and Greek native whose avocation was the history of religions; a Protestant nun from Bonn, Germany, who was spending the year (as I was) studying in Israel; a 23-year-old monk named Yoḥanan from Terra Sancta; and me, a Greek major and student of Rabbi Soloveitchik, newly graduated from Yeshiva University and planning to return for *smikha* (rabbinical) studies after this Israeli interlude.

The class met in the Givat Ram campus of the Hebrew University three times a week in a very large room (Professor Flusser generally lectured to overflow audiences); the three men sat in the front row, opposite Professor Flusser. All the way at the far end of the room – in splendid isolation, dressed in a gray habit – sat the Protestant nun. Although we were often engaged in lively discussion over the proper interpretation of a text, she never joined in; the only time she spoke was after class, privately, directly to the professor.

On the last day of the term, the nun approached me shyly with a question. She understood that I was a rabbinical student and wondered if I could direct her to a program leading to conversion to Judaism.

When I asked why she was interested in conversion, she explained that she had been taught at her seminary that because the Jews had rejected Jesus as the Messiah, they were doomed to wander stateless throughout the world. Once she realized that God had fulfilled His divine promise to us and that we had indeed returned to our ancient homeland, she questioned her previous theology and began exploring the Old Testament assiduously. Her friendship with a young religious woman had introduced her to the lifestyle of Sabbath and festival observance, and that had confirmed her decision to become Jewish.

Coincidentally, I had been studying Talmud privately that year with an older and very respected protégé of Rabbi Soloveitchik – Rabbi

Zev Gotthold. Rabbi Gotthold's official position in Israel was *Megayer HaMedina,* the one responsible for all conversions in the Jewish state. I introduced my classmate to Rabbi Gotthold with a warm endorsement.

About three years later, my wife and I came to Israel for the summer. Rabbi Gotthold told me that this nun had indeed converted, married a "Rav Arele" hasid, and dressed almost identically to the way she had dressed when I had known her in her former identity. She now had one baby and was pregnant with a second. "My husband and I agree on almost everything except for one issue," she told me when we finally got together. "I am a religious Zionist." My encounter with this former nun made me aware of two things: the significance of the reborn State of Israel in the revision of what had been accepted Christian doctrine, as well as how seamlessly a deeply religious and modest Christian can adapt into a hasidic religious lifestyle.

Brother Yoḥanan, Birkat Kohanim, and Christian persecution

I also got to spend time with Brother Yoḥanan. We were almost the same age, so we naturally became friends and spent every Saturday evening together at the movies. I shared with him a lot of my thoughts and dreams, including my desire to participate in *Birkat Kohanim* at the Kotel (which in 1961 was closed to Jews). One night, he said to me, "I have looked into the matter and I am sure that I can arrange to fulfill your dream." I asked him what I had to do and he told me that it was simply a matter of completing a form. "Meet me at the Garden of Terra Sancta and bring your American passport," he said. "Then I'll be able to admit you as a Passover pilgrim, you will be able to pray at the Western Wall, and if you can find a quorum of Jews, you can recite the priestly blessing."

I was very excited. I met him as arranged and he gave me the form to fill out which I did with alacrity. It asked some standard questions about my identity which I readily filled out, but at the end of the form the last line read, "I hereby attest to the fact I am a believing Christian." I could not possibly sign that; the pen almost fell from my hand. He looked crestfallen. "Why not?" he asked. "They are not going to ask you to baptize yourself. It doesn't really mean anything. Just sign it and then you will be able to visit the Western Wall." At that moment, I was overwhelmed by thoughts of all the massacres against the Jewish people perpetuated in the name of the founder of Christianity: the auto de fé, the deicide charges, the pogroms on Easter and Christmas. There were tears pouring down my cheeks. I screamed at him, "We can't even learn Torah on Christmas eve," *nittel nacht* (the night of the birth) was the night of pogroms, when it was forbidden for Jews to enter the beit midrash, the study hall which housed the communities' sacred Jewish texts. Were the Jews to have gathered to study that evening as they did every other evening, an entire community of men could be destroyed by simply torching the study hall.

He looked at me with absolute horror. "Then we can't be friends anymore, because you hate me." "I don't hate you at all," I protested. He insisted: "But you hate my god." No, I said, "We learned about Jesus together with Professor Flusser. I don't hate your god, who was a religious Jew. I hate what your religion *made* of your god, in whose name millions of my people were murdered." He walked away from me, bitterly calling out: "If you hate my religion, then you hate me. We can no longer be friends."

It was a difficult but sobering moment and from that conversation on, we never spoke again – although we continued to attend Professor Flusser's classes together.

Missionaries in Efrat: Strong measures must be taken to prevent fraudulent attempts to convert Jews to Christianity

In the late 1980s, the Jewish Agency arranged for seventy-two families from the former Soviet Union to come and make their homes in Efrat. Some Messianic Christian missionaries heard about our new arrivals and thought that these people would be easy prey. The missionaries placed copies of the Tanakh – the twenty-four books of the Bible – together with the New Testament in Hebrew and Russian in every mailbox in Efrat; the "Jewish" and Christian Testaments were bound together in one bind, so that the unsuspecting Russian Jews would think they were a single sacred text, with the Gospel as part of the Jewish Bible. The text was published in Hebrew on one side, Russian on the other.

As soon as I heard what had happened, I sent a letter to all the residents of Efrat, instructing them to publicly burn the entire Bible together with the Gospels. This was because the Talmud teaches that a *sefer Torah* (Bible scroll), which was written by a Jewish heretic or someone who is attempting to cause a Jew to renounce his religion (and anyone who accepts Jesus as a divinity and/or the Messiah has ipso facto renounced his privileges as a Jew), has to be burned (see Maimonides *Hilkhot Yesodei HaTorah* 6:8).

I have the utmost respect for the Gospels as the sacred literature of the Christians; however, when the two testaments are joined together and sent to unsuspecting Jews in order to convert them, I felt that I had to take so strong a stand as to disallow any credence to connecting the Gospels to the Jewish Bible, and in a manner which would leave no room for compromise or misunderstanding.

INTIMATIONS OF CHANGE WITHIN THE CHURCH

Most welcome Christian visitors arrive

When the second Intifada (Palestinian uprising) began, tourism to Israel came to a standstill. Efrat, especially, which is technically beyond the "Green Line," felt the isolation, even from friends and relatives. I then received a call from a woman who introduced herself as *Schwester* Marta, who asked if she could bring a busload of tourists from Germany to visit. Needless to say, I made an appointment to meet their bus at our parking lot the next day at 1:00 pm.

Nothing could have prepared me for the miraculous sight that greeted my eyes the following afternoon. Forty Protestant nuns, garbed in gray habits, descended from their tour bus, holding aloft Israeli flags and accompanying me to my office (Efrat is the main headquarters of the Ohr Torah Stone network), singing in Hebrew *Naḥamu naḥamu ami,* "Comfort ye, comfort ye my people," a verse from the prophet Isaiah. Hundreds of our students streamed out of our high schools to watch this stirring spectacle. *Schwester* Marta presented us with a textured tapestry of Jerusalem, featuring the verse from Psalms, "For the Sake of Jerusalem I dare not be silent." She then said – impromptu, and in front of the Ohr Torah Stone office building – "We want you to know that we have a special love for the Jewish people. We want to invite you to see our "kibbutz" in Darmstadt, Germany, called New Canaan. New Canaan also has a community of houses which we would like you to dedicate." The nuns then led the entire assemblage in the singing of the Hatikva national anthem, and took their leave.

I felt truly comforted by this experience, as if these nuns had given me the courage and faith to continue defending Efrat from Palestinian suicide bombers and drive-by shootings. I decided then and there that when I next visited our eleven rabbinic emissaries serving pulpits across Germany, I would investigate New Canaan.

What I found was a sweetly calm and laid-back verdant diamond, a perfectly tailored and beautifully appointed "kibbutz" with large and colorful farming areas for fruits, vegetables, and flowers. Upon entering, we first came upon an artificial stream with the words "River Jordan" announcing its namesake, and then twelve stones set in a row, each inscribed with the name of one of the twelve tribes of Israel. In the distance were clusters of home communes, modest but tasteful houses, in which the one-hundred forty nuns and sixty monks who comprised the village-kibbutz lived, and from where they raised and exported their produce, with all profits going to support *ḥesed* (loving-kindness) projects in Israel. One community of homes sported a sign which read Beth El, another Shiloh, a third Kiryat Arba, the largest Jerusalem – and then I came upon Efrat.

When I rose to "dedicate" Efrat, I quoted the verses from Isaiah (53) describing the travail of the suffering servant, who suffers for the sins of the world. "Whereas you believe that this text refers to the founder of Christianity, our major commentaries believe that it refers to the Jewish people entire (historic Israel); the scapegoat of the world, cast off of the craggy mountain peaks into the crematoria of Auschwitz and Treblinka. We must teach the world the morality of the Ten Commandments, we must hold aloft the banner of a God of love, morality, and peace. We must prevent a worldwide jihad of suicide bombers. And if we work and teach together, perhaps we will bring all the children of Abraham back to their father and to our Parent-in-Heaven."

As she accompanied me to my car, I asked the *Schwester* to explain the origin of New Canaan. "We were seven religious girlfriends, all of whose fathers had served in Hitler's Wehrmacht. We made a pact together to create New Canaan as a penance for our fathers' sins." She then led all the nuns in the singing of Hatikva. As I traveled back to Israel,

I felt that I had never before seen such an expression of repentance, a total rededication of life to atone for the sins of one's parents.

Israel faces fanatic Moslem foes and Christian religious friends

More and more Christians kept coming to Efrat, expressing love and support for the Jewish State of Israel, emphasizing our common heritage of the twenty-four books of the Bible, and seeking ways to help us socially and politically. I began to understand how crucial their newfound friendship was, given an international climate in which not only the Arab bloc, but also the European Union, the former FSU, more and more South American countries, and indeed, the United Nations as the "peacekeeping" force in the world, were questioning our legitimacy as a nation. They were condemning us left and right for protecting ourselves against Hamas rockets which were being hurled at our civilians and students (even within the "Green Line").

And political ties with the Christians assume even greater significance if one accepts the thesis of Harvard's Professor Samuel P. Huntington in his masterful work "Clash of Civilizations and the Remaking of World Order." Radical Islam is spreading its suicide-bombing terrorist tentacles throughout the globe, from Afghanistan to Indonesia to Pakistan to Lebanon to Chechnya to London to New York, creating an Iran-Al Quaeda-Syria-Hamas-Hezbollah axis of fanatic jihadism which threatens the entire free world. This present world war, in which the Israeli-Palestinian clashes are only small change, is primarily a religious war, in which Allah-turned-Satan by Wahhabi Islam is poised to overtake the God of love, compassion, morality, and peace of the Judeo-Christian tradition. Since we are fewer than thirteen million Jews worldwide, our forging an alliance with almost two billion Christians is not only politically clever, but becomes a crucial, planet-saving necessity.

But before I could embark on any kind of alliance with the Christian world, I had to entertain the possibility – given the past two thousand year-long history of Christian enmity against, and persecution and forced conversion of, the Jews – that our Christian friends were really wolves in sheep's clothing, that they were now embracing us only in order to convert us.

The Catholic Church reaches out

I quickly learned that as early as the 1960s, the Second Vatican Council embarked on a process of *aggiornamento* – the updating of Catholic doctrine, including a post-Holocaust and post-establishment of the Jewish state new look at the Catholic attitudes towards Jews and Judaism. (For much of what is to follow in this regard, I am deeply indebted to my colleague and partner Rabbi Dr. Eugene Korn, and his essay "The Man of Faith and Religious Dialogue: Reviewing 'Confrontation' After Forty Years," *Modern Judaism*, Volume 25, Issue 3).

It was within this context that at the Second Vatican Council, the Catholic Church under Pope Paul VI issued its landmark document *Nostra Aetate* ("In Our Time") in October 1965 (almost two years *after* Rabbi Soloveitchik's "Confrontation").

Nostra Aetate was accepted by a large majority of Roman Catholic bishops around the world and, as such, became part of the *magisterium* – the official teaching authority of the Roman Catholic Church. It set down three path-breaking departures from previous Catholic doctrine:

1. The repudiation of anti-Semitism: In *Nostra Aetate's* exact language, the Church "deplores all hatreds, persecutions, and displays of anti-Semitism leveled against the Jew." In two other authoritative Vatican documents, the "Guidelines" of 1974 and the "Notes" of 1985, the verb "deplores" is changed to "condemns," and Pope John Paul II (May 18, 1920-April 2, 2005) stated that anti-Semitism is a "sin against God and humanity."

2. The rejection of the collective charge of deicide against the Jews, "without distinction, then alive, nor against the Jews today...the Jews should not be presented as rejected or accused by God." *Nostra Aetate* did not *absolve* the Jewish people of the charge of deicide; it said the charge itself was completely false and invalid.

3. The rejection of the idea that our Jewish covenant with God has been cancelled, or superseded, by the Christians. "Jews are the people of God of the Old Covenant, which has never been revoked by God.... The permanence of Israel is a historic fact, to be interpreted within God's design. It (Israel) remains a chosen people."

Does this third point mean that the official Catholic Church now views Judaism for Jews as being just as salvific ("saving") as Christianity is for Christians? A number of American Catholic theologians maintained that it does, in a paper they published entitled "Reflections on Covenant and Mission" (August 12, 2002, United States Conference of Catholic Bishops), and they therefore maintain that targeting Jews for conversion to the Church is no longer acceptable Catholic theology. Cardinal Joseph Ratzinger (who became Pope Benedict), however, doesn't go so far; he insists that Christianity is the highest expression of God's revelation (*Many Religions, One Covenant*, Ignatius, San Francisco, 1999, pp. 70–71). But he also maintains that the conversion of the Jews "is hardly possible within our historical time and perhaps not even desirable" (p. 109). In Dr. Korn's words, he is an "eschatological supersessionalist." (I cannot find fault with this position, since I believe that Maimonides teaches in his Laws of Kings 12, 1 that in the eschaton, "all of humanity will return to the true religion" – that is, to Judaism, in accordance with the statement of Rabbi Shimon ben Elazar in the Babylonian Talmud (Berakhot 57b) and the words of the prophet Zephaniah (3:9). As long as we can respect each other in the fullness of our respective faith commitments without feeling beholden to convert the other, I can well appreciate the faith of each that he has the more perfect revelation, as will be proven by who converts to whom in the eschaton. This is also the position of Rabbi Soloveitchik, as I later explain in this paper.

It was clear to me that such profound theological changes could only have emerged from two realizations on the part of honest officials within the Catholic hierarchy:

1. Had it not been for the seeds of Christian anti-Semitism and anti-Judaism, sown far and wide by the Crusaders, Inquisitors, and pogromist-hooligans for close to two thousand years, the Holocaust could never have developed into the conflagration of decimation that consumed six million innocent men, women, and children. And so Pope John Paul II, when he visited the Yad Vashem Memorial and the Kotel in March 2000, said, "We are deeply saddened by the behavior of those who in the course of history have caused your children to suffer. Asking forgiveness,

we commit ourselves to genuine brotherhood with the people of the Covenant."

2. The State of Israel and its unprecedented success as a homeland for the Jewish people after their lengthy exile refuted the traditional Christian doctrine that the Jews were willed by God to wander stateless as punishment for their rejection of Jesus as the Messiah and son of God. And so, although it took twenty-nine years from the time of *Nostra Aetate* for the Church to recognize the State of Israel, it did so in June of 1994. The bishops at the Second Vatican Council would never have delivered the authoritative and groundbreaking theological position taken in *Nostra Aetate* without the knowledge that they had the support of a significant number of Catholic theologians and churchmen. (Note again that *Nostra Aetate* came almost two years *after* Rabbi Soloveitchik's article, "Confrontation").

The Evangelicals: A meeting with Pastor Hagee

The large numbers of Christians who were visiting Efrat – and especially those who were truly interested in studying – were mostly Evangelicals. I had become quite friendly with the charismatic Pastor Robert Stearns, who brought groups of Evangelicals of all ages who wanted to hear our biblical interpretations, study Talmud, and learn more about the Sabbath and the festivals. I understood that their intention was not conversion to Judaism; they merely wanted to live their lives more and more the way Jesus had lived his life. Having lived in America, they were never part of the Christian European anti-Semitic tradition; they also loved to study the Old Testament, which gave them a natural affinity for Jews and for the Land of Israel.

I felt instinctively the sincerity of their friendship, and it was mainly to satisfy their thirst for learning about Judaism, the Sabbath and the festivals, and their desire to strengthen their ties to us, to the Land of Israel, and to our right to our homeland, that I began to consider opening a Center for Jewish-Christian Understanding and Cooperation in Efrat. I received strong encouragement from Malcolm Hoenlein, a good friend and the Executive Vice President of Conference of Major American Jewish Organizations, as well as from leaders of AIPAC. I understood that an Orthodox rabbi – who accepted the divinity of the twenty-four books of the Bible – would be taken most seriously by the Evangelicals who share the same belief, and I had heard that, according to one study, Evangelicals comprise thirty-five percent of the American voting public.

At about this time, I visited San Antonio, Texas, where one of our young rabbinical emissaries had just been appointed assistant rabbi to Rabbi Aryeh Scheinberg. Rabbi Scheinberg is a beloved friend of long standing and a most respected colleague, who is known as Pastor John Hagee's "rabbi." Rabbi Scheinberg suggested that I meet this most influential pastor of the Evangelical world, which I was most anxious to do.

Pastor Hagee is a very impressive man with a clear, deep, articulate voice, and a warm and embracing manner. He looked at me intently and said, "Rabbi, I love the Jewish people; Rabbi, I love you, Rabbi."

The truth is that this extraordinary Christian leader puts his money where his mouth is; he dedicates much of his life to raising millions of dollars each year, which he distributes to help important social welfare and educational institutions throughout Israel. He really demonstrates the love he feels.

Nevertheless, since I was just at the cusp of announcing the opening of our Center for Jewish-Christian Understanding and Cooperation, I had to ask my question: "Tell me the truth, Pastor Hagee, do you love us because you want to convert us? Do you love us to death?" He flashed one of his signature smiles, amused by the *ḥutzpa*, or naivete, of my question. "No, Rabbi, I don't love you because I want to convert you; but neither do I love you purely out of altruistic consideration. I love you because of Genesis 12:3, where the Bible records that 'God said to Abraham, I will bless those who bless you, and those who curse you I shall curse.' Rabbi, I want to be blessed, not cursed!"

Pastor Hagee has a ministry which is measured in millions; he is undoubtedly the most successful pastor in our generation. Rabbi Scheinberg reported to me that during the forty-nine years he has lived in San Antonio, Pastor Hagee had not tried to convert even one Jew to Christianity. Given the overwhelming charisma of Pastor Hagee, this can only be because he truly does not believe that Jews must be converted to Christianity.

So I established the Center for Jewish-Christian Understanding and Cooperation in order to forge a political alliance against fundamentalist and radical Islamism and in order to forge a moral-ethical alliance against radical and materialistic secularism. We must convey our mutual belief in a God of love, compassion, and morality, the kind of absolute morality which would never refer to suicide bombers who murder innocent women and children as freedom fighters. I also felt humbled in the presence of a Christian who had such complete faith in the divine words of our Holy Bible.

GETTING INTO THE NITTY-GRITTY OF THE ISSUE

Are we permitted – or perhaps even mandated – to teach Torah to Christians?

Large numbers of Christians continued to come to our center; they were, however, less interested in discussing politics or in Israel's right to a Jewish state (which they took as an axiom, since the Land of Israel was promised to the Jewish people by the Creator of the heavens and earth Himself), and more interested in learning Torah: the Written Law, chiefly the Pentateuch (five books of Moses), in accordance with traditional Jewish commentaries, and the Oral Law, the talmudic Pharisaic tradition which had been studied by Jesus. Hence, I had to face a fundamental question: Are Jews permitted to teach Torah to Christians?

The great legalist-philosopher-decisor Maimonides (twelfth century) rules in one of his responsa (1:149, Blau edition) that "it is permissible to teach the Torah and commandments to the Christians and draw them close to our faith." This is very much in line with the Seforno (1475–1550) in his commentary to God's exhortation (preceding the revelation of the Decalogue) that Israel be a "kingdom of priest-teachers and a holy nation" (Ex. 19:6). The Seforno says there:

> As a result of this teaching function, you will be a treasure for all (of the nations); you (all of Israel) will be a kingdom of priest-teachers to bring understanding and instruction in Torah to all of humanity, "to call out to everyone in the name of God so that everyone will be enabled to serve God with one accord (Zeph. 3:9)." As it is said (in Scripture), "and you (Israel) shall

be called the priest-teachers of the Lord (Is. 61:6)," and as it is said, "From Zion shall go forth Torah" (Is 2:3).

Maimonides speaks in perfectly consistent tones regarding the Jewish obligation to teach Torah to the world in his "Book of the Commandments" (*Sefer HaMitzvot*), Positive Commandment 3. Here, in analyzing the command to "love the Lord your God with all your heart, with all your soul, and all your might," Maimonides equates "loving" God with "knowing" God; we achieve the performance of this commandment by "delving deeply and becoming knowledgeable in God's commandments and deeds (the two revelations of Torah and Creation, the commandments and the sciences; he may also be including philosophy, which is allied to physics and cosmogony, as well as history) so that we may come to know Him."

Maimonides then adds a most crucial addendum as part and parcel of this commandment to love – or know – God: "This commandment also includes seeking out and calling every human being to the service of God (*avodat Hashem*), may He be blessed, and to belief in Him ... For when one truly loves (knows) God – to whatever the extent that it is possible for one to grasp divine truth – one will undoubtedly seek out and summon the deniers and fools to the true understanding which one has achieved.

In the language of the *Sifrei*, "You shall love the Lord your God" means "make God beloved to every human being in the world as did your father Abraham," as it is written, "the Souls whom they made in *Haran*" in accord with the greatness of (Abraham's) love did he seek out people for the faith."

How much of the Torah do we teach?

At this point in our discussion, the reader may be a bit perplexed. Is Maimonides declaring Judaism to be a missionizing religion, with an obligation upon every Jew to bear witness to the world regarding the 613 commandments? This would certainly go against conventional wisdom. Maimonides does definitively rule that the Jews are obligated to teach – and even coerce – the gentiles into accepting the seven Noahide laws of morality: not murdering, not stealing, not committing sexual immorality, not eating the limb of a living animal, not worshipping idols, not blaspheming God, and establishing courts to enforce the first six laws (Laws of Kings 8, 10). This is in line with God's election of Abraham, in order that he instruct his household after him to "observe the ways of the Lord by doing acts of compassionate righteousness and moral justice" (Gen. 18:18, 19), as well as the divine charge to the first Hebrew and the "father of a multitude of nations" that "through you shall be blessed all the families of the earth" (Gen. 12:3). According to at least one view of the Talmud, these laws of morality are sufficient to gain for the gentiles a share in the World to Come, and are certainly necessary to secure a world without bloodshed which would not destroy itself if universally accepted.

From these sources it should be indubitably clear that if we are to teach the Christians the commandments (at least the commandments of Noahide morality, perhaps all the commandments of compassionate righteousness and moral justice), as well as a deeper understanding of God (remember, the Noahide laws do not include faith in God, and Maimonides derives outreach to the gentiles from the command to "know and love God"), how can we *not* be speaking to the Christians in theological terms? After all, when one teaches, one must always listen to one's students and learn from their responses. Theology means the study of God. Making God known and beloved to the gentile world is *all* about theological dialogue!

Even in terms of the nature of the corpus of commandments that we are permitted and even encouraged to share with the Christian world, it is clear that Maimonides goes beyond the seven Noahide laws. To be sure, we have already said that the positive and obligatory command for us to "missionize" and even coerce gentile acceptance of these laws refers only to the seven Noahide laws, which are necessary for a civilized society and a world of peace.

However, we have already seen how, in his *Book of Commandments* (Positive Commandment 3), Maimonides advocates spreading knowledge of God by means of spreading the "commandments" – not merely the seven Noahide laws. In his responsum permitting teaching Torah to Christians (1:149), he again speaks of teaching *the commandments*, and *thus drawing them closer to our faith (dateinu)*, going on to write "and perhaps, *yah'zeru l'mutav*, they will return to the best path" (ibid.). And so, in the last chapter of his *Mishneh Torah*, in speaking of the Messianic Age in the eschaton, Maimonides says, "everyone will return to the true religion" (*dat ha'emet* – Kings 12, 1), adding "they (the gentiles) will neither rob nor destroy; rather they will eat permitted foods in peace and quiet together with (or like) the Israelites" – which, to me, implies that they will keep our laws of *kashrut*, but probably within a vegetarian context. Moreover, within his *Guide for the Perplexed*, Maimonides refers to the Sabbath on which – in the eschaton – all humanity will rest; "therefore, we are told in the law to honor this (Sabbath) day – in order to confirm thereby the principle of Creation which will spread in the world when all people keep the Sabbath on the same day" (*Guide* 11:31).

In sum, Maimonides would maintain that the gentiles need not convert, but that it is salutary to expose them to the Torah commandments and – in the eschaton – they will convert or at least come to acceptance of many of the commandments, more than the seven Noahide laws.[1]

And so the *Mekhilta DeRabbi Yishmael* (in its introduction to the giving of the Torah, in *Parashat Yitro*) asserts: "The Torah was given in an open-spaced no-man's land (desert, *parousia*) because, had it been

---

1. See the difference of opinion, cited above on p. 301 n. 33, between Menaḥem Kellner (the gentiles will convert to Judaism in the eschaton), Chaim Rapaport (the gentiles will accept only the Noahide laws), and Gerald Blidstein, who ends up somewhere in between, as I do. The reader will also note that in his responsum 1:149 (Blau edition), Maimonides only permits the teaching of Torah to Christians but NOT to Moslems, who do not accept the validity of the Bible and will therefore use our teachings against Judaism and against the Jews. However, Rabbi Ḥaim David HaLevi (*Asei Lekha Rav* Part 7, 48), the former chief rabbi of Tel Aviv, also permits teaching Torah to Moslems, since the only time we prohibit Torah study at all to gentiles is before they accept the Noahide laws, and Moslems are monotheists. Indeed, Maimonides himself contrasts a gentile who does not yet keep the seven Noahide laws – and who may neither be occupied in the other commandments of the Torah nor may he rest on the Sabbath – with the children of Noah, who may keep all of the rest of the commandments, and if he is occupied in Torah, he may be compared to a High Priest (see the contrast in Sanhedrin 49, Avoda Zara 3). A child of Noah receives reward for any additional commandment he performs, he may bring whole burnt offerings to the Temple, and his charitable gifts are to be gratefully distributed among the poor of Israel (Laws of Kings 10:10).

given in the Land of Israel, the Israelites would say to the nations of the world: 'You have no share in it.' But the Torah was given in the free-to-all desert, so that anyone in the world who wishes to accept it may come and accept it."

Finally, Maimonides – although he considered Christianity to be idolatry (unlike the overwhelming majority of Middle-Age decisors who did not believe Christianity to be idolatry for the Christians) – nevertheless highly respected the successful activity of Christianity to spread major concepts of positive Judeo-Christian ideals and values to the farthest recesses of the globe:

> It is beyond the human mind to fathom the designs of the Creator, for our ways are not His ways, and neither are our thoughts His thoughts. All these matters relating to Jesus of Nazareth and the Ishmaelite (Mohammed) who came after him only served to pave the way for King Messiah, and to prepare the entire world to worship God together as one, as it is written, "For then will I turn to the peoples a pure language, that they may all call upon the name of the Lord to serve Him with one accord" (Zeph. 3:9). Thus, the Messianic hope, the Torah, and the commandments have become familiar topics of conversation among inhabitants of the far isles and (were brought) to many peoples uncircumcised of heart and flesh." (Laws of Kings, XI:4, unexpurgated version of Rabbi Kapah)

These words of the greatest philosopher and halakhic authority in Jewish history after Moses can only serve to underscore the importance of dialogue with the Christians and conveying the theological truths about God, Torah, and the Messianic Age which must (and will eventually be) accepted by a receptive world.

Hence, it is indubitably clear that we may teach Torah to the gentiles – the seven Noahide laws as compulsory, and as much of the rest of it that they would wish to learn. And that is precisely what our Center for Jewish-Christian Understanding and Cooperation does: we teach the Hebraic roots of Christianity, the basic lessons of our Written and Oral Torah as studied and practiced by Jesus.

It goes without saying that a great part of Torah is predicated upon the Land of Israel, from the commandments of proper tithing and the Sabbatical year, which are rooted in the produce from the soil of the Holy Land, to the great Jewish leaders from Abraham to Rabbi Avraham Yitzḥak HaKohen Kook, whose physical remains have been fused with the eternity of the soil of the homeland of historic Israel (*Knesset Yisrael*). Any honest study of Torah must serve to strengthen the bond between Israel and its land in the eyes and hearts of all who learn it – and teaching the Christians goes a long way in strengthening their commitment to Israel as a Jewish state.

One of the center's earliest experiences clearly demonstrates this point. In 2009, twenty-four Evangelical pastors came to our center for one week on a mission to study the Hebraic roots of Christianity through the sacred texts of our holy books and tours of our holy land. (As it turned out, they were snowed in for two days, so the hours of text study overpowered the hours of touring.) The result was twenty-four CUFI (Christians United for Israel) evenings which took place in twenty-four churches on the eastern seaboard of the United States – all dedicated to celebrating the State of Israel as a model for emulation and raising funds to help the indigent in Israel.

RABBI SOLOVEITCHIK'S "CONFRONTATION"

Background and overview

As mentioned, my revered teacher and mentor, Rabbi Joseph B. Soloveitchik, published a groundbreaking essay on Christian-Jewish dialogue in the journal *Tradition*, a publication of the Rabbinical Council of America, in the Spring-Summer edition of 1964, almost two years before the Second Vatican Council ratified *Nostra Aetate* in October 1965 (the essay was penned at least two years before).

This was at a time when the Catholic Church was rethinking its relationship to the Jews (in the wake of the Holocaust as well as the unexpected and unprecedented phoenix-like rebirth of the Jewish State of Israel) and was beginning to cultivate Catholic-Jewish inter-religious dialogue within this context of *aggiornamento* – the updating of doctrine. Rabbi Soloveitchik was legitimately concerned, lest such dialogue at this early and delicate stage lead to Jewish recapitulation on fundamental Jewish truths, which would obviously be disastrous. It was to this end that Rabbi Soloveitchik, the internationally renowned halakhic and theological leader of Yeshiva University-style Orthodox Jewry – the Lubavitcher Rebbe called him *lamdan ha'dor,* the greatest talmudic scholar of the generation – penned his far-reaching and penetrating essay, "Confrontation."

The essay begins and ends with biblical exegeses, opening with a masterful commentary on the biblical chapters on Creation and their ramifications for understanding the human existential mission and predicament, and concluding with the confrontation between Jacob and Esau after the patriarch leaves Laban and is returning to his ancestral home. Obviously, Jacob represents Israel and Esau is the midrashic symbol for Rome and the Vatican. The major piece of this theological tour de force is dedicated to Israel's relationship towards or confrontation with the world – and the concomitant obligations this engenders – as well as Israel's confrontation with its religious faith counterpart, Christianity, and to what extent dialogue in that setting is desirable, or even possible.

Contrary to what many Orthodox rabbis have maintained, "Confrontation" is not to be seen as a cut-and-dried halakhic responsum permitting Jewish-Christian dialogue on "universal problems," which are "economic, social, scientific, and ethical," but categorically forbidding dialogue in areas of "faith, religious law, doctrine, and ritual" (Rabbinical Council of America, Mid-Winter Conference, February 1966). Were that the case, Rabbi Soloveitchik would have written just such a precise halakhic responsum setting down these guidelines replete with talmudic citations and halakhic precedents, rather than the highly nuanced, theologically rich, and dialectically infused "Confrontation." Moreover, the very RCA statement of 1966 forbidding discussions of "faith and religious law" concludes (italics are mine): "To repeat, we are ready to discuss universal religious problems. We will resist any attempt to debate our private, individual faith commitment."

Apparently, how to define "religious" issues is neither simple nor clear-cut. In fact, Rabbi Soloveitchik defined his philosophical school of thought as that of a "Halakhic Existentialist" – committed to the proposition that halakha deals with the most fundamental existential problems of *humanity*! Rabbi Soloveitchik himself often cited in his writings Christian theologians such as Soren Kierkegaard, Karl Barth, and Rudolf Otto (see, for example, the beginnings of *Halakhic Man*) and the first reading that he gave of his "Lonely Man of Faith" essay prior to its publication took place at an inter-faith seminar (sic) at St. John's Seminary in Brighton, Massachusetts (see Korn, "The Man of Faith and Religious Dialogue," Note 8).

Perhaps, what the RCA was really saying in its 1966 statement was that "we resist any attempt to *debate* our private faith commitment," whereas "*discussion* (or dialogue) of universal religious problems" is perfectly permissible. Perhaps, much more in line with Rabbi Soloveitchik's thought is the statement adopted by the RCA [and probably written by Rabbi Soloveitchik himself] at its Mid-Winter Conference in February 1964, which is appended to the "Confrontation" article in *Tradition* 1964 and calls for a "harmonious relationship among all faiths" in order to combat the "threat of secularism and materialism and the modern atheistic negation of religion and religious values." Combating the negation of religion requires, at the very least, basic theological discourse defining "religious" values.

Indeed, I believe that a careful reading of "Confrontation" will more than justify the salutary benefits of religious dialogue today, albeit in accordance with the very specific guidelines and limitations expressed by Rabbi Soloveitchik and to which we at the Center for Jewish-Christian Understanding and Cooperation carefully adhere.

Let us explore together Rabbi Soloveitchik's "Confrontation" utilizing, as much as possible, his own words to attempt to fully understand his position.

Adam in the Garden of Eden: Non-confronted vs. confronted man

Rabbi Soloveitchik typologically explains the initial biblical description of man as "natural man," who sees himself as part and parcel of the natural world around him, non-confronted by it and bearing no responsibility towards it. "And the Lord God planted a garden in Eden eastwards, and he put there the man whom He had formed" – in the midst of all of the alluring and seductive vegetation all around (Gen. 2:8, 9). Natural man is egocentric and hedonistic, driven only by instinctive pleasures, devoid of individuation and self awareness. In short: non-confronted man.

Six verses later we see the emergence of a different man, a confronting and confronted man, who looks at the world, understands his power over it and his responsibilities towards it, and who accepts a commanding God setting limits to his conquests: "And the Lord God took the man and He placed him in the Garden of Eden to work it and to preserve it…and the Lord God commanded the man, saying… (2:15, 16)." Man has a kerygma, a mission, to perfect and preserve the world, to attempt to subdue the other, lesser creatures roundabout, and to agree to submit to – and be subdued by – the Creator of the universe. He says – and lives – "I am responsible, therefore I am." Confronted and confronting man has now emerged.

Confronting and confronted man is filled with self-awareness; he recognizes his position in the universe as unique (because he can control and conquer) and tragic (because he, too, will be subject to conquest by evil and by death), and he is beset by profound and debilitating loneliness ("It is not good for the human to be alone," Gen.2:18). And so, in addition to the universe, he confronts Eve, his life-partner, with whom he can establish a community by means of verbal communication – or dialogue (2:23) – a counterpart with whom to confront the world.

Words, however, are a double edged sword; they express "what is common in two existences," the similarities between two individuals joining their lives and destinies, but also the "singularity and uniqueness of each existence," what is separate and distinct for each one respectively. And, of course, the wages of sin are felt when the one attempts to control and subdue the other (3:16: "He shall rule over her").

From this paradigm, it is clear that confrontation is positive, salutary, even redemptive. And so, Rabbi Soloveitchik goes on to write that Jews engage in a double confrontation, with the universe as well as with God, through our covenant as Jews. And while "westernized" Jews may think that it is impossible to engage in both the universal and the covenantal confrontations – they may think that that they are mutually exclusive, that concern for world obviates and even drowns out the concern for a unique and separate covenantal identity – the very opposite is the truth.

Indeed, it is the covenantal confrontation which defines and directs our national kerygma (mission) towards the universal and the universe: "Through you shall be blessed all the families of the earth," was God's charge to Abraham. "But only in this (not in wisdom or strength or wealth) shall be praised the one who is to be praised: be intelligent, and come to know (understand) Me, that I am the Lord who does (acts) of loving-kindness, moral justice, and compassionate righteousness on earth (the whole of the earth), for in these do I delight, says God," was Jeremiah's message to the Israelites, as well as the citation with which Maimonides concludes his final magnum opus, *Guide for the Perplexed*.

Moreover, continues Rabbi Soloveitchik as he goes on to deal with Jewish-Christian confrontation and dialogue: "Involvement with the rest of mankind in the cosmic confrontation does not rule out the second personal confrontation of two faith communities, each aware of both what it shares with the other and what is singularly its own. In the same manner as Adam and Eve…encountered each other as two separate individuals, cognizant of their incommensurability and uniqueness, so also two faith communities – which coordinate their efforts when confronted by the same cosmic order – may face each other in the full knowledge of their distinctness and individuality. We reject the theory of a single confrontation and instead insist upon the indispensability of the double confrontation" (*Tradition*, volume 6, number. 2, Spring-Summer 1964).

The only reason why Rabbi Soloveitchik questions a confrontational dialogue with the "other faith community," which would be as salutary as Adam's confrontation with Eve, is because the Church historically treated us as inferior beings. In Rabbi Soloveitchik's own words, "Unfortunately, however, non-Jewish society has confronted us throughout the ages in a mood of defiance, as if we were part of the subhuman objective order separated by an abyss from the human" (ibid., pp. 19, 20):

> A confrontation of two faith communities is possible only if it is accompanied by a clear assurance that both parties will enjoy equal rights and full religious freedom… A democratic confrontation certainly does not demand that we submit to an attitude of self-righteousness taken by the community of the many which,

while debating whether or not to "absolve" the community of the few of some mythical guilt (i.e., deicide!), completely ignores its own historical responsibility for the suffering and martyrdom (it has inflicted) upon the few, the weak and the persecuted... there should be insistence upon one's inalienable rights as a human being created by God... we do not intend to play the part of the object encountered by dominating man," the Christian. (p. 21)

In other words, Rabbi Soloveitchik is not against religious dialogue with Christians; that is why this essay is entitled "Confrontation," and not "Non-Confrontation." The only thing he insists upon, however, is that the confrontation be in the spirit of religious equality, of mutual respect for the individual faith commitments of each which are not subject to logical debate, or traded compromises, in matters of our unique covenantal faith values and rituals.

Red lines and preconditions

These are the three things that Rabbi Soloveitchik was against and these are, likewise, my red lines in dialogue with Christians:

1. We will never dialogue with Christians if they represent missionary movements, if their avowed or surreptitious purpose is to convert Jews.

2. We will never *debate* unique Jewish ritual or faith issues with Christians. We will attempt to share with them unique Jewish points of theology and ritual practice if they wish to better understand them, but we and they must realize that each faith community has religious expressions which transcend rational logical discourse and which are not subject to debate.

3. We will never enter into dialogue with Christians in which we are expected to compromise our religious values or doctrines in order that they be more in consonance with Christianity.

Here are Rabbi Soloveitchik's words, published in "Confrontation," in which he set down his preconditions for Jewish-Christian dialogue, which are my preconditions as well:

> In light of this analysis, it would be reasonable to state that in any confrontation we must insist upon four basic conditions in order to safeguard our individuality and freedom of action.
>
> First, we must state, in unequivocal terms, the following. We are a totally independent faith community. We do not revolve as a satellite in any orbit. (p. 21)

Rabbi Soloveitchik was afraid that since Christianity claimed that it had superseded Judaism, this is what they would attempt to foist on us in any debate and – since they were the many and we were the few – we would be forced into a difficult position. Hence, our independence in faith has to be accepted and respected.

> Second, the *logos*, the word, in which the multifarious religious experience is expressed, does not lend itself to standardization or universalization. (p. 23)

Here, he emphasized that we are not one religious faith community with Christianity. He went on to write, "We must always remember that our singular commitment to God, and our hope and indomitable will for survival, are non-negotiable and non-rationalizable, and are not subject to debate and argumentation" (p. 24).

> Third, we members of the community of the few should always act with tact and understanding and refrain from suggesting to the community of the many, which is both proud and prudent, changes in ritual or emendations of its texts. (pp. 24–25)

We do not want Christians to ask us to change our religious texts and so we ought not expect of them to change their religious texts. I would submit that we can and must, however, share with them the pain in our hearts and injuries to our bodies that we have experienced as a result of certain of their sacred texts, as in the statements in the Gospel which refer to the historic Jewish collective guilt for deicide and the references in their writ and liturgy to convert the Jews now. Rabbi Soloveitchik continues:

Fourth, we certainly have not been authorized by our history, sanctified by the martyrdom of millions...to revise historical (Jewish) attitudes, to trade favors pertaining to fundamental matters of faith, and to reconcile "some" differences... We cannot command the respect of our confronters by displaying a servile attitude. Only a candid, frank, and unequivocal policy reflecting unconditional commitment to our God, a sense of dignity, pride, and inner joy in being what we are, believing with great passion in the ultimate truthfulness of our views, praying fervently for and expecting confidently the fulfillment of our eschatological vision when our faith will rise from particularity to universality, will impress the peers of the other faith community among whom we have both adversaries and friends. (p. 25)

Here, Rabbi Soloveitchik is expressing the view of Maimonides that ultimately, in the eschaton, everyone will turn to the Jewish faith. In the meantime, however, in our confrontation with the other faith community, we must express passionate commitment towards our unique religion without holding back the intensity of our intellectual and emotional fervor; only then, will our peers in the other faith community truly respect us.

It should be obvious that the four preconditions stipulated by Rabbi Soloveitchik for Jewish-Christian dialogue have largely been accepted by the Catholic and Evangelical churches, as well as by many Protestant church authorities. Nearly all churches today have rejected the collective deicide charge against the Jews, deplore anti-Semitism, asked for forgiveness for Christian persecution of Jews, and no longer maintain that Christianity has superseded the Jewish people's covenant with God.

In fact, we do enter Jewish-Christian dialogue very much as equals – and even as "equals plus." Our very existence in history – despite destruction, exile, and global persecution – affirms God's covenant with us as well as His existence on earth ("you are My witnesses says God," Is. 43:10), and our return to our homeland, Israel, after close to two thousand years of exile, confirms the divine biblical prophecies of Deuteronomy 30:1–10 and Isaiah 11:11.

While many of our Christian brothers and sisters believe that in the eschaton everyone will become Christian, we see that Maimonides believes that in the eschaton, everyone will become Jewish! As long as the group with whom we dialogue respects us as we are now in the fullness of our differences, we can very well agree that the eventual Messiah will tell us who is converting to whom (if indeed a conversion will be necessary at that time).

Understand the differences from generation to generation
As for those Jews to whom the Christian involvement in Jewish persecution culminating in the Holocaust makes it emotionally impossible to participate in any kind of Jewish-Christian discourse – for whom the very idea of delving into Jesus' Jewish identity cannot escape their lips or enter their hearts since so many atrocities were perpetrated against innocent Jews in his name – I can only urge that they revisit the biblical commandment, "Remember the days of old, consider the years of many generations; ask thy father, and he will declare unto thee, thine elders, and they will tell thee" (Deut. 32:7). Rabbi Saadia Gaon lists this verse as one of the 613 commandments, as exhortation to study history.

Rabbi Samson Raphael Hirsch goes one step further, interpreting the Hebrew *shnot* not as "years" (from the Hebrew *shana*), but rather as differences (from the Hebrew *shinui*). Be sensitive to the changes in history and respond accordingly: be sensitive to the evil empire of radical Islam threatening to destroy Israel and the entire free world in a "religious" war of the civilizations; be sensitive to the fundamental doctrinal changes within contemporary Christianity; be sensitive to the outstretched hands of so many in the Christian world offering friendship and support. Have we the moral and religious right to reject their overtures in the present climate of widespread Israel hatred and delegitimization?

Confrontation desired
What emerges most decisively from Rabbi Soloveitchik's "Confrontation" is how Rabbi Soloveitchik always emphasizes the importance of confrontation – dialogue – with the other faith community:

> We insist upon the indispensability of the double confrontation…
> As a charismatic faith community, we have to meet the challenge
> of confronting the general, non-Jewish faith community. We are
> called upon to tell this community not only the story it already
> knows – that we are human beings committed to the general wel-
> fare and progress of humanity, that we are interested in combating
> disease, in alleviating human suffering, in protecting man's rights, in
> helping the needy, etc. – but also what is still unknown to it, namely
> our otherness as a metaphysical covenantal community. (pp. 20–21)

In addition to universal social human concerns, Rabbi Soloveitchik
wants us to communicate what we believe in the secret chambers of
our hearts, the differences in our religious commitments. He opposes
a debate on these unique issues with the other faith community, *but
not our teaching of these issues to the other faith community*. Remember,
the RCA statement read: "To repeat, we are ready to discuss (dialogue)
universal religious problems. We will resist any attempt to debate our
private individual faith commitments" (Statement of the Rabbinical
Council of America, February 1966).

However, what is most important to emphasize is that if indeed
Rabbi Soloveitchik permits dialogue with Christians on ethical, social,
and political issues, surely such subjects are not merely part of a secular
weltanschauung, divorced hermetically from the religious and theological. Is it then possible to have ethical discussion without invoking the
creation of human being in God's image, or political dialogue concerning the State of Israel without citing God's covenant with Abraham?!

Moreover, allow me to quote Rabbi Soloveitchik's own words to
Cardinal Johannes Willebrands in March, 1971: "All dialogue between
Jews and Christians cannot but be religious and theological, for you are
a priest and I am a rabbi. Can we speak otherwise than at the level of
religion? Our culture is certainly a religious one" (see Korn, "The Man
of Faith and Religious Dialogue: Revisiting Confrontation," Note 17).

Conclusion

And so, we established a Center for Jewish-Christian Understanding
and Cooperation (CJCUC) in Efrat, Israel. In 2011, more than seven

thousand Christians from all over the world entered our portals to study the Hebraic roots of Christianity, and our faculty has taught many more thousands via DVDs, television programs, and lectures in Evangelical churches throughout North America. We have given teaching seminars to pastors and seminarians and inspired scores of "Nights to Honor Israel" in Evangelical churches all over the United States.

We have initiated an Institute for Theological Inquiry in partnership with the Witherspoon Institute of Princeton, NJ, to provide a forum for theological discussion among recognized Christian and Jewish theologians. The result of our dialogues will soon appear in a book entitled *Covenant and Hope in the Human Future*, which emphasizes our united mission to bring a God of compassion, morality, freedom, and peace into a world caught between the twin dangers of radical jihadist terrorism on the one hand and rampant secular materialism on the other. Our next project will be dialogue on "Religion, War and Violence" as well as "The Significance of the Jewish Return to Zion." Additionally, we effectuated the first Jewish-Evangelical Colloquium ever at Emory University, which resulted in the emergence of a paper by the Evangelical theologians stating unequivocally that the Christian mission to bear witness is for the gentiles; there is no necessity to convert Jews. All of our dialogues are clearly within the four official constraint parameters established by Rabbi Soloveitchik in "Confrontation."

It is to be hoped that the CJCUC and the Jewish-Christian dialogue it engenders will be a fitting addition to the "beginning of the sprouting of our redemption" in the era of our return to homeland, responsibility, and history. May it hasten the time when God will "turn to His nations with a clear language to call out to all of them in the name of the Lord to serve Him shoulder to shoulder" (Zeph. 3:9), and bring about "the perfection of the world in the kingship of the Almighty," when "nation will not lift sword against nation and humankind will not learn war anymore" (Is. 2, Mic. 4).

Land for Peace: A Halakhic and Theological Overview[1]

T he "Declaration of Principles" signed by Prime Minister of Israel Yitzḥak Rabin and PLO leader Yasser Arafat on the White House lawn some two decades ago has given rise to political debate and polarization within the State of Israel, centering around our right – or obligation – to give up land for peace. Within the yeshiva world, the argument is no less vociferous, with such eminent authorities as the late Rabbi Shlomo Goren, former Ashkenazic chief rabbi of Israel, and Rabbi Ovadia Yosef, former Sephardic chief rabbi of Israel, at opposite ends of the spectrum. The task of this essay is threefold: first, to explore the halakhic parameters for allowing a non-Jew to live in the Land of Israel; second, to attempt to define the unique sanctity of Israel, which might require it to remain under Jewish national sovereignty; and third, to examine the role of political, military, and popular consensus as factors to consider in the halakhic deliberations regarding ceding territories.

---

1. An earlier version of this article appeared in Hebrew in *Teḥumin* vol. 16, Zomet Institute.

THE BIBLICAL MANDATE

The Bible explicitly states that the Almighty, or His angel-messenger, will bring the People of Israel to the Land of Israel and that He will, in His own good time, drive out the earlier inhabitants of the land: "Not in one year, lest the land become desolate... [but] little by little shall I drive them out from before you, until you shall increase and inherit the land" (Ex. 23:23–31).

This verse does not mean that our acquisition of the land is totally dependent upon God's intervention and requires no human endeavor. The Bible typically attributes to God even those actions initiated by the Israelites which express the realization of the divine will. Hence, we are told about God's battle against Amalek despite the fact that the war was waged by the People of Israel (Ex. 17:14–16), and it is related that God brought the Jewish people into the land despite the numerous battles fought by Joshua and his armies (Joshua 24:8).

Nevertheless, the text does lend itself to an almost prophetic interpretation, affirming that gentiles will live on the Land of Israel until enough Jews decide that it is necessary to reclaim the land and they are numerous enough to populate it.

The Bible also explains the order of events in which the land is to be reclaimed. First, we must establish sovereign control over our national boundaries, "And I shall set your borders from the Sea of Reeds to the Sea of Philistines [the Mediterranean] and from the wilderness until the [Euphrates] River" (Ex. 23:31). After the borders have been established we are not to make any covenants with the local gentiles or their gods. Following this, the Bible commands that the gentiles are "not to dwell in your land lest they cause you to sin against Me, for you will serve their gods, that will be a snare for you" (Ex. 23:32–33).

According to this account, our takeover of the land will come in stages, and even more relevant to our present concern, the prohibitions against gentiles dwelling in our land, and against our entering into treaties with them, do not appear to commence until after we have gained sovereign control over all the territories within our promised borders, at least according to the simple meaning of the biblical text. Moreover, the reason for these prohibitions seems to be based on the idolatrous practices of the gentile inhabitants.

Later, the Bible exhorts us to "inherit/drive out the inhabitants of the land and to dwell therein" (Num. 33:53). The premier eleventh-century Ashkenazic commentator Rashi explains this practical two-part process. God says to the Israelites: First, you must drive out the inhabitants of the land. This is a necessary prerequisite to dwelling in the land: "You shall conquer the land from her inhabitants and *then* you shall dwell in it [the land], *and you will be able to survive in it*" (Rashi, ad loc., italics added). When the land was originally conquered in the time of Joshua, it was necessary for the Israelites to drive out the inhabitants of the land in order to live in peace.

Nahmanides, the famed thirteenth-century mystical Sephardic commentator and decisor, understood the same verse as a commandment that applies in every generation, in accordance with the idea that God expects us to actively conquer the Land of Israel, whenever possible and in every generation, and not merely wait for His redeeming hand.

In the last Book of the Pentateuch, the Bible specifies by name the seven indigenous nations that dwelled in Canaan, and commands the Israelites to "utterly destroy them, do not establish a covenant with them, and do not grant them a resting place" (Deut. 7:2).[2] The reason given by the Bible for this wholesale destruction is a repetition of what we have seen earlier: "You shall break down their altars and smash to pieces their pillars and hew down their sacred trees and burn their graven images with fire" (Deut. 7:5; and again in 20:16–18).

RABBINIC COMMENTARY: THREE OPINIONS REGARDING GENTILE RESIDENCE IN ISRAEL

Among the halakhic decisors known as the *Rishonim* (11th to 16th centuries), there is a fascinating three-way difference of opinion concerning the proper interpretation of these verses, with critical ramifications for our times. The discussion centers around the prohibitions forbidding gentiles to dwell in the Land of Israel. There are two prohibitions: "Thou shalt not allow them a resting place" (Deut. 7:2) – that is, they may not

---

2. Alternate interpretations exist for *lo tenaḥem*, such as "show them no mercy," but the classical commentators interpret the phrase to mean "do not grant them a resting place" in accordance with Gittin 45a.

establish a permanent abode in Israel, and, "They shall not dwell in your land" (Ex. 23:33) – meaning, they may not even have temporary homes in Israel. Do these prohibitions apply to anyone who does not accept the seven Noahide laws,[3] or only to an idolater, or specifically to the seven indigenous nations of Canaan? Our attitude as to the rights of Arabs to live in the Land of Israel today will depend directly on which of the above three possibilities we accept as halakhically operative.

Maimonides maintains that the prohibition applies to all those who do not accept the seven Noahide laws of morality. He codifies his position in his *Mishneh Torah*, Laws of Idolatry, chapter 10, law 6:

> Whenever Israel has sovereignty over the gentiles, it is forbidden for us to allow idolaters in our midst, even to dwell for a temporary period or even to pass from place to place to engage in commerce; they may not pass through our land until they accept upon themselves the seven Noahide commandments, as it is written "They shall not dwell in your land" – even temporarily. And when they accept upon themselves the seven [Noahide] commandments, they are considered resident aliens (*gerei toshav*).

The term "resident alien" refers to one who is permitted to reside in the Land of Israel even though he is not an Israelite. Maimonides concludes his discussion of this law averring that we do not accept resident aliens when the Jubilee year is not operable. This might lead us to surmise that nowadays, since there is no Jubilee, there is also no resident alien status, meaning that no non-Jew may be permitted to dwell in Israel at this time.

However, the *Kesef Mishneh* (Rabbi Yosef Karo, renowned sixteenth-century compiler of the *Shulḥan Arukh*) insists that this would not be a valid understanding of Maimonides' position. Rabbi Karo maintains that Maimonides only intended to restrict the ability of a modern Jewish court to confer on a non-Jew official status as a resident alien, a

---

3. The seven Noahide laws are the prohibitions against idolatry, murder, theft, blasphemy, sexual immorality, and the consumption of blood or meat from still-living animals, as well as the positive commandment to establish courts of law.

Given this background, is it any wonder that Jews continued to mourn the destruction of the Temple for close to two thousand years? They expressed their yearning for Israel and Jerusalem as part of their blessings at the conclusion of each formal meal and in a prayer for the restoration of Jerusalem, recited thrice daily in the *Amida*. It is this loyal commitment to the Land of Israel which prevented even an assimilated Jew like Theodore Herzl from trading in Israel for Uganda, and which gave Yitzḥak Tabenkin, a secularist-socialist Labor leader, the courage to reject one of the early partition plans, which would have granted the Jews a very paltry portion of land in the area of Israel. Tabenkin initially said that he had first to seek counsel with two individuals before giving his final decision; when he ultimately rejected the plan, he explained to his fellow Labor Zionists that he had sought the counsel of his grandfather who had died, and of his grandson who had not yet been born.

In fact, Jews have lived in Israel in a virtually unbroken chain for the past 3,500 years, despite two exiles and difficult persecutions. They began to politically lobby for a Jewish state after the Treaty of Versailles, which followed the First World War, resolved to provide the Jewish people with sovereignty over both sides of the Jordan River.

But aside from these biblical-historical foundations, can we provide a clear religio-legal definition for the sanctity of the Land of Israel? Several different approaches are apparent in Jewish halakhic literature.

Sanctity of the land is based on commandments pertaining to the land

Rashbatz (Rabbi Shimon ben Tzemaḥ Duran, 1361–1444) maintains that in Judaism, sanctity is a function of divine command (mitzva): an individual becomes holy if and when he performs commandments by means of and upon his person, and the Land of Israel is rendered holy insofar as biblical and rabbinic commandments are performed upon its land and produce (the Sabbatical year, tithes, etc.).

Hence, the Rashbatz writes that if Rabbi Yehuda HaNasi exempted the city of Bet She'an from the laws of tithes (*trumot* and *ma'aserot*, as per Ḥullin 7a), he was likewise excluding Bet She'an from the sanctity of Israel and from the commandment of *aliya* (*Responsa Tashbatz*, Part III, siman 200). This is similar to the opinion of Rabbi

permanent legal status which could be transmitted to his progeny; "but if he himself accepts the seven [Noahide] commandments, we do not prevent him from dwelling in the land" (*Kesef Mishneh*, ad loc.).

The Rabad of Posquieres, a thirteenth-century Sephardic contemporary of Maimonides, seems to interpret Maimonides in a similar manner to the *Kesef Mishneh*, since he comments on Maimonides' words, "When the Jubilee is not operable, we only accept righteous proselytes," with the limitation: "I would not compare this with dwelling in the land" (*Strictures on Rambam, Mishneh Torah*, ad loc.). The Rabad apparently distinguishes between our responsibility to *support* the resident alien – a law which only applies when the Jubilee year is operative (Maimonides, Laws of Idolatry 10:5) – and the permission to allow the resident alien to *dwell* in Israel, which applies to whoever accepts the seven Noahide commandments.

The Rabad does, however, strongly disagree with the basic position of Maimonides which prohibits anyone who doesn't accept the seven Noahide laws from living in Israel. He insists that the various prohibitions pertaining to dwelling in or passing through the Land of Israel only apply to the seven indigenous nations: "This [statement by Maimonides, that the prohibitions apply to every gentile who has not accepted the seven Noahide laws] has not been found and has not been heard at any time. The verse which he cites applies to the seven indigenous nations." (Rabad, *Strictures on Rambam, Mishneh Torah*, ad loc.). Hence, according to the Rabad, there would be no limitations whatsoever today on any Arab owning land or houses in Israel, since Jewish tradition teaches that King Sennacherib of Assyria confounded the seven indigenous nations, who have since assimilated completely and disappeared from sight (Berakhot 28a).

The third and most generally accepted interpretation limits the prohibition of living in Israel to idolaters. This view is based on an explicit talmudic passage:

It states in the Torah: "They shall not dwell in your land," and one might think that this biblical prohibition even applies to a gentile who has accepted upon himself not to serve idols. [That would be an incorrect assumption, however, since] the Torah teaches us "he [who agrees not to serve idols] shall dwell with you." (Gittin 45a)

This seems to be the position of Nahmanidies in his commentary to Deuteronomy 20:18, as well as of Maimonides in his *Sefer HaMitzvot* (*Book of Commandments*):

> We are warned against settling idolaters in our land in order that we not learn from their heresies, as it says, "They shall not dwell in your land lest they cause you to sin against Me," and if an idolater were to desire to remain in our land it would not be permitted for us [to allow him to remain] until he accepts upon himself not to serve idols. (*Sefer HaMitzvot*, Negative Commandment 51)

The *Sefer HaHinukh* (commandment 94) concurs with this position, as do the Rashba (*Responsa*, Part 1, siman 8), and the Meiri (*Commentary to* Avoda Zara 20a). Rashi defines a resident alien as one who accepts upon himself not to serve idols (Arakhin 29a), but it is not necessary for him to observe the seven Noahide laws. The *Tur* (Rabbi Yaakov ben Asher, Baal HaTurim, 1270–1340) writes: "It is forbidden to give a free gift to an idolater." The *Bah* (Rabbi Joel Sirkes, 1561–1640) takes this to mean that one is allowed to present a gift to an "Ishmaelite" or Muslim Arab who is not considered an idolater; the *Tur* and the *Bah* both maintain that the prohibition "Thou shalt not give a free gift or provide a permanent resting place" (Deut. 7:2) does not apply to a Muslim monotheist (*Tur, Hoshen Mishpat* 249, 2 and *Bah*, ad loc.).

The *SMA* (*Sefer Meirat Ainayim*, Rabbi Joshua Falk on *Shulhan Arukh, Hoshen Mishpat* 249) argues that we may sell any object or parcel of land in Israel to an Ishmaelite or anyone who is not an idolater, thus concurring with the *Bah* that the sole necessary criterion for sale of land is that the purchaser not be an idolater.

In modern times, the first Ashkenazi chief rabbi of Israel, Rabbi Avraham Yitzhak HaKohen Kook, approved the sale of Israeli land to Arabs on the basis of all the earlier authorities just cited (*Mishpat Kohen*, 63, pp. 128–129, Mossad HaRav Kook, 1985). His son, Rabbi Tzvi Yehuda Kook, in his notes to his father's responsa, states explicitly:

> So we have found a midway category between gentile and r alien (*ger toshav*) and this is, as explained … one who accep himself not to serve idols, and who is [considered] a resid as far as living in Israel is concerned … He is not a comp dent alien, but nevertheless concerning the matter of d Israel, he is similar to a resident alien and is not prohib dwelling there. (ibid., p. 365, based on Gittin 45a)

Hence the majority of commentaries and codifiers would it is halakhically permissible to allow Arabs to live in Israel provide them with land to live on.

THE UNIQUE SANCTITY OF THE LAND OF ISRAEL FOR THE PEOPLE OF ISRAEL

The second issue with which we must deal is the sanct of Israel, a historical-halakhic-mystical-metaphysical expresses the unique bond between the nation of Isra of Israel. The ramifications of this issue are quite signif is one thing to allow Palestinians to live in our land; i to cede portions of sacred Israel to another sovereign

The very first commandment to the first Jew, A forth for your sake, from your country, your birthpla house to the Land [of Israel] which I shall show yo Almighty then promised Abraham that "unto your land" (12:7). The initial "Covenant between the P with the promise of the greater borders of the Land be home for Abraham's descendants (15:18–21). reiterated to each of the patriarchs as well as to t

The leitmotif of the Bible may very well you a rose garden." What God *did* pledge was a eternity of the Jewish people and – despite dif pogrom, and decimation – the eventual return the Land of Israel (Lev. 26:27–46; Deut. 4:25– you be scattered to the ends of the heavens, fi you and from there will He take you … and Land … and you will be more numerous tha

Ḥaim HaKohen cited in the *Baalei Tosafot*: If objective physical conditions make it too difficult for Jews to perform the commandments dependent on the Land of Israel, then they no longer have an obligation to live there (Ketubbot 110b).

Sanctity of the land is based on divine mandate

The opposite view maintained by the *Ḥatam Sofer* (Rabbi Moses Sofer of Pressburg, 1762–1839) who insists that there exists a higher, metaphysical sanctity to Israel, regardless of whether or not commandments are performed there:

> It is not because of the commandments dependent upon the land and Jerusalem that one can force one's spouse to move there, but rather it is because of the sanctity itself, that "anyone who lives outside of Israel is likened to one without God…" We are not dealing with the questions of whether commandments are or are not in force, or whether a ritually impure individual may enter there or not, but rather [we are dealing with] a higher sanctity which [exalts] Jerusalem as the Gate of Heaven forever. Even when the Jebusites inhabited Jerusalem and the Canaanites and Perizites were then in the land, the Divine Presence (*Shekhina*) did not and will not move from the Western Wall – even upon its destruction. (*Ḥatam Sofer, Yoreh De'ah*, Responsum 234, based upon the *Maharit*, 2nd part, *Yoreh De'ah* 28)

In a more contemporary vein, this same difference of opinion is maintained between Rabbi Kook and Rabbi Yaakov David Slutzker (the Rydbaz), chief rabbi of Safed. It is well known that Rabbi Kook published a book, *Shabbat HaAretz*, for the specific purpose of presenting halakhic justification for selling the topsoil of the Land of Israel to the Arabs before the Sabbatical year. Such a sale would enable the Jews to benefit from the soil's produce, a most welcome (and perhaps necessary) solution for an agricultural community struggling to exist. The Slutzker Rav (as he was called), who was a devoted friend of Rabbi Kook, nevertheless vehemently disagreed with this option. He argued that Rabbi Kook was effectively throwing out the baby with the bath water. After all, the Slutzker Rav said, once we sell the Land of Israel to Arabs and divest it of the obligations of the Sabbatical year, we have also divested it of its sanctity and of its uniqueness for Jewish settlement (*Tashbetz* and Rabbi Ḥaim HaKohen, op. cit.). Rabbi Kook countered that the sale was only efficacious concerning the suspension of commandments pertaining to the land, such as the necessity to bring tithes or to refrain from the produce of the Sabbatical year, but that nothing could suspend the intrinsic sanctity of the land, which "God's eyes view constantly" and whose "quotient" of divinity can never be destroyed no matter how often or to whom it is sold.[4]

Sanctity of the land is based on Jews inhabiting Israel

A third view concerning the sanctity of Israel, which I find the most compelling, is a compromise between the two more extreme positions cited above.

Maimonides maintains that the sanctity of Israel depends in great measure on the Jewish people living in it and thereby sanctifying it, as I shall attempt to prove. Before analyzing Maimonides' position in detail, I would venture to suggest that his stand concerning the sanctity of Israel emerges from a deeper perspective on the biblical view of sanctity in general.

The Bible delineates three types of sanctity or *kedusha*, a term reserved for that which is specifically informed with the Divine. There is sanctity of time (as in the Days of Holy Convocation), sanctity of object and place (as in the Holy Temple and the Holy Land), and sanctity of the human being ("and the Almighty created the human being in His image," Gen. 1:27).

The first two categories of sanctity are fundamentally dependent upon the third. For example, we human beings established the calendar and thereby established our holy days. During the period when there was a functioning Sanhedrin, the month was sanctified as a result of a declaration by the rabbinic members of the Great Court – sometimes even in contradiction to the precise astronomic calculation (Mishna Rosh HaShana, chapter 4).

---

4. Rabbi Avraham Yitzḥak HaKohen, *Shabbat HaAretz*, Introduction and chapter 15, based on *Ḥatam Sofer*, op. cit.).

Additionally, we sanctify a specific area, such as the Temple, through acts of human dedication, and we sanctify specific objects by using them "for the sake of heaven." The opposite is also true: a sefer Torah written by a heretic – albeit with all the correct details of scribal law but with incorrect and misguided inner conviction – is to be burned (Gittin 45b).

This vision of dedicated human action as the ultimate bestower of sanctity is beautifully articulated by Rabbi Meir Simḥa HaKohen of Dvinsk in his biblical commentary on Moses' shattering of the Tablets (*Meshekh Ḥokhmah* on Ex. 32:19). He asks how Moses could have shattered the holiest object in the world, the Two Tablets of Divine Testimony, when he discovered the Jews worshipping the Golden Calf? Was he not adding insult to injury? And how was it possible that he even received divine approbation for his action? The sage explains:

> To demonstrate that there is no created object with intrinsic sanctity; [sanctity is achieved] only when Israel observes the Torah in accordance with the will of the Creator, may His Name be blessed, the Holy One.

Apparently, Rabbi Meir Simḥa maintains that since the People of Israel impose sanctity through their actions, the tablets could only reflect the sanctity of the Jews who observed their commandments. When the Jews served the Golden Calf, they effectively divested the tablets of their sanctity by their act of profanation. Again, in this view, human beings have the ability to endow sanctity and to remove it.

Maimonides' view of the sanctity of the Land of Israel is a complex one, since he distinguishes between different areas of the land. Maimonides (and later, the *Ḥatam Sofer*) insists that the sanctity of Jerusalem is eternal, and that this sanctity is totally independent of any human behavior, good or bad: "The sanctity of the Sanctuary and Jerusalem exists because of the Divine Presence [*Shekhina*] and the Divine Presence cannot be nullified" (Maimonides, *Mishneh Torah*, Laws of the Chosen Dwelling Place 6:16).

Maimonides also attributes eternal sanctity to those areas to which Jews returned after the Babylonian exile, but his reasoning is radically different from that regarding Jerusalem: "Because when Ezra came up and sanctified [the land], he did not sanctify it with conquest [which would dissipate with the next conquest], but with presumptive right of ownership based upon their dwelling in it after having previously lived there (*beḥazakah sheheḥeziku bah*)." In other words, Maimonides teaches that when the Jews returned to their ancient homeland they, by their act of return, endowed these territories with eternal sanctity.

A complete study of Maimonides' statements concerning the sanctity of Israel yields the following picture: Jerusalem mystically "contains" the eternal sanctity of the Divine Presence and its holiness is permanent. After the Babylonian conquest, the parts of the country which had originally been occupied by the Israelites who came from Egypt still retained their holiness – but only in potential. This holiness was actualized only when Jews returned from the Babylonian Diaspora and re-inhabited these areas. By their return, the Jews demonstrated their eternal relationship with the land despite foreign conquest. Therefore, only the areas to which the Babylonian exiles returned became endowed with eternal sanctity.

However, there still remains a residual potential sanctity in all of Israel, even extending beyond the areas inhabited by the returnees from Babylon. This is clear from Maimonides' ruling that in areas which had been populated by the Israelites in the time of Joshua – and to which the Babylonian exiles did not return – work on the Sabbatical year is nevertheless forbidden, although the vegetation which grows there is permitted for general consumption (*Mishneh Torah*, Laws of Shmitta and Yovel 4:26, based on Mishna Shevi'it 6:1). Similarly, Maimonides rules that, although the traditional *smikha* (rabbinical ordination) can only be conferred in Israel, "all of the Land of Israel which was occupied by those who went up from Egypt is worthy of being considered Israel regarding conferring *smikha*." (*Hilkhot Sanhedrin* 4:6).

On the basis of these rulings, it can certainly be argued in the name of Maimonides that the land's potential sanctity can be actualized by Jewish settlement even after the period of the Babylonian returnees, including in our own times. Hence, Rabbi Yaakov Baal HaTurim maintains that if any city in Israel, within the boundaries set by those who came up from Egypt, is later populated by Jews, it too becomes endowed with sanctity (*Hilkhot Eretz Yisrael*, attributed to the *Tur*, concerning the Laws of Hallah, paragraph 10). In the same vein, the Rashash (Rabbi Shimshon MeShantz) insists that according to Maimonides an individual Jew who purchases land in Israel within the boundaries established by those who came from Egypt, even if it is not necessarily within the boundaries established by those who returned from Babylon, has nevertheless ipso facto endowed the land with sanctity by his purchase! (Commentary on Mishna Eduyot 8:6).

What emerges from Maimonides' writings is the critical importance of a Jewish return to the Land of Israel, and the significance of continued Jewish presence in the land for the establishment of its sanctity. The original ḥalutzim of the first and second *aliyot*, as well as the present-day inhabitants of Judea, Samaria, and the Golan, can be seen as fulfilling the dictates of this great medieval sage. Further, Maimonides would certainly require that we take Jewish settlements very seriously, and think long and hard before – if ever – dismantling any of them!

CONQUEST OF THE LAND OF ISRAEL

The final question we must deal with is: When may we, or even must we, wage war to conquer the Land of Israel? If the commandment to conquer Israel applies in our generation, does the commandment of obligatory warfare extend even to the defense of Jewish settlements in Judea and Samaria? Does it matter if the United Nations recognizes the sovereign State of Israel, but denies its right to Judea and Samaria? Does the overriding principle of saving Jewish lives (*pikuaḥ nefesh*) take precedence in this instance, or does settling the land rank higher in the hierarchy of commandments than saving an individual life? Is the mitzva of settling the land on a par with the commandments against idolatry, adultery, and murder, concerning which our sages have taught that one must be prepared to die rather than transgress them – *yehareg v'al ya'avor* (Sanhedrin 73a)?

Undoubtedly, peace is the great biblical ideal, and the creation of a world of peace is the ultimate mission of our nation. King David was forbidden to build the Holy Temple because he had been a warrior for so much of his life ("You have shed much blood and you have waged great wars; you shall not build a house to My Name" – 1 Chron. 22:8).

Neither can the stones of the Temple altar be hewn by an implement of destruction, as the verse commands, "Thou shalt not lift an axe to hew the altar stones" (Ex. 20:22). The Midrash explains, "The altar was created to lengthen the life of humanity and the axe to shorten the life of humanity; that which shortens [life] may not come into contact with that which lengthens [it]" (*Mekhilta*, end of *Parashat Yitro*). Additionally, the prophets constantly yearn for the period when "nation will not lift up sword against nation, and humanity will not learn war any more" (Is. 2:4).

Despite our ideals, we live in an as-yet unredeemed world in which warfare is an unfortunate fact of life. Biblical Jewish law provides for the right – and occasionally the obligation – to wage battle (Deut. 20:1–20). The Talmud, on the basis of the biblical prescription, delineates two types of wars: voluntary and obligatory.

Voluntary war (*milḥemet reshut*) requires advance confirmation by the Great Court in Jerusalem (the Sanhedrin), in addition to the nation's political ruler. Exemptions from military service are granted to certain soldiers: "One who is engaged to a woman he has not yet married, one who has built a house he has not yet occupied, one who has planted a vineyard whose fruit he has not yet tasted, one who is fearful and one who is tender-hearted" (ibid., 5:10).[5]

Obligatory war (*milḥemet mitzva*) calls for a universal draft – "even the bridegroom from his chamber and the bride from her wedding canopy" – and requires no prior confirmation other than the decision of the ruler of Israel. (Sota 44a, b; *Mishneh Torah*, Laws of Kings 5, 2).

Obligatory and voluntary warfare: Maimonides' view

The task of precisely defining which type of war is obligatory and which is voluntary is not so simple. Maimonides offers the following formulation:

> A king must first wage an obligatory war. And which is an obligatory war? A war against the seven indigenous Canaanite nations, a war against Amalek, and [a war] to save Israel from the hand

---

5. This topic is also discussed in my article "The Torah of Mother Rebecca: *Yeshivot Hesder*," which appears in this volume.

of an enemy who is rising against us. Afterwards he may wage a voluntary war, which is a war against the rest of the nations in order to expand the borders of Israel and to add to its [Israel's] greatness and renown. (Laws of Kings 5:1)

It is important to note that Maimonides does not define obligatory war as a battle for the Land of Israel, akin to Joshua's battles more than four thousand years ago. He does mention Joshua's wars, but not as paradigms for today. Joshua's wars are only relevant as examples of the biblically mandated wars against the seven nations which originally inhabited Canaan. Since these seven indigenous nations no longer exist ("Sennacherib came and confounded the nations" – Berakhot 28a, *Mishneh Torah*, Laws of Kings 5:4), an automatic command to go to battle against gentile occupiers of Israel would not apply nowadays.

The Talmud states, "Rabbi Yehuda would define a voluntary war as when we attack them, and an obligatory war as when they attack us." (Y. Sota 8, 10). This is evidently Maimonides' source for an obligatory war being a battle in self-defense against an attacking enemy – a situation which certainly has present-day applications. Elsewhere, the Talmud comments: "The wars of conquest [against the seven nations] waged by Joshua are agreed by everyone to have been obligatory. The wars of expansion waged by the Davidic dynasty are agreed by everyone to have been voluntary. About which do they disagree? [A war waged] to weaken the gentiles so that they do not attack us [i.e., preventive warfare]. One authority [Rabbi Yehuda] calls it obligatory and the other calls it voluntary" (Sota 44b).

Maimonides' position is therefore eminently logical. He defines obligatory warfare as self-defense, and voluntary warfare as anything other than that, such as wars of expansion (even to our divinely-promised potential borders) and preventive battles (such as the 1981 Israeli bombing of the Iraqi nuclear reactor in Osirak).

The *Leḥem Mishneh* (Abraham di Boton, d. 1609) even suggests that Maimonides refers to preventive warfare in his words, "to add to [Israel's] greatness and renown." The reasoning is that a battle fought for the sake of strengthening Israel's reputation as a powerful nation will prevent those who might attack from doing so – especially if the recipient of Israel's military prowess is a potential aggressor (*Mishneh Torah*, ibid.).

The moral justification for an obligatory war of self-defense is the eminently logical talmudic dictum: "If one is poised to murder you, you must attempt to kill him first" (Sanhedrin 72a).[6] However, since a voluntary war – even of the preventive variety – is not as morally clear-cut as a war of self-defense, it requires the imprimatur of the Great Court or Sanhedrin (Mishna Sanhedrin 1:1). Moreover, this type of war allows for military exemptions, even on the basis of conscientious objection.

Obligatory warfare: Nahmanidies' view

What about a war to conquer the Land of Israel today? What about a war initiated by Israel to establish Jewish national sovereignty, to gain or to maintain Jewish control over areas which have eternal sanctity? We have clearly seen that Maimonides does not subsume such a war under the category of obligatory war (*milḥemet mitzva*). Nahmanides strongly disagrees. He rules that there is a halakhic imperative in every generation to dwell in the Land of Israel and to conquer it – even after the seven indigenous nations have ceased to be identifiable:

> We have been commanded to inherit the land which the Almighty, may He be Blessed, gave to our fathers Abraham, Isaac, and Jacob, and not to abandon it to any of the nations or to desolation. And He said to them, "And you shall conquer the land and dwell in it for I have given the land to you to inherit, and you shall divide the land as an inheritance as I have sworn to your fathers." And this [the war to conquer the land] is what our sages refer to as an obligatory war, and this is what they said in Tractate Sota [44b]: Rabbi Yehuda said, "The war of Joshua to conquer, everyone agrees is obligatory. The war of David to expand, everyone agrees is voluntary."

---

6. This is patently ethically superior to the Gospel's instruction to "turn the other cheek," which would render society vulnerable to takeover by the most heinously insensitive and wantonly cruel forces.

And do not confuse [the issue and mistakenly interpret] that this commandment is the commandment to wage war against the seven indigenous nations we have been commanded to destroy, as it is written, "And you shall surely destroy them." For the matter is not so! Indeed, we are commanded to kill those idolaters [of the seven indigenous nations] if they wage war against us, and we must make peace with them if they wish to make peace, and allow them to remain in accordance with the known conditions, but we may never allow the land to be left in their hands nor in the hands of any of the other idolaters in any of the generations.

And [the sages further] said, "If you will enquire: Why did King David conquer Aram Naharayim and Aram Zova when the commandments are not operative there [for they are part of Syria, and not part of the promised borders of Eretz Yisrael]? The response is that King David did not act properly. The Torah stipulates that only after you conquer the Land of Israel are you permitted to conquer *hutz laaretz* [areas outside of Israel], and he did not act in this way."

According to this interpretation, we are commanded to conquer Israel in every generation; not only in the generation of Joshua but also in the generation of David and, by extrapolation, in our generation as well. In addition, a war waged for the sake of conquering the Land of Israel promised by God to the Jews can always be considered an obligatory war, even in our times.

Rabban Yoḥanan ben Zakkai vs. Rabbi Akiva

The difference of opinion between the two great Sephardic authorities, Maimonides and Nahmanidies, harks back to the mishnaic debate between two giants of Jewish history, Rabban Yoḥanan ben Zakkai and Rabbi Akiva, as recorded in the Talmud (Gittin 56, 57). At the time of the imminent destruction of the Second Temple (69 CE Rabban Yoḥanan ben Zakkai, great sage of Jerusalem, stood before Vespasian, general of the Roman army, and requested "Yavneh and her wise men," thereby relinquishing claims to the doomed Jerusalem and any hopes for national

sovereignty. Apparently, for Rabban Yoḥanan, the positive commandment of obligatory warfare to conquer or maintain national sovereignty
over Israel only applied in the time of Joshua – as Maimonides would
later codify. Perhaps, according to Rabban Yoḥanan, the biblical injunction "and you shall live [and not die] by My laws" (Lev. 18:5) prohibits
warfare on behalf of a Jewish settlement, and even on behalf of the holy
city of Jerusalem.

Rabbi Akiva, one generation later, vehemently disagreed. According to one talmudic rendering (Gittin 57b), Rabbi Akiva even castigated
the senior Rabban Yoḥanan, the teacher of Rabbi Akiva's teachers, with
the verse, "[God sometimes] turns wise men backwards and transforms
their wisdom into foolishness" (Is. 44:25). To Rabbi Akiva, the defense
of Jerusalem – and perhaps of any Jewish settlement within the borders
of the land promised by God to the Children of Israel – is an obligatory
war mandated by the Bible. As a consequence, such a commandment
must necessarily override the danger to human life engendered by warfare.[7] And indeed, Rabbi Akiva proceeded to inspire his nation, barely
sixty-five years after ben Zakkai's capitulation to Rome, to undertake
violent rebellion against the Romans.

Upon further analysis, however, it is not logically compelling
to link the positions of Rabban Yoḥanan ben Zakkai and Maimonides,
Rabbi Akiva and Nahmanidies in this way. After all, although Bar Kokhba
did succeed in establishing Jewish sovereignty for over three years, the
Bar Kokhba rebellion ultimately ended in abject defeat; in light of the
historical vindication of ben Zakkai, it would be difficult to suggest that
Nahmanidies nevertheless upholds the banner of Rabbi Akiva, no matter what. Moreover, although the obligation to live in Israel is indeed
incumbent upon every individual in every generation according to
Nahmanidies,[8] the obligation to conquer the Land of Israel applies only
to the entire nation when it is an achievable goal and not a suicide mission. It would be foolhardy to suggest that each individual must wage war
against the nation occupying Israel in his lifetime. Nahmanidies himself

---

7. See discussion of *Minḥat Ḥinukh*, mitzva 425.
8. Nahmanidies, *Glosses on Maimonides' Book of Commandments*, Positive Commandment 4.

did not spearhead a movement to climb the ramparts of Jerusalem and claim sovereignty over Israel. He satisfied his halakhic requirements by establishing a personal residence in Israel, despite the hardships incurred.

It appears to me that the disagreement of the talmudic sages concerns another matter altogether which, when properly understood, illuminates the position of Nahmanidies, and has crucial consequences for us today.

Obligatory war to protect the life of the Nation Israel

The *Minḥat Ḥinukh* (Joseph Babad, d. 1874) raises an obvious question relating to the entire issue of obligatory warfare. The Talmud clearly specifies that the most crucial imperative is, "And he shall live by them [My commands]" (Lev. 18:5). The sages commented on this verse, "live by them – and not die by them." This verse is the basis for the ruling that *pikuaḥ nefesh* (the saving of a human life) overrides every commandment of the Bible – with the exception of idolatry, adultery, and murder. If that is the case, how can we ever be commanded to engage in obligatory warfare? After all, in every military battle, the life of the soldier is placed at risk!

The *Minḥat Ḥinukh* (mitzva 425) explains that warfare is a unique commandment, in which danger to life is a built-in aspect of its performance. Hence, the commandment to wage war always overrides the consideration of *pikuaḥ nefesh*.

I once heard an extension of this idea from my teacher and mentor, Rabbi Joseph B. Soloveitchik. Obligatory warfare overrides danger to the life of the individual because it is waged in order to protect the life of the entire nation. It is because the protection of the life of the entire nation takes precedence over the protection of the life of the individual that we are commanded to participate in an obligatory war.

From this vantage point, the biblical commandment of an obligatory war against Amalek and the indigenous seven nations who inhabited the land of Canaan becomes eminently understandable. Unless Amalek, the avowed arch-enemy of Israel, had been destroyed, and unless the wandering Hebrews had established a homeland for themselves, the Israelite nation would have been a non-starter. This is the common-sense, sage manner in which Rashi interprets the biblical command:

"And you shall conquer the land and dwell therein" (Num. 33:53). Rashi explains, "You must expel the indigenous nations from the land in order that you may dwell therein"; two nations cannot inhabit the same place at the same time!

This reasoning is the source of Maimonides' *ḥiddush* (halakhic innovation) stating that were Amalek and the seven indigenous nations to accept the seven Noahide laws of morality, even they could remain in the Land of Israel as *gerim toshavim*, resident aliens. We cannot morally displace moral people from their land, and in most instances it would be possible for us to dwell in Israel together with gentiles as long as they were committed to living in peace and harmony together with us. However, if any enemy rises up to destroy our people, we are obligated to fight back and destroy them in order to guarantee the future existence of our nation.

When the destruction of the Second Temple was imminent, Rabban Yoḥanan ben Zakkai believed that to continue the battle against Rome would have been tantamount to engaging in a suicide mission; moreover, he was convinced that Israel could survive by reestablishing the Sanhedrin in Yavneh. Rabbi Akiva disagreed; he maintained that without national sovereignty, expressed through Jewish control over Jerusalem, the future of the Jewish people would be extremely precarious. He also believed that had the people of Israel been united, they could have held off the Roman conquerors. From his perspective, Rabban Yoḥanan had requested too little too soon.

Rabbi Akiva was of the firm opinion that Rabban Yoḥanan had made a tragic and fateful mistake. He convinced his generation, and embarked on a massive rebellion against Rome led by Bar Kokhba. Tragically, the battle was lost. Rabbi Akiva, the great sage and teacher, lived through the death of 24,000 of his disciples, witnessed enormous Jewish suffering and persecution, and was publicly tortured to death.

The response of halakhic Judaism was a vindication of Rabban Yoḥanan ben Zakkai; for the sake of the preservation of the Jewish people, Jewish sovereignty over the Land of Israel was moved to the back burner. Following the abortive rebellion against Rome, the sages of the Talmud outlined a social contract between Israel and the nations of the world, expressed in three oaths: the Almighty adjures Israel "not to rebel against the nations of the world; not to climb the ramparts of Jerusalem" – that is, not to attempt to forcibly conquer the Land of Israel and establish Jewish sovereignty; and, in response, the Almighty also adjures the nations of the world "not to subjugate and persecute Israel too much" (Ketubbot 111a).

It must be remembered that Jerusalem is synonymous with Jewish sovereignty; the destruction of the Temple in Jerusalem signaled not only the termination of the sacrificial rituals but, more importantly, the end of Jewish national sovereignty. Although Yavneh is within Israel, giving up Jerusalem for Yavneh paved the way for the legitimacy of flourishing Jewish communities throughout the world.

Maimonides and Nahmanidies regarding warfare on behalf of Israel today

What would be the position of these great sages today, given the new reality of the Jewish state? Profound changes have overtaken the Jewish people. The Emancipation that began in the middle of the eighteenth century resulted in the creation of the secular Jew and threatened heretofore insular and observant Jewish communities with the specter of assimilation. Worldwide nationalist movements left little opportunity for the Jewish citizen of the Diaspora yearning for equal citizenship with his gentile neighbor. Instead, the Jew's fraught position as a homeless "stranger" further encouraged virulent anti-Semitic persecution.

Jewish Diaspora survival appeared endangered for the first time since Rabban Yoḥanan ben Zakkai and, as a result, the students of the Vilna Gaon, the Baal Shem Tov, and the *Ḥatam Sofer* all made their way back home to Israel. Major religious personalities such as Rabbi Yehuda Alkalai and Rabbi Kook gave ideological support to the new religious Zionism, and Theodore Herzl warned secular Jews that only Israel could provide a refuge from the assimilation and anti-Semitism of the Diaspora.

The Nazi Holocaust, which was aided both actively and passively by the cooperation of the majority of nation-states, made a mockery of the oath which the Midrash attributed to the gentiles, that they "would not subjugate Israel too much," in exchange for the Jewish oaths "not to rebel against the nations of the world and not to climb the ramparts of Jerusalem." Soaring intermarriage rates around the globe merely compounded the impossibility of a successful Jewish Diaspora. The real threat of Jewish extinction, together with the UN partition vote that gave international sanction to the fledgling State of Israel, certainly freed the Jews from their oaths.

In today's world, the Jewish state is a basic condition for the preservation of the Jewish people. The military prowess of Israel, as demonstrated in our various victories against the Arab nations constantly threatening to destroy us, would probably lead the exponents of Nahmanidies to the inescapable conclusion that nowadays war on behalf of the Jewish state is a viable option. At the very least, they might argue, we must retain under our sovereign control over every area of Israel that we are halakhically enjoined "not to abandon to any other of the nations or to desolation" (Nahmanidies, *Strictures on Sefer HaMitzvot*, op. cit.). If the Palestinians or any Arab state should go to war against us as a result of our hold on these territories, the war would be considered an obligatory one in Nahmanidies' view, since it would be fought for the conquest of Israel at a time when such a conquest is attainable.

But what about Maimonides? As we have already seen, he does not classify a present-day war for the sake of conquering Israel – or even retaining part of it – as an obligatory war. But Maimonides certainly recognizes the ultimate value of living in Israel, as well as the eternal sanctity of those settlements within the promised borders of Israel which are Jewishly inhabited.

We may surmise from Maimonides' writings that he would also have recognized the profound significance of the Jewish state and its halakhic significance in terms of fulfilling *mitzvot* that pertain to the Land of Israel. For example, in the beginning of the first chapter of the Laws of Tithes in *Mishneh Torah*, Maimonides clearly defines Israel in terms of an Israeli sovereign government ruling the land. And in the beginning of his Laws of Ḥanukka he lauds the corrupt Hasmonean rulers "because they restored Israeli sovereignty for more than two hundred years." Hence, the reality of the State of Israel as a result of a United Nations declaration, and the eternal sanctity of the Jewish settlements, would certainly affect Maimonides' opinion concerning the maintenance of portions of Israel.

WHAT BRINGS GREATEST SECURITY?

As I have endeavored to demonstrate, the fundamental question facing Maimonides would have to be: which course is most likely to guarantee the abiding peace and security of the Jewish people? Clearly, the Diaspora is not a viable option anymore, so we must maintain the State of Israel. But must this maintenance extend to the disputed areas of Judea, Samaria, and the Golan, even to the point of warfare on their behalf? Maimonides might accept our giving up those areas of Judea and Samaria inhabited by Arabs in the interest of peace, as long as our security needs (such as the IDF's right of entry in the instance of hot pursuit and its ability to secure intelligence information and extirpate terrorist cells) can be guaranteed.

Maimonides might even be interpreted to justify ceding Arab-inhabited areas which retain the eternal sanctity bestowed upon them by the return of the Jewish people in the time of Ezra. There are precedents for this kind of concession. For example, King Solomon presented twenty cities of the Galilee to King Hiram of Tyre (I Kings, 9:11), in payment for the wood and gold the Tyrian king had provided the kings of Israel. Of course, it is possible that – despite the plain meaning of the text that Galilean cities were ceded – it was only the oil produce which was given away (Malbim, ad loc.). Another possibility raised by the Ralbag is that a trade was executed between the two kings of twenty cities for twenty cities ("It is already mentioned in the Book of Chronicles that Hiram also gave to Solomon cities in which to settle Israelites, and it is proper for this to be so, since it is impossible for a king to lessen the Land of Israel" (Ralbag, ad loc.). Or, perhaps King Solomon acted incorrectly.

Nevertheless, a precedent seems to have been established for ceding territory, at least according to the literal meaning of the text. Moreover, such a concession of Arab-inhabited lands might be considered a salutary security move for the Jewish state because it would remove the danger of hundreds of thousands of disgruntled Arab fifth columnists within our very gut. Additionally, one could make a spiritual-educational argument for ceding territory: sensitive morality becomes difficult to communicate to a young generation of Israelis forced into the role of conquerors.

However, Maimonides would undoubtedly judge the Jewish settlements with an entirely different yardstick. We have already analyzed the special sanctity of Jewish settlements according to Maimonides. Moreover, the transfer of Jews out of their homes in the Jewish homeland, a precedent-shattering exile imposed upon Jews by their own Jewish government, is the very antithesis of humane moral policy.[9] For contrast, let us recall the statement of Navot the Yizraeli to King Ahab, who merely wished to take away his vineyard: "It would be a desecration before God were I to give away to you the inheritance of my fathers" (1 Kings 21:3).

Picture the justifiable moral outrage which would ensue worldwide and in Israel were an Israeli government to suggest transferring innocent Arabs from their homes in Judea and Samaria! Why are the rights of innocent Jews less inviolate?

In addition, from a security vantage point, it's important to note that the Jewish settlements are in the main concentrated on mountain ranges, in the Jordan valley, in Greater Jerusalem, and in buffer zones important for the protection of Israel. Nor dare we overlook the psychology of the Arab mind that idealizes Saladin's expulsion of the Crusaders and glorifies terrorists. The transfer of Jews out of Israeli settlements would only fan the flames of those preparing for a "Judenrein" Middle East; it would play into the "today Golan-Judea-Samaria, tomorrow Tel Aviv" mentality of the extremist Arab world.

To be sure, in the absence of a clearly mandated biblical directive to establish Jewish sovereignty over Israel, it is possible to argue Maimonides' principle that in order to save the entire organism, a doctor is permitted, even duty-bound, to sacrifice a limb (*Mishneh Torah, Hilkhot Mamrin* 2:4). If, however, the limb in question is vital to the life of the organism (such as the heart or brain), or the one to whom we are sacrificing the limb is not a doctor who intends to heal but rather a murderer whose purpose is to weaken and eventually destroy, then ceding territory – any territory – may be tantamount to suicide.

---

9. Indeed, when Israel unilaterally pulled out of the settlements of Gush Katif, at the cost of deep trauma to most of the nation, the only tangible result was the rise of a terrorist regime in Gaza.

It is precisely because the question is so complex and the life of the nation hangs in the balance that the various sides in the debate are so intense and polarized. Will ceding territory lead to greater security for Israel and enable us to live in peace with our neighbors or will it lessen security by leading to the establishment of a hostile Palestinian state that would be a constant security threat? Will it lead to peace or will it lead to war?

THE CITIZENS OF ISRAEL MUST DECIDE

According to Maimonides, everything hangs on the question of which policy is most likely to bring the greatest security. Who makes such a momentous decision? In the case of a seriously ill patient, where treatment can either result in his life or death, the decision must be made by experts – that is, according to the counsel of the best doctors available (See Hershel Schachter, *Land for Peace*, p. 80). Extrapolating to our situation, we must seek the counsel of the best military strategists in Israel, including present and former chiefs of staff and generals. If they are divided in their assessments, however – as is the case today – we must return to our medical analogy. If the doctors cannot reach a clear, united opinion as to whether aggressive treatment would be salutary, we must ask the patient himself (Schachter, ibid., p. 79 and note 11; *Beit Yitzhak* 1986, p. 104).

In the instance of our agonizing political situation, there is even greater halakhic support for allowing the majority of the people to decide. We have already seen that, according to Maimonides, an obligatory war is decided upon by the king or ruler of Israel. This ruler must be either the heir of the previous ruler (optimally from the Davidic dynasty), or else be appointed by prophet, Sanhedrin, or – in the absence of these institutions – public election. Similarly, a voluntary war must be ratified by the Sanhedrin. If the Sanhedrin has ceased to exist, the voice of the majority of Jews in Israel serves as a substitute, according to Maimonides.

Maimonides' source for identifying the nation of Israel with the Sanhedrin may be the biblical passage which provides for a special sacrifice of atonement "if the entire congregation of Israel (*kol adat Yisrael*) errs" (Lev. 4:13). The Mishna interprets this to mean that a sacrifice is brought if the Sanhedrin erred (Mishna Horayot 1:5, and

Rashi on Bible ad loc. See also Sanhedrin 16a, "And 'the entire congregation' refers to the Sanhedrin"). Hence, any appointed position or decision of permanence which was to have been made by the Sanhedrin is to be made – in the absence of this august body of Torah sages – by a vote of the people themselves. Even the recreation of the divine ordination which made the Sanhedrin possible can be voted in by the people of Israel themselves (Maimonides, *Commentary on Mishna Sanhedrin* 1:1).

Therefore, a fateful question such as whether to cede territory or go to battle on behalf of Israel can only be decided by the majority of eligible voters who live in Israel. Furthermore, the decision of the people cannot be dependent on their having elected a specific prime minister if he did not clearly state his policy on the debated topic during his campaign. The issue of territorial compromise is important enough – a matter of *pikuaḥ nefesh* for the nation as well as for individual Jews – for it to be specifically decided upon by the majority of Jews living in Israel, those whose lives are most affected by such a decision.

There is another fascinating parallel to our situation which confirms the right of the people to determine the intention of the enemy, which I once heard from Rabbi J. David Bleich. The Bible mandates that if an individual's home is entered in the night by a burglar, the homeowner has the right to protect his property, even if it means taking the life of the intruder. However, this is only the case if the burglar is liable to kill the inhabitant in the course of his thievery. Who makes the determination as to the intention of the burglar? The homeowner himself, says Jewish law! Exodus 22:1 points out that if an aggressor clearly comes to murder you, it is forbidden for you to spare his life, but if he comes to steal from you, "his blood is permitted." The difference in formulation teaches that in the latter case, the victim of the crime makes the judgment call. Moreover, the *Shulḥan Arukh* (*Oraḥ Ḥaim* 329:6) permits the military protection of a border town necessary to Israeli security on the Sabbath, even if the enemy is only coming for "straw and hay." The implication is that the enemy who takes our produce today may well come to take our lives tomorrow and we dare not weaken our security provisions. It is the people whose lives are in question who must the call about the enemy's intentions.

The principle is clear: giving up or retaining territory can only be a function of determining the best safeguard of the Jewish nation. Under ordinary circumstances, expert military advice must be followed. In the absence of a military consensus, the citizenry of Israel – those who will live or die as a result of the decision – must arrive at the determination by clear majority vote, either by holding new elections based upon the debated security issue, or by public referendum. Any duly elected government of Israel, unless it ran on a very specific security platform, must understand that a critical decision of such life-and-death significance must be made by the people themselves. And may the Almighty grant the people of Israel the wisdom to make the right decision.

The fonts used in this book are from the Arno family